LEAGUE CRICKET YEARBOOK

The Midlands

Editor:
Andy Searle

Contributing Editors:
Nick Archer & Alan Rowley

Contributors:
Alex E. Davis, Nigel Staley, Graham Seal, Bill Naylor, Owen Griffiths, Chris Marsh, Peter Radburn, Richard Matthews, Chris Williams, Allan Smith, Ron Douglas, David Hudson-Wood, Paul Smith, Ken Widdows.

CONTENTS

LEAGUE CRICKET

YEARBOOK

The Midlands

Compiled and Edited by Andy Searle, Nick Archer & Alan Rowley

Know The Score Books Limited
118 Alcester Road, Studley
Warwickshire, B80 7NT
Tel: 01527 454482
Fax: 01527 452183
info@knowthescorebooks.com
www.knowthescorebooks.com

A CIP catalogue record is available for this book from the British Library

ISBN: 978-1-905449-72-9

Book and Jacket Design by Andy Searle

Printed and bound in Great Britain
by Cromwell Press, Trowbridge, Wiltshire

Contents

PREFACE

By Andy Searle, Editor

WELCOME to the first edition of what is hoped will be an annual publication providing the most comprehensive coverage of recreational cricket in the Midlands that there has ever been.

This project is the result of a co-operation between the publishers Know The Score Books and a number of individuals in Warwickshire, Worcestershire, Staffordshire, Nottinghamshire, Derbyshire and Leicestershire and I would like to thank them all for their assistance in producing what I believe is an invaluable document for cricket lovers in the region.

I would particularly like to thank Nick Archer, the General Manager of the Birmingham & District Premier League and Alan Rowley, who produces 'the follow on', a superb website on Derbyshire and Nottinghamshire cricket (www.thefollowon.com) for their hard work and enthusiasm in helping myself and Know The Score Books bring this project to fruition.

As can be seen from the depth of coverage within these pages, there is a vast amount of administrative work surrounding cricket in the region, much of which receives little or no coverage in the media. Thousands of volunteers give up their spare time in the summer and beyond keeping the grassroots of the sport afloat, yet, despite the fact that 90% of cricket played in this country is at the grassroots, little attempt is made by the national media to cover the sport in any depth. This book and its accompanying editions in other areas of the country are an attempt to redress that.

Any comments and feedback on any aspect of the book will be welcome. We are expecting the 2008 edition to be even bigger so please contact us at the email address cricket@knowthescorebooks.com.

The West Midlands

**Birmingham & District Premier League
The Warwickshire League
The Worcestershire League
Staffordshire Club Championship
North Staffs & South Cheshire
Premier League
Cotswold Hills League**

Birmingham & District Premier Cricket League

(sponsored by Birmingham Midshires)

League Officials

PRESIDENT
Graham Warner

CHAIRMAN & HON. TREASURER
Robin Viner
Tel: 07860 721595 (M) 01562 66066 (O) & (F)

GENERAL MANAGER
Nick Archer
P.O. Box 2481, Walsall WS1 1GF
Tel: 07767 775350 e-mail: nick@bdpcl55.fsnet.co.uk

MANAGEMENT BOARD REPRESENTATIVES
Steve Baker (Halesowen CC), Tony Cox (Fordhouses CC),
John Day (Water Orton CC), Jamie Fleet (Cannock CC),
Tom Gray (Barnt Green CC), Rex Ingram (Bromsgrove CC),
Ken Lancaster (Sutton Coldfield CC), David Manning (W'ton CC),
Alan Neal (Old Hill CC), Tim Phillips (Old Elizabethans CC),
Barry Stokes (Walmley CC), Bill Tansell (Old Elizabethans CC)

Wicker bowls Walsall to title

by Nick Archer

HAVING TRAILED leaders West Bromwich Dartmouth for the majority of the season, Walsall, finally, tracked their nearest rivals down and overtook them with one game of the season remaining. An emphatic win over Coventry & N.W. in the final game, as Dartmouth slumped to defeat, at relegated Old Hill, ensured that they clinched the Premier Division crown by a healthy 27-point margin, their first title success since 1999.

The key game took place, on 12th August, when Walsall visited Dartmouth at Sandwell Park. Two weeks previously the home side headed the table by 38 points, but Walsall's crushing five wicket victory, as well as reducing the deficit to seven points, shifted the balance of power and transferred the momentum for the run-in to the end of the season.

Leading performers for Walsall were Paul Wicker (47 wickets), Nambian Gerrie Snyman (336 runs and 35 wickets), Nathan Round (607 runs and 18 wickets) and former Nottinghamshire batsman Graeme Archer (622 runs). Wicker topped the Premier Division bowling averages and, also, won the League's Player of the Year Award, but his performances were eclipsed by the Kenilworth Wardens Indian professional, Shitansu Kotak, who earned seven 'Man of the Match' Awards during the season to clinch the £1,000 prize from League sponsors Birmingham Midshires. Kotak finished the season as the

Paul Wicker
2006 Player of the Year

Shitansu Kotak
Leading run-scorer and
wicket-taker in 2006

Division's highest run-scorer (756) and leading wicket-taker (83) but, as an Overseas Player, he was ineligible for the Player of the Season Award. Kidderminster Victoria's Will Gifford (640 runs at 58.18) finished top of the batting averages and 19 years-old Kenilworth Wardens batsman, Scott Stenning, clinched the Most Promising Young Player Award by scoring 682 runs at 40.12.

Four times National Knock-Out Champions, Old Hill, were relegated to Division One alongside Shrewsbury; the Shropshire Club continuing a five-year trend that has seen one of the newly promoted Clubs return to where they came from at the first time of asking.

Promoted to the Premier Division, from Division One, for the first time in their history, were Shifnal (Champions) and Walmley (Runners-Up) while two founder members of The Birmingham & District Cricket League (1888), Smethwick and Aston Unity, were relegated to Division Two. In a very competitive Division, Harborne, Sutton Coldfield, and Stratford-upon-Avon retained hopes of promotion until the last weekend of the season, but Unity, in particular, and Smethwick lost touch with the rest of the table very early in the season. Leading batsman in Division One was former Derbyshire man, Andrew Gait, who scored 840 runs at 76.36 for Wolverhampton, and the leading wicket-taker was Water Orton's Lesroy Irish, with 62.

The Division Two title was won by Cannock, who led the table from Week One. The Staffordshire Club were never seriously challenged, but there was a keen battle for the second promotion place, which was clinched by Aston Manor, who earned a third promotion in three years. In 2004, they won the Warwickshire Cricket League, in 2005, they were

Cannock CC 1st XI, 2nd Division Champions

runners-up, to Evesham, in Division Three, and now take a place in Division One in 2007. Fordhouses' South African Overseas Player, Nick Van Woerkom, was the outstanding talent in this Division, scoring 956 runs at 68.29 and taking 25 wickets at 20.92. Cannock's Guy Bulpitt (59 wickets at 11.41) finished top of the bowling averages, but the leading wicket-taker was Imran Sabir (Attock) with 61. Studley and Pelsall were relegated to Division Two.

Newport and Berkswell continue progress

Two sides promoted from Feeder Leagues at the end of the 2005 season, Newport (Shropshire Premier League) and Berkswell (Warwickshire Cricket League) made further progress in 2006 and find themselves in Division Two at the start of the 2007 season. Champions Newport owed much to their Indian professional, Rajiv Bhatia, who dominated most matches, finishing the season with 1124 runs at 93.67 and 80 wickets at 13.36. During the season he scored an unbeaten 200 against Ombersley. A week earlier, Berkswell's former Warwickshire batsman, Dominic Ostler, scored 202 not out against the same opposition. Ostler totalled 985 runs, just two more than Maisam Hasnain from Whitchurch. The relegated Clubs were Beacon (Staffordshire Club Cricket Championship), Kings Heath (Warwickshire Cricket League), Redditch and Worcester (both to the Worcestershire County Cricket League). A feature of the season was Berkswell's inclusion of Shoaib Akhtar as their Overseas Player for two matches in August, resulting in plenty of publicity and a visit to the Club by the Sky Television cameras. In two games, he took three wickets and hit a quick-fire half-century before re-joining the Pakistan squad for the One-Day International against England.

In the 2nd XI Competitions, Divisional titles were won by Leamington Spa, Attock, Bridgnorth and Evesham. Attock were accompanied into the Premier Division by Shrewsbury, while Tamworth and Beacon were runners-up in Division Two and Division Three. Sadly, Beacon 2nd XI was unable to take its place in Division Two, because the Club's 1st XI was relegated out of the League. Their promotion place was taken by Old Elizabethans. Whitchurch 2nd XI also benefited form the demise of those clubs whose 2nd XI was placed in a higher Division and they take a place in Division Two in 2007, even though they finished in a distant fourth place in Division Three.

The League's 40-over competition, The Graham Williamson Trophy, was retained by Old Hill, who easily defeated Walsall at the second attempt after the original game had been abandoned with the holders in a strong position. Losing semi-finalists were Shifnal and Knowle & Dorridge. The sixteen teams invited to enter the Competition each year are the 12 Premier Division Clubs, from the previous season, the Champions and Runners-up from Division One and the Champions from Division Two and Division Three.

Since 1958, the League has organized a successful midweek Knock-Out Competition, the Challenge Cup, in various guises. Previous formats have taken the shape of sixteen eight-ball over and fifteen eight ball over contests but, in 2006, the Competition was re-branded as the (Twenty20) Challenge Cup. Second Division side Attock were comfortable winners over two legs against Second Division Champions Cannock from an entry of 30 Clubs. Attock's Imran Sabir won the 'Man of the Match' Award from League sponsor, Birmingham Midshires.

20/20 Challenge Cup winners, Attock CC 1st XI

2006 League Tables

PREMIER 1st XI

	P	W1	W2	TD	WD	ED	LD	L	A	BtP	BwP	Pts
WALSALL	22	5	5	0	5	0	1	3	3	19	28	323
W.B.DARTMOUTH	22	6	3	0	3	0	1	4	5	20	21	296
KENILWORTH WDNS	22	1	5	0	8	0	6	2	0	35	45	280
HIMLEY	22	1	7	0	1	0	3	5	5	25	28	256
MOSELEY	22	3	4	0	2	0	0	7	6	22	26	246
WELLINGTON	22	2	5	0	1	1	1	6	6	12	30	235
KNOWLE & DORRIDGE	22	2	1	0	4	1	3	4	7	35	46	224
COVENTRY NW	22	2	3	1	2	0	2	7	5	24	38	223
BARNT GREEN	22	4	2	1	0	0	2	7	6	21	21	220
KIDDERMINSTER VIC	22	3	0	0	4	0	4	6	5	32	39	208
OLD HILL	22	3	2	0	1	0	5	6	5	20	30	195
SHREWSBURY	22	1	1	0	0	0	3	14	3	39	34	135

PENALTIES:

Pts	Team	Reason for penalty
3	KNOWLE & DORRIDGE	Slow over rate
10	OLD HILL	Disciplinary reasons
3	SHREWSBURY	Failing to Report Result to Results Service
1	WALSALL	Slow over rate

Walsall CC 1st XI, 2006 Premier Division Champions

FIRST DIVISION 1st XI

	P	W1	W2	TD	WD	ED	LD	L	A	BtP	BwP	Pts
SHIFNAL	22	5	6	0	3	0	2	2	4	15	21	321
WALMLEY	22	5	3	0	3	0	3	4	4	27	30	287
HARBORNE	22	5	2	0	3	0	1	4	7	28	26	275
SUTTON COLDFIELD	22	7	1	0	2	0	2	8	2	18	37	273
WOLVERHAMPTON	22	4	3	0	1	0	3	5	6	13	36	249
WATER ORTON	22	4	2	0	4	0	1	8	3	32	38	249
STRATFORD-ON-AVON	22	5	0	0	4	0	1	7	5	34	36	248
LEAMINGTON SPA	22	3	4	0	2	0	1	5	7	14	27	246
HALESOWEN	22	6	0	0	2	0	1	8	5	21	26	234
BROMSGROVE	22	5	2	0	0	0	3	8	4	17	27	229
SMETHWICK	22	1	1	0	4	0	5	5	6	27	42	184
ASTON UNITY	22	2	0	0	0	0	5	12	3	16	26	115

PENALTIES:

Pts	Team	Reason for penalty
1	BROMSGROVE	Slow over rate
3	SHIFNAL	Failing to report result to Results Service
1	SMETHWICK	Slow over rate
1	STRATFORD-ON-AVON	Slow over rate
6	WATER ORTON	Slow over rate

Shifnal CC 1st XI, 2006 First Division Champions

SECOND DIVISION 1st XI

	P	W1	W2	TD	WD	ED	LD	L	A	BtP	BwP	Pts
CANNOCK	22	10	1	0	2	0	2	3	4	17	18	335
ASTON MANOR	22	4	6	0	1	0	0	6	5	20	25	294
DORRIDGE	22	3	4	0	5	0	0	5	5	24	34	275
EVESHAM	22	3	4	1	3	0	3	5	3	22	31	258
OLD ELIZABETHANS	22	4	3	0	2	0	3	6	4	16	35	248
ATTOCK	22	3	4	0	2	0	5	7	1	26	40	243
PENN	22	5	1	0	2	0	2	8	4	31	34	242
TAMWORTH	22	4	3	0	2	0	2	8	3	19	31	241
FORDHOUSES	22	3	3	1	0	0	2	7	5	16	34	216
BRIDGNORTH	22	3	3	0	0	0	1	9	6	14	26	204
STUDLEY	22	1	1	0	6	0	2	8	4	32	46	191
PELSALL	22	1	3	0	1	0	4	7	6	27	28	182

PENALTIES:

Pts	Team	Reason for penalty
3	FORDHOUSES	Failing to Report Result to Results Service
1	OLD ELIZABETHANS	Slow over rate
3	PENN	Failing to Report Result to Results Service
3	STUDLEY	Failing to Report Result to Results Service
6	ATTOCK	Slow over Rate
3	PELSALL	Slow over rate

THIRD DIVISION 1st XI

	P	W1	W2	TD	WD	ED	LD	L	A	BtP	BwP	Pts
NEWPORT	22	6	4	0	4	0	2	4	2	26	31	326
BERKSWELL	22	9	2	0	1	0	4	2	4	18	17	324
ST. GEORGES	22	5	5	0	2	0	1	4	5	15	22	300
SOLIHULL BLOSS	22	3	5	0	2	0	1	5	6	15	25	254
COLESHILL	22	4	3	1	1	0	4	5	4	18	33	251
WOMBOURNE	22	3	4	0	2	0	1	6	6	27	27	251
WHITCHURCH	22	2	3	1	4	1	1	5	5	27	38	245
OMBERSLEY	22	2	4	0	2	0	2	6	6	32	29	238
BEACON	22	2	4	0	1	0	4	6	5	23	35	227
KINGS HEATH	22	2	1	0	4	0	0	9	6	33	39	202
REDDITCH	22	4	0	0	1	0	5	8	4	17	28	179
WORCESTER	22	1	0	0	1	1	0	18	1	33	44	119

PENALTIES:

Pts	Team	Reason for penalty
3	BERKSWELL	Failing to Report Result to Results Service
6	SOLIHULL BLOSS	Failing to Report Result to Results Service
1	NEWPORT	Slow over rate
1	OMBERSLEY	Slow over rate
3	WOMBOURNE	Slow over rate

PREMIER 2nd XI

	P	W1	W2	TD	WD	ED	LD	L	A	BtP	BwP	Pts
LEAMINGTON SPA	22	4	3	0	5	0	1	3	6	22	26	276
WOLVERHAMPTON	22	1	5	0	8	0	2	3	3	29	37	273
BARNT GREEN	22	2	4	0	5	0	3	2	6	25	37	266
KNOWLE & DORRIDGE	22	4	4	0	1	0	6	2	5	18	26	265
KIDDERMINSTER VIC	22	3	3	0	5	0	5	3	3	25	30	252
WALSALL	22	3	5	0	0	0	4	4	6	20	15	245
MOSELEY	22	3	1	0	4	0	3	3	8	27	31	228
WALMLEY	22	1	4	0	1	0	6	4	6	20	37	211
HARBORNE	22	1	1	0	5	0	3	6	6	38	38	196
COVENTRY NW	22	1	1	0	5	0	3	7	5	24	40	176
OLD HILL	22	1	1	0	1	0	3	9	7	22	25	140
HALESOWEN	22	0	1	0	1	0	2	11	7	27	29	120

PENALTIES:

Pts	Team	Reason for penalty
3	COVENTRY NW	Failing to Report Result to Results Service
3	HALESOWEN	Failing to Report Result to Results Service

FIRST DIVISION 2nd XI

	P	W1	W2	TD	WD	ED	LD	L	A	BtP	BwP	Pts
ATTOCK	22	8	2	0	6	0	1	3	2	25	31	348
SHREWSBURY	22	7	1	0	4	0	2	3	5	18	28	295
SUTTON COLDFIELD	22	3	4	0	5	0	2	3	5	25	31	277
SHIFNAL	22	1	5	0	6	0	3	3	4	29	31	258
HIMLEY	22	5	2	0	1	0	7	3	4	23	28	253
STRATFORD-ON-AVON	22	3	3	0	4	0	0	8	4	30	29	243
W.B.DARTMOUTH	22	3	1	0	4	0	2	6	6	36	28	222
KENILWORTH WDNS	22	3	2	0	2	0	2	6	7	22	26	215
WATER ORTON	22	4	1	0	1	0	8	4	4	20	30	207
DORRIDGE	22	2	2	0	1	0	6	4	7	23	30	196
REDDITCH	22	3	0	0	3	0	3	8	5	20	42	186
ASTON UNITY	22	2	0	0	0	0	1	15	3	18	33	68

PENALTIES:

Pts	Team	Reason for penalty
3	REDDITCH	Failing to Report Result to Results Service
3	WATER ORTON	Failing to Report Result to Results Service
48	ASTON UNITY	Failing to Fulfill Two Fixtures

SECOND DIVISION 2nd XI

	P	W1	W2	TD	WD	ED	LD	L	A	BtP	BwP	Pts
BRIDGNORTH	22	8	3	0	5	0	1	0	5	19	17	352
TAMWORTH	22	6	5	0	3	0	2	4	3	17	26	330
PENN	22	3	8	0	1	0	3	2	5	9	17	297
BROMSGROVE	22	4	5	0	1	0	2	5	5	20	19	272
WELLINGTON	22	4	2	0	3	0	0	5	8	22	22	241
SMETHWICK	22	5	3	0	2	0	1	5	6	22	14	240
PELSALL	22	4	3	0	0	0	3	7	5	11	22	220
CANNOCK	22	2	2	0	3	0	3	6	6	18	31	197
FORDHOUSES	22	1	3	0	2	0	3	9	4	19	32	174
ST. GEORGES	22	0	2	0	2	0	3	10	5	22	40	149
WORCESTER	22	1	1	0	4	0	0	14	2	22	30	135
KINGS HEATH	22	1	1	0	0	0	5	11	4	15	33	122

PENALTIES:

Pts	Team	Reason for penalty
3	BRIDGNORTH	Failing to Report Result to Results Service
3	FORDHOUSES	Failing to Report Result to Results Service
3	WELLINGTON	Failing to Report Result to Results Service
3	WORCESTER	Failing to Report Result to Results Service
24	SMETHWICK	Failing to Fulfill Fixture

THIRD DIVISION 2nd XI

	P	W1	W2	TD	WD	ED	LD	L	A	BtP	BwP	Pts
EVESHAM	22	6	5	0	4	0	1	2	4	19	24	341
BEACON	22	5	6	0	0	0	4	3	4	16	22	306
OLD ELIZABETHANS	22	3	5	0	6	0	1	3	4	31	31	304
WHITCHURCH	22	4	1	0	7	0	1	3	6	32	24	257
BERKSWELL	22	4	0	0	7	0	2	5	4	37	36	249
OMBERSLEY	22	4	2	0	1	0	5	6	4	24	39	234
STUDLEY	22	2	4	0	3	0	2	6	5	19	29	229
NEWPORT	22	4	0	0	3	0	1	10	4	28	41	211
ASTON MANOR	22	1	3	0	2	0	5	5	6	38	31	209
WOMBOURNE	22	1	3	0	3	0	4	7	4	23	36	195
SOLIHULL BLOSS	22	2	3	0	0	0	4	10	3	14	35	180
COLESHILL	22	1	1	0	0	0	6	10	4	20	34	130

PENALTIES:

Pts	Team	Reason for penalty
3	OMBERSLEY	Failing to Report Result to Results Service
3	WHITCHURCH	Failing to Report Result to Results Service

Challenge Cup Results

Final 2nd Leg

Cannock 145 for 8 (20 overs) lost to
Attock 171 for 3 (20 overs) by 26 runs

Final 1st Leg

Attock 116 (19.1 overs) defeated
Cannock 55 (10 overs) by 61 runs

Semi-Finals

Smethwick 188 all out (19.4 overs) lost to
Cannock 210 for 8 (20 overs) by 22 runs

Knowle & Dorridge 117 all out (18.4 overs) lost to
Attock 173 for 5 (20 overs) by 56 runs

Williamson Trophy Results

Final

Walsall 148 all out (38.3 overs) lost to
Old Hill 150 for 2 (28.3 overs) by 8 wickets

Semi-Finals

Old Hill 257 for 4 (38.5 overs) defeated
Shifnal 253 for 4 (40 overs) by 6 wickets

Walsall 206 for 8 (40 overs) defeated
Knowle & Dorridge 196 all out (39.1 overs) by 10 runs

Old Hill CC 1st XI easily defeated league champions Walsall in the Williamson Trophy Final, but the four-times National Knockout champions were relegated to Division One

2006 Averages

* Overseas player   + Contracted player

BATTING (top 6):

Premier League 1st XI

		Inns	NO	Runs	HS	Ave
W. Gifford+	Kidderminster Vic.	13	2	640	138	58.18
S. Kotak*	Kenilworth W.	22	8	756	131	54.00
N. Round	Walsall	19	6	607	104*	46.69
K.D. Bell	Coventry & N.W.	14	4	462	91	46.20
S. Lampitt	Himley	16	5	488	81	44.36
J. Dhillon	Himley	14	5	377	121	41.89

First Division 1st XI

		Inns	NO	Runs	HS	Ave
A. Gait	Wolverhamtpon	18	7	840	145*	76.36
D.A. Banks	Smethwick	12	6	437	109*	72.83
S. Gear	Harborne	16	6	620	89*	62.00
F. Shahid	Halesowen	18	6	699	139*	58.25
L. Parker+	Stratford upon A.	15	1	767	118	54.79
D. Pashley	Shifnal	12	4	428	118	53.50

Second Division 1st XI

		Inns	NO	Runs	HS	Ave
N. Van W'kom*	Fordhouses	19	5	956	120*	68.29
D. Ball*	Dorridge	16	6	674	126*	67.40
A. Hafeez	Dorridge	18	6	673	122*	56.08
D. Powles*	Cannock	19	3	831	128*	51.94
K. Ali+	Aston Manor	12	3	420	115	46.67
S. Macey	Old Elizabethans	20	3	742	82	43.65

Third Division 1st XI

		Inns	NO	Runs	HS	Ave
R. Bhatia*	Newport	22	10	1124	200*	93.67
M. Hasnain*	Whitchurch	18	5	983	195*	75.62
D. Ostler	Berkswell	18	2	985	202*	61.56
D. Catterall	Ombersley	18	5	763	111	58.69
R. Nelson*	Kings Heath	19	5	747	127*	53.36
Z. Suliman	Coleshill	17	4	631	144*	48.54

Premier League 2nd XI

		Inns	NO	Runs	HS	Ave
R. Milne	Harborne	12	3	486	103*	54.00
S.Drury	Wolverhampton	10	3	351	74*	50.14
J. Taplin	Coventry & N.W.	12	4	382	107	47.75
Abid Din	Moseley	11	4	334	71	47.71
S. Williams	Barnt Green	14	2	558	106*	46.50
G. Jones	Leamington	15	4	485	118*	44.09

First Division 2nd XI

		Inns	NO	Runs	HS	Ave
A. Thornley	Dorridge	12	2	715	178*	71.50
J. White	Dorridge	11	3	469	88*	58.63
J. Foster	Shrewsbury	13	5	450	83*	56.25
W. Clarke	Shifnal	13	5	412	74	51.50
J. Miller	Sutton Coldfield	10	2	370	65	46.25
P. Kalair	W.B. Dartmouth	10	1	407	88	45.22

Second Division 2nd XI

		Inns	NO	Runs	HS	Ave
M. Bennison	Bromsgrove	10	3	479	86*	68.43
G. Taylor	Tamworth	13	4	585	95*	65.00
A. Bristow	Wellington	10	3	392	103*	56.00
R. Mateen	Smethwick	13	2	568	110*	51.64
A. Gough	Tamworth	10	2	400	71	50.00
M. Liddington	Pelsall	10	2	368	133*	46.00

Third Division 2nd XI

		Inns	NO	Runs	HS	Ave
D. Powell	Beacon	10	5	337	66*	67.40
A. Forman	Aston Manor	10	2	454	116	56.75
P. Tongue	Ombersley	10	1	439	114	48.78
J. Gregory	Evesham	10	3	339	83	48.43
A. Rahim	Aston Manor	18	2	738	129	46.13
B. Jones	Beacon	10	4	266	66*	44.33

BOWLING (top 6):

Premier League 1st XI

		Ovs	Ms	Runs	Wkts	Ave
P. Wicker	Walsall	214.4	41	679	47	14.45
A. Khan	Coventry & N.W.	196.3	26	660	45	14.67
M. Robinson	Wellington	151.2	20	592	39	15.18
S. Kotak *	Kenilworth W.	362.3	42	1287	83	15.51
T. Friend *	Knowle & Dorridge	231.3	46	720	42	17.14
N. Tahir +	W.B. Dartmouth	131.1	22	430	25	17.20

First Division 1st XI

		Ovs	Ms	Runs	Wkts	Ave
N. Thompson	Sutton Coldfield	104.4	22	312	25	12.48
I. Ali *	Halesowen	278.2	59	761	57	13.35
L. Irish	Water Orton	265	68	828	62	13.35
C. Sayers *	Shifnal	209.1	42	685	51	13.43
A. Suman *	Sutton Coldfield	263.3	67	815	57	14.30
D. Culbard	Harborne	97.3	17	287	20	14.35

Second Division 1st XI

		Ovs	Ms	Runs	Wkts	Ave
G. Bulpitt	Cannock	240.5	77	673	59	11.41
N. Radford	Evesham	143.5	27	428	37	11.57
J. Gray	Tamworth	109	16	393	31	12.68
J. Benjamin	Aston Manor	214	38	722	49	14.73
S. Harris	Studley	123.4	0	295	20	14.75
M. Fayyaz *	Aston Manor	177	28	539	36	14.97

Third Division 1st XI

		Ovs	Ms	Runs	Wkts	Ave
S. Taylor	St. Georges	101	28	236	25	9.44
J. Hussain	Solihull Blossom.	117.4	19	283	23	12.30
R. Bhatia *	Newport	370.1	94	1069	80	13.36
A. Ali	Whitchurch	237.2	75	670	48	13.96
K. Threlkeld	Berkswell	139.2	30	549	36	15.25
A. Huxley	Whitchurch	126.5	13	522	30	17.40

Premier League 2nd XI

		Ovs	Ms	Runs	Wkts	Ave
G. Broome	Walmley	35.1	8	107	12	8.92
P. Mann	Barnt Green	85.5	28	248	23	10.78
D. Bennett	Wolverhampton	159	31	426	35	12.17
S. Lloyd	Kidderminster Vic.	61.4	17	214	16	13.38
M. Lilley	Coventry & N.W.	143	25	406	28	14.50
S. Ogrizovic	Coventry & N.W.	92	22	248	17	14.59

First Division 2nd XI

		Ovs	Ms	Runs	Wkts	Ave
W. Troughton	Stratford upon A.	120.2	31	326	27	12.07
R. Ahmed	Attock	116.3	23	352	28	12.57
M. Ball	Sutton Coldfield	80	10	244	19	12.84
R. Byrne	Himley	87	11	296	23	12.87
T. Collins	Shifnal	66.5	10	171	13	13.15
S. Hooper	Dorridge	70	9	239	18	13.28

Second Division 2nd XI

		Ovs	Ms	Runs	Wkts	Ave
D. Hampton	Wellington	58	22	97	18	5.39
J. Manuel	Tamworth	115	34	263	31	8.48
A. Brains	Penn	26	6	101	10	10.10
S. Caine	Bridgnorth	146.3	52	305	30	10.17
H. Patel	Penn	65.4	18	175	17	10.29
I. Gregory	Bridgnorth	35	10	115	10	11.50

Third Division 2nd XI

		Ovs	Ms	Runs	Wkts	Ave
I. Stowe	Evesham	30.1	6	79	11	7.18
A. Green	Beacon	45.3	13	121	14	8.64
A. Brookes	Evesham	57.3	10	151	14	10.79
J. Gregory	Evesham	68	15	201	15	13.40
R. Jones	Whitchurch	143	32	421	28	15.04
J. Anderson	Evesham	107.3	16	347	23	15.09

Birmingham Midshires
sign for three years

FOLLOWING their successful sponsorship, in 2006, Birmingham Midshires has agreed a new deal, with the Management Board of the League for the next three seasons, 2007, 2008 and 2009. The deal covers the League Programme and the (Twenty20) Challenge Cup Competition. The Company will again provide a cash prize of £1,000 to the player who wins the most 'Man of the Match' Awards, selected by the umpires at the end of each Premier Division match. There will, also, be an Award for the 'Man of the Match' in the (Twenty20) Challenge Cup Final.

The 2006 Champions, Walsall, will start as one of the favourites for the 2007 Premier Division title, having strengthened their side by signing opening bowler, Gareth Williams, from Barnt Green and hard-hitting batsman, Chris Tranter, from Old Wulfs Tettenhall. They have, also, re-signed their overseas player from last season, Gerrie Snyman, as they attempt to become the second team to retain the title since the League's formation in 1998. Runners-up, West Bromwich Dartmouth, will again be strong, even though they appear to have lost former England under 19 skipper, Moeen Ali, who looks likely to be allocated to a Worcestershire Club, as well as Huw Jones and Chris Boroughs. Former Derbyshire all-rounder Mohammed Sheikh returns to Sandwell Park from Smethwick despite strong overtures from Knowle & Dorridge and Walsall. 2005 Champions, Barnt Green, have also lost Matt Rawnsley (to Ombersley) and Paul Bedford (to Water Orton), but they have captured the services of Warwickshire all-rounder, Dougie Brown. Former Bears keeper, Tony Frost, takes over as skipper at Knowle & Dorridge, and he has persuaded a former team-mate, Moseley's Nick Warren, to join him at Station Road, where Travis Friend is retained as the Overseas Player.

Both relegated sides from the Premier Division, Old Hill and Shrewsbury are expected to challenge strongly for the Division One title, alongside Harborne, Water Orton and Stratford-upon-Avon.

Nigel Stockton (Chief Executive, Birmingham Midshires), Jamie Fleet (Marketing Chairman, BDPCL), Jason Robinson (Director of Savings & Investment, Birmingham Midshires) and Nick Archer (General Manager, BDPCL) celebrate the signing of the three-year sponsorship deal.

Wolverhampton, having lost their leading scorer, Andrew Gait, and left-arm opening bowler, Danny Smith (to Penn), will do well to finish in the top half, as will promoted Aston Manor and Bromsgrove. The other promoted Club, Cannock, should be comfortable in mid-table, alongside Halesowen and Sutton Coldfield.

In Division Two, relegated Smethwick and promoted Berskwell will expect to do well, as will Penn and Fordhouses, who have both recruited strongly, during the close season. Aston Unity look to be in 'free-fall' and Newport's chances will depend on the performances of Rajiv Bhatia, who has signed for the Shropshire Club for another season. Dorridge will fancy their chances of regaining the place they lost in Division One in 2005, but Bridgnorth and Tamworth may have to settle for mid-table security. Evesham and Attock, in particular, are unpredictable and their season will be shaped by results in early matches.

With four sides relegated out of the League at the end of each season, stress levels in Division Three remain high until the final game has been played. Studley and Pelsall will be eager to regain the places they have lost in a higher Division, but they will need a good start to avoid a relegation 'dog-fight'. The four promoted sides, Kington, Old Wulfs Tettenhall, Olton & W.W. and Wem are unknown quantities, but the sides from Shropshire are, traditionally, strong. On that basis, Wem will be expected to challenge for promotion, alongside St. Georges and Whitchurch, but Coleshill, Ombersley, Solihull Blossomfield and Wombourne, also, fall into the unknown category, where a poor start could leave them looking over their shoulders for the rest of the season.

Although relegated to Division One, Old Hill will start as favourites to retain the Graham Williamson Trophy for the third year in succession. The shorter form of the game suits their explosive batting line-up, but they can expect a strong challenge from previous winners, Barnt Green, as well as Knowle & Dorridge, Walsall and Shifnal.

2007 Member clubs

Aston Manor
Church Road,
Perry Barr,
Birmingham B42 2LA
Tel: 0121 356 6537

Aston Unity
Coppice Lane,
Bassett's Pole,
Sutton Coldfield B78 2BS
Tel: 0121 308 5857

Attock
Moseley School, Wake
Green Road, Moseley,
Birmingham B13 9UU
Tel: 0121 777 0333

Barnt Green
Cherry Hill Road,
Barnt Green,
Birmingham B45 8LN
Tel: 0121 445 1684

Berkswell
Meeting House Lane,
Balsall Common,
Coventry CV7 7GE
Tel: 01676 533962

Bridgnorth
Cricket Meadow,
Bridgnorth WV16 4LB
Tel: 01746 764919

Bromsgrove
St. Godwald's Park,
St. Godwald's Road,
Aston Field
Bromsgrove B60 3BW
Tel: 01527 570878

Cannock
The Morris Ground,
Church Lane, Hatherton,
Cannock WS11 1RR
Tel: 01543 502424

Coleshill
Memorial Park,
Parkfield Road, Coleshill
Tel: 01675 462120

Coventry & NW
Binley Road,
Coventry CV3 1HB
Tel: 024 7645 1426

Dorridge
John Woolman Ground,
Broadacre, Grange Road,
Dorridge, Solihull
Tel: 01564 772077

Evesham
Off Albert Road,
Evesham
Tel: 01386 446469

Fordhouses
Wobaston Road,
Pendeford,
Wolverhampton WV9 9EW
Tel: 01902 397038

Halesowen
Seth Somers Park,
Grange Road,
Halesowen B63 3EG
Tek: 0121 550 2744

Harborne
Old Church Avenue,
Harborne,
Birmingham B17 0BE
Tel: 0121 427 4110

Himley
Stourbridge Road (A449),
Himley DY3 3PH
Tel: 01902 898239

Kenilworth Wardens
Glasshouse Park,
Glasshouse Lane,
Kenilworth CV8 2AL
Tel: 01926 852476

Kidderminster Victoria
Chester Road North,
Kidderminster DY10 1TH
Tel: 01562 824175

Kington
The Recreation Ground
Mill Street, Kington,
Herefordshire HR5 3AT
Tel: 01544 230095

Knowle & Dorridge
Station Road, Dorridge,
Solihull B93 8ET
Tel: 01564 774338

Leamington Spa
Arlington Avenue,
Leamington Spa
Tel: 01926 423854

Moseley
'Scorers',
Streetsbrook Road,
Solihull B90 3PE
Tel: 0121 744 5694

Newport
Audley Avenue,
Newport,
Shropshire TF10 4AD
Tel: 01952 810403

Old Elizabethans
The Memorial Ground,
Perdiswell Park,
Worcester WR2 7SN
Tel: 01905 756617

Old Hill
Haden Park Road,
Haden Hill,
Cradley Heath B64 7HF
Tel: 01384 566827

Old Wulfs Tettenhall
253a Castlecroft Road,
Wolverhampton WV3 8NA
Tel: 01902 761410

Olton & West Warwickshire
Grange Road, Olton,
Solihull B91 1BA
Tel: 0121 706 2192

Ombersley
Main Road, Ombersley,
Worcester WR9 0ET
Tel: 01905 621469

Pelsall
Walsall Road, Pelsall,
Walsall WS3 4BP
Tel: 01922 682018

Penn
Mount Road, Penn,
Wolverhampton WV4 5RU
Tel: 01902 331546

Shifnal
Priorslee Road,
Shifnal
Tel: 01952 462033

Shrewsbury
London Road,
Shrewsbury SY2 6PT
Tel: 01743 363655

Smethwick
Broomfield, The Uplands,
Smethwick B67 6BJ
Tel: 0121 558 0084

Solihull Blossomfield
The Wardens,
Widney Lane, Solihull
Tel: 0121 705 3254

St Georges
Recreation Ground,
Church Street, St. Georges
Telford TF2 9LU
Tel: 01952 612911

Stratford Upon Avon
Swan's Nest Lane,
Stratford-upon-Avon
CV37 6LS
Tel: 01789 297968

Studley
Washford Fields,
Birmingham Road,
Studley B80 7BG
Tel: 01527 853668

Sutton Coldfield
Rectory Park,
Rectory Road,
Sutton Coldfield B75 7RS
Tel: 0121 378 1294

Tamworth
Hints Road, Hopwas,
Tamworth B78 3AT
Tel: 01827 63428

Walmley
Eldon Drive,
Walmley B76 1LT
Tel: 0121 351 1349

Walsall
Gorway, Gorway Road,
Walsall WS1 3BE
Tel: 01922 622094

Water Orton
Coleshill Road,
Water Orton,
Birmingham B46 1QX
Tel: 0121 747 7158

Wellington
Orleton Park,
Haygate Road,
Wellington,
Telford TF1 2BU
Tel: 01952 251539

Wem
The Kynaston Ground,
Soulton Road, Wem,
Shropshire SY4 5HR
Tel: 01939 234680

West Bromwich Dartmouth
Sandwell Park,
Birmingham Road,
West Bromwich B71
Tel: 0121 553 0168

Whitchurch
Heath Road,
Whitchurch,
Shropshire SY13 3JG
Tel: 01948 663923

Wolverhampton
Danescourt Road,
Tettenhall,
Wolverhampton
Tel: 01902 754053

Wombourne
Church Road, Wombourne,
Wolverhampton WV5 9EZ
Tel: 01902 895199

Birmingham & District Premier League

2007 Fixtures

PREMIER DIVISION 1ST XI

Sat 5th May (1.00 pm)
Cov. & N.W. vWellington
Himley vWalsall
Ken. Wdns vK & Dorridge
K'minster V. vMoseley
Shifnal vBarnt Green
Walmley vWB D'mouth

Sat 12th May (1 pm)
Barnt Green vK'minster V.
K & Dorridge vShifnal
Moseley vWalmley
Walsall vCov. & NW
Wellington vHimley
WB D'mouth vKen. Wdns

Sat 19th May (1 pm)
Cov. & NW vK'minster V.
Ken. Wdns vHimley
Shifnal vWB D'mouth
Walmley vBarnt Green
Walsall vMoseley
Wellington vK & Dorridge

Sat 26th May (1 pm)
Himley vWalmley
Ken. Wdns vWalsall
K'minster V. vShifnal
K & Dorridge vCov. & NW
Moseley vWellington
WB D'mouth vBarnt Green

Mon 28th May (1 pm)
Barnt Green vCov. & NW
K & Dorridge vK'minster V.
Moseley vHimley
Shifnal vWalmley
Walsall vWB D'mouth
Wellington vKen. Wdns

Sat 2nd June (1 pm)
Barnt Green vMoseley
Cov. & NW vHimley
Ken. Wdns vShifnal
Walmley vK'minster V.
Walsall vK & Dorridge
WB D'mouth vWellington

Sat 9th June (1 pm)
Cov. & NW vKen. Wdns
Himley vBarnt Green
K'minster V. vWB D'mouth
K & Dorridge vWalmley
Moseley vShifnal
Wellington vWalsall

Sat 16th June (1 pm)
Barnt Green vKen. Wdns
Himley vK & Dorridge
K'minster V. vWalsall
Shifnal vWellington
Walmley vCov. & NW
WB D'mouth vMoseley

Sat 23rd June (1 pm)
Cov. & NW vWB D'mouth
Ken. Wdns vK'minster V.
Moseley vK & Dorridge
Shifnal vHimley
Walmley vWellington
Walsall vBarnt Green

Sat 30th June (1 pm)
Cov. & NW vShifnal
Himley vWB D'mouth
Ken. Wdns vMoseley
K & Dorridge vBarnt Green
Walsall vWalmley
Wellington vK'minster V.

Sat 7th July (1 pm)
Barnt Green vWellington
K'minster V. vHimley
Moseley vCov. & NW
Shifnal vWalsall
Walmley vKen. Wdns
WB D'mouth vK & Dorridge

Sat 14th July (1 pm)
Barnt Green vShifnal
K & Dorridge vKen. Wdns
Moseley vK'minster V.
Walsall vHimley
Wellington vCov. & NW
WB D'mouth vWalmley

Sat 21st July (1 pm)
Cov. & NW vWalsall
Himley vWellington
Ken. Wdns vWB D'mouth
K'minster V. vBarnt Green
Shifnal vK & Dorridge
Walmley vMoseley

Sat 28th July (1 pm)
Barnt Green vWalmley
Himley vKen. Wdns
K'minster V. vCov. & NW
K & Dorridge vWellington
Moseley vWalsall
WB D'mouth vShifnal

Sat 4th August (12.30 pm)
Barnt Green vWB D'mouth
Cov. & NW vK & Dorridge
Shifnal vK'minster V.
Walmley vHimley
Walsall vKen. Wdns
Wellington vMoseley

Sat 11th August (12.30 pm)
Cov. & NW vBarnt Green
Himley vMoseley
Ken. Wdns vWellington
K'minster V. vK & Dorridge
Walmley vShifnal
WB D'mouth vWalsall

Sat 18th August (12.30 pm)
Himley vCov. & NW
K'minster V. vWalmley
K & Dorridge vWalsall
Moseley vBarnt Green
Shifnal vKen. Wdns
Wellington vWB D'mouth

Sat 25th August (12.30 pm)
Barnt Green vHimley
Ken. Wdns vCov. & NW
Shifnal vMoseley
Walmley vK & Dorridge
Walsall vWellington
WB D'mouth vK'minster V.

Mon 27th August (12.30 pm)
Cov. & NW vWalmley
Ken. Wdns vBarnt Green
K & Dorridge vHimley
Moseley vWB D'mouth
Walsall vK'minster V.
Wellington vShifnal

Sat 1st September (12 pm)
Barnt Green vWalsall
Himley vShifnal
K'minster V. vKen. Wdns
K & Dorridge vMoseley
Wellington vWalmley
WB D'mouth vCov. & NW

Sat 8th September (12 pm)
Barnt Green vK & Dorridge
K'minster V. vWellington
Moseley vKen. Wdns
Shifnal vCov. & NW
Walmley vWalsall
WB D'mouth vHimley

Sat 15th September (12 pm)
Cov. & NW vMoseley
Himley vK'minster V.
Ken. Wdns vWalmley
K & Dorridge vWB D'mouth
Walsall vShifnal
Wellington vBarnt Green

FIRST DIVISION 1ST XI

Sat 5th May (1.00 pm)
Aston Manor vS'ford-up-Av
Halesowen vOld Hill
Harborne vS. Coldfield
L'ton Spa vBromsgrove
Shrewsbury vCannock
Water Orton vW'hampton

Sat 12th May (1 pm)
Bromsgrove vShrewsbury
Cannock vAston Manor
Old Hill vHarborne
S'ford-up-Av vWater Orton
S. Coldfield vHalesowen
W'hampton vL'ton Spa

Sat 19th May (1 pm)
Halesowen vAston Manor
L'ton Spa vHarborne
Old Hill vBromsgrove
Shrewsbury vW'hampton
S. Coldfield vS'ford-up-Av
Water Orton vCannock

Sat 26th May (1 pm)
Aston Manor vShrewsbury
Bromsgrove vHalesowen
Harborne vWater Orton
L'ton Spa vS. Coldfield
S'ford-up-Av vOld Hill
W'hampton vCannock

Mon 28th May (1 pm)
Bromsgrove vAston Manor
Cannock vHalesowen
Old Hill vL'ton Spa
Shrewsbury vWater Orton
S'ford-up-Av vHarborne
S. Coldfield vW'hampton

Sat 2nd June (1 pm)
Cannock vS'ford-up-Av
Halesowen vHarborne
L'ton Spa vShrewsbury
S. Coldfield vBromsgrove
Water Orton vAston Manor
W'hampton vOld Hill

Sat 9th June (1 pm)
Aston Manor vW'hampton
Bromsgrove vWater Orton
Halesowen vL'ton Spa
Harborne vCannock
Old Hill vS. Coldfield
S'ford-up-Av vShrewsbury

Sat 16th June (1 pm)
Aston Manor vS. Coldfield
Cannock vL'ton Spa
Harborne vBromsgrove
Shrewsbury vOld Hill
Water Orton vHalesowen
W'hampton vS'ford-up-Av

Sat 23rd June (1 pm)
Halesowen vW'hampton
L'ton Spa vAston Manor
Shrewsbury vHarborne
S'ford-up-Av vBromsgrove
S. Coldfield vCannock
Water Orton vOld Hill

Sat 30th June (1 pm)
Bromsgrove vCannock
Halesowen vShrewsbury
Harborne vW'hampton
L'ton Spa vS'ford-up-Av
Old Hill vAston Manor
S. Coldfield vWater Orton

Sat 7th July (1 pm)
Aston Manor vHarborne
Cannock vOld Hill
Shrewsbury vS. Coldfield
S'ford-up-Av vHalesowen
Water Orton vL'ton Spa
W'hampton vBromsgrove

Sat 14th July (1 pm)
Bromsgrove vL'ton Spa
Cannock vShrewsbury
Old Hill vHalesowen
S'ford-up-Av vAston Manor
S. Coldfield vHarborne
W'hampton vWater Orton

Sat 21st July (1 pm)
Aston Manor vCannock
Halesowen vS. Coldfield
Harborne vOld Hill
L'ton Spa vW'hampton
Shrewsbury vBromsgrove
Water Orton vS'ford-up-Av

Sat 28th July (1 pm)
Aston Manor vHalesowen
Bromsgrove vOld Hill
Cannock vWater Orton
Harborne vL'ton Spa
S'ford-up-Av vS. Coldfield
W'hampton vShrewsbury

Sat 4th August (12.30 pm)
Cannock vW'hampton
Halesowen vBromsgrove
Old Hill vS'ford-up-Av
Shrewsbury vAston Manor
S. Coldfield vL'ton Spa
Water Orton vHarborne

Sat 11th August (12.30 pm)
Aston Manor vBromsgrove
Halesowen vCannock
Harborne vS'ford-up-Av
L'ton Spa vOld Hill
Water Orton vShrewsbury
W'hampton vS. Coldfield

Sat 18th August (12.30 pm)
Aston Manor vWater Orton
Bromsgrove vS. Coldfield
Harborne vHalesowen
Old Hill vW'hampton
Shrewsbury vL'ton Spa
S'ford-up-Av vCannock

Sat 25th August (12.30 pm)
Cannock vHarborne
L'ton Spa vHalesowen
Shrewsbury vS'ford-up-Av
S. Coldfield vOld Hill
Water Orton vBromsgrove
W'hampton vAston Manor

Mon 27th August (12.30 pm)
Bromsgrove vHarborne
Halesowen vWater Orton
L'ton Spa vCannock
Old Hill vShrewsbury
S'ford-up-Av vW'hampton
S. Coldfield vAston Manor

Sat 1st September (12 pm)
Aston Manor vL'ton Spa
Bromsgrove vS'ford-up-Av
Cannock vS. Coldfield
Harborne vShrewsbury
Old Hill vWater Orton
W'hampton vHalesowen

Sat 8th September (12 pm)
Aston Manor vOld Hill
Cannock vBromsgrove
Shrewsbury vHalesowen
S'ford-up-Av vL'ton Spa
Water Orton vS. Coldfield
W'hampton vHarborne

Sat 15th September (12 pm)
Bromsgrove vW'hampton
Halesowen vS'ford-up-Av
Harborne vAston Manor
L'ton Spa vWater Orton
Old Hill vCannock
S. Coldfield vShrewsbury

Birmingham & District Premier League

SECOND DIVISION 1ST XI

Sat 5th May (1 pm)
Berkswell vAttock
Dorridge vEvesham
Fordhouses vBridgnorth
Newport vTamworth
Old Elizab's vAston Unity
Penn vSmethwick

Sat 12th May (1 pm)
Aston Unity vNewport
Attock v Penn
Bridgnorth vDorridge
Evesham vOld Elizab's
Smethwick vBerkswell
Tamworth vFordhouses

Sat 19th May (1 pm)
Attock vTamworth
Berkswell vDorridge
Fordhouses vAston Unity
Newport v Penn
Old Elizab's vBridgnorth
Smethwick vEvesham

Sat 26th May (1 pm)
Aston Unity vBridgnorth
Dorridge vFordhouses
Evesham vAttock
Newport vSmethwick
Penn vOld Elizab's
Tamworth vBerkswell

Mon 28th May (1 pm)
Attock vNewport
Bridgnorth vBerkswell
Evesham v Penn
Fordhouses vOld Elizab's
Smethwick vAston Unity
Tamworth vDorridge

Sat 2nd June (1 pm)
Aston Unity vAttock
Berkswell v Penn
Bridgnorth vEvesham
Newport vFordhouses
Old Elizab's vDorridge
Smethwick vTamworth

Sat 9th June (1 pm)
Attock vSmethwick
Berkswell vNewport
Dorridge vAston Unity
Evesham vFordhouses
Penn vBridgnorth
Tamworth vOld Elizab's

Sat 16th June (1 pm)
Aston Unity vEvesham
Bridgnorth vNewport
Dorridge vSmethwick
Fordhouses vAttock
Old Elizab's vBerkswell
Penn vTamworth

Sat 23rd June (1 pm)
Berkswell vAston Unity
Evesham vTamworth
Fordhouses v Penn
Newport vDorridge
Old Elizab's vAttock
Smethwick vBridgnorth

Sat 30th June (1 pm)
Attock vDorridge
Berkswell vFordhouses
Newport vEvesham
Penn vAston Unity
Smethwick vOld Elizab's
Tamworth vBridgnorth

Sat 7th July (1 pm)
Aston Unity vTamworth
Bridgnorth vAttock
Dorridge v Penn
Evesham vBerkswell
Fordhouses vSmethwick
Old Elizab's vNewport

Sat 14th July (1 pm)
Aston Unity vOld Elizab's
Attock vBerkswell
Bridgnorth vFordhouses
Evesham vDorridge
Smethwick v Penn
Tamworth vNewport

Sat 21st July (1 pm)
Berkswell vSmethwick
Dorridge vBridgnorth
Fordhouses vTamworth
Newport vAston Unity
Old Elizab's vEvesham
Penn vAttock

Sat 28th July (1 pm)
Aston Unity vFordhouses
Bridgnorth vOld Elizab's
Dorridge vBerkswell
Evesham vSmethwick
Penn vNewport
Tamworth vAttock

Sat 4th August (12.30 pm)
Attock vEvesham
Berkswell vTamworth
Bridgnorth vAston Unity
Fordhouses vDorridge
Old Elizab's v Penn
Smethwick vNewport

Sat 11th August (12.30 pm)
Aston Unity vSmethwick
Berkswell vBridgnorth
Dorridge vTamworth
Newport vAttock
Old Elizab's vFordhouses
Penn vEvesham

Sat 18th August (12.30 pm)
Attock vAston Unity
Dorridge vOld Elizab's
Evesham vBridgnorth
Fordhouses vNewport
Penn vBerkswell
Tamworth vSmethwick

Sat 25th August (12.30 pm)
Aston Unity vDorridge
Bridgnorth v Penn
Fordhouses vEvesham
Newport vBerkswell
Old Elizab's vTamworth
Smethwick vAttock

Mon 27th August (12.30 pm)
Attock vFordhouses
Berkswell vOld Elizab's
Evesham vAston Unity
Newport vBridgnorth
Smethwick vDorridge
Tamworth v Penn

Sat 1st September (12 pm)
Aston Unity vBerkswell
Attock vOld Elizab's
Bridgnorth vSmethwick
Dorridge vNewport
Penn vFordhouses
Tamworth vEvesham

Sat 8th September (12 pm)
Aston Unity v Penn
Bridgnorth vTamworth
Dorridge vAttock
Evesham vNewport
Fordhouses vBerkswell
Old Elizab's vSmethwick

Sat 15th September (12 pm)
Attock vBridgnorth
Berkswell vEvesham
Newport vOld Elizab's
Penn vDorridge
Smethwick vFordhouses
Tamworth vAston Unity

THIRD DIVISION 1ST XI

Sat 5th May (1 pm)
Kington   vStudley
Olton & WW   vSol B'field
Old W Tett.   vOmbersley
Pelsall   vColeshill
St. Georges   v Wem
Whitchurch   vWombourne

Sat 12th May (1 pm)
Coleshill   vOld W Tett.
Ombersley   vWhitchurch
Sol B'field   vSt. Georges
Studley   vPelsall
Wem   vOlton & WW
Wombourne   vKington

Sat 19th May (1 pm)
Kington   vOmbersley
Old W Tett.   vStudley
Pelsall   vOlton & WW
Sol B'field   vWombourne
St. Georges   vWhitchurch
Wem   vColeshill

Sat 26th May (1 pm)
Coleshill   vSt. Georges
Olton & WW   vKington
Pelsall   vSol B'field
Studley   vOmbersley
Whitchurch   vOld W Tett.
Wombourne   v Wem

Mon 28th May (1 pm)
Coleshill   vWhitchurch
Old W Tett.   vKington
Ombersley   vSt. Georges
Sol B'field   vStudley
Wem   vPelsall
Wombourne   vOlton & WW

Sat 2nd June (1 pm)
Kington   vWhitchurch
Ombersley   vWombourne
Pelsall   vOld W Tett.
Sol B'field   vColeshill
St. Georges   vOlton & WW
Studley   v Wem

Sat 9th June (1 pm)
Coleshill   vKington
Olton & WW   vOmbersley
St. Georges   vPelsall
Wem   vSol B'field
Whitchurch   vStudley
Wombourne   vOld W Tett.

Sat 16th June (1 pm)
Kington   vSt. Georges
Olton & WW   vColeshill
Old W Tett.   v Wem
Ombersley   vPelsall
Studley   vWombourne
Whitchurch   vSol B'field

Sat 23rd June (1 pm)
Kington   v Wem
Old W Tett.   vOlton & WW
Pelsall   vWhitchurch
Sol B'field   vOmbersley
St. Georges   vStudley
Wombourne   vColeshill

Sat 30th June (1 pm)
Coleshill   vOmbersley
Olton & WW   vStudley
Pelsall   vWombourne
Sol B'field   vKington
St. Georges   vOld W Tett.
Wem   vWhitchurch

Sat 7th July (1 pm)
Kington   vPelsall
Old W Tett.   vSol B'field
Ombersley   v Wem
Studley   vColeshill
Whitchurch   vOlton & WW
Wombourne   vSt. Georges

Sat 14th July (1 pm)
Coleshill   vPelsall
Ombersley   vOld W Tett.
Sol B'field   vOlton & WW
Studley   vKington
Wem   vSt. Georges
Wombourne   vWhitchurch

Sat 21st July (1 pm)
Kington   vWombourne
Olton & WW   v Wem
Old W Tett.   vColeshill
Pelsall   vStudley
St. Georges   vSol B'field
Whitchurch   vOmbersley

Sat 28th July (1 pm)
Coleshill   v Wem
Olton & WW   vPelsall
Ombersley   vKington
Studley   vOld W Tett.
Whitchurch   vSt. Georges
Wombourne   vSol B'field

Sat 4th August (12.30 pm)
Kington   vOlton & WW
Old W Tett.   vWhitchurch
Ombersley   vStudley
Sol B'field   vPelsall
St. Georges   vColeshill
Wem   vWombourne

Sat 11th August (12.30 pm)
Kington   vOld W Tett.
Olton & WW   vWombourne
Pelsall   v Wem
St. Georges   vOmbersley
Studley   vSol B'field
Whitchurch   vColeshill

Sat 18th August (12.30 pm)
Coleshill   vSol B'field
Olton & WW   vSt. Georges
Old W Tett.   vPelsall
Wem   vStudley
Whitchurch   vKington
Wombourne   vOmbersley

Sat 25th August (12.30 pm)
Kington   vColeshill
Old W Tett.   vWombourne
Ombersley   vOlton & WW
Pelsall   vSt. Georges
Sol B'field   v Wem
Studley   vWhitchurch

Mon 27th August (12.30 pm)
Coleshill   vOlton & WW
Pelsall   vOmbersley
Sol B'field   vWhitchurch
St. Georges   vKington
Wem   vOld W Tett.
Wombourne   vStudley

Sat 1st September (12 pm)
Coleshill   vWombourne
Olton & WW   vOld W Tett.
Ombersley   vSol B'field
Studley   vSt. Georges
Wem   vKington
Whitchurch   vPelsall

Sat 8th September (12 pm)
Kington   vSol B'field
Old W Tett.   vSt. Georges
Ombersley   vColeshill
Studley   vOlton & WW
Whitchurch   v Wem
Wombourne   vPelsall

Sat 15th September (12 pm)
Coleshill   vStudley
Olton & WW   vWhitchurch
Pelsall   vKington
Sol B'field   vOld W Tett.
St. Georges   vWombourne
Wem   vOmbersley

Birmingham & District Premier League

PREMIER DIVISION 2ND XI

Sat 5th May (1.30 pm)
Attock vCov. & NW
Barnt Green vShrewsbury
K & Dorridge vL'ton Spa
Moseley vK'minster V.
Walsall vHarborne
W'hampton vWalmley

Sat 12th May (1.30 pm)
Cov. & NW vWalsall
Harborne vAttock
K'minster V. vBarnt Green
L'ton Spa vW'hampton
Shrewsbury vK & Dorridge
Walmley vMoseley

Sat 19th May (1.30 pm)
Barnt Green vWalmley
Harborne vL'ton Spa
K'minster V. vCov. & NW
K & Dorridge vAttock
Moseley vWalsall
W'hampton vShrewsbury

Sat 26th May (1.30 pm)
Attock vMoseley
Barnt Green vW'hampton
Cov. & NW vK & Dorridge
Shrewsbury vK'minster V.
Walmley vHarborne
Walsall vL'ton Spa

Mon 28th May (1.30 pm)
Cov. & NW vBarnt Green
Harborne vMoseley
K'minster V. vK & Dorridge
L'ton Spa vAttock
Walmley vShrewsbury
W'hampton vWalsall

Sat 2nd June (1.30 pm)
Attock vW'hampton
Harborne vCov. & NW
K'minster V. vWalmley
K & Dorridge vWalsall
Moseley vBarnt Green
Shrewsbury vL'ton Spa

Sat 9th June (1.30 pm)
Barnt Green vHarborne
L'ton Spa vCov. & NW
Shrewsbury vMoseley
Walmley vK & Dorridge
Walsall vAttock
W'hampton vK'minster V.

Sat 16th June (1.30 pm)
Attock vShrewsbury
Cov. & NW vWalmley
K & Dorridge vHarborne
L'ton Spa vBarnt Green
Moseley vW'hampton
Walsall vK'minster V.

Sat 23rd June (1.30 pm)
Attock vWalmley
Barnt Green vWalsall
Harborne vShrewsbury
K'minster V. vL'ton Spa
K & Dorridge vMoseley
W'hampton vCov. & NW

Sat 30th June (1.30 pm)
Barnt Green vK & Dorridge
K'minster V. vAttock
Moseley vL'ton Spa
Shrewsbury vCov. & NW
Walmley vWalsall
W'hampton vHarborne

Sat 7th July (1.30 pm)
Attock vBarnt Green
Cov. & NW vMoseley
Harborne vK'minster V.
K & Dorridge vW'hampton
L'ton Spa vWalmley
Walsall vShrewsbury

Sat 14th July (1.30 pm)
Cov. & NW vAttock
Harborne vWalsall
K'minster V. vMoseley
L'ton Spa vK & Dorridge
Shrewsbury vBarnt Green
Walmley vW'hampton

Sat 21st July (1.30 pm)
Attock vHarborne
Barnt Green vK'minster V.
K & Dorridge vShrewsbury
Moseley vWalmley
Walsall vCov. & NW
W'hampton vL'ton Spa

Sat 28th July (1.30 pm)
Attock vK & Dorridge
Cov. & NW vK'minster V.
L'ton Spa vHarborne
Shrewsbury vW'hampton
Walmley vBarnt Green
Walsall vMoseley

Sat 4th August (1 pm)
Harborne vWalmley
K'minster V. vShrewsbury
K & Dorridge vCov. & NW
L'ton Spa vWalsall
Moseley vAttock
W'hampton vBarnt Green

Sat 11th August (1 pm)
Attock vL'ton Spa
Barnt Green vCov. & NW
K & Dorridge vK'minster V.
Moseley vHarborne
Shrewsbury vWalmley
Walsall vW'hampton

Sat 18th August (1 pm)
Barnt Green vMoseley
Cov. & NW vHarborne
L'ton Spa vShrewsbury
Walmley vK'minster V.
Walsall vK & Dorridge
W'hampton vAttock

Sat 25th August (1 pm)
Attock vWalsall
Cov. & NW vL'ton Spa
Harborne vBarnt Green
K'minster V. vW'hampton
K & Dorridge vWalmley
Moseley vShrewsbury

Mon 27th August (1 pm)
Barnt Green vL'ton Spa
Harborne vK & Dorridge
K'minster V. vWalsall
Shrewsbury vAttock
Walmley vCov. & NW
W'hampton vMoseley

Sat 1st Sept (12.30 pm)
Cov. & NW vW'hampton
L'ton Spa vK'minster V.
Moseley vK & Dorridge
Shrewsbury vHarborne
Walmley vAttock
Walsall vBarnt Green

Sat 8th Sept (12.30 pm)
Attock vK'minster V.
Cov. & NW vShrewsbury
Harborne vW'hampton
K & Dorridge vBarnt Green
L'ton Spa vMoseley
Walsall vWalmley

Sat 15th Sept (12.30 pm)
Barnt Green vAttock
K'minster V. vHarborne
Moseley vCov. & NW
Shrewsbury vWalsall
Walmley vL'ton Spa
W'hampton vK & Dorridge

FIRST DIVISION 2ND XI

Sat 5th May (1.30 pm)
Bridgnorth   vShifnal
Old Hill   vHalesowen
S'ford-up-Av   vDorridge
S. Coldfield   vHimley
Tamworth   vKen. Wdns
WB D'mouth   vWater Orton

Sat 12th May (1.30 pm)
Dorridge   vBridgnorth
Halesowen   vS. Coldfield
Himley   vOld Hill
Ken. Wdns   vWB D'mouth
Shifnal   vTamworth
Water Orton   vS'ford-up-Av

Sat 19th May (1.30 pm)
Bridgnorth   vWater Orton
Dorridge   vHalesowen
Himley   vKen. Wdns
S'ford-up-Av   vS. Coldfield
Tamworth   vOld Hill
WB D'mouth   vShifnal

Sat 26th May (1.30 pm)
Bridgnorth   vWB D'mouth
Halesowen   vTamworth
Old Hill   vS'ford-up-Av
Shifnal   vDorridge
S. Coldfield   vKen. Wdns
Water Orton   vHimley

Mon 28th May (1.30 pm)
Dorridge   vTamworth
Halesowen   vBridgnorth
Himley   vS'ford-up-Av
Ken. Wdns   vOld Hill
Water Orton   vShifnal
WB D'mouth   vS. Coldfield

Sat 2nd June (1.30 pm)
Dorridge   vWater Orton
Himley   vHalesowen
Old Hill   vWB D'mouth
Shifnal   vKen. Wdns
S'ford-up-Av   vBridgnorth
Tamworth   vS. Coldfield

Sat 9th June (1.30 pm)
Bridgnorth   vHimley
Ken. Wdns   vHalesowen
Shifnal   vS'ford-up-Av
S. Coldfield   vOld Hill
Water Orton   vTamworth
WB D'mouth   vDorridge

Sat 16th June (1.30 pm)
Halesowen   vWater Orton
Ken. Wdns   vBridgnorth
Old Hill   vShifnal
S'ford-up-Av   vWB D'mouth
S. Coldfield   vDorridge
Tamworth   vHimley

Sat 23rd June (1.30 pm)
Bridgnorth   vS. Coldfield
Dorridge   vKen. Wdns
Himley   vShifnal
Old Hill   vWater Orton
Tamworth   vS'ford-up-Av
WB D'mouth   vHalesowen

Sat 30th June (1.30 pm)
Bridgnorth   vTamworth
Dorridge   vOld Hill
Shifnal   vHalesowen
S'ford-up-Av   vKen. Wdns
Water Orton   vS. Coldfield
WB D'mouth   vHimley

Sat 7th July (1.30 pm)
Halesowen   vS'ford-up-Av
Himley   vDorridge
Ken. Wdns   vWater Orton
Old Hill   vBridgnorth
S. Coldfield   vShifnal
Tamworth   vWB D'mouth

Sat 14th July (1.30 pm)
Dorridge   vS'ford-up-Av
Halesowen   vOld Hill
Himley   vS. Coldfield
Ken. Wdns   vTamworth
Shifnal   vBridgnorth
Water Orton   vWB D'mouth

Sat 21st July (1.30 pm)
Bridgnorth   vDorridge
Old Hill   vHimley
S'ford-up-Av   vWater Orton
S. Coldfield   vHalesowen
Tamworth   vShifnal
WB D'mouth   vKen. Wdns

Sat 28th July (1.30 pm)
Halesowen   vDorridge
Ken. Wdns   vHimley
Old Hill   vTamworth
Shifnal   vWB D'mouth
S. Coldfield   vS'ford-up-Av
Water Orton   vBridgnorth

Sat 4th August (1 pm)
Dorridge   vShifnal
Himley   vWater Orton
Ken. Wdns   vS. Coldfield
S'ford-up-Av   vOld Hill
Tamworth   vHalesowen
WB D'mouth   vBridgnorth

Sat 11th August (1 pm)
Bridgnorth   vHalesowen
Old Hill   vKen. Wdns
Shifnal   vWater Orton
S'ford-up-Av   vHimley
S. Coldfield   vWB D'mouth
Tamworth   vDorridge

Sat 18th August (1 pm)
Bridgnorth   vS'ford-up-Av
Halesowen   vHimley
Ken. Wdns   vShifnal
S. Coldfield   vTamworth
WB D'mouth   vOld Hill
Water Orton   vDorridge

Sat 25th August (1 pm)
Dorridge   vWB D'mouth
Halesowen   vKen. Wdns
Himley   vBridgnorth
Old Hill   vS. Coldfield
S'ford-up-Av   vShifnal
Tamworth   vWater Orton

Mon 27th August (1 pm)
Bridgnorth   vKen. Wdns
Dorridge   vS. Coldfield
Himley   vTamworth
Shifnal   vOld Hill
Water Orton   vHalesowen
WB D'mouth   vS'ford-up-Av

Sat 1st Sept (12.30 pm)
Halesowen   vWB D'mouth
Ken. Wdns   vDorridge
Shifnal   vHimley
S'ford-up-Av   vTamworth
S. Coldfield   vBridgnorth
Water Orton   vOld Hill

Sat 8th Sept (12.30 pm)
Halesowen   vShifnal
Himley   vWB D'mouth
Ken. Wdns   vS'ford-up-Av
Old Hill   vDorridge
S. Coldfield   vWater Orton
Tamworth   vBridgnorth

Sat 15th Sept (12.30 pm)
Bridgnorth   vOld Hill
Dorridge   vHimley
Shifnal   vS. Coldfield
S'ford-up-Av   vHalesowen
Water Orton   vKen. Wdns
WB D'mouth   vTamworth

Birmingham & District Premier League

SECOND DIVISION 2ND XI

Sat 5th May (1.30 pm)
Aston Unity vOld Elizab's
Bromsgrove vPelsall
Cannock vFordhouses
Evesham vWhitchurch
Smethwick v Penn
Wellington vSt. Georges

Sat 12th May (1.30 pm)
Fordhouses vBromsgrove
Old Elizab's vEvesham
Pelsall vAston Unity
Penn vWellington
St. Georges vSmethwick
Whitchurch vCannock

Sat 19th May (1.30 pm)
Aston Unity vFordhouses
Bromsgrove vWellington
Cannock vOld Elizab's
Evesham vSmethwick
Penn vPelsall
Whitchurch vSt. Georges

Sat 26th May (1.30 pm)
Cannock vAston Unity
Fordhouses vWhitchurch
Old Elizab's v Penn
Smethwick vPelsall
St. Georges vBromsgrove
Wellington vEvesham

Mon 28th May (1.30 pm)
Aston Unity vSmethwick
Old Elizab's vFordhouses
Pelsall vWellington
Penn vEvesham
St. Georges vCannock
Whitchurch vBromsgrove

Sat 2nd June (1.30 pm)
Bromsgrove vSmethwick
Evesham vCannock
Fordhouses vPelsall
Penn vSt. Georges
Wellington vAston Unity
Whitchurch vOld Elizab's

Sat 9th June (1.30 pm)
Aston Unity vWhitchurch
Cannock v Penn
Fordhouses vEvesham
Old Elizab's vBromsgrove
Pelsall vSt. Georges
Smethwick vWellington

Sat 16th June (1.30 pm)
Bromsgrove v Penn
Evesham vAston Unity
Pelsall vCannock
Smethwick vWhitchurch
St. Georges vOld Elizab's
Wellington vFordhouses

Sat 23rd June (1.30 pm)
Aston Unity vSt. Georges
Bromsgrove vEvesham
Cannock vSmethwick
Penn vFordhouses
Wellington vOld Elizab's
Whitchurch vPelsall

Sat 30th June (1.30 pm)
Aston Unity v Penn
Cannock vBromsgrove
Evesham vPelsall
Fordhouses vSt. Georges
Old Elizab's vSmethwick
Whitchurch vWellington

Sat 7th July (1.30 pm)
Bromsgrove vAston Unity
Pelsall vOld Elizab's
Penn vWhitchurch
Smethwick vFordhouses
St. Georges vEvesham
Wellington vCannock

Sat 14th July (1.30 pm)
Fordhouses vCannock
Old Elizab's vAston Unity
Pelsall vBromsgrove
Penn vSmethwick
St. Georges vWellington
Whitchurch vEvesham

Sat 21st July (1.30 pm)
Aston Unity vPelsall
Bromsgrove vFordhouses
Cannock vWhitchurch
Evesham vOld Elizab's
Smethwick vSt. Georges
Wellington v Penn

Sat 28th July (1.30 pm)
Fordhouses vAston Unity
Old Elizab's vCannock
Pelsall v Penn
Smethwick vEvesham
St. Georges vWhitchurch
Wellington vBromsgrove

Sat 4th August (1 pm)
Aston Unity vCannock
Bromsgrove vSt. Georges
Evesham vWellington
Pelsall vSmethwick
Penn vOld Elizab's
Whitchurch vFordhouses

Sat 11th August (1 pm)
Bromsgrove vWhitchurch
Cannock vSt. Georges
Evesham v Penn
Fordhouses vOld Elizab's
Smethwick vAston Unity
Wellington vPelsall

Sat 18th August (1 pm)
Aston Unity vWellington
Cannock vEvesham
Old Elizab's vWhitchurch
Pelsall vFordhouses
Smethwick vBromsgrove
St. Georges v Penn

Sat 25th August (1 pm)
Bromsgrove vOld Elizab's
Evesham vFordhouses
Penn vCannock
St. Georges vPelsall
Wellington vSmethwick
Whitchurch vAston Unity

Mon 27th August (1 pm)
Aston Unity vEvesham
Cannock vPelsall
Fordhouses vWellington
Old Elizab's vSt. Georges
Penn vBromsgrove
Whitchurch vSmethwick

Sat 1st Sept (12.30 pm)
Evesham vBromsgrove
Fordhouses v Penn
Old Elizab's vWellington
Pelsall vWhitchurch
Smethwick vCannock
St. Georges vAston Unity

Sat 8th Sept (12.30 pm)
Bromsgrove vCannock
Pelsall vEvesham
Penn vAston Unity
Smethwick vOld Elizab's
St. Georges vFordhouses
Wellington vWhitchurch

Sat 15th Sept (12.30 pm)
Aston Unity vBromsgrove
Cannock vWellington
Evesham vSt. Georges
Fordhouses vSmethwick
Old Elizab's vPelsall
Whitchurch v Penn

THIRD DIVISION 2ND XI

Sat 5th May (1.30 pm)
Coleshill vNewport
Ombersley vOld W Tett.
Sol B'field vOlton & WW
Studley vKington
Wem vBerkswell
Wombourne vAston Manor

Sat 12th May (1.30 pm)
Aston Manor vOmbersley
Berkswell vSol B'field
Kington vWombourne
Newport vStudley
Old W Tett. vColeshill
Olton & WW v Wem

Sat 19th May (1.30 pm)
Aston Manor vBerkswell
Coleshill v Wem
Olton & WW vNewport
Ombersley vKington
Studley vOld W Tett.
Wombourne vSol B'field

Sat 26th May (1.30 pm)
Berkswell vColeshill
Kington vOlton & WW
Old W Tett. vAston Manor
Ombersley vStudley
Sol B'field vNewport
Wem vWombourne

Mon 28th May (1.30 pm)
Aston Manor vColeshill
Berkswell vOmbersley
Kington vOld W Tett.
Newport v Wem
Olton & WW vWombourne
Studley vSol B'field

Sat 2nd June (1.30 pm)
Aston Manor vKington
Coleshill vSol B'field
Old W Tett. vNewport
Olton & WW vBerkswell
Wem vStudley
Wombourne vOmbersley

Sat 9th June (1.30 pm)
Kington vColeshill
Newport vBerkswell
Old W Tett. vWombourne
Ombersley vOlton & WW
Sol B'field v Wem
Studley vAston Manor

Sat 16th June (1.30 pm)
Berkswell vKington
Coleshill vOlton & WW

Newport vOmbersley
Sol B'field vAston Manor
Wem vOld W Tett.
Wombourne vStudley

Sat 23rd June (1.30 pm)
Aston Manor vNewport
Coleshill vWombourne
Olton & WW vOld W Tett.
Ombersley vSol B'field
Studley vBerkswell
Wem vKington

Sat 30th June (1.30 pm)
Aston Manor v Wem
Kington vSol B'field
Old W Tett. vBerkswell
Ombersley vColeshill
Studley vOlton & WW
Wombourne vNewport

Sat 7th July (1.30 pm)
Berkswell vWombourne
Coleshill vStudley
Newport vKington
Olton & WW vAston Manor
Sol B'field vOld W Tett.
Wem vOmbersley

Sat 14th July (1.30 pm)
Aston Manor vWombourne
Berkswell v Wem
Kington vStudley
Newport vColeshill
Old W Tett. vOmbersley
Olton & WW vSol B'field

Sat 21st July (1.30 pm)
Coleshill vOld W Tett.
Ombersley vAston Manor
Sol B'field vBerkswell
Studley vNewport
Wem vOlton & WW
Wombourne vKington

Sat 28th July (1.30 pm)
Berkswell vAston Manor
Kington vOmbersley
Newport vOlton & WW
Old W Tett. vStudley
Sol B'field vWombourne
Wem vColeshill

Sat 4th August (1 pm)
Aston Manor vOld W Tett.
Coleshill vBerkswell
Newport vSol B'field
Olton & WW vKington
Studley vOmbersley
Wombourne v Wem

Sat 11th August (1 pm)
Coleshill vAston Manor
Old W Tett. vKington
Ombersley vBerkswell
Sol B'field vStudley
Wem vNewport
Wombourne vOlton & WW

Sat 18th August (1 pm)
Berkswell vOlton & WW
Kington vAston Manor
Newport vOld W Tett.
Ombersley vWombourne
Sol B'field vColeshill
Studley v Wem

Sat 25th August (1 pm)
Aston Manor vStudley
Berkswell vNewport
Coleshill vKington
Olton & WW vOmbersley
Wem vSol B'field
Wombourne vOld W Tett.

Mon 27th August (1 pm)
Aston Manor vSol B'field
Kington vBerkswell
Old W Tett. v Wem
Olton & WW vColeshill
Ombersley vNewport
Studley vWombourne

Sat 1st SepT (12.30 pm)
Berkswell vStudley
Kington v Wem
Newport vAston Manor
Old W Tett. vOlton & WW
Sol B'field vOmbersley
Wombourne vColeshill

Sat 8th Sept (12.30 pm)
Berkswell vOld W Tett.
Coleshill vOmbersley
Newport vWombourne
Olton & WW vStudley
Sol B'field vKington
Wem vAston Manor

Sat 15th Sept (12.30 pm)
Aston Manor vOlton & WW
Kington vNewport
Old W Tett. vSol B'field
Ombersley v Wem
Studley vColeshill
Wombourne vBerkswell

Clubs in the Top Flight

A HISTORY OF THE BIRMINGHAM & DISTRICT CRICKET LEAGUE

(With thanks to Alex E. Davis, author of 'First in the Field')

IN 1998, the Oldest Cricket League in the World, the Birmingham & District Cricket League, became the first League to be accredited as a Premier League, by the newly created England & Wales Cricket Board. After numerous meetings, plenty of soul-searching and some tough negotiating, the Management Committee agreed that BDCL should become the Premier Division of The Birmingham & District Premier Cricket League, with clubs from the Midland Club Cricket Championship forming Division One and clubs from the Midland Combined Counties League forming Division Two. Further successful negotiations saw Leagues in Shropshire, Staffordshire, Warwickshire and Worcestershire agree to become Feeder Leagues to the Premier League and the League, now, encompasses 48 clubs, covering an area from Whitchurch, in the North, to Evesham, in the South, and from Kington, in the West, to Coventry & N.W. in the East.

This is a very different scenario to 1888, when the Birmingham & District Cricket League comprised the following clubs: - Aston Unity, Handsworth Wood, Kings Heath, Mitchells, Salters, Walsall and West Bromwich Dartmouth. Within a year, Kings Heath changed its name, after a merger, to Moseley, although a Kings Heath Cricket Club was, subsequently, reformed and re-entered the League, in Division One, in 1998. Aston Unity, Walsall and West Bromwich Dartmouth have retained unbroken membership of the League since 1888, but Walsall is the only club to play its cricket, since then entirely in the top Division. Aston Unity has slipped into Division Two but West Bromwich Dartmouth has experienced a welcome resurgence following two seasons, in Division One, in 2002 and 2003. Fittingly, both remaining Founder Members, in the Premier Division, finished Champions and Runners-Up in 2006.

41

Of the remaining Founder Members, Mitchells left the League, after the 1892 season, but were re-admitted four years later, becoming Mitchells & Butlers, in 1898 following the amalgamation of two brewery firms. They remained members of the League, until 1994, when the Company withdrew its support, and their superb ground, at Portland Road, became a football pitch. Salters, a West Bromwich Company, resigned after one season but Handsworth Wood struggled on, until 1919, before they were voted out of the League because they had lost their permanent ground.

Although Smethwick had been invited to join the League, in 1888, their Committee declined the offer but a change of direction, in 1891, saw the club's application accepted and they have retained unbroken membership, since then, albeit in four different Divisions. Wednesbury, playing where they do, now, in Wood Green Road, were members from 1890 to 1893 and Small Heath joined the League in 1892. Like Wednesbury, they struggled, and left the League after three seasons.

Warwickshire County Cricket Club entered its Club & Ground side, in 1894, but on being admitted to the County Championship, in 1895, withdrew its membership. The season in the League had been unsatisfactory and the strength of the side was dependent on County calls, varying from extremely strong to very weak.

A strong Worcestershire influence entered the League, in the mid 1890's, with the election of the following clubs: Dudley (1893), Stourbridge (1894) and Kidderminster (1895) and, by 1896, the League comprised 10 clubs - Aston Unity, Dudley, Handsworth Wood, Kidderminster, Mitchells & Butlers, Moseley, Smethwick, Stourbridge, Walsall and West Bromwich Dartmouth. With the exception of Old Hill's election, in 1920, in place of Handsworth Wood, the constitution of the League remained the same until 1975, the year that the League season was extended, by four weeks, to include two additional teams.

Those teams were Warwickshire C.C.C. 2nd XI and Worcestershire C.C.C. 2nd XI, but the latter struggled to field a balanced side each week and Duport took their place in 1977. Basically a works side, they attempted to strengthen their team but, after cutbacks in financial support from the works sports club, they withdrew, in 1981, to be replaced by Worcester City. After 12 years, they folded and were replaced by Stratford-upon-Avon.

In 1985, Dudley was forced to resign from the League, after the closure of its ground by the Local Council because it was in an area subject to subsidence caused by old limestone workings. The place was filled by Coventry & N.W. who joined from the Midlands Club Cricket Championship, as did Wolverhampton in 1989 when they replaced Warwickshire, who changed policy, preferring their players to be allocated to clubs, around the League, rather than playing together on a Saturday afternoon.

A final change occurred in 1995 when Barnt Green took the place of Mitchells & Butlers, which meant that by the time the League was accredited with Premier League status, in 1998, the 12 member clubs were Aston Unity, Barnt Green, Coventry & N.W., Kidderminster, Moseley, Old Hill, Smethwick, Stourbridge, Stratford-upon-Avon, Walsall, West Bromwich Dartmouth and Wolverhampton. At various times, since the formation of the Premier Division, another 12 clubs have, also, sampled life in the top flight - Cannock, Halesowen, Himley, Harborne, Kenilworth Wardens, Knowle & Dorridge, Leamington Spa, Shifnal, Shrewsbury, Walmley, Water Orton and Wellington.

First in the Field - a History of the Birmingham & District Cricket League was published in 1888 to celebrate the centenary of the world's first cricket league

Gunpowder, Cricket and Beer

By Andy Searle

CLUB CRICKET has suffered as much as any sport in the last 20 years by the dwindling number of active players and consequent closure and merger of clubs. Therefore, it is heartening to report that a Midlands pub and its owner have received planning position to convert the fields at the back of the pub into a cricket pitch in one of the most picturesque and historical parts of Warwickshire.

The Throckmorton Arms is situated on the A435 between Studley and Alcester. It gets its name from the Throckmorton family, whose ancestral home from the early 16th Century has been Coughton Court on the opposite side of the road. The Throckmortons are famous as one of England's leading Catholic families and infamous for the role they played in the 1605 Gunpowder Plot.

Robert Catesby, who devised the plan to blow up the Houses of Parliament, was the son of Anne Throckmorton and used Coughton Court as one of the many places to hide fellow conspirators after the failed plot. Indeed, because its expansive views over the surrounding Warwickshire and Worcestershire countryside, ideal to watch out for government troops, it had often been used to shelter Catholics on the run.

Nigel Staley, landlord of the Throckmorton Arms, is hoping for fireworks of a different kind in the not too distant future. Having gained change of use approval from the local council

The Throckmorton Arms

to convert the fields that go with the pub to a cricket pitch, he is searching for a development partner - be it an existing club, an individual, a group of individuals or a company - to help him bear the financial burden.

The estimated cost of such a venture is between £20,000 and £25,000, of which Mr Staley expects to put in a third, a third from any interested party and the other third from the various grants and assistance available for sports clubs these days from a number of schemes. Moreover, Mr Staley is then planning to allow the new or existing club to play on the site on a long 25-year lease and at the peppercorn rent of £1 a year.

It's an ambitious but wholly achievable plan. The site is perfect for cricket, picturesque and with the soil having been tested by an ECB ground inspector for suitability. The cost of levelling the fields are minimal and Richard Cox of the Warwickshire Cricket Board has stated that he would like to see junior county representative cricket on the site in the future.

On top of all this is the obvious advantage of being attached to the pub - a major consideration for cricketers through the ages. In an area rich in cricket and history it is good to see the potential for further growth. Anyone interested in talking to Nigel Staley about this project should contact him on 01285 720020 or by email at nigel.staley@btconnect.com. The website of the pub is www.throckmortonarms.co.uk

The site of the potential cricket ground.

The Warwickshire Cricket League

(sponsored by Boundary Sports)

Management Committee

Chairman - Graham Seal
For Phone enquiries (H) 02476 615124
(M) 07802 496776

General Manager - Jim Hartley
For Email enquiries: Jimwarcl@aol.com

Cricket Sub Committee
Roy Wilson

Finance Sub Committee
Feraz Mustafa

Disciplinary Sub Committee
Feraz Mustafa (acting)

Grounds Liaison
Neil Garland

Umpires Sub Committee
Peter Cox

Marketing
Mike Kiernan

Olton & West Warwicks Birmingham-bound

by Graham Seal

THE 2006 SEASON for the Warwickshire Cricket League ran from 6th of May and over the following four and a half months 85 clubs turned out 178 teams in 17 divisions to play 1712 games of cricket. In 2007 the league will expand to 90 teams and the number of matches will total nearly 1800. The standards vary dramatically from those clubs in the premier division striving to gain promotion into the Birmingham and District Premier League to some newly formed clubs starting out in the lower divisions. The Warwickshire Cricket League welcomes all and caters for all levels and all abilities within the recreational level of the game.

In 2006, the Premier Division was very competitive and Olton & West Warwicks' achievement in winning and gaining promotion to the Birmingham & District League was very much down to their development of youth over the last few years. In addition, both second and third placed teams, Bedworth and North Warwickshire, relied heavily on players developed from a young age at their clubs.

Bablake Old Boys were the club of the year in the league, winning Division One with over 400 points, whilst a resurgent Warwick, having gained promotion in 2005, repeated the feat in 2006 by winning Division Two.

Unfortunately, at the business end of the season there were several wet Saturdays. So much so that during the close season the rain rules were reviewed to try and get a more balanced approach when rain interferes, several clubs feeling their season's position was determined as much by the weather as their ability.

At the Annual Dinner at Drayton Manor Park, attended by 280 people, Simon Hughes was the guest speaker and in between the several

good natured jibes at Neil Smith (who was also present) he mixed well with the players and guests attending. In addition to club awards for the 17 divisional winners and runners up, the divisional players of the year were presented with bats donated by sponsor Boundary Sports.

Matt Pickering of Atherstone was the top player with seven man of the match awards, strange to see however that whilst he had a batting average of 91 he did not lead the division batting averages. This honour fell to Richard Adams of North Warwickshire, opening the batting for his side with an average over 98.

Warwick and Willow take club awards

Two club awards were also run, one for the best administered club, the 2006 winners being Warwick, and one for the most sporting - each club in a division marking its opposition out of 100 for all teams run and the club with the highest average winning the award - 2006 winners being Willow, who achieved an 89% average mark.

There are now seven divisions with each team having a second team section. From this season all these clubs have to have sightscreens and covers (at least tarpaulin sheets). When the league embarked on this it was thought to be an ambitious target, but all clubs have managed to comply with the request.

In 2006, there were three divisions for the Single Team Competition, which is mainly for 3rd & 4th teams but does include a growing number of clubs who only run one team. This competition is becoming ever more popular and a fourth division has been added in 2007.

As with most cricket leagues, getting qualified Umpires for all games is an issue. Although the Warwickshire League does better than most, with 60 plus umpires available on any particular Saturday, 2006 saw the Premier Division Clubs along with the committee looking to introduce club-appointed umpires to second team fixtures in the top division in 2007.

2006 League Tables

Premier Division - 1st XI

	P	W	L	T	D	A	RP	BP	Ded	Pts
OLTON & WW	22	10	2	0	7	3	280	50	0	330
BEDWORTH	22	10	3	0	6	3	246	46	0	292
NORTH WARWICKSHIRE	22	9	3	0	4	6	242	44	0	286
ATHERSTONE	22	5	5	0	6	6	194	70	0	264
NUNEATON	22	6	6	0	7	3	196	65	0	261
BRONZE	22	5	4	0	8	5	174	76	4	246
MOSELEY ASHFIELD	22	3	5	0	9	5	158	87	1	244
HIGHWAY	22	4	3	1	7	7	168	68	0	236
OLD EDWARDIANS	22	5	7	0	4	6	156	62	0	218
KENILWORTH	22	2	5	0	10	5	118	76	0	194
PICKWICK POST & MAIL	22	3	9	1	2	7	108	52	23	137
MARSTON GREEN	22	1	11	0	4	6	64	59	21	102

Division 1 - 1st XI

	P	W	L	T	D	A	RP	BP	Ded	Pts
BABLAKE OLD BOYS	22	16	0	0	2	4	396	17	0	413
FILLONGLEY	22	11	3	1	5	2	280	50	0	330
WISHAW	22	9	3	0	6	4	250	45	0	295
WALSALL YMF	22	9	7	0	2	4	232	36	0	268
CAMP HILL OLD EDWARDIANS	22	6	8	0	6	2	176	71	0	247
ANSLEY SPORTS	22	6	7	1	4	4	186	56	0	242
SHELDON MARLBOROUGH	22	4	5	0	9	4	170	75	4	241
STOCKTON	22	6	4	0	7	5	188	52	0	240
STREETLY	22	5	8	0	5	4	162	61	0	223
SOUTHAM	22	6	9	0	5	2	152	60	0	212
BOURNVILLE	22	2	12	0	3	5	90	61	0	151
HAMPTON	22	0	14	0	4	4	28	59	31	56

Division 2 - 1st XI

	P	W	L	T	D	A	RP	BP	Ded	Pts
WARWICK	22	13	2	0	6	1	304	42	0	346
ROWLAND UNITED	22	11	4	0	3	4	284	43	0	327
HANDSWORTH	22	10	3	0	5	4	282	46	3	325
OFFCHURCH / LAPWORTH	22	9	5	0	4	4	244	51	0	295
AMBLESIDE	22	8	4	0	5	5	240	46	0	286
CIVIL SERVICE	22	8	5	0	5	4	234	56	15	275
RUGBY	22	7	5	0	5	5	198	47	0	245
SPHINX	22	5	7	0	6	4	144	66	0	210
FOUR OAKS SAINTS	22	3	10	0	6	3	118	73	1	190
GRIFF & COTON	22	3	10	0	4	5	110	55	0	165
ELFORD	22	3	12	0	6	1	90	73	0	163
WARD END UNITY	22	2	15	0	1	4	70	70	0	140

Division 3 - 1st XI

	P	W	L	T	D	A	RP	BP	Ded	Pts
LYNDWORTH	18	10	3	0	3	2	260	22	0	282
NETHER WHITACRE	18	9	0	0	5	4	242	32	0	274
ATTLEBOROUGH CC	18	8	0	0	7	3	232	40	5	267
ERDINGTON COURT	18	6	3	0	6	3	166	49	16	199
JAGUAR DAIMLER	18	6	6	0	0	6	152	39	0	191
FIVE WAYS OE	18	4	5	0	4	5	140	43	1	182
PAKSHAHEEN	18	1	5	0	7	5	100	70	5	165
BULKINGTON	18	3	9	0	2	4	88	56	0	144
WEOLEY HILL	18	1	8	0	2	7	62	50	0	112
WYTHALL	18	2	11	0	2	3	60	52	0	112

Division 4 - 1st XI

	P	W	L	T	D	A	RP	BP	Ded	Pts
CASTLE BROMWICH	18	11	2	0	2	3	272	18	0	290
KNOWLE & DORRIDGE	18	8	3	0	5	2	220	45	0	265
COVENTRY COLLIERY	18	9	3	0	2	4	236	27	0	263
CORLEY	18	5	6	0	4	3	154	51	2	203
WALSALL YPF	18	6	5	0	2	5	172	32	1	203
COPSEWOOD WI WNDS	18	5	6	0	3	4	130	43	0	173
THIMBLEMILL	18	4	7	0	2	5	116	33	0	149
SOLIHULL MUNICIPAL	18	4	5	0	6	3	106	32	0	138
COLLYCROFT	18	3	10	0	2	3	88	47	15	120
HAUNCHWOOD	18	3	11	0	0	4	84	35	0	119

Division 5 - 1st XI

	P	W	L	T	D	A	RP	BP	Ded	Pts
BARBY	18	12	2	0	1	3	266	10	0	276
ASTON OE	18	8	5	0	3	2	202	44	0	246
OAKFIELD	18	8	2	0	2	6	202	24	0	226
HUNNINGHAM	18	6	6	0	2	4	166	32	0	198
KNOWLE VILLAGE	18	6	7	0	1	4	154	35	0	189
WILCLARE FUJITTSU	18	6	8	0	0	4	152	36	0	188
WILNECOTE	18	5	8	0	2	3	136	46	0	182
WOLVEY	18	4	5	0	5	4	120	52	0	172
PEUGEOT	18	5	11	0	1	1	116	41	1	156
STOCKINGFORD	18	3	9	0	3	3	84	41	0	125

Division 6 - 1st XI

	P	W	L	T	D	A	RP	BP	Ded	Pts
NEWDIGATE	18	12	3	0	1	2	260	16	0	276
COV. UNIV	18	8	3	0	1	6	206	27	0	233
NEWBOLD	18	8	3	0	3	4	208	24	0	232
MASSEY FERG	18	7	2	0	4	5	204	28	0	232
BRIDGE TRUST	18	5	4	0	5	4	168	44	15	197
DUNLOP	18	5	6	0	2	5	144	33	30	147
STANDARD	18	2	8	0	5	3	84	47	0	131
BEDWORTH	18	3	7	0	3	5	98	32	15	115
PRINCE OF WALES	18	3	10	0	3	2	98	48	33	113
NUNEATON	18	1	8	0	7	2	58	54	0	112

Premier Division - 2nd XI

	P	W	L	T	D	A	RP	BP	Ded	Pts
NUNEATON	22	11	3	0	4	4	284	45	2	327
BEDWORTH	22	6	3	0	10	3	228	76	0	304
ATHERSTONE	22	9	6	0	4	3	240	51	0	291
OLD EDWARDIANS	22	6	2	0	8	6	220	60	0	280
MOSELEY ASHFIELD	22	6	2	0	8	6	206	64	0	270
BRONZE	22	5	6	0	8	3	162	81	0	243
BOURNVILLE	22	6	6	0	6	4	188	51	0	239
KENILWORTH	22	3	4	1	9	5	152	72	0	224
HIGHWAY	22	6	8	1	4	3	170	53	0	223
SOUTHAM	22	3	5	0	9	5	136	59	0	195
OLTON & WW	22	3	7	0	8	4	124	68	0	192
MARSTON GREEN	22	1	13	0	2	6	52	51	0	103

Division 1 - 2nd XI

	P	W	L	T	D	A	RP	BP	Ded	Pts
SHELDON MARLBOROUGH	22	11	3	0	5	3	292	50	0	342
BABLAKE OLD BOYS	22	9	3	0	6	4	266	54	0	320
FILLONGLEY	22	11	4	0	3	4	276	35	0	311
PICKWICK POST & MAIL	22	9	2	0	6	5	262	44	0	306
WISHAW	22	8	5	0	8	1	198	59	0	257
WALSALL YMF	22	7	5	0	4	6	210	42	3	249
AMBLESIDE	22	7	6	0	4	5	172	39	0	211
NORTH WARWICKSHIRE	22	5	8	0	4	5	158	49	0	207
CAMP HILL OLD EDWARD'S	22	5	8	0	4	5	150	54	0	204
STREETLY	22	4	11	0	1	6	126	63	15	174
RUGBY	22	4	12	0	3	3	108	47	15	140
HAMPTON	22	1	14	0	2	5	52	41	19	74

Division 2 - 2nd XI

	P	W	L	T	D	A	RP	BP	Ded	Pts
ANSLEY SPORTS	22	11	5	0	2	4	280	35	0	315
HANDSWORTH	22	10	5	0	5	2	268	45	0	313
OFFCHURCH / LAPWORTH	22	10	4	0	4	4	262	34	0	296
ROWLAND UNITED	22	11	5	0	3	3	262	25	0	287
WARWICK	22	10	2	0	4	6	252	33	0	285
SPHINX	22	7	4	0	6	5	186	48	0	234
WARD END UNITY	22	5	9	0	5	3	162	61	5	218
STOCKTON	22	7	9	0	1	5	178	37	0	215
CIVIL SERVICE	22	6	10	0	2	4	158	38	20	176
FOUR OAKS SAINTS	22	3	10	0	5	4	118	51	0	169
GRIFF & COTON	22	3	10	0	4	5	106	51	0	157
ELFORD	22	3	13	0	3	3	98	39	2	135

Division 3 - 2nd XI

	P	W	L	T	D	A	RP	BP	Ded	Pts
LYNDWORTH	18	8	0	0	6	4	256	49	0	305
JAGUAR DAIMLER	18	7	2	0	5	4	182	29	0	211
FIVE WAYS OE	18	6	4	0	3	5	166	44	0	210

The Warwickshire League

	P	W	L	T	D	A	RP	BP	Ded	Pts
THIMBLEMILL	18	5	3	0	4	6	172	33	0	205
ATTLEBOROUGH	18	5	5	0	4	4	156	43	0	199
WEOLEY HILL	18	6	5	0	2	5	146	35	15	166
ERDINGTON COURT	18	4	7	0	5	2	130	49	15	164
HAUNCHWOOD	18	4	8	0	3	3	116	38	0	154
NETHER WHITACRE	18	2	7	0	4	5	82	54	0	136
WYTHALL	18	2	8	0	4	4	78	40	0	118

Division 4 - 2nd XI

	P	W	L	T	D	A	RP	BP	Ded	Pts
KNOWLE & DORRIDGE	18	12	1	0	1	4	276	11	0	287
CASTLE BROMWICH	18	11	1	0	3	3	260	23	0	283
COVENTRY COLLIERY	18	8	2	0	5	3	238	39	15	262
WALSALL YPF	18	8	4	0	3	3	208	35	0	243
BULKINGTON	18	6	8	0	0	4	148	22	0	170
COPSEWOOD WI WDRS	18	3	7	0	4	4	110	41	0	151
KNOWLE VILLAGE	18	4	9	0	2	3	104	41	0	145
PAKSHAHEEN	18	4	9	0	2	3	104	38	0	142
CORLEY	18	4	10	0	1	3	94	33	0	127
COLLYCROFT	18	3	12	0	1	2	76	29	0	105

Division 5 - 2nd XI

	P	W	L	T	D	A	RP	BP	Ded	Pts
STOCKINGFORD	18	13	1	0	0	4	292	6	0	298
BARBY	18	8	2	0	4	4	204	29	0	233
ASTON OE	18	7	3	0	3	5	198	31	0	229
HUNNINGHAM	18	6	3	0	4	5	182	34	0	216
SOLIHULL MUNICIPAL	18	5	4	0	6	3	152	60	0	212
OAKFIELD	18	4	8	0	3	3	112	54	0	166
WILCLARE FUJITTSU	18	4	7	0	3	4	114	52	0	166
WILNECOTE	18	4	9	0	2	3	108	36	2	142
BRIDGE TRUST	18	2	8	0	4	4	90	51	15	126
COV. UNIV	18	3	11	0	1	3	94	28	34	88

Division 6 - 2nd XI

	P	W	L	T	D	A	RP	BP	Ded	Pts
NEWDIGATE	18	11	2	0	1	4	246	12	0	258
NEWBOLD	18	9	3	0	1	5	218	23	0	241
WOLVEY	18	8	4	0	1	5	196	22	0	218
DUNLOP	18	7	4	1	1	5	204	20	15	209
MASSEY FERG	18	6	4	0	2	6	170	22	0	192
NUNEATON	18	3	8	1	2	4	106	43	0	149
PEUGEOT	18	3	9	0	4	2	94	50	0	144
STANDARD	18	5	7	0	1	5	128	14	15	127
BEDWORTH	18	4	7	0	2	5	112	20	30	102
PRINCE OF WALES	18	3	11	0	1	3	90	38	47	81

Single Teams 1

	P	W	L	T	D	A	RP	BP	Ded	Pts
FOUR OAKS	16	10	0	1	2	3	242	20	0	262
SMALL HEATH	16	9	2	0	2	3	220	21	-1	242
LEEK WOOTTON	16	9	3	1	0	3	210	17	-1	228
BABLAKE OLD BOYS	16	6	5	0	2	3	148	21	-5	174
A J K	16	5	5	0	1	5	130	28	-3	161
OLTON & WW	16	2	6	0	5	3	78	41	-7	126
BRAUNSTON PADDOX	16	3	10	0	1	2	82	37	-2	121
SPHINX	16	2	9	0	1	4	64	27	-7	98
CLEVELAND	16	1	7	0	2	6	54	21	29	46

Single Teams 2

	P	W	L	T	D	A	RP	BP	Ded	Pts
AMBLESIDE	14	8	1	0	2	3	202	14	-2	218
ANSLEY SPORTS	14	6	4	0	3	1	158	36	-5	199
HANDSWORTH	14	6	4	0	3	1	164	28	-5	197
CRESCENT	14	8	3	0	2	1	180	12	-3	195
WARWICK	14	3	3	0	4	4	102	34	-6	142
BERKSWELL	14	2	5	0	2	5	88	31	0	119
WILLOW	14	2	8	0	0	4	56	20	-3	79
ATHERSTONE	14	0	7	0	2	5	28	26	-4	58
WATER ORTON	16	0	11	0	2	3	32	38	65	5
ERDINGTON COURT	0	0	0	0	0	0	0	0	72	-72

Single Teams 3

	P	W	L	T	D	A	RP	BP	Ded	Pts
RIVERSIDE ROYALS	16	10	1	0	3	2	274	25	0	299
BABLAKE OLD BOYS	16	9	1	0	3	3	230	26	-2	258
SELLY PARK	16	8	4	0	2	2	204	27	-4	235
BRONZE	16	7	5	0	2	2	168	23	-3	194
COLESHILL	16	5	7	0	3	1	128	40	-6	174
HIGHWAY	16	5	7	0	1	3	128	28	-6	162
ANSLEY SPORTS	16	4	7	0	3	2	104	28	-3	135
BRAUNSTON PADDOX	16	3	8	0	3	2	80	26	-4	110
GRIFF & COTON	12	0	9	0	1	2	18	9	88	-61

2006 Averages

BATTING (Top six):

Premier Division - 1st XI

		Inns	NO	Runs	HS	Ave
Richard Adams	North Warwickshire	15	6	883	156*	98.11
Matt Pickering	Atherstone	18	2	1450	300*	90.63
R Qayyum	Bronze	14	5	762	147*	84.67
Scott Friswell	Bedworth	13	3	546	90*	54.60
Steve Kelly	North Warwickshire	15	3	611	99	50.92
Marc Webb	Olton and WW	12	0	568	151	47.33

Division 1 - 1st XI

		Inns	NO	Runs	HS	Ave
C Moore	Streetly	17	4	781	108*	60.08
M Hughes	Stockton	18	5	777	158	59.77
J Street	Stockton	13	4	416	119*	46.22
T Cooper	Stockton	12	3	372	81	41.33
Richard Swaffield	Bablake OB	17	2	618	94	41.20
P Burnell	Southam	14	5	361	0	40.11

Division 2 - 1st XI

		Inns	NO	Runs	HS	Ave
R Hooper	Handsworth	15	3	762	150 *	63.50
T Briscoe	Warwick	15	4	642	112*	58.36
Junaid Ahmed	Civil Service	20	3	968	171*	56.94
A Passey	Warwick	15	7	440	74*	55.00
Steve Hurt	Rugby	16	3	683	109*	52.54
S Marillier	Offchurch Lapworth	17	2	784	113*	52.27

Division 3 - 1st XI

		Inns	NO	Runs	HS	Ave
Russell Rice	Attleborough	12	4	588	181	73.50
S Levy	Nether Whitacre	16	6	708	117*	70.80
M Lawrence	Nether Whitacre	13	5	534	115*	66.75
Shakeel Khan	Lyndworth	11	2	492	106*	54.67
A Wier	Nether Whitacre	12	3	448	96*	49.78
Raju Sharma	Attleborough	12	3	392	117*	43.56

Division 4 - 1st XI

		Inns	NO	Runs	HS	Ave
David Rogers	Corley	12	3	449	78	49.89
Richard Harriman	Collycroft	9	1	374	91*	46.75
M. Mulla	Coventry Colliery	12	0	550	164	45.83
Guy Fathers	Knowle & Dorridge	11	0	489	110	44.45
H.Gul Khan	Coventry Colliery	8	0	345	110	43.13
Paul Williams	Corley	14	0	580	117	41.43

Division 5 - 1st XI

		Inns	NO	Runs	HS	Ave
Rob Field	Barby	12	5	544	101*	77.71
R Burnett	Oakfield	12	2	676	137	67.60
Paul Upton	Wolvey	10	2	450	88*	56.25
Neil Chippington	Barby	14	4	489	110	48.90
G Kilroy	Knowle Village	9	3	291	81	48.50
Ritesh Patel	Willclare	11	0	473	96	43.00

Division 6 - 1st XI

		Inns	NO	Runs	HS	Ave
S Cross	Bridge Trust	12	4	932	142*	116.50
Raja Nawaz	Coventry University	12	3	700	127	77.78
John Basset	Newdigate	9	3	370	69	61.67
Chris Layton	Massey Ferguson	14	2	687	171	57.25
Paul Evans	Newbold	11	2	499	149	55.44
A Smith	Bridge Trust	12	3	441	90*	49.00

Premier Division - 2nd XI

		Inns	NO	Runs	HS	Ave
Ehsan Yousaf	Bournville	13	4	551	100	61.22
R Boal	Atherstone	11	3	459	81	57.38
Evans	Nuneaton	12	2	503	113	50.30
Gazanfer Ali	Old Edwardians	10	2	381	105*	47.63
M Wisdish	Kenilworth	13	1	534	115	44.50
Mike McDermott	Highway	7	0	306	158	43.71

Division 1 - 2nd XI

		Inns	NO	Runs	HS	Ave
A Massey	Wishaw	15	4	624	76	56.73
Jim Rasin	Sheldon Marlbourgh	17	2	846	105	56.40
Martin Wheatley	Bablake OB	12	2	545	80	54.50
John Bromley	Fillongley	10	1	374	86	41.56
Ansel Pottinger	Sheldon Marlbourgh	20	1	782	141	41.16
T Masood	Sheldon Marlbourgh	10	3	285	114*	40.71

Division 2 - 2nd XI

		Inns	NO	Runs	HS	Ave
M Daniels	Griff & Coton	10	4	446	108*	74.33
D Robbins	Warwick	10	4	386	74*	64.33
G Philogen	Handsworth	8	2	355		59.17
Sean Troth	Offchurch/Lapworth	12	2	525	108	52.50
J Davis	Warwick	12	4	416	101*	52.00
Joe Troth	Offchurch/Lapworth	16	4	608	154*	50.67

Division 3 - 2nd XI

		Inns	NO	Runs	HS	Ave
C Titmus	Nether Whitacre	9	1	421	156	52.63
Graham Jones	Erdington Court	14	1	541	114*	41.62
S Comfort	Nether Whitacre	9	0	372	83	41.33
Paul Barnes	Attleborough	10	2	315	59*	39.38
Mohammed Nisar	Lyndworth	10	1	337	96	37.44
Babar Khan	Lyndworth	14	1	485	170	37.31

The Warwickshire League

Division 4 - 2nd XI

		Inns	NO	Runs	HS	Ave
E.Iassin	Coventry Colliery	14	3	695	120	63.18
Amjad Mahmood	Solihull Municipal	8	0	439	207	54.88
Ray Mian	Solihull Municipal	8	2	318	112	53.00
Andy Chaplin	Castle Bromwich	9	2	344	135	49.14
Don Clarkson	Castle Bromwich	15	4	516	72*	46.91
John Stanley	Solihull Municipal	8	2	239	76*	39.83

Division 5 - 2nd XI

		Inns	NO	Runs	HS	Ave
Darren Williams	Willclare	8	0	539	90	67.38
D.Alford	Aston OE	8	1	285	168	40.71
A.Parsons	Aston OE	6	1	195	69	39.00
D Smith	Knowle Village	10	3	268	64	38.29
Matthew Glenn	Barby	8	1	250	76*	35.71
P Brough	Oakfield	7	1	211	90	35.17

Division 6 - 2nd XI

		Inns	NO	Runs	HS	Ave
Terry Gough	Dunlop	8	1	475	105*	67.86
Graeme Pykett	Bedworth	8	2	322	127*	53.67
Matthew Glenn	Barby	8	1	250	76*	35.71
Tony Brookes	Dunlop	9	1	250	65	31.25
S Hinds	Standard	11	2	273		30.33
Jack Bennett	Barby	9	1	238	73*	29.75

Single Teams 1

		Inns	NO	Runs	HS	Ave
M Burton	Four Oaks	10	4	527	111*	87.83
S Neilson	Four Oaks	12	4	601	107	75.13
Ian Cox	Leek Wootton	10	3	449	92*	64.14
Keith Bennett	Leek Wootton	10	6	236	48*	59.00
Keith Scott	Olton and WW	10	3	294	123*	42.00
John Hough	Olton and WW	10	3	291	71*	41.57

Single Teams 2

		Inns	NO	Runs	HS	Ave
Asif Patel	Crescent	11	4	612	125*	87.43
R Haddon	Ansley Sports	7	1	329	106*	54.83
I Tracey	Berkswell	6	0	208	79	34.67
James Doan	Ambleside	8	1	183	87	26.14
Haydon Wood	Ambleside	5	0	128	39	25.60
S Walton	Ansley Sports	11	0	269	90	24.45

Single Teams 3

		Inns	NO	Runs	HS	Ave
Andy Russell	Bablake OB	11	6	517	168*	103.40
Chris Crocker	Riverside	8	1	424	87	60.57
O Kirkland	Selly Park	10	2	402	78	50.25
Tom Holt	Riverside	11	0	552	139	50.18
M Hubbard	Ansley Sports	11	5	269	59*	44.83
R Emery	Ansley Sports	7	1	246	88*	41.00

BOWLING (Top six):

Premier Division - 1st XI

		O	M	R	W	S/R	Ave
Heath Parnell	Bedworth	134.1	34	407	34	3.94	11.97
Sunil Vyakaranam	Olton and WW	123	23	477	30	4.10	15.90
K Sadiq	Bronze	143	20	660	40	3.58	16.50
B Macey	Bronze	72	4	409	24	3.00	17.04
Dennis Oakes	Bedworth	75.5	6	385	22	3.43	17.50
I.Carey	Mosley Ashfield	109	17	417	23	4.74	18.13

Division 1 - 1st XI

		O	M	R	W	S/R	Ave
O Chagar	Wishaw	86	16	318	27	3.19	11.78
Steven Swaffield	Bablake OB	173.1	42	495	40	4.33	12.38
Leron Barker	Bablake OB	109	17	320	25	4.36	12.80
Ian Webster	Fillongley	94	18	293	22	4.27	13.32
N Parmer	Stockton	121	28	308	23	5.26	13.39
Tom Cowley	Bablake OB	100.4	16	347	25	4.02	13.88

Division 2 - 1st XI

		O	M	R	W	S/R	Ave
Mark Randle	Rowland United	324	85	857	71	4.56	12.07
E Ramsey	Handsworth	363	65	1124	84	4.32	13.38
Neil Walton	Rowland United	69.1	8	291	21	3.29	13.86
A Passey	Warwick	190	25	755	54	3.52	13.98
Ilyas Shaikh	Civil Service			464	32		14.50
Danny Simms	Rowland United	152.2	25	537	35	4.35	15.34

Division 3 - 1st XI

		O	M	R	W	S/R	Ave
Sajid Baig	Lyndworth	138	46	356	29	4.76	12.28
Shakeel Khan	Lyndworth	136	22	482	35	3.89	13.77
Stewart Hall	Jaguar Daimler	163		705	51	3.20	13.82
Dave Perks	Wythall	136	16	512	31	4.39	16.52
B Smith	Bulkington	146.4	21	551	33	4.44	16.70
Julian Jones	Erdington Court	105	17	369	22	4.77	16.77

Division 4 - 1st XI

		O	M	R	W	S/R	Ave
Paul Miller	Castle Bromwich	76	24	143	24	3.17	5.96
Peter Jablonski	Castle Bromwich	45	13	162	19	2.37	8.53
Palle Quinn	Castle Bromwich	121	35	321	37	3.27	8.68
S.Khan	Coventry Colliery	147	21	379	36	4.08	10.53
Richard Poulton	Castle Bromwich	112	21	340	30	3.73	11.33
Dan Ward	Kn & Dorridge	145.2	34	489	39	3.72	12.54

Division 5 - 1st XI

		O	M	R	W	S/R	Ave
P Dodson	Peugeot	63	12	197	16	3.94	12.31
D.Maskell	Hunningham			471	35	0.00	13.46

Dave Norton	Barby	210.3	36	690	51	4.12	13.53
Neil Buddhia	Willclare	79.3		326	24	3.30	13.58
Stev Stipanovic	Barby	110.5	29	299	22	5.02	13.59
G.Goadby	Aston OE	183	38	585	43	4.26	13.60

Division 6 - 1st XI

		O	M	R	W	S/R	Av
Adie Parker	Newdigate	175.5	14	421	39	4.50	10.79
Darren Wood	Newbold	99.5	21	256	22	4.52	11.64
Darren Parker	Newdigate	53	7	190	16	3.31	11.88
Zulfchar Khan	Coventry Uni.	63	8	205	17	3.71	12.06
Andy Buckton	Bedworth	115.5	31	293	23	5.02	12.74
Chris Frost	Newdigate	133.1	21	466	34	3.91	13.71

Premier Division - 2nd XI

		O	M	R	W	S/R	Ave
Dan Bates	Highway	77.2	15	228	21	3.68	10.86
R Lacy	Bronze	46	4	175	16	2.88	10.94
Lester	Nuneaton	115.3	25	334	27	4.27	12.37
A Kennell	Kenilworth	221.1	51	573	46	4.81	12.46
Paul Lovick	Bedworth	164.5	19	474	38	4.33	12.47
B Macey	Bronze	81	15	222	17	4.76	13.06

Division 1 - 2nd XI

		O	M	R	W	S/R	Ave
Graham Eyles	Bablake OB	96.5	37	201	23	4.20	8.74
Steve Mullard	Sheldon Marl.	88.4	14	279	30	2.95	9.30
C Pearce	Camp Hill OE	86.13	22	243	24	3.59	10.13
Salman Ahmad	Bablake OB	152.5	28	520	38	4.01	13.68
George Rubery	Bablake OB	154.3	39	347	25	6.17	13.88
Matt Read	Sheldon Marl.	141	33	409	26	5.42	15.73

Division 2 - 2nd XI

		O	M	R	W	S/R	Ave
A Beale	Ansley	172	40	424	58	2.97	7.31
S Jayes	Stockton	101.1	25	235	22	4.60	10.68
V Clarke	Handsworth	135	28	347	32	4.22	10.84
O Brown	Handsworth	209	48	502	45	4.64	11.16
A Stock	Rowland United	248.4	55	703	60	4.14	11.72
M Sharples	Stockton	180.4	40	454	38	4.75	11.95

Division 3 - 2nd XI

		O	M	R	W	S/R	Ave
Babar Khan	Lyndworth	75	14	173	38	1.97	4.55
Sultan Afsar	Lyndworth	145	33	253	22	6.59	11.50
Dave Stringer	Attleborough	119.1	31	396	31	3.84	12.77
Anthony Harris	Erdington Court	80	6	329	25	3.20	13.16
H Clay	Weoley Hill	72.3	15	248	18	4.02	13.78
Glenn Foster	Attleborough	117	22	363	26	4.50	13.96

Division 4 - 2nd XI

		O	M	R	W	S/R	Ave
J Peters	Bulkington	110.3	20	398	34	3.24	11.71
Dan Ward	Castle Bromwich	52	8	211	17	3.06	12.41
M.Ikhlaq	Coventry Colliery	118	17	337	26	4.54	12.96
R.Memi	Coventry Colliery	38	5	200	15	2.53	13.33
Scot White	Castle Bromwich	130	18	465	33	3.94	14.09
A Riley	Bulkington	96	11	345	22	4.36	15.68

Division 5 - 2nd XI

		O	M	R	W	S/R	Ave
C.Williams	Hunningham			136	17	0.00	8.00
Lee Jones	Stockingford	303	95	674	62	4.89	10.87
Upen Randhawa	Willclare	60		203	16	3.75	12.69
Nigel Hancock	Barby	107.4	19	368	28	3.84	13.14
M.Studholme	Aston OE	63.2	6	217	16	3.95	13.56
M.Mundy	Hunningham			221	15	0.00	14.73

Division 6 - 2nd XI

		O	M	R	W	S/R	Ave
Dave Cheney	Newbold	128.5	43	273	33	3.89	8.27
P J McManus	Peugeot	164.8	29	487	43	3.83	11.33
David Elvidge	Dunlop	137	37	401	34	4.03	11.79
Will Mulheron	Nuneaton	157.4	38	449	35	4.50	12.83
Nigel Hancock	Barby	107.4	19	368	28	3.84	13.14
James Kirkham	Wolvey	96	12	356	25	3.84	14.24

Single Teams 1

		O	M	R	W	S/R	Ave
Simon Stapley	Braunston Padd.	73.3	13	156	17	4.31	9.18
R.Sudat	Small Heath	110.5	28	304	31	3.56	9.81
I.Godfree	Small Heath	74	16	167	17	4.35	9.82
Ian Cox	Leek Wootton	74.5	16	204	17	4.38	12.00
Paul Beck	Braunston Padd.	66.5	12	233	17	3.91	13.71
K.Singh	Small Heath	65.5	20	166	12	5.46	13.83

Single Teams 2

		O	M	R	W	S/R	Ave
R Gordon	Handsworth	33	2	69	17	1.94	4.06
Tom Rumble	Ambleside	57.2	11	117	21	2.72	5.57
K Smith	Handsworth	30	2	118	17	1.76	6.94
I Stockley	Berkswell	45	14	110	12	3.75	9.17
Shafiq Patel	Crescent	64	15	153	16	4.00	9.56
P Hardwick	Warwick	51	16	117	12	4.25	9.75

Single Teams 3

		O	M	R	W	S/R	Ave
Dave Beardsmore	Riverside	33	5	87	12	2.75	7.25
Joseph Henry	Bablake OB	52	15	151	17	3.06	8.88
Dan McKenzie	Riverside	77	19	219	24	3.21	9.13
Dave Bevan	Riverside	88	10	293	32	2.75	9.16
A Williams	Selly Park	70.4	10	184	19	3.71	9.68
Chris Crocker	Riverside	79	15	203	19	4.16	10.68

The Origins of Premier League Cricket in Warwickshire

BEFORE 1989, league cricket in the Midlands consisted of several independent leagues with between 12 and 18 clubs playing each other home and away - no promotion or relegation. This meant that teams of varying degrees of ability were kept together for several years and sometimes to compensate for playing better teams, opposition captains would play very defensively to achieve a draw.

In 1989 two leagues suggested a merger, the Central League and the Willis Coroon and although this did not come to fruition, Gordon Sharpe on behalf of the Worcestershire League and Geoff Gale of The Warwickshire & Staffordshire League got together and after several meetings between the two committees these two agreed to merge. As these discussions went on other leagues wanted to be involved and by not taking set positions on the "batting order", these leagues i.e. The James Travel and the Print Line combined with the other two to form the Midlands Combined Counties League, with promotion and relegation between five divisions on a two up, two down basis. An umpires' panel was set up so that neutral umpires could officiate.

Several years later the ECB floated the idea of Premier Leagues formed on a countywide basis. Leicestershire was one of the early counties to go down this road and so the Leicestershire based clubs in the Central League left leaving several clubs on their own. However, immediately and with the same "goodwill" as in 1989, the MCCL invited these clubs into the top division - having to relegate some clubs to make room for them, again believing that in time clubs would again find their own level. The formation of a Premier League in the West Midlands took much longer, as the Birmingham League found it harder to convince its 12 clubs to accept the idea of promotion and relegation. However, very much due to the work of Tony Cross of the Warwickshire County Cricket Club, a Birmingham & District Premier League was set up. It consisted of the 12 clubs in the Birmingham League, clubs in the Debenham Tewson League and the top clubs in the MCCL.

At that time, it was requested by the ECB that below the level of the Birmingham League, cricket should be organised on a county basis and so several other clubs left the MCCL to go into the Staffordshire Club Championship & the Worcestershire County League. The remaining clubs from the MCCL stayed to form the Warwickshire League and later the Coventry & District League joined taking the full membership up to 90 + clubs.

Thus the pyramid system in the West Midlands was in place, at the top, the Birmingham & District League, and then four feeder leagues - Warwickshire, Staffordshire, Worcestershire and Shropshire.

2007 Member clubs

Ambleside
Ambleside Way
Nuneaton CV11 6AT
Tel: 02476 371033

Ansley Sports
Behind Ansley Hall
Nuneaton Road
Ansley
Tel: 07967 164581

Aston Oe
The Memorial Ground
Sunnybank Avenue
Perry Common
Birmingham B44 OHP
Tel: 0121 373 5746

Atherstone
Ratcliffe Road
Atherstone
Warwickshire
Tel: 01827 714934

Attleborough
Marston Lane
Attleborough
Nuneaton
Tel: 02476 328716

Bablake Old Boys
Norman Place Road
Coundon
Coventry CV6 2BU
Tel: 02476 271275

Barby
Longdown Lane
Barby
Rugby
Tel: 07930 555654

Bedworth
Miners Welfare Park
Rye Piece Ringway
Bedworth CV12 8JH
Tel: 02476 315296

Bourneville
Bourneville Lane
Birmingham B30
Tel: 07974 245679

Braunston Paddox
Braunston Playing Fields
Barby Lane
Braunston
Northants
Tel: 01788 890475

Bridge Trust
Romilly Avenue
Off Wood Lane
Handsworth Wood
Birmingham B20 2AT
Tel: 0121 554 3015

Bronze
Chapel Lane
Great Barr
Birmingham B43 7BD
Tel: 0121 358 4060

Bulkington
Pavilion
Recreation Ground
Bulkington
Nr Nuneaton CV12 9JB
Tel: 02476 643240

Camp Hill Old Edwardians
Rumbush Park
Rumbush Lane
Earlswood
Solihull B94 5NA
Tel: 07788 103616

Castle Bromwich
Rear Of Arden Hall
Water Orton Road
Castle Bromwich B36
Tel: 0121-748-1704

Civil Service
Old Damson Lane, Elmdon
Solihull B92 9ED
Tel: 0121 782 2151

Cleveland

Coleshill
The Coleshill School
Coventry Road
Coleshill B46 3EX

Collycroft
Heckley Fields
Coventry Rd
Exhall CV7 9EU
Tel: 02476 392164

Corley
Tamworth Road
Coventry CV7 8AA
Tel: 01676 542470

Coventry University & RM
Coventry University Sports Ground
Westwood Heath Road
Coventry CV4 8GP
Tel: 02476 465642

Coventry Colliery
Coventry Colliery
Sports & Social
Bennettts Road North
Keresley
Coventry CV7 8JW
Tel: 02476 332722

Crescent
123 Norman Avenue
Nuneaton CV11 5NY
Tel: 07974 414551

Dunlop
Burnaby Road
Holbrooks
Coventry
Tel: 02476 662394

Elford
Brickhouse Lane
Elford
Tamworth B79 9DE

Erdington Court
Bowling Green Close
Off Goosemoor Lane
Erdington B23 5QU
Tel: 0121 382 7565

Fillongley
The Parks
Blackhall Lane
Fillongley
Tel: 07976 310887

Five Ways Oe
'masshouse'
Ash Lane
Hopwood B48 7BD
Tel: 0121 445 4909

Four Oaks
Roger Smolden Ground
Sutton Coldfield Rugby
Club
Walmley Road
Sutton Coldfield.
Tel: 07986 891 222

Four Oaks Saints
Clarence Road
Four Oaks
Sutton Coldfield B74 4LT
Tel: 0121 353 4923

Griff & Coton
Heath End Road
Nuneaton CV10 7JQ
Tel: 02476 386798

Hampton & Solihull
Marsh Lane
Solihull B91 2PF
Tel: 0121 705 5271

Handsworth
Handsworth Park
Hinstock Road
Handsworth B21
Tel: 07817 979111

Handsworth Recreation

Haunchwood
Park Lane
Galley Common
Nuneaton
Tel: 02476 395221

Highway
Fletchamstead Highway
Coventry CV4 9BY
Tel: 02476 675615

Hunningham
Behind The Red Lion
Main Street
Hunningham CV33 9DY
Tel: 01926 402926

Jaguar Daimler
Alvis Sports Ground
Green Lane
Coventry
Tel: 02476 678486

Kenilworth
Warwick Road
Kenilworth CV8 1FB
Tel: 01926 853872

Knowle & Dorridge
239 - 293 Lugtrout Lane
Solihull B91 2RX
Tel: 0121 711 2338

Knowle Village
Hampton Road
Knowle
Solihull B93 0NX
Tel: 01564 771117

Leek Wootton
Off Quarry Close
Leek Wootton CV35 7QJ
Tel: 01926 852231

Lyndworth
19-21 Lyndworth Road
Stirchley
Birmingham
Tel: 0121 444 0418

Marston Green
Bickenhill Road
Marston Green
Solihull
Tel:0121 779 4092

Massey Ferguson
Bannerbrook Park
Banner Lane
Coventry CV5 9HG
Tel: 02476694202

Moseley Ashfield
Yardley Wood Road
Moseley
Birmingham
Tel: 01214493595

Nether Whitacre
Coton Road
Whitacre Heath
Nr. Coleshill B46 2HL
Tel: 07940 302344

Newbold
Parkfield Rd
Newbold
Rugby CV21 1EZ

Newdigate
Smorrall Lane
Bedworth CV12 0JP
Tel: 02476 366004

The Warwickshire League

Plastic Engineering

North Warwickshire
Hermitage Hill
Polesworth B78 1HT
Tel: 01827 892482

Nuneaton
Weddington Rd
Nuneaton CV10 0AL
Tel: 02476 382734

Oakfield
Sheaf And Sickle
Coventry Road
Long Lawford
Rugby CV23 9DT
Tel: 01788 544622

Offchurch/ Lapworth
Hunningham Road
Offchurch
Tel: 01926 420122

Old Edwardians
Streetsbrook Rd
Solihull B90 3PE
Tel: 0121 744 6831

Pakshaheen
Newbold Comyn
Newbold Terrace East
Leamington Spa
CV32 4EW
Tel: 02476 4221553

Peugeot
Gate 3, Humber Road
Coventry CV3 1BD

Pickwick Post & Mail
Windermere Rd
Moseley B13 9QD
Tel: 07866 725293

Prince Of Wales
By Railway Bridge
Tamworth Road
Sutton Coldfield B74
Tel: 07973 346731

Riverside Royals

Rowland United
Lutterworth Road
Swinford
Nr Rugby
Tel: 01788 832373

Rugby
The Cricket Ground
Webb Ellis Road
Rugby
Tel: 01788 561408

Saffron

Selly Park

Sheldon Marlborough
Foliot Fields
Off Stoney Lane
Yardley B25 8RF
Tel: 0121 784 9191

Small Heath
Civil Service
Old Damson Lane
Solihull

Solihull Municipal
Brick Kiln Lane
Off Widney Lane
Solihull B91 3LE
Tel: 0121 705-1192

Southam
The Old Road
Southam
Leamington Spa CV47
Tel: 01926 814735

Sphinx
Sphinx Sports Ground
Sphinx Drive
Off Siddeley Avenue
Coventry CV3 1WA
Tel: 02476 451361

St Johns

Standard
Tanners Lane
Coventry
Tel: 02476 679733

Stockingford
Ansley Road
Stockingford
Nuneaton CV10
Tel: 02476 387743

Stockton
The Town Piece
Napton Road
Stockton CV47 1AE
Tel: 01926 813960

Streetly
Briar Avenue
Streetly
Sutton Coldfield B74 3HQ
Tel: 0121 353 0958

Thimblemill
Pavillion Sports Ground
Thimblemill Road
Smethwick B66
Tel: 0121 420 3505

Walsall Ymf
Old Walsall
Phoenix Ground
The Grange Arboretum
Sutton Road
Walsall
Tel: 07776 200224

Ward End Unity
The Marriotts
Rear Of 118

Stechford Road
Hodge Hill B34
Tel: 0121 783 2755

Warwick
Hampton Road
Warwick CV35 8HA
Tel: 01926 491569

Weoley Hill
Valley Parkway
Weoley Hill
Selly Oak
Birmingham B29 4XX
Tel: 0121 475 3639

**Copsewood West
Indian Wanderers**
Allard Way
Copsewood
Coventry
Warwickshire CV3 1HQ
Tel: 02476 635992

Willclare Fujitsu
Willclare Road
Sheldon
Birmingham B26
Tel: 0121 743 6368

Willow

Wilnecote

Wishaw
Church Lane
Wishaw
Sutton Coldfield B76 9QD
Tel: 0121 313 1564

Wolvey

Wythall

**Warwick CC 1st XI, who had such a succesful season in 2006.
From left to right
Back Row - Rob Codderington, Steve Webb, Steve Smith,
Matt Sarson, Francis Batt, Adrian Passey, 'TAFF' (scorer)
Front Row - Niel Turner, Paul Jackson, Dave Griffith
(Capt), Jamie Coleman (Wkt), Craig Downing.**

2007 Fixtures

Premier Division 1st XI

Sat 5th May - 1.30pm
N. Warwick.	vKings Heath
Kenilworth	vHighway
Mos. Ashfield	vNuneaton
O. Edward's	vAtherstone
Bablake OB	vBedworth
Fillongley	vBronze

Sat 12th May - 1.30pm
Kings Heath	vFillongley
Bedworth	vN. Warwick.
Atherstone	vBablake OB
Nuneaton	vO. Edward's
Highway	vMos. Ashfield
Bronze	vKenilworth

Sat 19th May - 1.30pm
N. Warwick.	vAtherstone
Kings Heath	vBedworth
Mos. Ashfield	vBronze
O. Edward's	vHighway
Bablake OB	vNuneaton
Fillongley	vKenilworth

Sat 26th May - 1.30pm
Bedworth	vFillongley
Atherstone	vKings Heath
Nuneaton	vN. Warwick.
Highway	vBablake OB
Bronze	vO. Edward's
Kenilworth	vMos. Ashfield

Mon 28th May - 1.30pm
N. Warwick.	vHighway
Kings Heath	vNuneaton
Bedworth	vAtherstone
O. Edward's	vKenilworth
Bablake OB	vBronze
Fillongley	vMos. Ashfield

Sat 2nd June - 1.30pm
Fillongley	vAtherstone
Nuneaton	vBedworth
Highway	vKings Heath
Bronze	vN. Warwick.
Kenilworth	vBablake OB
Mos. Ashfield	vO. Edward's

Sat 9th June - 1.30pm
N. Warwick.	vKenilworth
Kings Heath	vBronze
Bedworth	vHighway
Atherstone	vNuneaton

Bablake OB	vMos. Ashfield
Fillongley	vO. Edward's

Sat 16th June - 1.30pm
Nuneaton	vFillongley
Highway	vAtherstone
Bronze	vBedworth
Kenilworth	vKings Heath
Mos. Ashfield	vN. Warwick.
O. Edward's	vBablake OB

Sat 23rd June - 1.30pm
N. Warwick.	vO. Edward's
Kings Heath	vMos. Ashfield
Bedworth	vKenilworth
Atherstone	vBronze
Nuneaton	vHighway
Fillongley	vBablake OB

Sat 30th June - 1.30pm
Bronze	vNuneaton
Kenilworth	vAtherstone
Mos. Ashfield	vBedworth
O. Edward's	vKings Heath
Bablake OB	vN. Warwick.
Fillongley	vHighway

Sat 7th July - 1.30pm
N. Warwick.	vFillongley
Kings Heath	vBablake OB
Bedworth	vO. Edward's
Atherstone	vMos. Ashfield
Nuneaton	vKenilworth
Highway	vBronze

Sat 14th July - 1.30pm
Kings Heath	vN. Warwick.
Highway	vKenilworth
Nuneaton	vMos. Ashfield
Atherstone	vO. Edward's
Bedworth	vBablake OB
Bronze	vFillongley

Sat 21st July - 1.30pm
Fillongley	vKings Heath
N. Warwick.	vBedworth
Bablake OB	vAtherstone
O. Edward's	vNuneaton
Mos. Ashfield	vHighway
Kenilworth	vBronze

Sat 28th July - 1.30pm
Atherstone	vN. Warwick.
Bedworth	vKings Heath
Bronze	vMos. Ashfield
Highway	vO. Edward's

Nuneaton	vBablake OB
Kenilworth	vFillongley

Sat 4th Aug - 1.30pm
Fillongley	vBedworth
Kings Heath	vAtherstone
N. Warwick.	vNuneaton
Bablake OB	vHighway
O. Edward's	vBronze
Mos. Ashfield	vKenilworth

Sat 11th Aug - 1.30pm
Highway	vN. Warwick.
Nuneaton	vKings Heath
Atherstone	vBedworth
Kenilworth	vO. Edward's
Bronze	vBablake OB
Mos. Ashfield	vFillongley

Sat 18th Aug - 1pm
Atherstone	vFillongley
Bedworth	vNuneaton
Kings Heath	vHighway
N. Warwick.	vBronze
Bablake OB	vKenilworth
O. Edward's	vMos. Ashfield

Sat 25th Aug - 1pm
Kenilworth	vN. Warwick.
Bronze	vKings Heath
Highway	vBedworth
Nuneaton	vAtherstone
Mos. Ashfield	vBablake OB
O. Edward's	vFillongley

Mon 27th Aug - 1pm
Fillongley	vNuneaton
Atherstone	vHighway
Bedworth	vBronze
Kings Heath	vKenilworth
N. Warwick.	vMos. Ashfield
Bablake OB	vO. Edward's

Sat 1st Sept - 1pm
O. Edward's	vN. Warwick.
Mos. Ashfield	vKings Heath
Kenilworth	vBedworth
Bronze	vAtherstone
Highway	vNuneaton
Bablake OB	vFillongley

Sat 8st Sept - 12.30pm
Nuneaton	vBronze
Atherstone	vKenilworth
Bedworth	vMos. Ashfield
Kings Heath	vO. Edward's

N. Warwick.   vBablake OB
Highway   vFillongley

Sat 15st Sept - 12.30pm
Fillongley   vN. Warwick.
Bablake OB   vKings Heath
O. Edward's   vBedworth
Mos. Ashfield   vAtherstone
Kenilworth   vNuneaton
Bronze   vHighway

Division 1 - 1st XI

Sat 5th May - 1.30pm
Stockton   vStreetly
Rowland Utd   vAnsley Sp.
CH O. Ed's   vMar. Green
Warwick   vPickwick P&M
Handsworth   vSoutham
Sh. Marlb.   vWishaw

Sat 12th May - 1.30pm
Streetly   vSh. Marlb.
Southam   vStockton
Pickwick P&M   vHandsworth
Mar. Green   vWarwick
Ansley Sp.   vCH O. Ed's
Wishaw   vRowland Utd

Sat 19th May - 1.30pm
Stockton   vPickwick P&M
Streetly   vSoutham
CH O. Ed's   vWishaw
Warwick   vAnsley Sp.
Handsworth   vMar. Green
Sh. Marlb.   vRowland Utd

Sat 26th May - 1.30pm
Southam   vSh. Marlb.
Pickwick P&M   vStreetly
Mar. Green   vStockton
Ansley Sp.   vHandsworth
Wishaw   vWarwick
Rowland Utd   vCH O. Ed's

Mon 28th May - 1.30pm
Stockton   vAnsley Sp.
Streetly   vMar. Green
Southam   vPickwick P&M
Warwick   vRowland Utd
Handsworth   vWishaw
Sh. Marlb.   vCH O. Ed's

Sat 2nd June - 1.30pm
Sh. Marlb.   vPickwick P&M
Mar. Green   vSoutham
Ansley Sp.   vStreetly
Wishaw   vStockton
Rowland Utd   vHandsworth
CH O. Ed's   vWarwick

Sat 9th June - 1.30pm
Stockton   vRowland Utd
Streetly   vWishaw
Southam   vAnsley Sp.
Pickwick P&M   vMar. Green
Handsworth   vCH O. Ed's
Sh. Marlb.   vWarwick

Sat 16th June - 1.30pm
Mar. Green   vSh. Marlb.
Ansley Sp.   vPickwick P&M
Wishaw   vSoutham
Rowland Utd   vStreetly
CH O. Ed's   vStockton
Warwick   vHandsworth

Sat 23rd June - 1.30pm
Stockton   vWarwick
Streetly   vCH O. Ed's
Southam   vRowland Utd
Pickwick P&M   vWishaw
Mar. Green   vAnsley Sp.
Sh. Marlb.   vHandsworth

Sat 30th June - 1.30pm
Wishaw   vMar. Green
Rowland Utd   vPickwick P&M
CH O. Ed's   vSoutham
Warwick   vStreetly
Handsworth   vStockton
Sh. Marlb.   vAnsley Sp.

Sat 7th July - 1.30pm
Stockton   vSh. Marlb.
Streetly   vHandsworth
Southam   vWarwick
Pickwick P&M   vCH O. Ed's
Mar. Green   vRowland Utd
Ansley Sp.   vWishaw

Sat 14th July - 1.30pm
Streetly   vStockton
Ansley Sp.   vRowland Utd
Mar. Green   vCH O. Ed's
Pickwick P&M   vWarwick
Southam   vHandsworth
Wishaw   vSh. Marlb.

Sat 21st July - 1.30pm
Sh. Marlb.   vStreetly
Stockton   vSoutham
Handsworth   vPickwick P&M
Warwick   vMar. Green
CH O. Ed'sv   vAnsley Sp.
Rowland Utd   vWishaw

Sat 28th July - 1.30pm
Pickwick P&M   vStockton
Southam   vStreetly
Wishaw   vCH O. Ed's
Ansley Sp.   vWarwick
Mar. Green   vHandsworth
Rowland Utd   vSh. Marlb.

Sat 4th Aug - 1.30pm
Sh. Marlb.   vSoutham
Streetly   vPickwick P&M
Stockton   vMar. Green
Handsworth   vAnsley Sp.
Warwick   vWishaw
CH O. Ed's   vRowland Utd

Sat 11th Aug - 1.30pm
Ansley Sp.   vStockton
Mar. Green   vStreetly
Pickwick P&M   vSoutham
Rowland Utd   vWarwick
Wishaw   vHandsworth
CH O. Ed's   vSh. Marlb.

Sat 18th Aug - 1pm
Pickwick P&M   vSh. Marlb.
Southam   vMar. Green
Streetly   vAnsley Sp.
Stockton   vWishaw
Handsworth   vRowland Utd
Warwick   vCH O. Ed's

Sat 25th Aug - 1pm
Rowland Utd   vStockton
Wishaw   vStreetly
Ansley Sp.   vSoutham
Mar. Green   vPickwick P&M
CH O. Ed's   vHandsworth
Warwick   vSh. Marlb.

Mon 27th Aug - 1pm
Sh. Marlb.   vMar. Green
Pickwick P&M   vAnsley Sp.
Southam   vWishaw
Streetly   vRowland Utd
Stockton   vCH O. Ed's
Handsworth   vWarwick

Sat 1st Sept - 1pm
Warwick   vStockton
CH O. Ed's   vStreetly
Rowland Utd   vSoutham
Wishaw   vPickwick P&M
Ansley Sp.   vMar. Green
Handsworth   vSh. Marlb.

The Warwickshire League

Sat 8st Sept - 12.30pm
Mar. Green   vWishaw
Pickwick P&M   vRowland Utd
Southam   vCH O. Ed's
Streetly   vWarwick
Stockton   vHandsworth
Ansley Sp.   vSh. Marlb.

Sat 15st Sept - 12pm
Sh. Marlb.   vStockton
Handsworth   vStreetly
Warwick   vSoutham
CH O. Ed's   vPickwick P&M
Rowland Utd   vMar. Green
Wishaw   vAnsley Sp.

Division 2 - 1st XI

Sat 5th May - 1.30pm
Bournville   vHam. & Sol.
Ambleside   vLyndworth
Griff & Coton   vRugby
Offch./Lap.   vCivil Service
N. Whitacre   vSphinx
Attleborough   vF. Oaks Sts

Sat 12th May - 1.30pm
Ham. & Sol.   vAttleborough
Sphinx   vBournville
Civil Service   vN. Whitacre
Rugby   vOffch./Lap.
Lyndworth   vGriff & Coton
F. Oaks Sts   vAmbleside

Sat 19th May - 1.30pm V
Bournville   vCivil Service
Ham. & Sol.   vSphinx
Griff & Coton   vF. Oaks Sts
Offch./Lap.   vLyndworth
N. Whitacre   vRugby
Attleborough   vAmbleside

Sat 26th May - 1.30pm
Sphinx   vAttleborough
Civil Service   vHam. & Sol.
Rugby   vBournville
Lyndworth   vN. Whitacre
F. Oaks Sts   vOffch./Lap.
Ambleside   vGriff & Coton

Mon 28th May - 1.30pm
Bournville   vLyndworth
Ham. & Sol.   vRugby
Sphinx   vCivil Service
Offch./Lap.   vAmbleside
N. Whitacre   vF. Oaks Sts
Attleborough   vGriff & Coton

Sat 2nd June - 1.30pm
Civil Service   vAttleborough
Rugby   vSphinx
Lyndworth   vHam. & Sol.
F. Oaks Sts   vBournville
Ambleside   vN. Whitacre
Griff & Coton   vOffch./Lap.

Sat 9th June - 1.30pm
Bournville   vAmbleside
Ham. & Sol.   vF. Oaks Sts
Sphinx   vLyndworth
Civil Service   vRugby
N. Whitacre   vGriff & Coton
Attleborough   vOffch./Lap.

Sat 16th June - 1.30pm
F. Oaks Sts   vRugby
Ambleside   vCivil Service
Griff & Coton   vSphinx
Offch./Lap.   vHam. & Sol.
N. Whitacre   vBournville
Attleborough   vLyndworth

Sat 23rd June - 1.30pm
Bournville   vOffch./Lap.
Ham. & Sol.   vGriff & Coton
Sphinx   vAmbleside
Civil Service   vF. Oaks Sts
Rugby   vLyndworth
Attleborough   vN. Whitacre

Sat 30th June - 1.30pm
Rugby   vAttleborough
Lyndworth   vCivil Service
Sphinx   vF. Oaks Sts
Ambleside   vHam. & Sol.
Griff & Coton   vBournville
Offch./Lap.   vN. Whitacre

Sat 7th July - 1.30pm
Bournville   vAttleborough
Ham. & Sol.   vN. Whitacre
Sphinx   vOffch./Lap.
Griff & Coton   vCivil Service
Rugby   vAmbleside
Lyndworth   vF. Oaks Sts

Sat 14th July - 1.30pm
Ham. & Sol.   vBournville
Lyndworth   vAmbleside
Rugby   vGriff & Coton
Civil Service   vOffch./Lap.
Sphinx   vN. Whitacre
F. Oaks Sts   vAttleborough

Sat 21st July - 1.30pm
Attleborough   vHam. & Sol.
Bournville   vSphinx

N. Whitacre   vCivil Service
Offch./Lap.   vRugby
Griff & Coton   vLyndworth
Ambleside   vF. Oaks Sts

Sat 28th July - 1.30pm
Civil Service   vBournville
Sphinx   vHam. & Sol.
F. Oaks Sts   vGriff & Coton
Lyndworth   vOffch./Lap.
Rugby   vN. Whitacre
Ambleside   vAttleborough

Sat 4th Aug - 1.30pm
Attleborough   vSphinx
Ham. & Sol.   vCivil Service
Bournville   vRugby
N. Whitacre   vLyndworth
Offch./Lap.   vF. Oaks Sts
Griff & Coton   vAmbleside

Sat 11th Aug - 1.30pm
Lyndworth   vBournville
Rugby   vHam. & Sol.
Civil Service   vSphinx
Ambleside   vOffch./Lap.
F. Oaks Sts   vN. Whitacre
Griff & Coton   vAttleborough

Sat 18th Aug - 1pm
Attleborough   vCivil Service
Sphinx   vRugby
Ham. & Sol.   vLyndworth
Bournville   vF. Oaks Sts
N. Whitacre   vAmbleside
Offch./Lap.   vGriff & Coton

Sat 25th Aug - 1pm
Ambleside   vBournville
F. Oaks Sts   vHam. & Sol.
Lyndworth   vSphinx
Rugby   vCivil Service
Griff & Coton   vN. Whitacre
Offch./Lap.   vAttleborough

Mon 28th Aug - 1pm
Rugby   vF. Oaks Sts
Civil Service   vAmbleside
Sphinx   vGriff & Coton
Ham. & Sol.   vOffch./Lap.
Bournville   vN. Whitacre
Lyndworth   vAttleborough

Sat 1st Sept - 1pm
Offch./Lap.   vBournville
Griff & Coton   vHam. & Sol.
Ambleside   vSphinx
F. Oaks Sts   vCivil Service
Lyndworth   vRugby
N. Whitacre   vAttleborough

Sat 8st Sept - 12.30pm

Attleborough	vRugby
Civil Service	vLyndworth
F. Oaks Sts	vSphinx
Ham. & Sol.	vAmbleside
Bournville	vGriff & Coton
N. Whitacre	vOffch./Lap.

Sat 15th Sept - 12pm

Attleborough	vBournville
N. Whitacre	vHam. & Sol.
Offch./Lap.	vSphinx
Civil Service	vGriff & Coton
Ambleside	vRugby
F. Oaks Sts	vLyndworth

Division 3 - 1st XI

Sat 5th May - 1.30pm

Pakshaheen	vElford
Walsall Ymf	vWard End U.
Erdington Ct	vBulkington
K & Dorridge	vJag. Daimler
Five Ways Oe	vCastle Brom.

Sat 12th May - 1.30pm

Castle Brom.	vElford
Ward End U.	vK & Dorridge
Erdington Ct	vFive Ways Oe
Jag. Daimler	vWalsall Ymf
Bulkington	vPakshaheen

Sat 19th May - 1.30pm

Elford	vJag. Daimler
Ward End U.	vErdington Ct
Five Ways Oe	vK & Dorridge
Pakshaheen	vCastle Brom.
Walsall Ymf	vBulkington

Sat 26th May - 1.30pm

Erdington Ct	vElford
Five Ways Oe	vWard End U.
K & Dorridge	vWalsall Ymf
Jag. Daimler	vPakshaheen
Castle Brom.	vBulkington

Sat 2nd June - 1.30pm

Elford	vFive Ways Oe
Ward End U.	vCastle Brom.
Walsall Ymf	vErdington Ct
Bulkington	vJag. Daimler
Pakshaheen	vK & Dorridge

Sat 9th June - 1.30pm

Elford	vBulkington
Pakshaheen	vWard End U.
K & Dorridge	vErdington Ct
Jag. Daimler	vCastle Brom.
Five Ways Oe	vWalsall Ymf

Sat 16th June - 1.30pm

Walsall Ymf	vElford
Ward End U.	vJag. Daimler
Erdington Ct	vPakshaheen
Bulkington	vFive Ways Oe
Castle Brom.	vK & Dorridge

Sat 23rd June - 1.30pm

Elford	vWard End U.
Pakshaheen	vWalsall Ymf
Castle Brom.	vErdington Ct
Jag. Daimler	vFive Ways Oe
Bulkington	vK & Dorridge

Sat 30th June - 1.30pm

K & Dorridge	vElford
Ward End U.	vBulkington
Erdington Ct	vJag. Daimler
Walsall Ymf	vCastle Brom.
Five Ways Oe	vPakshaheen

Sat 7th July - 1.30pm

Elford	vPakshaheen
Ward End U.	vWalsall Ymf
Bulkington	vErdington Ct
Jag. Daimler	vK & Dorridge
Castle Brom.	vFive Ways Oe

Sat 14th July - 1.30pm

Elford	vCastle Brom.
K & Dorridge	vWard End U.
Five Ways Oe	vErdington Ct
Walsall Ymf	vJag. Daimler
Pakshaheen	vBulkington

Sat 21st July - 1.30pm

Jag. Daimler	vElford
Erdington Ct	vWard End U.
K & Dorridge	vFive Ways Oe
Castle Brom.	vPakshaheen
Bulkington	vWalsall Ymf

Sat 28th July - 1.30pm

Elford	vErdington Ct
Ward End U.	vFive Ways Oe
Walsall Ymf	vK & Dorridge
Pakshaheen	vJag. Daimler
Bulkington	vCastle Brom.

Sat 4th Aug - 1.30pm

Five Ways Oe	vElford
Castle Brom.	vWard End U.
Erdington Ct	vWalsall Ymf
Jag. Daimler	vBulkington
K & Dorridge	vPakshaheen

Sat 11th Aug - 1.30pm

Bulkington	vElford
Ward End U.	vPakshaheen
Erdington Ct	vK & Dorridge
Castle Brom.	vJag. Daimler
Walsall Ymf	vFive Ways Oe

Sat 18th Aug - 1pm

Elford	vWalsall Ymf
Jag. Daimler	vWard End U.
Pakshaheen	vErdington Ct
Five Ways Oe	vBulkington
K & Dorridge	vCastle Brom.

Sat 25th Aug - 1pm

Ward End U.	vElford
Walsall Ymf	vPakshaheen
Erdington Ct	vCastle Brom.
Five Ways Oe	vJag. Daimler
K & Dorridge	vBulkington

Sat 1st Sept - 1pm

Elford	vK & Dorridge
Bulkington	vWard End U.
Jag. Daimler	vErdington Ct
Castle Brom.	vWalsall Ymf
Pakshaheen	vFive Ways Oe

Division 4 - 1st XI

Sat 5th May - 1.30pm

Thimblemill	vHunningham
Barby	vCorley
Cop. WI Wds	vWeoley Hill
Aston OE	vOakfield
Sol. Municip.	vCov. Colliery

Sat 12th May - 1.30pm

Sol. Municip.	vHunningham
Corley	vAston OE
Cop. WI Wds	vCov. Colliery
Oakfield	vBarby
Weoley Hill	vThimblemill

Sat 19th May - 1.30pm

Hunningham	vOakfield
Corley	vCop. WI Wds
Cov. Colliery	vAston OE
Thimblemill	vSol. Municip.
Barby	vWeoley Hill

Sat 26th May - 1.30pm

Cop. WI Wds	vHunningham
Cov. Colliery	vCorley
Aston OE	vBarby
Oakfield	vThimblemill
Sol. Municip.	vWeoley Hill

The Warwickshire League

Sat 2nd June - 1.30pm

Hunningham	vCov. Colliery
Corley	vSol. Municip.
Barby	vCop. WI Wds
Weoley Hill	vOakfield
Thimblemill	vAston OE

Sat 9th June - 1.30pm

Hunningham	vWeoley Hill
Thimblemill	vCorley
Aston OE	vCop. WI Wds
Oakfield	vSol. Municip.
Cov. Colliery	vBarby

Sat 16th June - 1.30pm

Barby	vHunningham
Corley	vOakfield
Cop. WI Wds	vThimblemill
Weoley Hill	vCov. Colliery
Sol. Municip.	vAston OE

Sat 23rd June - 1.30pm

Hunningham	vCorley
Thimblemill	vBarby
Sol. Municip.	vCop. WI Wds
Oakfield	vCov. Colliery
Weoley Hill	vAston OE

Sat 30th June - 1.30pm

Aston OE	vHunningham
Corley	vWeoley Hill
Cop. WI Wds	vOakfield
Barby	vSol. Municip.
Cov. Colliery	vThimblemill

Sat 7th July - 1.30pm

Hunningham	vThimblemill
Corley	vBarby
Weoley Hill	vCop. WI Wds
Oakfield	vAston OE
Cov. Colliery	vSol. Municip.

Sat 14th July - 1.30pm

Hunningham	vSol. Municip.
Aston OE	vCorley
Cov. Colliery	vCop. WI Wds
Barby	vOakfield
Thimblemill	vWeoley Hill

Sat 21st July - 1.30pm

Oakfield	vHunningham
Cop. WI Wds	vCorley
Aston OE	vCov. Colliery
Sol. Municip.	vThimblemill
Weoley Hill	vBarby

Sat 28th July - 1.30pm

Hunningham	vCop. WI Wds
Corley	vCov. Colliery
Barby	vAston OE
Thimblemill	vOakfield
Weoley Hill	vSol. Municip.

Sat 4th Aug - 1.30pm

Cov. Colliery	vHunningham
Sol. Municip.	vCorley
Cop. WI Wds	vBarby
Oakfield	vWeoley Hill
Aston OE	vThimblemill

Sat 11th Aug - 1.30pm

Weoley Hill	vHunningham
Corley	vThimblemill
Cop. WI Wds	vAston OE
Sol. Municip.	vOakfield
Barby	vCov. Colliery

Sat 18th Aug - 1pm

Hunningham	vBarby
Oakfield	vCorley
Thimblemill	vCop. WI Wds
Cov. Colliery	vWeoley Hill
Aston OE	vSol. Municip.

Sat 25th Aug - 1pm

Corley	vHunningham
Barby	vThimblemill
Cop. WI Wds	vSol. Municip.
Cov. Colliery	vOakfield
Aston OE	vWeoley Hill

Sat 1st Sept - 1pm

Hunningham	vAston OE
Weoley Hill	vCorley
Oakfield	vCop. WI Wds
Sol. Municip.	vBarby
Thimblemill	vCov. Colliery

Division 5 - 1st XI

Sat 5th May - 1.30pm

Wilnecote	vCollycroft
Newdigate	vHaunchwood
Mass. Ferg.	vWolvey
Newbold	vKnowle Vill.
Cov. U. &RM	vWillclare

Sat 12th May - 1.30pm

Cov. U. &RM	vCollycroft
Haunchwood	vNewbold
Mass. Ferg.	vWillclare
Knowle Vill.	vNewdigate
Wolvey	vWilnecote

Sat 19th May - 1.30pm

Collycroft	vKnowle Vill.
Haunchwood	vMass. Ferg.
Willclare	vNewbold
Wilnecote	vCov. U. &RM
Newdigate	vWolvey

Sat 26th May - 1.30pm

Mass. Ferg.	vCollycroft
Willclare	vHaunchwood
Newbold	vNewdigate
Knowle Vill.	vWilnecote
Cov. U. &RM	vWolvey

Sat 2nd June - 1.30pm

Collycroft	vWillclare
Haunchwood	vCov. U. &RM
Newdigate	vMass. Ferg.
Wolvey	vKnowle Vill.
Wilnecote	vNewbold

Sat 9th June - 1.30pm

Collycroft	vWolvey
Wilnecote	vHaunchwood
Newbold	vMass. Ferg.
Knowle Vill.	vCov. U. &RM
Willclare	vNewdigate

Sat 16th June - 1.30pm

Newdigate	vCollycroft
Haunchwood	vKnowle Vill.
Mass. Ferg.	vWilnecote
Wolvey	vWillclare
Cov. U. &RM	vNewbold

Sat 23rd June - 1.30pm

Collycroft	vHaunchwood
Wilnecote	vNewdigate
Cov. U. &RM	vMass. Ferg.
Knowle Vill.	vWillclare
Wolvey	vNewbold

Sat 30th June - 1.30pm

Newbold	vCollycroft
Haunchwood	vWolvey
Mass. Ferg.	vKnowle Vill.
Newdigate	vCov. U. &RM
Willclare	vWilnecote

Sat 7th July - 1.30pm

Collycroft	vWilnecote
Haunchwood	vNewdigate
Wolvey	vMass. Ferg.
Knowle Vill.	vNewbold
Willclare	vCov. U. &RM

Division 6 - 1st XI

Sat 14th July - 1.30pm

Collycroft	vCov. U. &RM
Newbold	vHaunchwood
Willclare	vMass. Ferg.
Newdigate	vKnowle Vill.
Wilnecote	vWolvey

Sat 21st July - 1.30pm

Knowle Vill.	vCollycroft
Mass. Ferg.	vHaunchwood
Newbold	vWillclare
Cov. U. &RM	vWilnecote
Wolvey	vNewdigate

Sat 28th July - 1.30pm

Collycroft	vMass. Ferg.
Haunchwood	vWillclare
Newdigate	vNewbold
Wilnecote	vKnowle Vill.
Wolvey	vCov. U. &RM

Sat 4th Aug - 1.30pm

Willclare	vCollycroft
Cov. U. &RM	vHaunchwood
Mass. Ferg.	vNewdigate
Knowle Vill.	vWolvey
Newbold	vWilnecote

Sat 11th Aug - 1.30pm

Wolvey	vCollycroft
Haunchwood	vWilnecote
Mass. Ferg.	vNewbold
Cov. U. &RM	vKnowle Vill.
Newdigate	vWillclare

Sat 18th Aug - 1pm

Collycroft	vNewdigate
Knowle Vill.	vHaunchwood
Wilnecote	vMass. Ferg.
Willclare	vWolvey
Newbold	vCov. U. &RM

Sat 25th Aug - 1pm

Haunchwood	vCollycroft
Newdigate	vWilnecote
Mass. Ferg.	vCov. U. &RM
Willclare	vKnowle Vill.
Newbold	vWolvey

Sat 1st Sept - 1pm

Collycroft	vNewbold
Wolvey	vHaunchwood
Knowle Vill.	vMass. Ferg.
Cov. U. &RM	vNewdigate
Wilnecote	vWillclare

Sat 5th May - 1.30pm

Standard	vFour Oaks
Nuneaton III	vPeugeot
Dunlop	vBedworth III
Bab. OB III	vBridge Trust
Stockingford	vP. Of Wales

Sat 12th May - 1.30pm

Stockingford	vFour Oaks
Peugeot	vBab. OB III
Dunlop	vP. Of Wales
Bridge Trust	vNuneaton III
Bedworth III	vStandard

Sat 19th May - 1.30pm

Four Oaks	vBridge Trust
Peugeot	vDunlop
P. Of Wales	vBab. OB III
Standard	vStockingford
Nuneaton III	vBedworth III

Sat 26th May - 1.30pm

Dunlop	vFour Oaks
P. Of Wales	vPeugeot
Bab. OB III	vNuneaton III
Bridge Trust	vStandard
Stockingford	vBedworth III

Sat 2nd June - 1.30pm

Four Oaks	vP. Of Wales
Peugeot	vStockingford
Nuneaton III	vDunlop
Bedworth III	vBridge Trust
Standard	vBab. OB III

Sat 9th June - 1.30pm

Four Oaks	vBedworth III
Standard	vPeugeot
Bab. OB III	vDunlop
Bridge Trust	vStockingford
P. Of Wales	vNuneaton III

Sat 16th June - 1.30pm

Nuneaton III	vFour Oaks
Peugeot	vBridge Trust
Dunlop	vStandard
Bedworth III	vP. Of Wales
Stockingford	vBab. OB III

Sat 23rd June - 1.30pm

Four Oaks	vPeugeot
Standard	vNuneaton III
Stockingford	vDunlop
Bridge Trust	vP. Of Wales
Bedworth III	vBab. OB III

Sat 30th June - 1.30pm

Bab. OB III	vFour Oaks
Peugeot	vBedworth III
Dunlop	vBridge Trust
Nuneaton III	vStockingford
P. Of Wales	vStandard

Sat 7th July - 1.30pm

Four Oaks	vStandard
Peugeot	vNuneaton III
Bedworth III	vDunlop
Bridge Trust	vBab. OB III
P. Of Wales	vStockingford

Sat 14th July - 1.30pm

Four Oaks	vStockingford
Bab. OB III	vPeugeot
P. Of Wales	vDunlop
Nuneaton III	vBridge Trust
Standard	vBedworth III

Sat 21st July - 1.30pm

Bridge Trust	vFour Oaks
Dunlop	vPeugeot
Bab. OB III	vP. Of Wales
Stockingford	vStandard
Bedworth III	vNuneaton III

Sat 28th July - 1.30pm

Four Oaks	vDunlop
Peugeot	vP. Of Wales
Nuneaton III	vBab. OB III
Standard	vBridge Trust
Bedworth III	vStockingford

Sat 4th Aug - 1.30pm

P. Of Wales	vFour Oaks
Stockingford	vPeugeot
Dunlop	vNuneaton III
Bridge Trust	vBedworth III
Bab. OB III	vStandard

Sat 11th Aug - 1.30pm

Bedworth III	vFour Oaks
Peugeot	vStandard
Dunlop	vBab. OB III
Stockingford	vBridge Trust
Nuneaton III	vP. Of Wales

Sat 18th Aug - 1pm

Four Oaks	vNuneaton III
Bridge Trust	vPeugeot
Standard	vDunlop
P. Of Wales	vBedworth III
Bab. OB III	vStockingford

The Warwickshire League

Sat 25th Aug - 1pm

Peugeot   vFour Oaks
Nuneaton III   vStandard
Dunlop   vStockingford
P. Of Wales   vBridge Trust
Bab. OB III   vBedworth III

Sat 1st Sept - 1pm

Four Oaks   vBab. OB III
Bedworth III   vPeugeot
Bridge Trust   vDunlop
Stockingford   vNuneaton III
Standard   vP. Of Wales

Premier Division
2nd XI

Sat 5th May - 1.30pm

Kings Heath   vBournville
Highway   vKenilworth
Nuneaton   vMos. Ashfield
Atherstone   vO. Edward's
Bedworth   vBablake OB
Bronze   vSh. Marlb.

Sat 12th May - 1.30pm

Sh. Marlb.   vKings Heath
Bournville   vBedworth
Bablake OB   vAtherstone
O. Edward's   vNuneaton
Mos. Ashfield vHighway
Kenilworth   vBronze

Sat 19th May - 1.30pm

Atherstone   vBournville
Bedworth   vKings Heath
Bronze   vMos. Ashfield
Highway   vO. Edward's
Nuneaton   vBablake OB
Kenilworth   vSh. Marlb.

Sat 26th May - 1.30pm

Sh. Marlb.   vBedworth
Kings Heath   vAtherstone
Bournville   vNuneaton
Bablake OB   vHighway
O. Edward's   vBronze
Mos. Ashfield vKenilworth

Mon 28th May - 1.30pm

Highway   vBournville
Nuneaton   vKings Heath
Atherstone   vBedworth
Kenilworth   vO. Edward's
Bronze   vBablake OB
Mos. Ashfield vSh. Marlb.

Sat 2nd June - 1.30pm

Atherstone   vSh. Marlb.
Bedworth   vNuneaton
Kings Heath   vHighway
Bournville   vBronze
Bablake OB   vKenilworth
O. Edward's   vMos. Ashfield

Sat 9th June - 1.30pm

Kenilworth   vBournville
Bronze   vKings Heath
Highway   vBedworth
Nuneaton   vAtherstone
Mos. Ashfield vBablake OB
O. Edward's   vSh. Marlb.

Sat 16th June - 1.30pm

Sh. Marlb.   vNuneaton
Atherstone   vHighway
Bedworth   vBronze
Kings Heath   vKenilworth
Bournville   vMos. Ashfield
Bablake OB   vO. Edward's

Sat 23rd June - 1.30pm

O. Edward's   vBournville
Mos. Ashfield vKings Heath
Kenilworth   vBedworth
Bronze   vAtherstone
Highway   vNuneaton
Bablake OB   vSh. Marlb.

Sat 30th June - 1.30pm

Nuneaton   vBronze
Atherstone   vKenilworth
Bedworth   vMos. Ashfield
Kings Heath   vO. Edward's
Bournville   vBablake OB
Highway   vSh. Marlb.

Sat 7th July - 1.30pm

Sh. Marlb.   vBournville
Bablake OB   vKings Heath
O. Edward's   vBedworth
Mos. Ashfield vAtherstone
Kenilworth   vNuneaton
Bronze   vHighway

Sat 14th July - 1.30pm

Bournville   vKings Heath
Kenilworth   vHighway
Mos. Ashfield vNuneaton
O. Edward's   vAtherstone
Bablake OB   vBedworth
Sh. Marlb.   vBronze

Sat 21st July - 1.30pm

Kings Heath   vSh. Marlb.
Bedworth   vBournville
Atherstone   vBablake OB

Nuneaton   vO. Edward's
Highway   vMos. Ashfield
Bronze   vKenilworth

Sat 28th July - 1.30pm

Bournville   vAtherstone
Kings Heath   vBedworth
Mos. Ashfield vBronze
O. Edward's   vHighway
Bablake OB   vNuneaton
Sh. Marlb.   vKenilworth

Sat 4th Aug - 1.30pm

Bedworth   vSh. Marlb.
Atherstone   vKings Heath
Nuneaton   vBournville
Highway   vBablake OB
Bronze   vO. Edward's
Kenilworth   vMos. Ashfield

Sat 11th Aug - 1.30pm

Bournville   vHighway
Kings Heath   vNuneaton
Bedworth   vAtherstone
O. Edward's   vKenilworth
Bablake OB   vBronze
Sh. Marlb.   vMos. Ashfield

Sat 18th Aug - 1pm

Sh. Marlb.   vAtherstone
Nuneaton   vBedworth
Highway   vKings Heath
Bronze   vBournville
Kenilworth   vBablake OB
Mos. Ashfield vO. Edward's

Sat 25th Aug - 1pm

Bournville   vKenilworth
Kings Heath   vBronze
Bedworth   vHighway
Atherstone   vNuneaton
Bablake OB   vMos. Ashfield
Sh. Marlb.   vO. Edward's

Mon 27th Aug - 1pm

Nuneaton   vSh. Marlb.
Highway   vAtherstone
Bronze   vBedworth
Kenilworth   vKings Heath
Mos. Ashfield vBournville
O. Edward's   vBablake OB

Sat 1st Sept - 1pm

Bournville   vO. Edward's
Kings Heath   vMos. Ashfield
Bedworth   vKenilworth
Atherstone   vBronze
Nuneaton   vHighway
Sh. Marlb.   vBablake OB

Sat 8th Sept - 12.30pm
Bronze   vNuneaton
Kenilworth   vAtherstone
Mos. Ashfield   vBedworth
O. Edward's   vKings Heath
Bablake OB   vBournville
Sh. Marlb.   vHighway

Sat 15th Sept - 12pm
Bournville   vSh. Marlb.
Kings Heath   vBablake OB
Bedworth   vO. Edward's
Atherstone   vMos. Ashfield
Nuneaton   vKenilworth
Highway   vBronze

Division 1 - 2nd XI

Sat 5th May - 1.30pm
Streetly   vN. Warwick.
Ansley Sp.   vAmbleside
Mar. Green   vCH O. Ed's
Pickwick P&M   vOffch./Lap.
Southam   vHandsworth
Wishaw   vFillongley

Sat 12th May - 1.30pm
Fillongley   vStreetly
N. Warwick.   vSoutham
Handsworth   vPickwick P&M
Offch./Lap.   vMar. Green
CH O. Ed's   vAnsley Sp.
Ambleside   vWishaw

Sat 19th May - 1.30pm
Pickwick P&M   vN. Warwick.
Southam   vStreetly
Wishaw   vCH O. Ed's
Ansley Sp.   vOffch./Lap.
Mar. Green   vHandsworth
Ambleside   vFillongley

Sat 26th May - 1.30pm
Fillongley   vSoutham
Streetly   vPickwick P&M
N. Warwick.   vMar. Green
Handsworth   vAnsley Sp.
Offch./Lap.   vWishaw
CH O. Ed's   vAmbleside

Mon 28th May - 1.30pm
Ansley Sp.   vN. Warwick.
Mar. Green   vStreetly
Pickwick P&M   vSoutham
Ambleside   vOffch./Lap.
Wishaw   vHandsworth
CH O. Ed's   vFillongley

Sat 2nd June - 1.30pm
Pickwick P&M   vFillongley
Southam   vMar. Green
Streetly   vAnsley Sp.
N. Warwick.   vWishaw
Handsworth   vAmbleside
Offch./Lap.   vCH O. Ed's

Sat 9th June - 1.30pm
Ambleside   vN. Warwick.
Wishaw   vStreetly
Ansley Sp.   vSoutham
Mar. Green   vPickwick P&M
CH O. Ed's   vHandsworth
Offch./Lap.   vFillongley

Sat 16th June - 1.30pm
Fillongley   vMar. Green
Pickwick P&M   vAnsley Sp.
Southam   vWishaw
Streetly   vAmbleside
N. Warwick.   vCH O. Ed's
Handsworth   vOffch./Lap.

Sat 23rd June - 1.30pm
Offch./Lap.   vN. Warwick.
CH O. Ed's   vStreetly
Ambleside   vSoutham
Wishaw   vPickwick P&M
Ansley Sp.   vMar. Green
Handsworth   vFillongley

Sat 30th June - 1.30pm
Mar. Green   vWishaw
Pickwick P&M   vAmbleside
Southam   vCH O. Ed's
Streetly   vOffch./Lap.
N. Warwick.   vHandsworth
Ansley Sp.   vFillongley

Sat 7th July - 1.30pm
Fillongley   vN. Warwick.
Handsworth   vStreetly
Offch./Lap.   vSoutham
CH O. Ed's   vPickwick P&M
Ambleside   vMar. Green
Wishaw   vAnsley Sp.

Sat 14th July - 1.30pm
N. Warwick.   v Streetly
Ambleside   vAnsley Sp.
CH O. Ed's   vMar. Green
Offch./Lap.   vPickwick P&M
Handsworth   vSoutham
Fillongley   vWishaw

Sat 21st July - 1.30pm
Streetly   vFillongley
Southam   vN. Warwick.
Pickwick P&M   vHandsworth
Mar. Green   vOffch./Lap.
Ansley Sp.   vCH O. Ed's
Wishaw   vAmbleside

Sat 28th July - 1.30pm
N. Warwick.   vPickwick P&M
Streetly   vSoutham
CH O. Ed's   vWishaw
Offch./Lap.   vAnsley Sp.
Handsworth   vMar. Green
Fillongley   vAmbleside

Sat 4th Aug - 1.30pm
Southam   vFillongley
Pickwick P&M   vStreetly
Mar. Green   vN. Warwick.
Ansley Sp.   vHandsworth
Wishaw   vOffch./Lap.
Ambleside   vCH O. Ed's

Sat 11th Aug - 1.30pm
N. Warwick.   vAnsley Sp.
Streetly   vMar. Green
Southam   vPickwick P&M
Offch./Lap.   vAmbleside
Handsworth   vWishaw
Fillongley   vCH O. Ed's

Sat 18th Aug - 1pm
Fillongley   vPickwick P&M
Mar. Green   vSoutham
Ansley Sp.   vStreetly
Wishaw   vN. Warwick.
Ambleside   vHandsworth
CH O. Ed's   vOffch./Lap.

Sat 25th Aug - 1pm
N. Warwick.   vAmbleside
Streetly   vWishaw
Southam   vAnsley Sp.
Pickwick P&M   vMar. Green
Handsworth   vCH O. Ed's
Fillongley   vOffch./Lap.

Mon 27th Aug - 1pm
Mar. Green   vFillongley
Ansley Sp.   vPickwick P&M
Wishaw   vSoutham
Ambleside   vStreetly
CH O. Ed's   vN. Warwick.
Offch./Lap.   vHandsworth

Sat 1st Sept - 1pm
N. Warwick.   vOffch./Lap.
Streetly   vCH O. Ed's

The Warwickshire League

Southam   vAmbleside
Pickwick P&M   vWishaw
Mar. Green   vAnsley Sp.
Fillongley   vHandsworth

Sat 8th Sept - 12.30pm
Wishaw   vMar. Green
Ambleside   vPickwick P&M
CH O. Ed's   vSoutham
Offch./Lap.   vStreetly
Handsworth   vN. Warwick.
Fillongley   vAnsley Sp.

Sat 15th Sept - 12pm
N. Warwick.   vFillongley
Streetly   vHandsworth
Southam   vOffch./Lap.
Pickwick P&M   vCH O. Ed's
Mar. Green   vAmbleside
Ansley Sp.   vWishaw

Division 2 - 2nd XI

Sat 5th May - 1.30pm
Ham. & Sol.   vStockton
Lyndworth   vRowland Utd
Rugby   vGriff & Coton
Civil Service vWarwick
Sphinx   vN. Whitacre
F. Oaks Sts   vAttleborough

Sat 12th May - 1.30pm
Attleborough   vHam. & Sol.
Stockton   vSphinx
N. Whitacre   vCivil Service
Warwick   vRugby
Griff & Coton vLyndworth
Rowland Utd   vF. Oaks Sts

Sat 19th May - 1.30pm
Civil Service vStockton
Sphinx   vHam. & Sol.
F. Oaks Sts   vGriff & Coton
Lyndworth   vWarwick
Rugby   vN. Whitacre
Rowland Utd   vAttleborough

Sat 26th May - 1.30pm
Attleborough   vSphinx
Ham. & Sol.   vCivil Service
Stockton   vRugby
N. Whitacre   vLyndworth
Warwick   vF. Oaks Sts
Griff & Coton vRowland Utd

Mon 28th May - 1.30pm
Lyndworth   vStockton
Rugby   vHam. & Sol.
Civil Service vSphinx
Rowland Utd   vWarwick

F. Oaks Sts   vN. Whitacre
Griff & Coton vAttleborough

Sat 2nd June - 1.30pm
Attleborough   vCivil Service
Sphinx   vRugby
Ham. & Sol.   vLyndworth
Stockton   vF. Oaks Sts
N. Whitacre   vRowland Utd
Warwick   vGriff & Coton

Sat 9th June - 1.30pm
Rowland Utd   vStockton
F. Oaks Sts   vHam. & Sol.
Lyndworth   vSphinx
Rugby   vCivil Service
Griff & Coton vN. Whitacre
Warwick   vAttleborough

Sat 16th June - 1.30pm
Rugby   vF. Oaks Sts
Civil Service vRowland Utd
Sphinx   vGriff & Coton
Ham. & Sol.   vWarwick
Stockton   vN. Whitacre
Lyndworth   vAttleborough

Sat 23rd June - 1.30pm
Warwick   vStockton
Griff & Coton vHam. & Sol.
Rowland Utd   vSphinx
F. Oaks Sts   vCivil Service
Lyndworth   vRugby
N. Whitacre   vAttleborough

Sat 30th June - 1.30pm
Attleborough   vRugby
Civil Service vLyndworth
F. Oaks Sts   vSphinx
Ham. & Sol.   vRowland Utd
Stockton   vGriff & Coton
N. Whitacre   vWarwick

Sat 7th July - 1.30pm
Attleborough   vStockton
N. Whitacre   vHam. & Sol.
Warwick   vSphinx
Civil Service vGriff & Coton
Rowland Utd   vRugby
F. Oaks Sts   vLyndworth

Sat 14th July - 1.30pm
Stockton   vHam. & Sol.
Rowland Utd   vLyndworth
Griff & Coton vRugby
Warwick   vCivil Service
N. Whitacre   vSphinx
Attleborough   vF. Oaks Sts

Sat 21st July - 1.30pm
Ham. & Sol.   vAttleborough
Sphinx   vStockton
Civil Service vN. Whitacre
Rugby   vWarwick
Lyndworth   vGriff & Coton
F. Oaks Sts   vRowland Utd

Sat 28th July - 1.30pm
Stockton   vCivil Service
Ham. & Sol.   vSphinx
Griff & Coton vF. Oaks Sts
Warwick   vLyndworth
N. Whitacre   vRugby
Attleborough   vRowland Utd

Sat 4th Aug - 1.30pm
Sphinx   vAttleborough
Civil Service vHam. & Sol.
Rugby   vStockton
Lyndworth   vN. Whitacre
F. Oaks Sts   vWarwick
Rowland Utd   vGriff & Coton

Sat 11th Aug - 1.30pm
Stockton   vLyndworth
Ham. & Sol.   vRugby
Sphinx   vCivil Service
Warwick   vRowland Utd
N. Whitacre   vF. Oaks Sts
Attleborough   vGriff & Coton

Sat 18th Aug - 1pm
Civil Service vAttleborough
Rugby   vSphinx
Lyndworth   vHam. & Sol.
F. Oaks Sts   vStockton
Rowland Utd   vN. Whitacre
Griff & Coton vWarwick

Sat 25th Aug - 1pm
Stockton   vRowland Utd
Ham. & Sol.   vF. Oaks Sts
Sphinx   vLyndworth
Civil Service vRugby
N. Whitacre   vGriff & Coton
Attleborough   vWarwick

Mon 27th Aug - 1pm
F. Oaks Sts   vRugby
Rowland Utd   vCivil Service
Griff & Coton vSphinx
Warwick   vHam. & Sol.
N. Whitacre   vStockton
Attleborough   vLyndworth

Sat 1st Sept - 1pm
Stockton   vWarwick
Ham. & Sol.   vGriff & Coton

Sphinx   vRowland Utd
Civil Service vF. Oaks Sts
Rugby   vLyndworth
Attleborough   vN. Whitacre

Sat 8th Sept - 12.30pm
Rugby   vAttleborough
Lyndworth   vCivil Service
Sphinx   vF. Oaks Sts
Rowland Utd   vHam. & Sol.
Griff & Coton vStockton
Warwick   vN. Whitacre

Sat 15th Sept - 12pm
Stockton   vAttleborough
Ham. & Sol.   vN. Whitacre
Sphinx   vWarwick
Griff & Coton vCivil Service
Rugby   vRowland Utd
Lyndworth   vF. Oaks Sts

Division 3 - 2nd XI

Sat 5th May - 1.30pm
Elford   vThimblemill
Ward End U.   vWalsall Ymf
Weoley Hill   vErdington Ct
Jag. Daimler   vK & Dorridge
Castle Brom.   vFive Ways Oe

Sat 12th May - 1.30pm
Elford   vCastle Brom.
K & Dorridge   vWard End U.
Five Ways Oe   vErdington Ct
Walsall Ymf   vJag. Daimler
Thimblemill   vWeoley Hill

Sat 19th May - 1.30pm
Jag. Daimler   vElford
Erdington Ct   vWard End U.
K & Dorridge   vFive Ways Oe
Castle Brom.   vThimblemill
Weoley Hill   vWalsall Ymf

Sat 26th May - 1.30pm
Elford   vErdington Ct
Ward End U.   vFive Ways Oe
Walsall Ymf   vK & Dorridge
Thimblemill   vJag. Daimler
Weoley Hill   vCastle Brom.

Sat 2nd June - 1.30pm
Five Ways Oe   vElford
Castle Brom.   vWard End U.
Erdington Ct   vWalsall Ymf
Jag. Daimler   vWeoley Hill
K & Dorridge   vThimblemill

Sat 9th June - 1.30pm
Weoley Hill   vElford
Ward End U.   vThimblemill
Erdington Ct   vK & Dorridge
Castle Brom.   vJag. Daimler
Walsall Ymf   vFive Ways Oe

Sat 16th June - 1.30pm
Elford   vWalsall Ymf
Jag. Daimler   vWard End U.
Thimblemill   vErdington Ct
Five Ways Oe   vWeoley Hill
K & Dorridge   vCastle Brom.

Sat 23rd June - 1.30pm
Ward End U.   vElford
Walsall Ymf   vThimblemill
Erdington Ct   vCastle Brom.
Five Ways Oe   vJag. Daimler
K & Dorridge   vWeoley Hill

Sat 30th June - 1.30pm
Elford   vK & Dorridge
Weoley Hill   vWard End U.
Jag. Daimler   vErdington Ct
Castle Brom.   vWalsall Ymf
Thimblemill   vFive Ways Oe

Sat 7th July - 1.30pm
Thimblemill   vElford
Walsall Ymf   vWard End U.
Erdington Ct   vWeoley Hill
K & Dorridge   vJag. Daimler
Five Ways Oe   vCastle Brom.

Sat 14th July - 1.30pm
Castle Brom.   vElford
Ward End U.   vK & Dorridge
Erdington Ct   vFive Ways Oe
Jag. Daimler   vWalsall Ymf
Weoley Hill   vThimblemill

Sat 21st July - 1.30pm
Elford   vJag. Daimler
Ward End U.   vErdington Ct
Five Ways Oe   vK & Dorridge
Thimblemill   vCastle Brom.
Walsall Ymf   vWeoley Hill

Sat 28th July - 1.30pm
Erdington Ct   vElford
Five Ways Oe   vWard End U.
K & Dorridge   vWalsall Ymf
Jag. Daimler   vThimblemill
Castle Brom.   vWeoley Hill

Sat 4th Aug - 1.30pm
Elford   vFive Ways Oe
Ward End U.   vCastle Brom.
Walsall Ymf   vErdington Ct
Weoley Hill   vJag. Daimler
Thimblemill   vK & Dorridge

Sat 11th Aug - 1.30pm
Elford   vWeoley Hill
Thimblemill   vWard End U.
K & Dorridge   vErdington Ct
Jag. Daimler   vCastle Brom.
Five Ways Oe   vWalsall Ymf

Sat 18th Aug - 1.30pm
Walsall Ymf   vElford
Ward End U.   vJag. Daimler
Erdington Ct   vThimblemill
Weoley Hill   vFive Ways Oe
Castle Brom.   vK & Dorridge

Sat 25th Aug - 1.30pm
Elford   vWard End U.
Thimblemill   vWalsall Ymf
Castle Brom.   vErdington Ct
Jag. Daimler   vFive Ways Oe
Weoley Hill   vK & Dorridge

Sat 1st Sept - 1pm
K & Dorridge   vElford
Ward End U.   vWeoley Hill
Erdington Ct   vJag. Daimler
Walsall Ymf   vCastle Brom.
Five Ways Oe   vThimblemill

Division 4 - 2nd XI

Sat 5th May - 1.30pm
Hunningham   vPakshaheen
Haunchwood   vBarby
Bulkington   vCop. WI Wds
Knowle Vill.   vAston OE
Cov. Colliery vStockingford

Sat 12th May - 1.30pm
Hunningham   vStockingford
Aston OE   vHaunchwood
Cov. Colliery vCop. WI Wds
Barby   vKnowle Vill.
Pakshaheen   vBulkington

Sat 19th May - 1.30pm
Knowle VIll.   vHunningham
Cop. WI Wds   vHaunchwood
Aston OE   vCov. Colliery
Stockingford   vPakshaheen
Bulkington   vBarby

The Warwickshire League

Sat 26th May - 1.30pm

Hunningham	vCop. WI Wds
Haunchwood	vCov. Colliery
Barby	vAston OE
Pakshaheen	vKnowle Vill.
Bulkington	vStockingford

Sat 2nd June - 1.30pm

Cov. Colliery	vHunningham
Stockingford	vHaunchwood
Cop. WI Wds	vBarby
Knowle Vill.	vBulkington
Aston OE	vPakshaheen

Sat 9th June - 1.30pm

Bulkington	vHunningham
Haunchwood	vPakshaheen
Cop. WI Wds	vAston OE
Stockingford	vKnowle Vill.
Barby	vCov. Colliery

Sat 16th June - 1.30pm

Hunningham	vBarby
Knowle Vill.	vHaunchwood
Pakshaheen	vCop. WI Wds
Cov. Colliery	vBulkington
Aston OE	vStockingford

Sat 23rd June - 1.30pm

Haunchwood	vHunningham
Barby	vPakshaheen
Cop. WI Wds	vStockingford
Cov. Colliery	vKnowle Vill.
Aston OE	vBulkington

Sat 30th June - 1.30pm

Hunningham	vAston OE
Bulkington	vHaunchwood
Knowle Vill.	vCop. WI Wds
Stockingford	vBarby
Pakshaheen	vCov. Colliery

Sat 7th July - 1.30pm

Pakshaheen	vHunningham
Barby	vHaunchwood
Cop. WI Wds	vBulkington
Aston OE	vKnowle Vill.
Stockingford	vCov. Colliery

Sat 14th July - 1.30pm

Stockingford	vHunningham
Haunchwood	vAston OE
Cop. WI Wds	vCov. Colliery
Knowle Vill.	vBarby
Bulkington	vPakshaheen

Sat 21st July - 1.30pm

Hunningham	vKnowle Vill.
Haunchwood	vCop. WI Wds
Cov. Colliery	vAston OE
Pakshaheen	vStockingford
Barby	vBulkington

Sat 28th July - 1.30pm

Cop. WI Wds	vHunningham
Cov. Colliery	vHaunchwood
Aston OE	vBarby
Knowle Vill.	vPakshaheen
Stockingford	vBulkington

Sat 4th Aug - 1.30pm

Hunningham	vCov. Colliery
Haunchwood	vStockingford
Barby	vCop. WI Wds
Bulkington	vKnowle Vill.
Pakshaheen	vAston OE

Sat 11th Aug - 1.30pm

Hunningham	vBulkington
Pakshaheen	vHaunchwood
Aston OE	vCop. WI Wds
Knowle Vill.	vStockingford
Cov. Colliery	vBarby

Sat 18th Aug - 1pm

Barby	vHunningham
Haunchwood	vKnowle Vill.
Cop. WI Wds	vPakshaheen
Bulkington	vCov. Colliery
Stockingford	vAston OE

Sat 25th Aug - 1pm

Hunningham	vHaunchwood
Pakshaheen	vBarby
Stockingford	vCop. WI Wds
Knowle Vill.	vCov. Colliery
Bulkington	vAston OE

Sat 1st Sept - 1pm

Aston OE	vHunningham
Haunchwood	vBulkington
Cop. WI Wds	vKnowle Vill.
Barby	vStockingford
Cov. Colliery	vPakshaheen

Division 5 - 2nd XI

Sat 5th May - 1.30pm

Collycroft	vWilnecote
Corley	vNewdigate
Wolvey	vDunlop
Oakfield	vNewbold
Willclare	vSol. Municip.

Sat 12th May - 1.30pm

Collycroft	vSol. Municip.
Newbold	vCorley
Willclare	vDunlop
Newdigate	vOakfield
Wilnecote	vWolvey

Sat 19th May - 1.30pm

Oakfield	vCollycroft
Dunlop	vCorley
Newbold	vWillclare
Sol. Municip.	vWilnecote
Wolvey	vNewdigate

Sat 26th May - 1.30pm

Collycroft	vDunlop
Corley	vWillclare
Newdigate	vNewbold
Wilnecote	vOakfield
Wolvey	vSol. Municip.

Sat 2nd June - 1.30pm

Willclare	vCollycroft
Sol. Municip.	vCorley
Dunlop	vNewdigate
Oakfield	vWolvey
Newbold	vWilnecote

Sat 9th June - 1.30pm

Wolvey	vCollycroft
Corley	vWilnecote
Dunlop	vNewbold
Sol. Municip.	vOakfield
Newdigate	vWillclare

Sat 16th June - 1.30pm

Collycroft	vNewdigate
Oakfield	vCorley
Wilnecote	vDunlop
Willclare	vWolvey
Newbold	vSol. Municip.

Sat 23rd June - 1.30pm

Corley	vCollycroft
Newdigate	vWilnecote
Dunlop	vSol. Municip.
Willclare	vOakfield
Newbold	vWolvey

Sat 30th June - 1.30pm

Collycroft	vNewbold
Wolvey	vCorley
Oakfield	vDunlop
Sol. Municip.	vNewdigate
Wilnecote	vWillclare

Sat 7th July - 1.30pm
Wilnecote	vCollycroft
Newdigate	vCorley
Dunlop	vWolvey
Newbold	vOakfield
Sol. Municip.	vWillclare

Sat 14th July - 1.30pm
Sol. Municip.	vCollycroft
Corley	vNewbold
Dunlop	vWillclare
Oakfield	vNewdigate
Wolvey	vWilnecote

Sat 21st July - 1.30pm
Collycroft	vOakfield
Corley	vDunlop
Willclare	vNewbold
Wilnecote	vSol. Municip.
Newdigate	vWolvey

Sat 28th July - 1.30pm
Dunlop	vCollycroft
Willclare	vCorley
Newbold	vNewdigate
Oakfield	vWilnecote
Sol. Municip.	vWolvey

Sat 4th Aug - 1.30pm
Collycroft	vWillclare
Corley	vSol. Municip.
Newdigate	vDunlop
Wolvey	vOakfield
Wilnecote	vNewbold

Sat 11th Aug - 1.30pm
Collycroft	vWolvey
Wilnecote	vCorley
Newbold	vDunlop
Oakfield	vSol. Municip.
Willclare	vNewdigate

Sat 18th Aug - 1.30pm
Newdigate	vCollycroft
Corley	vOakfield
Dunlop	vWilnecote
Wolvey	vWillclare
Sol. Municip.	vNewbold

Sat 25th Aug - 1.30pm
Collycroft	vCorley
Wilnecote	vNewdigate
Sol. Municip.	vDunlop
Oakfield	vWillclare
Wolvey	vNewbold

Sat 1st Sept - 1.30pm
Newbold	vCollycroft
Corley	vWolvey

Dunlop	vOakfield
Newdigate	vSol. Municip.
Willclare	vWilnecote

Division 6 - 2nd XI

Sat 5th May - 1.30pm
Four Oaks	vStandard
Peugeot	vNuneaton IV
Bedworth IV	vMass. Ferg.
Bridge Trust	vBab. OB IV
P. Of Wales	vCov. U. &RM

Sat 12th May - 1.30pm
Four Oaks	vCov. U. &RM
Bab. OB IV	vPeugeot
P. Of Wales	vMass. Ferg.
Nuneaton IV	vBridge Trust
Standard	vBedworth IV

Sat 19th May - 1.30pm
Bridge Trust	vFour Oaks
Mass. Ferg.	vPeugeot
Bab. OB IV	vP. Of Wales
Cov. U. &RM	vStandard
Bedworth IV	vNuneaton IV

Sat 26th May - 1.30pm
Four Oaks	vMass. Ferg.
Peugeot	vP. Of Wales
Nuneaton IV	vBab. OB IV
Standard	vBridge Trust
Bedworth IV	vCov. U. &RM

Sat 2nd June - 1.30pm
P. Of Wales	vFour Oaks
Cov. U. &RM	vPeugeot
Mass. Ferg.	vNuneaton IV
Bridge Trust	vBedworth IV
Bab. OB IV	vStandard

Sat 9th June - 1.30pm
Bedworth IV	vFour Oaks
Peugeot	vStandard
Mass. Ferg.	vBab. OB IV
Cov. U. &RM	vBridge Trust
Nuneaton IV	vP. Of Wales

Sat 16th June - 1.30pm
Four Oaks	vNuneaton IV
Bridge Trust	vPeugeot
Standard	vMass. Ferg.
P. Of Wales	vBedworth IV
Bab. OB IV	vCov. U. &RM

Sat 23rd June - 1.30pm
Peugeot	vFour Oaks
Nuneaton IV	vStandard

Mass. Ferg.	vCov. U. &RM
P. Of Wales	vBridge Trust
Bab. OB IV	vBedworth IV

Sat 30th June - 1.30pm
Four Oaks	vBab. OB IV
Bedworth IV	vPeugeot
Bridge Trust	vMass. Ferg.
Cov. U. &RM	vNuneaton IV
Standard	vP. Of Wales

Sat 7th July - 1.30pm
Standard	vFour Oaks
Nuneaton IV	vPeugeot
Mass. Ferg.	vBedworth IV
Bab. OB IV	vBridge Trust
Cov. U. &RM	vP. Of Wales

Sat 14th July - 1.30pm
Cov. U. &RM	vFour Oaks
Peugeot	vBab. OB IV
Mass. Ferg.	vP. Of Wales
Bridge Trust	vNuneaton IV
Bedworth IV	vStandard

Sat 21st July - 1.30pm
Four Oaks	vBridge Trust
Peugeot	vMass. Ferg.
P. Of Wales	vBab. OB IV
Standard	vCov. U. &RM
Nuneaton IV	vBedworth IV

Sat 28th July - 1.30pm
Mass. Ferg.	vFour Oaks
P. Of Wales	vPeugeot
Bab. OB IV	vNuneaton IV
Bridge Trust	vStandard
Cov. U. &RM	vBedworth IV

Sat 4th Aug - 1.30pm
Four Oaks	vP. Of Wales
Peugeot	vCov. U. &RM
Nuneaton IV	vMass. Ferg.
Bedworth IV	vBridge Trust
Standard	vBab. OB IV

Sat 11th Aug - 1.30pm
Four Oaks	vBedworth IV
Standard	vPeugeot
Bab. OB IV	vMass. Ferg.
Bridge Trust	vCov. U. &RM
P. Of Wales	vNuneaton IV

Sat 18th Aug - 1.30pm
Nuneaton IV	vFour Oaks
Peugeot	vBridge Trust
Mass. Ferg.	vStandard
Bedworth IV	vP. Of Wales
Cov. U. &RM	vBab. OB IV

The Warwickshire League

Sat 25th Aug - 1.30pm
Four Oaks   vPeugeot
Standard   vNuneaton IV
Cov. U. &RM   vMass. Ferg.
Bridge Trust   vP. Of Wales
Bedworth IV   vBab. OB IV

Sat 1st Sept - 1.30pm
Bab. OB IV   vFour Oaks
Peugeot   vBedworth IV
Mass. Ferg.   vBridge Trust
Nuneaton IV   vCov. U. &RM
P. Of Wales   vStandard

Single Teams 1

Sat 5th May - 1.30pm
Wythall I   vHands. Rec.
Small H. I   vCrescent I
Leek W. I   vAmbleside III
Hands. III   vWarwick III
B. Paddox I   vAnsley Sp. III

Sat 12th May - 1.30pm
Ansley Sp. IIIvHands. Rec.
Warwick III   vSmall Heath I
B. Paddox I   vLeek W. I
Hands. III   vCrescent I
Ambleside III vWythall I

Sat 19th May - 1.30pm
Hands. Rec.   vHands. III
Small Heath IvLeek W. I
Warwick III   vB. Paddox I
Ansley Sp. IIIvWythall I
Crescent I   vAmbleside III

Sat 26th May - 1.30pm
Leek W. I   vHands. Rec.
B. Paddox I   vSmall Heath I
Crescent I   vWarwick III
Hands. III   vWythall I
Ansley Sp. IIIvAmbleside III

Sat 2nd June - 1.30pm
Hands. Rec.   vB. Paddox I
Small Heath IvAnsley Sp. III
Crescent I   vLeek W. I
Ambleside III vHands. III
Warwick III   vWythall I

Sat 9th June - 1.30pm
Hands. Rec.   vAmbleside III
Wythall I   vSmall Heath I
Warwick III   vLeek W. I
Hands. III   vAnsley Sp. III
B. Paddox I   vCrescent I

Sat 16th June - 1.30pm
Crescent I   vHands. Rec.
Small Heath IvHands. III
Wythall I   vLeek W. I
Ambleside III vB. Paddox I
Warwick III   vAnsley Sp. III

Sat 23rd June - 1.30pm
Hands. Rec.   vSmall Heath I
Wythall I   vCrescent I
Leek W. I   vAnsley Sp. III
Hands. III   vB. Paddox I
Ambleside III vWarwick III

Sat 30th June - 1.30pm
Hands. Rec.   vWarwick III
Small Heath IvAmbleside III
Leek W. I   vHands. III
Ansley Sp. IIIvCrescent I
B. Paddox I   vWythall I

Sat 7th July - 1.30pm
Hands. Rec.   vWythall I
Crescent I   vSmall Heath I
Ambleside III vLeek W. I
Warwick III   vHands. III
Ansley Sp. IIIvB. Paddox I

Sat 14th July - 1.30pm
Hands. Rec.   vAnsley Sp. III
Small Heath IvWarwick III
Leek W. I   vB. Paddox I
Crescent I   vHands. III
Wythall I   vAmbleside III

Sat 21st July - 1.30pm
Hands. III   vHands. Rec.
Leek W. I   vSmall Heath I
B. Paddox I   vWarwick III
Wythall I   vAnsley Sp. III
Ambleside III vCrescent I

Sat 28th July - 1.30pm
Hands. Rec.   vLeek W. I
Small Heath IvB. Paddox I
Warwick III   vCrescent I
Wythall I   vHands. III
Ambleside III vAnsley Sp. III

Sat 4th Aug - 1.30pm
B. Paddox I   vHands. Rec.
Ansley Sp. IIIvSmall Heath I
Leek W. I   vCrescent I
Hands. III   vAmbleside III
Wythall I   vWarwick III

Sat 11th Aug - 1.30pm
Ambleside III vHands. Rec.
Small Heath IvWythall I
Leek W. I   vWarwick III
Ansley Sp. IIIvHands. III
Crescent I   vB. Paddox I

Sat 19th Aug - 1pm
Hands. Rec.   vCrescent I
Hands. III   vSmall Heath I
Leek W. I   vWythall I
B. Paddox I   vAmbleside III
Ansley Sp. IIIvWarwick III

Sat 25th Aug - 1pm
Small Heath IvHands. Rec.
Crescent I   vWythall I
Ansley Sp. IIIvLeek W. I
B. Paddox I   vHands. III
Warwick III   vAmbleside III

Sat 1st Sept - 1pm
Warwick III   vHands. Rec.
Ambleside III vSmall Heath I
Hands. III   vLeek W. I
Crescent I   vAnsley Sp. III
Wythall I   vB. Paddox I

Single Teams 2

Sat 5th May - 1.30pm
Cov. Co. AJK vStock'ford III
Atherstone IIIvBronze III
Coleshill IV   vWillow I
Berkswell III vSelly Park I
River. Roy. I   vSphinx III

Sat 12th May - 1.30pm
Stock'ford III vRiver. Roy. I
Bronze III   vSelly Park I
Coleshill IV   vSphinx III
Atherstone IIIvBerkswell III
Willow I   vCov. Co. AJK

Sat 19th May - 1.30pm
Berkswell III vStock'ford III
Bronze III   vColeshill IV
Sphinx III   vSelly Park I
Cov. Coll. AJKvRiver. Roy. I
Atherstone IIIvWillow I

Sat 26th May - 1.30pm
Coleshill IV   vStock'ford III
Sphinx III   vBronze III
Selly Park I   vAtherstone III
Cov. Coll. AJKvBerkswell III
River. Roy. I   vWillow I

Sat 2nd June - 1.30pm
Sphinx III   vStock'ford III
Bronze III   vRiver. Roy. I
Atherstone III vColeshill IV
Cov. Coll. AJK vSelly Park I

Sat 9th June - 1.30pm
Willow I   vStock'ford III
Cov. Coll. AJK vBronze III
Selly Park I   vColeshill IV
River. Roy. I   vBerkswell III
Sphinx III   vAtherstone III

Sat 16th June - 1.30pm
Stock'ford III vAtherstone III
Berkswell III vBronze III
Coleshill IVvCov. Co. AJK
Willow I   vSphinx III
River. Roy. I   vSelly Park I

Sat 23rd June - 1.30pm
Bronze III   vStock'ford III
Cov. Coll. AJK vAtherstone III
River. Roy. I   vColeshill IV
Sphinx III   vBerkswell III
Willow I   vSelly Park I

Sat 30th June - 1.30pm
Stock'ford III vSelly Park I
Bronze III   vWillow I
Berkswell III vColeshill IV
Atherstone III vRiver. Roy. I
Sphinx III vCov. Co. AJK

Sat 7th July - 1.30pm
Stock'ford III vCov. Co. AJK
Bronze III   vAtherstone III
Willow I   vColeshill IV
Selly Park I   vBerkswell III
Sphinx III   vRiver. Roy. I

Sat 14th July - 1.30pm
Stock'ford III vBerkswell III
Coleshill IV   vBronze III
River. Roy. IvCov. Co. AJK
Willow I   vAtherstone III

Sat 21st July - 1.30pm
River. Roy. I   vStock'ford III
Selly Park I   vBronze III
Sphinx III   vColeshill IV
Berkswell III vAtherstone III
Cov. Coll. AJK vWillow I

Sat 28th July - 1.30pm
Atherstone III vStock'ford III
Bronze III   vBerkswell III
Cov. Coll. AJK vColeshill IV

Sphinx III   vWillow I
Selly Park I   vRiver. Roy. I

Sat 4th Aug - 1.30pm
Stock'ford III vSphinx III
River. Roy. I   vBronze III
Coleshill IV   vAtherstone III
Berkswell III vWillow I
Selly Park IvCov. Co. AJK

Sat 11th Aug - 1.30pm
Selly Park I   vStock'ford III
Willow I   vBronze III
Coleshill IV   vBerkswell III
River. Roy. I   vAtherstone III
Cov. Coll. AJK vSphinx III

Sat 18th Aug - 1pm
Stock'ford III vColeshill IV
Bronze III   vSphinx III
Atherstone III vSelly Park I
Berkswell IIIvCov. Co. AJK
Willow I   vRiver. Roy. I

Sat 25th Aug - 1pm
Stock'ford III vBronze III
Atherstone III vCov. Co. AJK
Coleshill IV   vRiver. Roy. I
Berkswell III vSphinx III
Selly Park I   vWillow I

Sat 1st Sept - 1pm
Stock'ford III vWillow I
Bronze III   vCov. Co. AJK
Coleshill IV   vSelly Park I
Berkswell III vRiver. Roy. I
Atherstone III vSphinx III

Sat 8th Sept - 1pm
Selly Park I   vSphinx III
Willow I   vBerkswell III

Single Teams 3 East

Sat 5th May - 1.30pm
Plastic Eng.   vNuneaton V
Ansley Sp. IV vB. Paddox II
Griff & C. III vHighway III

Sat 12th May - 1.30pm
Nuneaton V   vHighway III
L. Khalsa II   vB. Paddox II
Plastic Eng.   vOakfield III

Sat 19th May - 1.30pm
Plastic Eng.   vHighway III
B. Paddox II   vOakfield III
Nuneaton V   vL. Khalsa II

Sat 26th May - 1.30pm
Highway III   vB. Paddox II
L. Khalsa II   vAnsley Sp. IV
Griff & C. III vPlastic Eng.
Nuneaton V   vOakfield III

Sat 2nd June - 1.30pm
Highway III   vLeamington Khalsa 2nds
B. Paddox II   vNuneaton V
Griff & C. III vOakfield III

Sat 9th June - 1.30pm
Nuneaton V   vGriff & C. III
Ansley Sp. IV vPlastic Eng.
L. Khalsa II   vOakfield III

Sat 16th June - 1.30pm
Ansley Sp. IV vGriff & C. III
Plastic Eng.   vB. Paddox II
L. Khalsa II   vHighway III

Sat 23rd June - 1.30pm
Ansley Sp. IV vHighway III
L. Khalsa II   vGriff & C. III
B. Paddox II   vOakfield III

Sat 30th June - 1.30pm
Griff & C. III vB. Paddox II
Plastic Eng.   vL. Khalsa II

Sat 7th July - 1.30pm
Highway III   vGriff & C. III
B. Paddox II   vAnsley Sp. IV
Nuneaton V   vPlastic Eng.

Sat 14th July - 1.30pm
Highway III   vNuneaton V
Plastic Eng.   vOakfield III
B. Paddox II   vL. Khalsa II

Sat 21st July - 1.30pm
Highway III   vPlastic Eng.
Ansley Sp. IV vOakfield III
L. Khalsa II   vNuneaton V

Sat 28th July - 1.30pm
B. Paddox II   vHighway III
Ansley Sp. IV vLeamington Khalsa 2nds
Plastic Eng.   vGriff & C. III
Nuneaton V   vOakfield III

Sat 4th Aug - 1.30pm
Highway III   vOakfield III
Nuneaton V   vAnsley Sp. IV
Griff & C. III vL. Khalsa II

The Warwickshire League

Sat 11th Aug - 1.30pm
Highway III   vOakfield III
Plastic Eng.   vAnsley Sp. IV

Sat 18th Aug - 1pm
L. Khalsa II   vOakfield III
Griff & C. III   vAnsley Sp. IV

Sat 25th Aug - 1pm
Highway III   vAnsley Sp. IV
Nuneaton V   vB. Paddox II
Griff & C. III   vOakfield III

Sat 1st Sept - 1pm
L. Khalsa II   vPlastic Eng.
Ansley Sp. IV vNuneaton V
B. Paddox II   vGriff & C. III

Sat 8th Sept - 1pm
Ansley Sp. IV vOakfield III
B. Paddox II   vPlastic Eng.
Griff & C. III   vNuneaton V

Single Teams 3 West

Sat 5th May - 1.30pm
West Walsall   vSaffron
Five Ways   vN. War. III
SH Comm.   vW. Orton IV

Sat 12th May - 1.30pm
W. Orton IV   vWest Walsall
Saffron   vFive Ways
SH Comm.   vN. War. III

Sat 19th May - 1.30pm
W. Orton IV   vSaffron
SH Comm.   vFive Ways
West Walsall   vN. War. III

Sat 26th May - 1.30pm
Five Ways   vW. Orton IV
Saffron   vN. War. III
West Walsall   vSH Comm.

Sat 2nd June - 1.30pm
SH Comm.   vSaffron
Five Ways   vWest Walsall
W. Orton IV   vN. War. III

Sat 9th June - 1.30pm
Saffron   vWest Walsall
Five Ways   vN. War. III
W. Orton IV   vSH Comm.

Sat 16th June - 1.30pm
West Walsall   vW. Orton IV
Five Ways   vSaffron
SH Comm.   vN. War. III

Sat 23rd June - 1.30pm
Saffron   vW. Orton IV
Five Ways   vSH Comm.
West Walsall   vN. War. III

Sat 30th June - 1.30pm
W. Orton IV   vFive Ways
Saffron   vN. War. III
SH Comm.   vWest Walsall

Sat 7th July - 1.30pm
Saffron   vSH Comm.
West Walsall   vFive Ways
W. Orton IV   vN. War. III

Sat 14th July - 1.30pm
West Walsall   vSaffron
Five Ways   vN. War. III
SH Comm.   vW. Orton IV

Sat 21st July - 1.30pm
West Walsall   vW. Orton IV
Saffron   vFive Ways
SH Comm.   vN. War. III

Sat 28th July - 1.30pm
W. Orton IV   vSaffron
SH Comm.   vFive Ways
West Walsall   vN. War. III

Sat 4th Aug - 1.30pm
Five Ways   vW. Orton IV
Saffron   vN. War. III
West Walsall   vSH Comm.

Sat 11th Aug - 1.30pm
SH Comm.   vSaffron
Five Ways   vWest Walsall
W. Orton IV   vN. War. III

The Face that has watched a thousand matches.....

THE CLOCK which is fixed high in front of the pavilion at the Hampton Road ground of Warwick has already seen quite a full share of cricket during its life span.

For 65 years, the clock had pride of place at The County Ground, Edgbaston and was a gift to the Warwick Cricket Club when it was formed in 1960. It is an electric clock and received attention several times during its stay at The County Ground when the glass broken by big hits.

It is actually quite a fair way from the wicket to the pavilion at Hampton Road, as any outgoing batsman will testify, and the building is square to the wicket also, so it's doubtful whether it will ever be hit again. All the same, I wouldn't like to lay odds!

The clock is an excellent timepiece and residents of the neighbouring houses have been very quick in requesting it should be corrected in the unlikely event of a power failure. Indeed, many people make their way into and out of work, casting a cursory glance at the old stager as they pass by the Hampton Road, such is its size it is easily identifiable from the roadside some 300 yards away.

The clock, which is four feet in diameter, bares a scar which was inflicted by the committee of the County Club in the year of 1939 and at the outbreak of the Second World War it was decided that the clock would be stopped and not restarted until the war was over. The current was swictched off when the time on the clock showed 11.30, the usual starting time for a County Championship match. A close inspection of the timepiece would give the impression that there were four hands.

The club made a special request at the handing over ceremony in May 1960 that the face of the clock should not be cleaned in any way which would erase the scar of those war years, so next time you are near to it, take a good look to see if you can see the 'other hand'.

I wonder how many times the Captain of a side, whether it be in a Test Match, County or Club game has gazed anxiously at the clock due to the circumstances of the match.

If the clock could speak it would indeed have a very facinating tale to tell of the many great and exciting games and also, inevitably, the more lacklustre ones!

However, during every game played on the old ground, it has and always will play its part. Umpires from the League have said that they always played the match by the pavilion timepiece rather than that of the wristwatch they had on, even though the clock was very often fast or slow!

This piece was put together by the late Bill Naylor, a prolific writer in local newspapers and a wonderful servant to Warwick Cricket Club in his many years there. Bill, a long suffering Coventry fan and regular season ticket holder, had many stories to tell over the years and, like many of us, loved the wonderful game.

The Worcestershire County Cricket League

(sponsored by Crusader Sports)

League Officials

CHAIRMAN

Peter Radburn
01562 67053

TREASURER

Tony Cook
33 Anstruther Road
Edgbaston, Birmingham, B15 3NN
0121 455 6608

ADMINISTRATOR

Chris Marsh
10 Florence Avenue
Droitwich WR9 8NJ
Tel: 01905 778771 Fax 01905 776804
e-mail: admin@worcscl.org

UMPIRES SECRETARY: Mike Neal 01527523937
DISCIPLINARY PANEL CHAIRMAN: Bill Tansell 01905 456016
MINUTING SECRETARY: Tony Holland 01902 410640

League expansion gathers pace

by Chris Marsh

IN 2006, WHEN the weather permitted, 66 member clubs played a full programme of League and Knockout matches in the Crusader Worcestershire County League and provided results both to the league website and to some 20 local newspapers and periodicals. Tribute should be paid to the Committee members who have worked hard in carrying out 22 facility audits last season, including most of the one team Division Four clubs for the first time. Moreover, David Thomas continued his Sterling work of arranging and distributing several thousands of pounds worth of junior equipment and courses to clubs via Sportsmatch.

The Annual Dinner, with guest Pat Murphy from Radio Five Live, was a great success and this year's event on October 20th will have Mike Smith from Gloucestershire and England as the guest speaker.

It is pleasing to report that this season only a couple of cricket balls caused enough concern to be returned and that the league concluded negotiations with the present sponsor to supply the same standard cricket balls at reduced prices for the next three years, responding to the member clubs' wishes.

Kington triumphed from Division One, holding off the strong challenges from both Droitwich and Brockhampton and a late surge by Astwood Bank. We wish Kington every success in the Birmingham League next season. In Division Two, Stourbridge were easily returned as Champions with Worcester Nomads runners up.

The newly created Division Three North saw Oldswinford as Champions and Feckenham, returning to Division Two after two seasons, were runners up. In Division Three South, the honours were chased by all three new member clubs and it was Wormelow and Monmouth respectively who finished at the top, with Colwall having to play outside Division Two for at least one more year. The one team section had Champions in Divisions 4 to 8 of Barnards Green 3rds, Knighton on Teme, Halesowen 3rds, Netherton 3rds and Coombs Wood 3rds respectively.

The 1st XI League knockout Cup was won by Astwood Bank, who defeated Coombs Wood at Kidderminster and the following week, Barnards Green fended off Coombs Wood 2nds in their final.

The new "Saturday Cup" competition for one team clubs below Division Four saw Evesham 3rds defeat Vine in an exciting final, with Worcester Nomads 3rds beating Droitwich 3rds to win the Plate.

Our senior league representative side had more success with the weather and beat sides from both Warwickshire and Staffordshire in 2006. The under 19s suffered the fate of last year's seniors as only half a game was played on a wet Lapworth wicket against Warwickshire.

Excessive appealing and sledging on increase

There were not very many disciplinary problems dealt with by the Committee, but the groundswell of Umpires' opinions, through formal and informal reports, are that excessive appealing and childish sledging are on the increase the higher that one goes up the league. It is intended to continue trying to eradicate these in 2007 to ensure that everyone - including officials - enjoy the matches. The average mark for Umpires was up about 0.3 of a mark to 7.7, but there is still an urgent need to train and recruit more.

Once again new teams enquired about joining the league in 2006 and yet another new structure to better suit the needs of our clubs has been unveiled.

2006 League Tables

Division One 1st XI

	Pld	W	L	D	T	Ab	Pts
KINGTON	22	13	2	2	0	5	357
DROITWICH	22	8	3	6	0	5	316
BROCKHAMPTON	22	9	6	3	0	4	284
ASTWOOD BANK	22	7	5	6	0	4	277
EASTNOR	22	6	5	5	0	6	253
PERSHORE	22	6	4	7	0	5	250
BROMYARD	22	7	3	7	0	5	246
CHADDESLEY CORBETT	22	5	7	7	0	3	209
BEWDLEY	22	6	8	3	0	5	207
BARNARDS GREEN	22	2	8	6	0	6	191
ALVECHURCH	22	2	11	5	0	4	189
ROMSLEY	22	3	12	1	0	6	143

Division Two 1st XI

	Pld	W	L	D	T	Ab	Pts
STOURBRIDGE	22	12	1	3	0	6	366
WORCESTER NOMADS	22	9	2	6	0	5	311
LYE	22	8	5	4	0	5	266
COOMBS WOOD	22	7	3	6	0	6	260
BELBROUGHTON	22	6	6	6	0	4	246
MALVERN	22	6	8	3	0	5	240
NETHERTON	22	4	6	7	0	5	227
LUCTONIANS	22	3	8	8	0	3	227
HAGLEY	22	4	4	9	0	5	208
HARBORNE	22	4	5	5	0	8	207
AVONCROFT	22	2	11	4	0	5	165
KIDDERMINSTER VICTORIA	22	3	9	5	0	5	160

Division Three North 1st XI

	Pld	W	L	D	T	Ab	Pts
OLDSWINFORD	22	10	1	4	0	7	316
FECKENHAM	22	9	3	7	0	3	314
CUTNALL GREEN	22	10	4	4	0	4	301
OLD HALESONIANS	22	6	4	6	0	6	288
STOURPORT	22	6	4	6	0	6	280
PEDMORE	22	8	3	4	0	7	278
ENVILLE	22	7	6	5	0	4	269
COOKLEY	22	6	6	5	0	5	247
STOURBRIDGE	22	4	10	2	0	6	195
AMBLECOTE & WOLLASTON	22	2	10	3	0	7	170
ALVELEY	22	3	9	5	0	5	160
CLAVERLEY	22	0	11	5	0	6	104

Division 3 South 1st Division

	Pld	W	L	D	T	Ab	Pts
WORMELOW	22	14	3	2	0	3	371
MONMOUTH	22	12	2	5	0	3	362
COLWALL	22	13	1	2	0	6	359
MARTLEY	22	9	5	4	0	4	300
OLD VIGORNIANS	22	7	5	6	0	4	279
HIMBLETON	22	6	6	6	0	4	251
WORCS DOMINIES	22	5	6	6	0	5	232
RUSHWICK	22	6	8	5	0	3	228
BIRLINGHAM	22	4	8	5	0	5	197
TENBURY	22	3	10	2	0	7	156
OLD ELIZABETHANS	22	1	11	6	0	4	153
HANLEY CASTLE	22	1	16	1	0	4	97

Division One 2nd XI

	Pld	W	L	D	T	Ab	Pts
DROITWICH	22	12	0	4	0	6	315
BROCKHAMPTON	22	8	6	4	0	4	295
ASTWOOD BANK	22	8	4	3	0	7	275
ALVECHURCH	22	8	4	4	0	6	271
KINGTON	22	7	8	2	0	5	266
BEWDLEY	22	7	5	2	0	8	247
PERSHORE	22	7	7	2	0	6	245
BARNARDS GREEN	22	5	9	2	0	6	229
BROMYARD	22	5	7	3	0	7	228
CHADDESLEY CORBETT	22	6	7	5	0	4	224
EASTNOR	22	5	11	2	0	4	200
ROMSLEY	22	2	12	1	0	7	124

Division Two 2nd XI

	Pld	W	L	D	T	Ab	Pts
BELBROUGHTON	22	10	1	7	0	4	331
WORCESTER NOMADS	22	9	5	2	0	6	292
HARBORNE	22	8	5	4	0	5	269
COOMBS WOOD	22	8	2	6	0	6	264
HAGLEY	22	7	6	3	0	6	262
NETHERTON	22	8	1	6	0	7	259
LYE	22	5	7	5	0	5	234
AVONCROFT	22	5	4	9	0	4	218
STOURBRIDGE	22	3	6	8	0	5	218
KIDDERMINSTER VICT	22	2	12	3	0	5	148
LUCTONIANS	22	1	11	3	0	7	135
MALVERN	22	2	8	4	0	8	127

Division Three South 2nd XI

	Pld	W	L	D	T	Ab	Pts
COLWALL	22	13	2	3	0	4	361
MONMOUTH	22	13	1	3	0	5	357
WORCS DOMINIES	22	11	3	4	0	4	341
WORMELOW	22	8	6	3	0	5	268
OLD ELIZABETHANS	22	9	8	2	0	3	258
TENBURY	22	7	6	5	0	4	254
OLD VIGORNIANS	22	6	9	1	0	6	224
MARTLEY	22	7	8	2	0	5	222
HIMBLETON	22	4	8	4	0	6	201
RUSHWICK	22	6	11	1	0	4	196
BIRLINGHAM	22	4	9	5	0	4	151
HANLEY CASTLE	22	0	17	1	0	4	59

Division Three North 2nd XI

	Pld	W	L	D	T	Ab	Pts
PEDMORE	22	11	3	3	0	5	330
STOURPORT	22	7	3	6	0	6	288
COOKLEY	22	9	7	2	0	4	273
OLDSWINFORD	22	6	4	5	0	7	261
AMBLECOTE & WOLLASTON	22	8	7	1	0	6	260
ENVILLE	22	7	5	4	0	6	251
CUTNALL GREEN	22	4	4	7	0	7	230
FECKENHAM	22	6	9	0	0	7	219
OLD HALESONIANS	22	5	7	4	0	6	214
STOURBRIDGE	22	5	7	5	0	5	178
CLAVERLEY	22	4	6	6	0	6	162
ALVELEY	22	2	12	1	0	7	115

Division Four

	Pld	W	L	D	T	Ab	Pts
BARNARDS GREEN	18	9	1	3	0	5	274
KIDDERMINSTER VICT	18	7	4	3	0	4	240
BADSEY	18	4	3	6	0	5	221
CHAIN WIRE	18	6	4	2	0	6	201
HIGHLEY	18	5	3	3	0	7	198
BRINTONS	18	4	6	4	0	4	191
CLEOBURY	18	4	4	4	0	6	183
BELBROUGHTON	18	4	1	7	0	6	173
STONE	18	0	8	5	0	5	97
HEWELL	18	1	10	3	0	4	83

Division Five

	Pld	W	L	D	T	Ab	Pts
KNIGHTON ON TEME	14	11	0	1	0	2	267
VINE	14	8	3	2	0	1	233
STOURBRIDGE SOCIAL	14	4	3	3	0	4	161
BARNARDS GREEN	14	6	5	0	0	3	154
DROITWICH	14	3	4	3	0	4	139
HALLOW	14	2	6	3	0	3	102
OMBERSLEY	14	3	8	0	0	3	101
WORCESTER	14	1	9	2	0	2	70

Division Six

	Pld	W	L	D	T	Ab	Pts
HALESOWEN	14	9	1	2	0	2	241
EVESHAM	14	6	2	3	0	3	204
WEST MALVERN	14	6	2	4	0	2	192
OLD HILL	14	5	6	2	0	1	138
STOURBRIDGE SOCIAL	14	4	6	1	0	3	123
BEWDLEY	14	3	8	1	0	2	117
ENVILLE	14	2	5	5	0	2	108
BELBROUGHTON	14	2	7	2	0	3	92

Division Seven

	Pld	W	L	D	T	Ab	Pts
NETHERTON	14	9	2	1	0	2	244
THE LENCHES	14	8	3	1	0	2	230
COLWALL	14	6	5	1	0	2	182
HARBORNE	14	4	2	4	0	4	165
PERSHORE	14	5	6	1	0	2	151
CHADDESLEY CORBETT	14	2	6	3	0	3	113
WORCESTER NOMADS	14	1	5	4	0	4	109
AVONCROFT	14	1	7	3	0	3	82

Division Eight

	Pld	W	L	D	T	Ab	Pts
COOMBS WOOD	12	6	1	3	0	2	187
BARNT GREEN	12	5	1	3	0	3	171
ALVECHURCH	12	5	1	3	0	3	152
ASTWOOD BANK	12	4	3	2	0	3	136
EVESHAM	12	2	5	1	0	4	92
HALESOWEN	12	1	6	1	0	4	75
AMBLECOTE & WOLLASTON	12	0	6	3	0	3	41

2006 Averages

BATTING (top 6 unless stated - qualification 250 runs):

Division One 1st XI

		Inns	NO	Runs	HS	Ave
A.Bullock	Bromyard	15	6	578	100*	64.22
O.Bailey	Bromyard	16	1	777	188	51.80
B.Stebbings	Kington	11	2	435	107	48.33
P.Bryan	Droitwich	14	5	411	92*	45.67
L.Wilks	Pershore	13	2	499	78*	45.36
M.Edward	Chaddesley Corb.	17	2	650	89	43.33

Division Two 1st XI

		Inns	NO	Runs	HS	Ave
M.Mitchell	Stourbridge	13	9	531	79	132.75
B.Raj	Harborne	6	2	432	140	108.00
M.Lowden	Luctonians	14	2	768	160	64.00
C.Beams	Harborne	6	1	302	104*	60.40
M.Craig *	Coombs Wood	17	3	771	138	55.07
H.Farhat *	Stourbridge	18	3	814	116	54.27

Division Three South 1st XI

		Inns	NO	Runs	HS	Ave
D.Powell	Colwall	14	4	980	138	98.00
P.Bibby	Martley	14	2	911	133	75.92
A.Fiaz	Old Vigornians	16	5	718	120	65.27
H.Nicholls	Old Elizabethans	5	0	302	154	60.40
A.Howorth	Himbleton	11	3	482	146	60.25
D.Teague	Monmouth	18	5	751	99	57.77

Division Three North 1st XI

		Inns	NO	Runs	HS	Ave
D.Cook	Stourport	10	4	519	83	86.50
D.Attwood	Oldswinford	16	6	749	104*	74.90
N.Fletcher	Cutnall Green	19	3	1121	180*	70.06
M.Branch	Enville	20	6	810	130*	57.86
M.Jarrett	Pedmore	7	1	316	124	52.67
N.Barrett	Pedmore	8	2	310	87	51.67

Division One 2nd XI

		Inns	NO	Runs	HS	Ave
P.Boycott	Astwood Bank	4	2	287	119*	143.50
S.Churchley	Astwood Bank	4	0	258	91	64.50
S.Smith	Alvechurch & Hop.	8	3	308	73	61.60

O.Thomas	Bromyard	7	1	359	92	59.83
A.Fletcher	Droitwich	12	5	379	86*	54.14
R.Bond	Chaddesley Corb.	16	4	646	99*	53.83

Division Two 2nd XI

		Inns	NO	Runs	HS	Ave
G.Ross	Belbroughton	6	3	446	125	148.67
A.Biddle	Stourbridge	4	1	251	80	83.67
M.Patel	Netherton	7	1	396	100	66.00
A.Leach	Worcester Nom.	13	4	492	78*	54.67
S.Jessop	Belbroughton	7	1	327	121*	54.50
T.Pardoe	Belbroughton	12	3	450	82	50.00

Division Three South 2nd XI

		Inns	NO	Runs	HS	Ave
D.Taylor	Colwall	13	7	742	116*	123.67
I.Morgan	Monmouth	14	4	814	113*	81.40
M.Oliver	Worcester Dom.	10	2	572	150*	71.50
J.Prime	Wormelow	9	2	468	83	66.86
P.Mackie	Old Vigornians	11	3	450	137*	56.25
A.Jones	Monmouth	8	3	275	82	55.00

Division Three North 2nd XI

		Inns	NO	Runs	HS	Ave
B.Colley	Stourport	6	3	410	126*	136.67
R.Palmer	Enville	8	4	317	79*	79.25
B.Whitticase	Oldswinford	12	1	585	94	53.18
C.Judd	Stourport	16	3	564	71	43.38
W.Etheridge	Claverley	13	4	384	80*	42.67
J.Holloway	Oldswinford	13	2	452	120	41.09

Division Four

		Inns	NO	Runs	HS	Ave
M.Burrows	Belbroughton	5	1	294	n/a	73.50
N.Griffiths	Cleobury Mortimer	11	2	643	188*	71.44
J.Doughty	Barnards Green	13	4	604	119	67.11
A.Cowley	Badsey	8	3	331	78*	66.20
A.Maiden	Brintons	13	2	671	171	61.00
N.Humphries	Highley	9	1	457	103*	57.13

Division Five

		Inns	NO	Runs	HS	Ave
R.Perkins	Vine	15	4	910	199*	82.73
R.Passey	Vine	14	4	554	83	55.40
M.Mangan	Stourbridge Social	11	4	369	n/a	52.71
D.Finch	Vine	16	3	538	75	41.38

R.Lewis	Barnards Green	12	2	405	88*	40.50
I.Hatton	Stourbridge Social	11	0	433	n/a	39.36

Division Six

		Inns	NO	Runs	HS	Ave
S.Baker	Halesowen	5	2	298	109*	99.33
S.Wright	West Malvern	11	4	607	111*	86.71
C.F.Hodges	Enville	9	4	338	79	67.60
M.Groves	West Malvern	8	0	429	115	53.63
G.Southall	Stourbridge Social	6	0	257	n/a	42.83
C.Cartwright	Stourbridge Social	9	1	296	n/a	37.00

Division Seven

		Inns	NO	Runs	HS	Ave
T.Riley	Colwall	7	4	383	127	127.67
D.Selvey	The Lenches	12	0	758	180	63.17
J.Taylor	Pershore	8	1	388	102	55.43
T.Murray	Avoncroft	9	2	307	59*	43.86
P.Taylor	Pershore	8	1	307	86*	43.86
S.Tedstone	Avoncroft	10	2	322	71*	40.25

Division Eight (only two qualified)

		Inns	NO	Runs	HS	Ave
L.Nolan	Barnt Green	8	2	320	75	53.33
P.Coldicott	Coombs Wood	8	2	318	108	53.00

BOWLING (top 6 unless stated - qaulification 15 wickets):

Division One 1st XI

		Ovs	Ms	Runs	Ws	Ave
O.Price	Kington	184.4	34	566	44	12.86
Atiq	Eastnor	52.3	9	249	17	14.65
A.Rouf	Brockhampton	242.5	39	895	59	15.17
D.Gamage	Kington	180.1	39	546	34	16.06
J.Sandford	Eastnor	67.4	12	242	15	16.13
M.Rogers	Droitwich	195.1	25	708	43	16.47

Division Two 1st XI

		Ovs	Ms	Runs	Ws	Ave
H.Farhat	Stourbridge	254.1	49	689	53	13.00
D.Hall	Lye	79.1	16	252	16	15.75
M.Mitchell	Stourbridge	63.2	11	250	15	16.67
H.Raza	Lye	74.5	10	317	19	16.68
G.Taylor	Worcester Nom.	190	33	595	34	17.50
R.Hawk	Belbroughton	185.1	38	639	33	19.36

The Worcestershire County League

Division Three South 1st XI

		Ovs	Ms	Runs	Ws	Ave
C.Griffiths	Colwall	186	61	458	39	11.74
A.Riaz	Old Vigornians	116.4	15	397	32	12.41
P.Guy	Himbleton	41.5	2	193	15	12.87
I.Turner	Rushwick	180.3	42	533	39	13.67
N.Trigg	Worcester Dom.	140.4	36	469	34	13.79
J.Basford	Martley	156.2	30	528	35	15.09

Division Three North 1st XI

		Ovs	Ms	Runs	Ws	Ave
S.Soucup	Oldswinford	188	40	570	46	12.39
P.Monk	Feckenham	208.5	52	647	52	12.44
D.Bloomer	Feckenham	101	36	317	20	15.85
T.Blunt	Oldswinford	101.1	31	298	17	17.53
R.Musk	Pedmore	140.2	33	434	24	18.08
R.Ali	Old Halesonians	n/a	n/a	551	29	19.00

Division One 2nd XI

		Ovs	Ms	Runs	Ws	Ave
T.Mole	Chaddesley Corb.	89.2	6	326	23	14.17
M.Woodward	Droitwich	247.1	71	719	49	14.67
R.Williams	Brockhampton	200.5	47	642	39	16.46
I.Macklin	Brockhampton	73.5	19	284	17	16.71
Holly Pen'den	Pershore	59.2	10	268	16	16.75
D.Jones	Bewdley	97	15	402	23	17.48

Division Two 2nd XI

		Ovs	Ms	Runs	Ws	Ave
B.Adams	Harborne	71.6	13	198	18	11.00
S.Ahmed	Harborne	92.3	31	233	21	11.10
A.Burkes	Kidderminster V.	134.2	31	283	24	11.79
L.Pennington	Belbroughton	118.2	12	544	40	13.60
Z.Tariq	Netherton	83	10	336	21	16.00
N.Lloyd	Worcester Nom.	133.2	18	513	32	16.03

Division Three South 2nd XI

		Ovs	Ms	Runs	Ws	Ave
J.Wyatt	Rushwick	52	9	157	17	9.24
G.Humphries	Worcester Dom.	164.3	31	552	48	11.50
D.Kendrick	Old Vigornians	50.3	2	195	16	12.19
Matt King	Colwall	163	38	503	40	12.58
R.Bennett	Colwall	110	18	329	25	13.16
I.Leonard	Monmouth	300.3	73	821	58	14.16

Division Three North 2nd XI

		Ovs	Ms	Runs	Ws	Ave
S.Such	Enville	135	31	338	33	10.24
J.King	Enville	81	12	303	26	11.65
L.Small	Enville	63	13	193	16	12.06
M.Pearson	Amblecote & W.	98.5	10	281	21	13.38
M.Hand	Oldswinford	69.3	13	244	18	13.56
B.Davies	Cookley	67	6	238	17	14.00

Division Four

		Ovs	Ms	Runs	Ws	Ave
A.Cowley	Badsey	61	10	206	17	12.12
R.A.Brown	Barnards Green	75	12	294	19	15.47
A.Pountney	Belbroughton	66	9	277	17	16.29
J.Rine	Kidderminster V.	76	12	283	16	17.69
G.Bryan	Brintons	124.2	24	444	25	17.76
L.Stuart	Chainwire	64.4	1	314	16	19.63

Division Five

		Ovs	Ms	Runs	Ws	Ave
M.James	Knighton on T.	76.2	17	214	30	7.13
I.Scullion	Barnards Green	67	14	185	19	9.74
M.Evans	Knighton on T.	75.2	15	233	18	12.94
M.Jones	Vine	152.3	38	428	33	12.97
D.Pullen	Knighton on T.	89	22	255	19	13.42
P.Perkins	Vine	82.1	6	387	26	14.88

Division Six (only five qualified)

		Ovs	Ms	Runs	Ws	Ave
M.Webb	Stourbridge Social	53	9	168	15	11.20
L.Fisher	Evesham	40	5	178	15	11.87
D.Cowdery	Bewdley	66.4	9	235	15	15.67
M.Groves	West Malvern	75	8	265	15	17.67
A.Stannard	Bewdley	90	11	371	15	24.73

Division Seven (only four qualified)

		Ovs	Ms	Runs	Ws	Ave
E.Cottrill	The Lenches	135.1	28	464	32	14.50
A.Madzarevic	Worcester Nomads	112	16	394	23	17.13
A.Pittam	Avoncroft	75	8	327	19	17.21
M.Gould	Avoncroft	118	25	407	20	20.35

Division Eight (only four qualified)

		Ovs	Ms	Runs	Ws	Ave
R.Shilvock	Coombs Wood	94	26	316	23	13.74
S.Crayton	Barnt Green	55.4	7	244	17	14.35
J.Niblett	Evesham	53	11	248	15	16.53
T.Cross	Coombs Wood	95	23	309	16	19.31

£10,000 Lottery Grant

by Peter Radburn, Chairman

THE LEAGUE will begin its ninth season as a feeder league to the Birmingham and District Premier Cricket League and continues to grow. Once again, generous support comes from Crusader (Sports & Leisure Ltd.), who are in their fifth year as the League's main sponsors. For 2007 a significant grant of £10,000 has been awarded to the League by the National Lottery community funding scheme "Awards for All". With the additional help of a small residue provided by the government Sportsmatch scheme, the League has been able to provide substantial subsidies for players and officials to attend First Aid, Child Protection and Coaching courses.

Once again, standards have remained high and that the quality of cricket continues to improve and another season of competitive cricket played in a positive spirit is anticipated.

Sadly, two teams will be joining the Worcestershire League from the Premier League structure – Redditch and Worcester. They replace Division 1 champions Kington, who the League wishes luck in the Birmingham & District Premier League for 2007. The 1st Division will be completed with the addition of newly promoted Stourbridge and Worcester Nomads. Two new clubs are welcomed – Canon Frome and Ross-on-Wye. These additions make the League the largest ever and an extra division has been added to the two teams section to accommodate all clubs. We can be sure that, wherever they play, teams will experience some challenging cricket in 2007.

Clubs and other visitors can keep up with the action throughout the season by visiting the website: www.worcscl.org. We wish all Clubs and Umpires an enjoyable 2007 season.

2007 Member clubs

ALVECHURCH & HOPWOOD
Rear of 6, Birmingham Rd.
Alvechurch B48 7TA
Tel: 0121 445 1023

ALVELEY
Recreation Ground,
Alveley WV15 6JT
Tel: 07894 461299

AMBLECOTE & WOLLASTON
Kinver Community Centre,
Legion Drive, Off HIgh St.,
Kinver DY7 6ER
Tel: 01384 872932

ASTWOOD BANK
Samborne Lane,
Astwood Bank,
Redditch B96 6EP
Tel: 07776 404282

AVONCROFT
Hanbury Road,
Stoke Heath,
Bromsgrove
Tel: 07963 532170

BADSEY
Brewers Lane, Badsey,
EveshamWR11 4EU
Tel: 01386 830867

BARNARDS GREEN
North End Lane,
Malvern WR14 2ET
Tel: 01684 575962

BARNT GREEN
Cherry Hill Road,
Barnt Green B45 8LN
Tel: 0121 445 1684

BELBROUGHTON
Hackman's Gate Lane,
Belbroughton DY9 0DL
Tel: 01562 73106

BEWDLEY
Lower Park,
Bewdley DY12 2DP
Tel: 07842 602233

BIRLINGHAM
Church Lane, Birlingham,
Nr. Pershore WR10 3AA
Tel: 07834 422281 or
07766 543025

BRINTONS
Chainwire Sports Ground
Zortech Rd
Kidderminster DY11 7EW
Tel: 01562 69392

BROCKHAMPTON
The Parks,
Brockhampton HR1 4TQ
Tel: 07752 487974

BROMYARD
Flaggoners Green,
Bromyard,
Herefordshire. HR7 4QR
Tel: 01885 488152

CANON FROME
Walsopthorne Farm,
Ashperton,
Ledbury HR8 2SB
Tel: 07979 556202

CHADDESLEY CORBETT
Longmore,
Chaddesley Corbett
DY10 4RE
Tel: 01562 777691

CHAINWIRE
Oldington Leisure Centre,
Zortech Ave.
Kidderminster DY11 7EW
Tel: 01562 69392

CLAVERLEY
Sandford Park, Claverley,
Shropshire
WV5 7AF

CLEOBURY MORTIMER
Love Lane,
Cleobury Mortimer,
Worcs DY14 8PE
Tel: 01299 271448

COLWALL
Stowe Lane, Colwall,
Herefordshire WR14 6EH
Tel: 01684 541050

COOKLEY
Lea Lane, Cookley,
Kidderminster DY10 3RH
Tel: 01562 850055

COOMBS WOOD
Coombs Rd, Halesowen,
West Midlands B62 8AF
Tel: 0121 561 1932

CUTNALL GREEN
Addis Lane,
Cutnall Green WR9 OPN
Tel: 01299 851408

DROITWICH
St. Peter's Field,
St. Peter's Lane,
Droitwich WR9 7AN
Tel: 01905 770325

The Worcestershire County League

EASTNOR
Clenchers Mill Lane,
Eastnor,
Herefordshire HR8 1RW
Tel: 07815 476659

ENVILLE
Hall Drive, Enville,
Stourbridge DY7 5HB
Tel: 01384 872368

EVESHAM
Evesham Sports Club,
Albert Rd WR11 4LE
Tel: 01386 446469

FECKENHAM
Mill Lane,
Feckenham B96 6HY
Tel: 01527 893167

HAGLEY
Hagley Hall DY9 9LG
Tel: 07900 476534

HALESOWEN
Earls High School,
Furnace Lane,
Halesowen B63 3SL
Tel: 0121 550 2744

HALLOW
Main Road,
Hallow WR2 6PW
Tel: 07837 104697

HANLEY CASTLE
The Glebe,
Hanley Castle WR8 0BJ

HARBORNE
Old Church Ave, Harborne,
Birmingham B17 0BE
Tel: 0121 427 4110

HEWELL
Donkey Hole Lane,
off Hewell Lane
Bromsgrove

HIGHLEY
Severn Centre, Highley,
Bridgnorth,
Salop WV16 6JG
Tel: 01746 860000

HIMBLETON
Neight Hill, Himbleton,
Worcestershire, WR9 7LE
Tel: 01905 391626

KIDDERMINSTER VICTORIA
Chester Road North,
Kidderminster DY10 1TH
Tel: 01562 824175

KNIGHTON -ON-TEME
Newnham Court Farm,
Newnham Bridge,
Tenbury Wells WR15 8JF
Tel: 07752 718238

LUCTONIANS
Mortimer Park,
Kingsland HR6 8SB
Tel: 01568 709080

LYE
Stourbridge Road,
Lye DY9 7PP
Tel: 07889 113017

MALVERN
Regency Road, Malvern
WR14 1EB

MARTLEY
Jewry Field,
Martley WR6 6PY
Tel: 07878 560337

MONMOUTH
Chippenham Sport Ground,
Monmouth NP25 3EQ.
Tel: 07790 703398

NETHERTON
Highbridge
Road,Netherton,
Dudley DY2 0HU
Tel: 01384 457834

OLD ELIZABETHANS
Neel Park, Perdiswell Park,
Droitwich Rd,
Worcester WR3 7SN
Tel: 01905 756617

OLD HALESONIANS
Wassell Grove,
Hagley
Stourbridge DY9 9JP
Tel: 01562 883036

OLD HILL
off Haden Park Road,
Cradley Heath,
West Midlands B64 7HF
Tel: 01384 566827

OLDSWINFORD
The Ken Turner Pavilion,
Bigmore Playing Field,
Albemarle Road,
Stourbridge DY8 2BG
Tel: 01384 374387

OLD VIGORNIANS
Slingpool Walk,
Bromwich Road, St Johns,
Worcester WR2 4AD

OMBERSLEY
Main Road,
Ombersley WR9 0ET
Tel: 01905 621469

PEDMORE
Rectory Glebe,
Pedmore Hall Lane,
Pedmore DY9 0ST
Tel: 01562 883648

PERSHORE
The Bottoms,
Defford Road,
Pershore WR10 1HU
Tel: 01386 552856

REDDITCH
Bromsgrove Road,
Redditch B97 4SP
Tel: 01527 62807

ROMSLEY & HUNNINGTON
Rear of 332,
Bromsgrove Rd,
Hunnington B62 0JW
Tel: 0121 602 2085

ROSS ON WYE
The Park, Wilton Rd.
Ross-on-Wye HR9 5JA
Tel: 07814 982985

RUSHWICK
Upper Wick Lane,
Rushwick WR2 5SU
Tel: 07738 837543

STONE
Worcester Road.
Shenstone,
Worcs DY10 4BU
Tel: 07970 785 967

STOURBRIDGE
Memorial Ground,
Amblecote, DY8 4HN
Tel: 01384 396878

STOURBRIDGE SOCIAL
Norwood Rd.
Brierley Hill, DY5 3XF
Tel: 07703 335337

STOURPORT
Walshes Meadows,
Dunley Rd. DY13 0AA
Tel: 01299 822210

TENBURY
'Penlu' Worcester Rd,
Tenbury Wells WR15 8AP
Tel: 01584 810456

THE LENCHES
Ab Lench Rd,
Church Lench,
Nr. Evesham WR11 4UQ
Tel: 07775 660065

VINE
Cadbury Ground,
Unit 54 Blackpole Trading Estate,
Worcester

WEST MALVERN
Mathon Court,
West Malvern WR13 5NZ
Tel: 07743 903189

WORCESTER
Gordon Jones
Memorial Ground,
Brockhill Lane,
Worcester
Tel: 01905 351222

WORCESTER DOMINIES & GUILD
Brockhill Lane, Norton,
Worcester WR5 2PD
Tel: 01905 351222

WORCESTER NOMADS
Whitegates Farm,
Bransford
Worcester WR6 5JH
Tel: 01886 833171

WORMELOW
Kennel Field, Wormelow,
Hereford HR2 8EJ
Tel: 07796813068

The Worcestershire County League

2007 Fixtures

DIVISION ONE 1ST XI

Saturday 28th April 1.30pm
Astwood B'k v Bewdley
Dr'wich Spa v Pershore
Chadd. Cor. v Redditch
Stourbridge v Bromyard
Worcester v Brock'ton
Worcs Noms v Eastnor

Saturday 5th May 1.30pm
Bewdley v Worcs Noms
Brock'ton v Astwood B'k
Bromyard v Worcester
Chadd. Cor. v Stourbridge
Eastnor v Pershore
Redditch v Dr'wich Spa

Saturday 12th May 1.30pm
Astwood B'k v Bromyard
Bewdley v Brock'ton
Redditch v Eastnor
Stourbridge v Dr'wich Spa
Worcester v Chadd. Cor.
Worcs Noms v Pershore

Saturday 19th May 1.30pm
Brock'ton v Worcs Noms
Bromyard v Bewdley
Chadd. Cor. v Astwood B'k
Dr'wich Spa v Worcester
Eastnor v Stourbridge
Pershore v Redditch

Saturday 26th May 1.30pm
Astwood B'k v Dr'wich Spa
Bewdley v Chadd. Cor.
Brock'ton v Bromyard
Stourbridge v Pershore
Worcester v Eastnor
Worcs Noms v Redditch

Monday 28th May 1.30pm
Bromyard v Worcs Noms
Chadd. Cor. v Brock'ton
Dr'wich Spa v Bewdley
Eastnor v Astwood B'k
Pershore v Worcester
Redditch v Stourbridge

Saturday 2nd June 1.30pm
Astwood B'k v Pershore
Bewdley v Eastnor
Bromyard v Chadd. Cor.
Dr'wich Spa v Brock'ton
Worcester v Redditch
Worcs Noms v Stourbridge

Saturday 9th June 1.30pm
Bromyard v Dr'wich Spa
Chadd. Cor. v Worcs Noms
Eastnor v Brock'ton
Pershore v Bewdley
Redditch v Astwood B'k
Stourbridge v Worcester

Saturday 16th June 1.30pm
Astwood B'k v Stourbridge
Bewdley v Redditch
Brock'ton v Pershore
Bromyard v Eastnor
Chadd. Cor. v Dr'wich Spa
Worcs Noms v Worcester

Saturday 23rd June 1.30pm
Eastnor v Chadd. Cor.
Pershore v Bromyard
Redditch v Brock'ton
Stourbridge v Bewdley
Worcester v Astwood B'k
Worcs Noms v Dr'wich Spa

Saturday 30th June 1.30pm
Astwood B'k v Worcs Noms
Bewdley v Worcester
Bromyard v Redditch
Dr'wich Spa v Eastnor
Pershore v Chadd. Cor.
Stourbridge v Brock'ton

Saturday 7th July 1.30pm
Bewdley v Astwood B'k
Brock'ton v Worcester
Bromyard v Stourbridge
Redditch v Chadd. Cor
Eastnor v Worcs Noms
Pershore v Dr'wich Spa

Saturday 14th July 1.30pm
Astwood B'k v Brock'ton
Dr'wich Spa v Redditch
Pershore v Eastnor
Stourbridge v Chadd. Cor.
Worcester v Bromyard
Worcs Noms v Bewdley

Saturday 21st July 1.30pm
Brock'ton v Bewdley
Bromyard v Astwood B'k
Chadd. Cor. v Worcester
Dr'wich Spa v Stourbridge
Eastnor v Redditch
Pershore v Worcs Noms

Saturday 28th July 1.30pm
Astwood B'k v Chadd. Cor.
Bewdley v Bromyard
Redditch v Pershore
Stourbridge v Eastnor

Worcester v Dr'wich Spa
Worcs Noms v Brock'ton

Saturday 4th August 1.30pm
Bromyard v Brock'ton
Chadd. Cor. v Bewdley
Dr'wich Spa v Astwood B'k
Eastnor v Worcester
Pershore v Stourbridge
Redditch v Worcs Noms

Saturday 11th August 1.30pm
Dr'wich Spa v Chadd. Cor.
Eastnor v Bromyard
Pershore v Brock'ton
Redditch v Bewdley
Stourbridge v Astwood B'k
Worcester v Worcs Noms

Saturday 18th August 1.00pm
Brock'ton v Dr'wich Spa
Chadd. Cor. v Bromyard
Eastnor v Bewdley
Pershore v Astwood B'k
Redditch v Worcester
Stourbridge v Worcs Noms

Saturday 25th August 1.00pm
Astwood B'k v Redditch
Bewdley v Pershore
Brock'ton v Eastnor
Dr'wich Spa v Bromyard
Worcester v Stourbridge
Worcs Noms v Chadd. Cor.

Monday 27th August 1.00pm
Astwood B'k v Eastnor
Bewdley v Dr'wich Spa
Brock'ton v Chadd. Cor.
Stourbridge v Redditch
Worcester v Pershore
Worcs Noms v Bromyard

Saturday 1st Sept 12.30pm
Astwood B'k v Worcester
Bewdley v Stourbridge
Brock'ton v Redditch
Bromyard v Pershore
Chadd. Cor. v Eastnor
Dr'wich Spa v Worcs Noms

Saturday 8th Sept 12.30pm
Brock'ton v Stourbridge
Chadd. Cor. v Pershore
Eastnor v Dr'wich Spa
Redditch v Bromyard
Worcester v Bewdley
Worcs Noms v Astwood B'k

DIVISION TWO 1ST XI

Saturday 28th April 1.30pm
Belbr'ghton   v Lye
Coombs Wd   v Feckenham
Malvern   v Monmouth
Alvechurch   v Netherton
Oldswinford   v Luctonians
Wormelow   v Barnards Gr

Saturday 5th May 1.30pm
Alvechurch   v Belbr'ghton
Barnards Gr   v Monmouth
Feckenham   v Wormelow
Luctonians   v Coombs Wd
Lye   v Oldswinford
Malvern   v Netherton

Saturday 12th May 1.30pm
Belbr'ghton   v Malvern
Coombs Wd   v Lye
Feckenham   v Luctonians
Netherton   v Barnards Gr
Oldswinford   v Alvechurch
Wormelow   v Monmouth

Saturday 19th May 1.30pm
Alvechurch   v Coombs Wd
Barnards Gr   v Belbr'ghton
Luctonians   v Wormelow
Lye   v Feckenham
Malvern   v Oldswinford
Monmouth   v Netherton

Saturday 26th May 1.30pm
Belbr'ghton   v Monmouth
Coombs Wd   v Malvern
Feckenham   v Alvechurch
Luctonians   v Lye
Oldswinford   v Barnards Gr
Wormelow   v Netherton

Monday 28th May 1.30pm
Alvechurch   v Luctonians
Barnards Gr   v Coombs Wd
Lye   v Wormelow
Malvern   v Feckenham
Monmouth   v Oldswinford
Netherton   v Belbr'ghton

Saturday 2nd June 1.30pm
Coombs Wd   v Monmouth
Feckenham   v Barnards Gr
Luctonians   v Malvern
Lye   v Alvechurch
Oldswinford   v Netherton
Wormelow   v Belbr'ghton

Saturday 9th June 1.30pm
Alvechurch   v Wormelow
Barnards Gr   v Luctonians
Belbr'ghton   v Oldswinford
Malvern   v Lye
Monmouth   v Feckenham
Netherton   v Coombs Wd

Saturday 16th June 1.30pm
Alvechurch   v Malvern
Coombs Wd   v Belbr'ghton
Feckenham   v Netherton
Luctonians   v Monmouth
Lye   v Barnards Gr
Wormelow   v Oldswinford

Saturday 23rd June 1.30pm
Barnards Gr   v Alvechurch
Belbr'ghton   v Feckenham
Monmouth   v Lye
Netherton   v Luctonians
Oldswinford   v Coombs Wd
Wormelow   v Malvern

Saturday 30th June 1.30pm
Belbr'ghton   v Luctonians
Coombs Wd   v Wormelow
Feckenham   v Oldswinford
Lye   v Netherton
Malvern   v Barnards Gr
Monmouth   v Alvechurch

Saturday 7th July 1.30pm
Netherton   v Alvechurch
Barnards Gr   v Wormelow
Feckenham   v Coombs Wd
Luctonians   v Oldswinford
Lye   v Belbr'ghton
Monmouth   v Malvern

Saturday 14th July 1.30pm
Belbr'ghton   v Alvechurch
Coombs Wd   v Luctonians
Monmouth   v Barnards Gr
Netherton   v Malvern
Oldswinford   v Lye
Wormelow   v Feckenham

Saturday 21st July 1.30pm
Alvechurch   v Oldswinford
Barnards Gr   v Netherton
Luctonians   v Feckenham
Lye   v Coombs Wd
Malvern   v Belbr'ghton
Monmouth   v Wormelow

Saturday 28th July 1.30pm
Belbr'ghton   v Barnards Gr
Coombs Wd   v Alvechurch

Feckenham   v Lye
Netherton   v Monmouth
Oldswinford   v Malvern
Wormelow   v Luctonians

Saturday 4th August 1.30pm
Alvechurch   v Feckenham
Barnards Gr   v Oldswinford
Lye   v Luctonians
Malvern   v Coombs Wd
Monmouth   v Belbr'ghton
Netherton   v Wormelow

Saturday 11th August 1.30pm
Barnards Gr   v Lye
Belbr'ghton   v Coombs Wd
Malvern   v Alvechurch
Monmouth   v Luctonians
Netherton   v Feckenham
Oldswinford   v Wormelow

Saturday 18th August 1.00pm
Alvechurch   v Lye
Barnards Gr   v Feckenham
Belbr'ghton   v Wormelow
Malvern   v Luctonians
Monmouth   v Coombs Wd
Netherton   v Oldswinford

Saturday 25th August 1.00pm
Coombs Wd   v Netherton
Feckenham   v Monmouth
Luctonians   v Barnards Gr
Lye   v Malvern
Oldswinford   v Belbr'ghton
Wormelow   v Alvechurch

Monday 27th August 1.00pm
Belbr'ghton   v Netherton
Coombs Wd   v Barnards Gr
Feckenham   v Malvern
Luctonians   v Alvechurch
Oldswinford   v Monmouth
Wormelow   v Lye

Saturday 1st Sept 12.30pm
Alvechurch   v Barnards Gr
Coombs Wd   v Oldswinford
Feckenham   v Belbr'ghton
Luctonians   v Netherton
Lye   v Monmouth
Malvern   v Wormelow

Saturday 8th Sept 12.30pm
Alvechurch   v Monmouth
Barnards Gr   v Malvern
Luctonians   v Belbr'ghton
Netherton   v Lye
Oldswinford   v Feckenham
Wormelow   v Coombs Wd

The Worcestershire County League

DIVISION THREE 1ST XI

Saturday 28th April 1.30pm
Avoncroft   v Colwall
Harborne   v Old Vig'ians
K'minster V.   v Old Hale'ons
Pedmore   v Hagley
Romsley & H   v Cutnall Gr
Stourport   v Martley

Saturday 5th May 1.30pm
Colwall   v Stourport
Cutnall Gr   v Avoncroft
Hagley   v Romsley & H
Harborne   v Pedmore
K'minster V.   v Old Vig'ians
Old Hale'ons   v Martley

Saturday 12th May 1.30pm
Avoncroft   v Hagley
Cutnall Gr   v Colwall
Martley   v Old Vig'ians
Pedmore   v K'minster V.
Romsley & H   v Harborne
Stourport   v Old Hale'ons

Saturday 19th May 1.30pm
Cutnall Gr   v Stourport
Hagley   v Colwall
Harborne   v Avoncroft
K'minster V.   v Romsley & H
Martley   v Pedmore
Old Hale'ons   v Old Vig'ians

Saturday 26th May 1.30pm
Colwall   v Harborne
Hagley   v Cutnall Gr
K'minster V.   v Avoncroft
Old Vig'ians   v Stourport
Pedmore   v Old Hale'ons
Romsley & H   v Martley

Monday 28th May 1.30pm
Harborne   v Cutnall Gr
K'minster V.   v Colwall
Martley   v Avoncroft
Old Hale'ons   v Romsley & H
Old Vig'ians   v Pedmore
Stourport   v Hagley

Saturday 2nd June 1.30pm
Avoncroft   v Old Hale'ons
Martley   v Colwall
Cutnall Gr   v K'minster V.
Hagley   v Harborne
Romsley & H   v Old Vig'ians
Stourport   v Pedmore

Saturday 9th June 1.30pm
Avoncroft   v Old Vig'ians
Harborne   v Stourport
K'minster V.   v Hagley
Martley   v Cutnall Gr
Old Hale'ons   v Colwall
Pedmore   v Romsley & H

Saturday 16th June 1.30pm
Colwall   v Old Vig'ians
Cutnall Gr   v Old Hale'ons
Hagley   v Martley
Harborne   v K'minster V.
Pedmore   v Avoncroft
Stourport   v Romsley & H

Saturday 23rd June 1.30pm
Colwall   v Pedmore
Cutnall Gr   v Old Vig'ians
K'minster V.   v Stourport
Martley   v Harborne
Old Hale'ons   v Hagley
Romsley & H   v Avoncroft

Saturday 30th June 1.30pm
Avoncroft   v Stourport
Colwall   v Romsley & H
Hagley   v Old Vig'ians
Harborne   v Old Hale'ons
Martley   v K'minster V.
Pedmore   v Cutnall Gr

Saturday 7th July 1.30pm
Avoncroft   v K'minster V.
Cutnall Gr   v Hagley
Harborne   v Colwall
Martley   v Romsley & H
Old Hale'ons   v Pedmore
Stourport   v Old Vig'ians

Saturday 14th July 1.30pm
Avoncroft   v Cutnall Gr
Martley   v Old Hale'ons
Old Vig'ians   v K'minster V.
Pedmore   v Harborne
Romsley & H   v Hagley
Stourport   v Colwall

Saturday 21st July 1.30pm
Colwall   v Cutnall Gr
Hagley   v Avoncroft
Harborne   v Romsley & H
K'minster V.   v Pedmore
Old Hale'ons   v Stourport
Old Vig'ians   v Martley

Saturday 28th July 1.30pm
Avoncroft   v Harborne
Colwall   v Hagley

Old Vig'ians   v Old Hale'ons
Pedmore   v Martley
Romsley & H   v K'minster V.
Stourport   v Cutnall Gr

Saturday 4th August 1.30pm
Colwall   v Avoncroft
Cutnall Gr   v Romsley & H
Hagley   v Pedmore
Martley   v Stourport
Old Hale'ons   v K'minster V.
Old Vig'ians   v Harborne

Saturday 11th August 1.30pm
Avoncroft   v Pedmore
K'minster V.   v Harborne
Martley   v Hagley
Old Hale'ons   v Cutnall Gr
Old Vig'ians   v Colwall
Romsley & H   v Stourport

Saturday 18th August 1.00pm
Harborne   v Hagley
K'minster V.   v Cutnall Gr
Colwall   v Martley
Old Hale'ons   v Avoncroft
Old Vig'ians   v Romsley & H
Pedmore   v Stourport

Saturday 25th August 1.00pm
Colwall   v Old Hale'ons
Cutnall Gr   v Martley
Hagley   v K'minster V.
Old Vig'ians   v Avoncroft
Romsley & H   v Pedmore
Stourport   v Harborne

Monday 27th August 1.00pm
Avoncroft   v Martley
Colwall   v K'minster V.
Cutnall Gr   v Harborne
Hagley   v Stourport
Pedmore   v Old Vig'ians
Romsley & H   v Old Hale'ons

Saturday 1st Sept 12.30pm
Avoncroft   v Romsley & H
Hagley   v Old Hale'ons
Harborne   v Martley
Old Vig'ians   v Cutnall Gr
Pedmore   v Colwall
Stourport   v K'minster V.

Saturday 8th Sept 12.30pm
Cutnall Gr   v Pedmore
K'minster V.   v Martley
Old Hale'ons   v Harborne
Old Vig'ians   v Hagley
Romsley & H   v Colwall
Stourport   v Avoncroft

DIVISION FOUR NORTH
1ST XI

Saturday May 5th 1.30pm
Alveley   v Amb & Woll
Belbr'ghton v Barnt Green
Evesham   v Cookley
Halesowen   v Claverley
Stourbridge v Enville

Saturday May 12th 1.30pm
Amb & Woll   v Stourbridge
Barnt Green v Alveley
Claverley   v Belbr'ghton
Cookley   v Halesowen
Enville   v Evesham

Saturday May 19th 1.30pm
Alveley   v Claverley
Amb & Woll   v Barnt Green
Belbr'ghton v Cookley
Halesowen   v Enville
Stourbridge v Evesham

Saturday May 26th 1.30pm
Barnt Green v Stourbridge
Claverley   v Amb & Woll
Cookley   v Alveley
Enville   v Belbr'ghton
Evesham   v Halesowen

Saturday June 2nd 1.30pm
Alveley   v Enville
Amb & Woll   v Cookley
Barnt Green v Claverley
Belbr'ghton v Evesham
Stourbridge v Halesowen

Saturday June 9th 1.30pm
Claverley   v Stourbridge
Cookley   v Barnt Green
Enville   v Amb & Woll
Evesham   v Alveley
Halesowen   v Belbr'ghton

Saturday June 16th 1.30pm
Alveley   v Halesowen
Amb & Woll   v Evesham
Barnt Green v Enville
Claverley   v Cookley
Stourbridge v Belbr'ghton

Saturday June 23rd 1.30pm
Cookley   v Stourbridge
Enville   v Claverley
Evesham   v Barnt Green
Halesowen   v Amb & Woll
Belbr'ghton v Alveley

Saturday June 30th 1.30pm
Alveley   v Stourbridge
Amb & Woll   v Belbr'ghton
Barnt Green v Halesowen
Claverley   v Evesham
Cookley   v Enville

Saturday July 7th 1.30pm
Amb & Woll   v Alveley
Barnt Green v Belbr'ghton
Claverley   v Halesowen
Cookley   v Evesham
Enville   v Stourbridge

Saturday July 14th 1.30pm
Alveley   v Barnt Green
Belbr'ghton v Claverley
Evesham   v Enville
Halesowen   v Cookley
Stourbridge v Amb & Woll

Saturday July 21st 1.30pm
Barnt Green v Amb & Woll
Claverley   v Alveley
Cookley   v Belbr'ghton
Enville   v Halesowen
Evesham   v Stourbridge

Saturday July 28th 1.30pm
Alveley   v Cookley
Amb & Woll   v Claverley
Belbr'ghton v Enville
Halesowen   v Evesham
Stourbridge v Barnt Green

Saturday August 4th 1.30pm
Claverley   v Barnt Green
Cookley   v Amb & Woll
Enville   v Alveley
Evesham   v Belbr'ghton
Halesowen   v Stourbridge

Saturday August 11th 1.30pm
Alveley   v Evesham
Amb & Woll   v Enville
Barnt Green v Cookley
Belbr'ghton v Halesowen
Stourbridge v Claverley

Saturday August 18th 1.00pm
Belbr'ghton v Stourbridge
Cookley   v Claverley
Enville   v Barnt Green
Evesham   v Amb & Woll
Halesowen   v Alveley

Saturday August 25th 1.00pm
Alveley   v Belbr'ghton
Amb & Woll   v Halesowen
Barnt Green v Evesham
Claverley   v Enville
Stourbridge v Cookley

Saturday Sept 1st 1.00pm
Belbr'ghton v Amb & Woll
Enville   v Cookley
Evesham   v Claverley
Halesowen   v Barnt Green
Stourbridge v Alveley

DIVISION FOUR SOUTH
1ST XI

Saturday May 5th 1.30pm
Barnards Gr   v Birlingham
Old Eliz's   v W'cester Do
Ross on Wye   v H'ley Ca & U
Rushwick   v Himbleton
Tenbury   v Canon Fr.

Saturday May 12th 1.30pm
Birlingham   v W'cester Do
Canon Fr.   v Barnards Gr
H'ley Ca & U v Rushwick
Himbleton   v Tenbury
Old Eliz's   v Ross on Wye

Saturday May 19th 1.30pm
Barnards Gr   v Himbleton
Birlingham   v Canon Fr.
Rushwick   v Old Eliz's
Tenbury   v H'ley Ca & U
W'cester Do   v Ross on Wye

Saturday May 26th 1.30pm
Canon Fr.   v W'cester Do
H'ley Ca & U v Barnards Gr
Himbleton   v Birlingham
Old Eliz's   v Tenbury
Ross on Wye   v Rushwick

Saturday June 2nd 1.30pm
Barnards Gr   v Old Eliz's
Birlingham   v H'ley Ca & U
Canon Fr.   v Himbleton
Tenbury   v Ross on Wye
W'cester Do   v Rushwick

Saturday June 9th 1.30pm
H'ley Ca & U v Canon Fr.
Himbleton   v W'cester Do
Old Eliz's   v Birlingham
Ross on Wye   v Barnards Gr
Rushwick   v Tenbury

Saturday June 16th 1.30pm
Barnards Gr   v Rushwick
Birlingham   v Ross on Wye
Canon Fr.   v Old Eliz's
Himbleton   v H'ley Ca & U
W'cester Do   v Tenbury

The Worcestershire County League

Saturday June 23rd 1.30pm
H'ley Ca & U   v W'cester Do
Old Eliz's   v Himbleton
Ross on Wye   v Canon Fr.
Rushwick   v Birlingham
Tenbury   v Barnards Gr

Saturday June 30th 1.30pm
Barnards Gr   v W'cester Do
Birlingham   v Tenbury
Canon Fr.   v Rushwick
H'ley Ca & U   v Old Eliz's
Himbleton   v Ross on Wye

Saturday July 7th 1.30pm
Birlingham   v Barnards Gr
Canon Fr.   v Tenbury
H'ley Ca & U   v Ross on Wye
Himbleton   v Rushwick
W'cester Do   v Old Eliz's

Saturday July 14th 1.30pm
Barnards Gr   v Canon Fr.
Ross on Wye   v Old Eliz's
Rushwick   v H'ley Ca & U
Tenbury   v Himbleton
W'cester Do   v Birlingham

Saturday July 21st 1.30pm
Canon Fr.   v Birlingham
H'ley Ca & U   v Tenbury
Himbleton   v Barnards Gr
Old Eliz's   v Rushwick
Ross on Wye   v W'cester Do

Saturday July 28th 1.30pm
Barnards Gr   v H'ley Ca & U
Birlingham   v Himbleton
Rushwick   v Ross on Wye
Tenbury   v Old Eliz's
W'cester Do   v Canon Fr.

Saturday August 4th 1.30pm
H'ley Ca & U   v Birlingham
Himbleton   v Canon Fr.
Old Eliz's   v Barnards Gr
Ross on Wye   v Tenbury
Rushwick   v W'cester Do

Saturday August 11th 1.30pm
Barnards Gr   v Ross on Wye
Birlingham   v Old Eliz's
Canon Fr.   v H'ley Ca & U
Tenbury   v Rushwick
W'cester Do   v Himbleton

Saturday August 18th 1.00pm
H'ley Ca & U   v Himbleton
Old Eliz's   v Canon Fr.
Ross on Wye   v Birlingham
Rushwick   v Barnards Gr
Tenbury   v W'cester Do

Saturday August 25th 1.00pm
Barnards Gr   v Tenbury
Birlingham   v Rushwick
Canon Fr.   v Ross on Wye
Himbleton   v Old Eliz's
W'cester Do   v H'ley Ca & U

Saturday Sept 1st 1.00pm
Old Eliz's   v H'ley Ca & U
Ross on Wye   v Himbleton
Rushwick   v Canon Fr.
Tenbury   v Birlingham
W'cester Do   v Barnards Gr

DIVISION ONE 2ND XI

Saturday 28th April 1.30pm
Redditch   v Alvechurch
Barnards Gr   v Worcs Noms
Bewdley   v Astwood B'k
Brock'ton   v Worcester
Bromyard   v Belbr'ghton
Pershore   v Dr'wich Spa

Saturday 5th May 1.30pm
Astwood B'k   v Brock'ton
Belbr'ghton   v Alvechurch
Dr'wich Spa   v Redditch
Pershore   v Barnards Gr
Worcester   v Bromyard
Worcs Noms   v Bewdley

Saturday 12th May 1.30pm
Alvechurch   v Worcester
Barnards Gr   v Redditch
Brock'ton   v Bewdley
Bromyard   v Astwood B'k
Dr'wich Spa   v Belbr'ghton
Pershore   v Worcs Noms

Saturday 19th May 1.30pm
Astwood B'k   v Alvechurch
Belbr'ghton   v Barnards Gr
Bewdley   v Bromyard
Redditch   v Pershore
Worcester   v Dr'wich Spa
Worcs Noms   v Brock'ton

Saturday 26th May 1.30pm
Alvechurch   v Bewdley
Barnards Gr   v Worcester
Bromyard   v Brock'ton
Dr'wich Spa   v Astwood B'k
Pershore   v Belbr'ghton
Redditch   v Worcs Noms

Monday 28th May 1.30pm
Astwood B'k   v Barnards Gr
Belbr'ghton   v Redditch

Bewdley   v Dr'wich Spa
Brock'ton   v Alvechurch
Worcester   v Pershore
Worcs Noms   v Bromyard

Saturday 2nd June 1.30pm
Alvechurch   v Bromyard
Barnards Gr   v Bewdley
Belbr'ghton   v Worcs Noms
Brock'ton   v Dr'wich Spa
Pershore   v Astwood B'k
Redditch   v Worcester

Saturday 9th June 1.30pm
Astwood B'k   v Redditch
Bewdley   v Pershore
Brock'ton   v Barnards Gr
Dr'wich Spa   v Bromyard
Worcester   v Belbr'ghton
Worcs Noms   v Alvechurch

Saturday 16th June 1.30pm
Barnards Gr   v Bromyard
Belbr'ghton   v Astwood B'k
Dr'wich Spa   v Alvechurch
Pershore   v Brock'ton
Redditch   v Bewdley
Worcester   v Worcs Noms

Saturday 23rd June 1.30pm
Alvechurch   v Barnards Gr
Astwood B'k   v Worcester
Bewdley   v Belbr'ghton
Brock'ton   v Redditch
Bromyard   v Pershore
Dr'wich Spa   v Worcs Noms

Saturday 30th June 1.30pm
Alvechurch   v Pershore
Barnards Gr   v Dr'wich Spa
Brock'ton   v Belbr'ghton
Redditch   v Bromyard
Worcester   v Bewdley
Worcs Noms   v Astwood B'k

Saturday 7th July 1.30pm
Astwood B'k   v Bewdley
Belbr'ghton   v Bromyard
Dr'wich Spa   v Pershore
Alvechurch   v Redditch
Worcester   v Brock'ton
Worcs Noms   v Barnards Gr

Saturday 14th July 1.30pm
Alvechurch   v Belbr'ghton
Barnards Gr   v Pershore
Bewdley   v Worcs Noms
Brock'ton   v Astwood B'k
Bromyard   v Worcester
Redditch   v Dr'wich Spa

Saturday 21st July 1.30pm
Astwood B'k   v Bromyard
Belbr'ghton   v Dr'wich Spa
Bewdley   v Brock'ton
Redditch   v Barnards Gr
Worcester   v Alvechurch
Worcs Noms   v Pershore

Saturday 28th July 1.30pm
Alvechurch   v Astwood B'k
Barnards Gr   v Belbr'ghton
Brock'ton   v Worcs Noms
Bromyard   v Bewdley
Dr'wich Spa   v Worcester
Pershore   v Redditch

Saturday 4th August 1.30pm
Astwood B'k   v Dr'wich Spa
Belbr'ghton   v Pershore
Bewdley   v Alvechurch
Brock'ton   v Bromyard
Worcester   v Barnards Gr
Worcs Noms   v Redditch

Saturday 11th August 1.30pm
Alvechurch   v Dr'wich Spa
Astwood B'k   v Belbr'ghton
Bewdley   v Redditch
Brock'ton   v Pershore
Bromyard   v Barnards Gr
Worcs Noms   v Worcester

Saturday 18th August 1.00pm
Astwood B'k   v Pershore
Bewdley   v Barnards Gr
Bromyard   v Alvechurch
Dr'wich Spa   v Brock'ton
Worcester   v Redditch
Worcs Noms   v Belbr'ghton

Saturday 25th August 1.00pm
Alvechurch   v Worcs Noms
Barnards Gr   v Brock'ton
Belbr'ghton   v Worcester
Bromyard   v Dr'wich Spa
Pershore   v Bewdley
Redditch   v Astwood B'k

Monday 27th August 1.00pm
Alvechurch   v Brock'ton
Barnards Gr   v Astwood B'k
Bromyard   v Worcs Noms
Dr'wich Spa   v Bewdley
Pershore   v Worcester
Redditch   v Belbr'ghton

Saturday 1st Sept 12.30pm
Barnards Gr   v Alvechurch
Belbr'ghton   v Bewdley
Pershore   v Bromyard

Redditch   v Brock'ton
Worcester   v Astwood B'k
Worcs Noms   v Dr'wich Spa

Saturday 8th Sept 12.30pm
Astwood B'k   v Worcs Noms
Belbr'ghton   v Brock'ton
Bewdley   v Worcester
Bromyard   v Redditch
Dr'wich Spa   v Barnards Gr
Pershore   v Alvechurch

DIVISION TWO 2ND XI

Saturday 28th April 1.30pm
Netherton   v Chadd. Cor.
Eastnor   v Wormelow
Feckenham   v Coombs Wd
Luctonians   v Oldswinford
Lye   v Stourbridge
Monmouth   v Malvern

Saturday 5th May 1.30pm
Coombs Wd   v Luctonians
Monmouth   v Eastnor
Netherton   v Malvern
Oldswinford   v Lye
Stourbridge   v Chadd. Cor.
Wormelow   v Feckenham

Saturday 12th May 1.30pm
Chadd. Cor.   v Oldswinford
Eastnor   v Netherton
Luctonians   v Feckenham
Lye   v Coombs Wd
Malvern   v Stourbridge
Monmouth   v Wormelow

Saturday 19th May 1.30pm
Coombs Wd   v Chadd. Cor.
Feckenham   v Lye
Netherton   v Monmouth
Oldswinford   v Malvern
Stourbridge   v Eastnor
Wormelow   v Luctonians

Saturday 26th May 1.30pm
Chadd. Cor.   v Feckenham
Eastnor   v Oldswinford
Lye   v Luctonians
Malvern   v Coombs Wd
Monmouth   v Stourbridge
Netherton   v Wormelow

Monday 28th May 1.30pm
Coombs Wd   v Eastnor
Feckenham   v Malvern
Luctonians   v Chadd. Cor.
Oldswinford   v Monmouth
Stourbridge   v Netherton
Wormelow   v Lye

Saturday 2nd June 1.30pm
Chadd. Cor.   v Lye
Eastnor   v Feckenham
Malvern   v Luctonians
Monmouth   v Coombs Wd
Netherton   v Oldswinford
Stourbridge   v Wormelow

Saturday 9th June 1.30pm
Coombs Wd   v Netherton
Feckenham   v Monmouth
Luctonians   v Eastnor
Lye   v Malvern
Oldswinford   v Stourbridge
Wormelow   v Chadd. Cor.

Saturday 16th June 1.30pm
Eastnor   v Lye
Malvern   v Chadd. Cor.
Monmouth   v Luctonians
Netherton   v Feckenham
Oldswinford   v Wormelow
Stourbridge   v Coombs Wd

Saturday 23rd June 1.30pm
Chadd. Cor.   v Eastnor
Coombs Wd   v Oldswinford
Feckenham   v Stourbridge
Luctonians   v Netherton
Lye   v Monmouth
Malvern   v Wormelow

Saturday 30th June 1.30pm
Chadd. Cor.   v Monmouth
Eastnor   v Malvern
Luctonians   v Stourbridge
Netherton   v Lye
Oldswinford   v Feckenham
Wormelow   v Coombs Wd

Saturday 7th July 1.30pm
Coombs Wd   v Feckenham
Malvern   v Monmouth
Chadd. Cor.   v Netherton
Oldswinford   v Luctonians
Stourbridge   v Lye
Wormelow   v Eastnor

Saturday 14th July 1.30pm
Chadd. Cor.   v Stourbridge
Eastnor   v Monmouth
Feckenham   v Wormelow
Luctonians   v Coombs Wd
Lye   v Oldswinford
Malvern   v Netherton

Saturday 21st July 1.30pm
Coombs Wd   v Lye
Feckenham   v Luctonians
Netherton   v Eastnor

The Worcestershire County League

Oldswinford v Chadd. Cor.
Stourbridge v Malvern
Wormelow v Monmouth

Saturday 28th July 1.30pm
Chadd. Cor. v Coombs Wd
Eastnor v Stourbridge
Luctonians v Wormelow
Lye v Feckenham
Malvern v Oldswinford
Monmouth v Netherton

Saturday 4th August 1.30pm
Coombs Wd v Malvern
Feckenham v Chadd. Cor.
Luctonians v Lye
Oldswinford v Eastnor
Stourbridge v Monmouth
Wormelow v Netherton

Saturday 11th August 1.30pm
Chadd. Cor. v Malvern
Coombs Wd v Stourbridge
Feckenham v Netherton
Luctonians v Monmouth
Lye v Eastnor
Wormelow v Oldswinford

Saturday 18th August 1.00pm
Coombs Wd v Monmouth
Feckenham v Eastnor
Luctonians v Malvern
Lye v Chadd. Cor.
Oldswinford v Netherton
Wormelow v Stourbridge

Saturday 25th August 1.00pm
Chadd. Cor. v Wormelow
Eastnor v Luctonians
Malvern v Lye
Monmouth v Feckenham
Netherton v Coombs Wd
Stourbridge v Oldswinford

Monday 27th August 1.00pm
Chadd. Cor. v Luctonians
Eastnor v Coombs Wd
Lye v Wormelow
Malvern v Feckenham
Monmouth v Oldswinford
Netherton v Stourbridge

Saturday 1st Sept 12.30pm
Eastnor v Chadd. Cor.
Monmouth v Lye
Netherton v Luctonians
Oldswinford v Coombs Wd
Stourbridge v Feckenham
Wormelow v Malvern

Saturday 8th Sept 12.30pm
Coombs Wd v Wormelow
Feckenham v Oldswinford
Lye v Netherton
Malvern v Eastnor
Monmouth v Chadd. Cor.
Stourbridge v Luctonians

DIVISION THREE 2ND XI

Saturday 28th April 1.30pm
Colwall v Avoncroft
Cutnall Gr v Romsley & H
Hagley v Pedmore
Martley v Stourport
Old Hale'ons v K'minster V.
Old Vig'ians v Harborne

Saturday 5th May 1.30pm
Avoncroft v Cutnall Gr
Martley v Old Hale'ons
Old Vig'ians v K'minster V.
Pedmore v Harborne
Romsley & H v Hagley
Stourport v Colwall

Saturday 12th May 1.30pm
Colwall v Cutnall Gr
Hagley v Avoncroft
Harborne v Romsley & H
K'minster V. v Pedmore
Old Hale'ons v Stourport
Old Vig'ians v Martley

Saturday 19th May 1.30pm
Avoncroft v Harborne
Colwall v Hagley
Old Vig'ians v Old Hale'ons
Pedmore v Martley
Romsley & H v K'minster V.
Stourport v Cutnall Gr

Saturday 26th May 1.30pm
Avoncroft v K'minster V.
Cutnall Gr v Hagley
Harborne v Colwall
Martley v Romsley & H
Old Hale'ons v Pedmore
Stourport v Old Vig'ians

Monday 28th May 1.30pm
Avoncroft v Martley
Colwall v K'minster V.
Cutnall Gr v Harborne
Hagley v Stourport
Pedmore v Old Vig'ians
Romsley & H v Old Hale'ons

Saturday 2nd June 1.30pm
Colwall v Martley
Harborne v Hagley

K'minster V. v Cutnall Gr
Old Hale'ons v Avoncroft
Old Vig'ians v Romsley & H
Pedmore v Stourport

Saturday 9th June 1.30pm
Colwall v Old Hale'ons
Cutnall Gr v Martley
Hagley v K'minster V.
Old Vig'ians v Avoncroft
Romsley & H v Pedmore
Stourport v Harborne

Saturday 16th June 1.30pm
Avoncroft v Pedmore
K'minster V. v Harborne
Martley v Hagley
Old Hale'ons v Cutnall Gr
Old Vig'ians v Colwall
Romsley & H v Stourport

Saturday 23rd June 1.30pm
Avoncroft v Romsley & H
Hagley v Old Hale'ons
Harborne v Martley
Old Vig'ians v Cutnall Gr
Pedmore v Colwall
Stourport v K'minster V.

Saturday 30th June 1.30pm
Cutnall Gr v Pedmore
K'minster V. v Martley
Old Hale'ons v Harborne
Old Vig'ians v Hagley
Romsley & H v Colwall
Stourport v Avoncroft

Saturday 7th July 1.30pm
Colwall v Harborne
Hagley v Cutnall Gr
K'minster V. v Avoncroft
Old Vig'ians v Stourport
Pedmore v Old Hale'ons
Romsley & H v Martley

Saturday 14th July 1.30pm
Colwall v Stourport
Cutnall Gr v Avoncroft
Hagley v Romsley & H
Harborne v Pedmore
K'minster V. v Old Vig'ians
Old Hale'ons v Martley

Saturday 21st July 1.30pm
Avoncroft v Hagley
Cutnall Gr v Colwall
Martley v Old Vig'ians
Pedmore v K'minster V.
Romsley & H v Harborne
Stourport v Old Hale'ons

Saturday 28th July 1.30pm

Cutnall Gr	v Stourport
Hagley	v Colwall
Harborne	v Avoncroft
K'minster V.	v Romsley & H
Martley	v Pedmore
Old Hale'ons	v Old Vig'ians

Saturday 4th August 1.30pm

Avoncroft	v Colwall
Harborne	v Old Vig'ians
K'minster V.	v Old Hale'ons
Pedmore	v Hagley
Romsley & H	v Cutnall Gr
Stourport	v Martley

Saturday 11th August 1.30pm

Colwall	v Old Vig'ians
Cutnall Gr	v Old Hale'ons
Hagley	v Martley
Harborne	v K'minster V.
Pedmore	v Avoncroft
Stourport	v Romsley & H

Saturday 18th August 1.00pm

Avoncroft	v Old Hale'ons
Cutnall Gr	v K'minster V.
Hagley	v Harborne
Martley	v Colwall
Romsley & H	v Old Vig'ians
Stourport	v Pedmore

Saturday 25th August 1.00pm

Avoncroft	v Old Vig'ians
Harborne	v Stourport
K'minster V.	v Hagley
Martley	v Cutnall Gr
Old Hale'ons	v Colwall
Pedmore	v Romsley & H

Monday 27th August 1.00pm

Harborne	v Cutnall Gr
K'minster V.	v Colwall
Martley	v Avoncroft
Old Hale'ons	v Romsley & H
Old Vig'ians	v Pedmore
Stourport	v Hagley

Saturday 1st Sept 12.30pm

Colwall	v Pedmore
Cutnall Gr	v Old Vig'ians
K'minster V.	v Stourport
Martley	v Harborne
Old Hale'ons	v Hagley
Romsley & H	v Avoncroft

Saturday 8th Sept 12.30pm

Avoncroft	v Stourport
Colwall	v Romsley & H
Hagley	v Old Vig'ians
Harborne	v Old Hale'ons

Martley	v K'minster V.
Pedmore	v Cutnall Gr

DIVISION FOUR NORTH
2ND XI

Saturday May 5th 1.30pm

Amb & Woll	v Alveley
Barnt Green	v Belbr'ghton
Claverley	v Halesowen
Cookley	v Evesham
Enville	v Stourbridge

Saturday May 12th 1.30pm

Alveley	v Barnt Green
Belbr'ghton	v Claverley
Evesham	v Enville
Halesowen	v Cookley
Stourbridge	v Amb & Woll

Saturday May 19th 1.30pm

Barnt Green	v Amb & Woll
Claverley	v Alveley
Cookley	v Belbr'ghton
Enville	v Halesowen
Evesham	v Stourbridge

Saturday May 26th 1.30pm

Alveley	v Cookley
Amb & Woll	v Claverley
Belbr'ghton	v Enville
Halesowen	v Evesham
Stourbridge	v Barnt Green

Saturday June 2nd 1.30pm

Claverley	v Barnt Green
Cookley	v Amb & Woll
Enville	v Alveley
Evesham	v Belbr'ghton
Halesowen	v Stourbridge

Saturday June 9th 1.30pm

Alveley	v Evesham
Amb & Woll	v Enville
Barnt Green	v Cookley
Belbr'ghton	v Halesowen
Stourbridge	v Claverley

Saturday June 16th 1.30pm

Belbr'ghton	v Stourbridge
Cookley	v Claverley
Enville	v Barnt Green
Evesham	v Amb & Woll
Halesowen	v Alveley

Saturday June 23rd 1.30pm

Alveley	v Belbr'ghton
Amb & Woll	v Halesowen
Barnt Green	v Evesham
Claverley	v Enville
Stourbridge	v Cookley

Saturday June 30th 1.30pm

Belbr'ghton	v Amb & Woll
Enville	v Cookley
Evesham	v Claverley
Halesowen	v Barnt Green
Stourbridge	v Alveley

Saturday July 7th 1.30pm

Alveley	v Amb & Woll
Belbr'ghton	v Barnt Green
Evesham	v Cookley
Halesowen	v Claverley
Stourbridge	v Enville

Saturday July 14th 1.30pm

Amb & Woll	v Stourbridge
Barnt Green	v Alveley
Claverley	v Belbr'ghton
Cookley	v Halesowen
Enville	v Evesham

Saturday July 21st 1.30pm

Alveley	v Claverley
Amb & Woll	v Barnt Green
Belbr'ghton	v Cookley
Halesowen	v Enville
Stourbridge	v Evesham

Saturday July 28th 1.30pm

Barnt Green	v Stourbridge
Claverley	v Amb & Woll
Cookley	v Alveley
Enville	v Belbr'ghton
Evesham	v Halesowen

Saturday August 4th 1.30pm

Alveley	v Enville
Amb & Woll	v Cookley
Barnt Green	v Claverley
Belbr'ghton	v Evesham
Stourbridge	v Halesowen

Saturday August 11th 1.30pm

Claverley	v Stourbridge
Cookley	v Barnt Green
Enville	v Amb & Woll
Evesham	v Alveley
Halesowen	v Belbr'ghton

Saturday August 18th 1.00pm

Alveley	v Halesowen
Amb & Woll	v Evesham
Barnt Green	v Enville
Claverley	v Cookley
Stourbridge	v Belbr'ghton

Saturday August 25th 1.00pm

Belbr'ghton	v Alveley
Cookley	v Stourbridge
Enville	v Claverley

The Worcestershire County League

Evesham v Barnt Green
Halesowen v Amb & Woll

Saturday Sept 1st 1.00pm
Alveley v Stourbridge
Amb & Woll v Belbr'ghton
Barnt Green v Halesowen
Claverley v Evesham
Cookley v Enville

DIVISION FOUR SOUTH
2ND XI

Saturday May 5th 1.30pm
Birlingham v Barnards Gr
Canon Fr. v Tenbury
H'ley Ca & U v Ross on Wye
Himbleton v Rushwick
W'cester Do v Old Eliz's

Saturday May 12th 1.30pm
Barnards Gr v Canon Fr.
Ross on Wye v Old Eliz's
Rushwick v H'ley Ca & U
Tenbury v Himbleton
W'cester Do v Birlingham

Saturday May 19th 1.30pm
Canon Fr. v Birlingham
H'ley Ca & U v Tenbury
Himbleton v Barnards Gr
Old Eliz's v Rushwick
Ross on Wye v W'cester Do

Saturday May 26th 1.30pm
Barnards Gr v H'ley Ca & U
Birlingham v Himbleton
Rushwick v Ross on Wye
Tenbury v Old Eliz's
W'cester Do v Canon Fr.

Saturday June 2nd 1.30pm
H'ley Ca & U v Birlingham
Himbleton v Canon Fr.
Old Eliz's v Barnards Gr
Ross on Wye v Tenbury
Rushwick v W'cester Do

Saturday June 9th 1.30pm
Barnards Gr v Ross on Wye
Birlingham v Old Eliz's
Canon Fr. v H'ley Ca & U
Tenbury v Rushwick
W'cester Do v Himbleton

Saturday June 16th 1.30pm
H'ley Ca & U v Himbleton
Old Eliz's v Canon Fr.
Ross on Wye v Birlingham
Rushwick v Barnards Gr
Tenbury v W'cester Do

Saturday June 23rd 1.30pm
Barnards Gr v Tenbury
Birlingham v Rushwick
Canon Fr. v Ross on Wye
Himbleton v Old Eliz's
W'cester Do v H'ley Ca & U

Saturday June 30th 1.30pm
Old Eliz's v H'ley Ca & U
Ross on Wye v Himbleton
Rushwick v Canon Fr.
Tenbury v Birlingham
W'cester Do v Barnards Gr

Saturday July 7th 1.30pm
Barnards Gr v Birlingham
Old Eliz's v W'cester Do
Ross on Wye v H'ley Ca & U
Rushwick v Himbleton
Tenbury v Canon Fr.

Saturday July 14th 1.30pm
Birlingham v W'cester Do
Canon Fr. v Barnards Gr
H'ley Ca & U v Rushwick
Himbleton v Tenbury
Old Eliz's v Ross on Wye

Saturday July 21st 1.30pm
Barnards Gr v Himbleton
Birlingham v Canon Fr.
Rushwick v Old Eliz's
Tenbury v H'ley Ca & U
W'cester Do v Ross on Wye

Saturday July 28th 1.30pm
Canon Fr. v W'cester Do
H'ley Ca & U v Barnards Gr
Himbleton v Birlingham
Old Eliz's v Tenbury
Ross on Wye v Rushwick

Saturday August 4th 1.30pm
Barnards Gr v Old Eliz's
Birlingham v H'ley Ca & U
Canon Fr. v Himbleton
Tenbury v Ross on Wye
W'cester Do v Rushwick

Saturday August 11th 1.30pm
H'ley Ca & U v Canon Fr.
Himbleton v W'cester Do
Old Eliz's v Birlingham
Ross on Wye v Barnards Gr
Rushwick v Tenbury

Saturday August 18th 1.00pm
Barnards Gr v Rushwick
Birlingham v Ross on Wye
Canon Fr. v Old Eliz's

Himbleton v H'ley Ca & U
W'cester Do v Tenbury

Saturday August 25th 1.00pm
H'ley Ca & U v W'cester Do
Old Eliz's v Himbleton
Ross on Wye v Canon Fr.
Rushwick v Birlingham
Tenbury v Barnards Gr

Saturday Sept 1st 1.00pm
Barnards Gr v W'cester Do
Birlingham v Tenbury
Canon Fr. v Rushwick
H'ley Ca & U v Old Eliz's
Himbleton v Ross on Wye

DIVISION FIVE

Saturday May 5th 1.30pm
Badsey v Vine
Brintons v K'minster V.
Cl'bury Mort. v Highley
Droitwich v S'bridge Soc
K'ton on T. v Chainwire

Saturday May 12th 1.30pm
Badsey v Cl'bury Mort.
Brintons v S'bridge Soc
Droitwich v Chainwire
K'minster V. v Vine
K'ton on T. v Highley

Saturday May 19th 1.30pm
Brintons v Chainwire
Highley v Droitwich
K'minster V. v S'bridge Soc
K'ton on T. v Badsey
Vine v Cl'bury Mort.

Saturday May 26th 1.30pm
Chainwire v K'minster V.
Cl'bury Mort. v K'ton on T.
Droitwich v Badsey
Highley v Brintons
S'bridge Soc v Vine

Saturday June 2nd 1.30pm
Badsey v Brintons
Chainwire v S'bridge Soc
Droitwich v Cl'bury Mort.
K'minster V. v Highley
K'ton on T. v Vine

Saturday June 9th 1.30pm
Badsey v Highley
Chainwire v Cl'bury Mort.
Droitwich v K'minster V.
K'ton on T. v S'bridge Soc
Vine v Brintons

Saturday June 16th 1.30pm
Brintons   v K'ton on T.
Cl'bury Mort.   v K'minster V.
Droitwich   v Vine
Highley   v Chainwire
S'bridge Soc   v Badsey

Saturday June 23rd 1.30pm
Chainwire   v Badsey
Cl'bury Mort.   v S'bridge Soc
Droitwich   v Brintons
Highley   v Vine
K'minster V.   v K'ton on T.

Saturday June 30th 1.30pm
Brintons   v Vine
Cl'bury Mort.   v Chainwire
Highley   v Badsey
K'minster V.   v Droitwich
S'bridge Soc   v K'ton on T.

Saturday July 7th 1.30pm
Badsey   v K'ton on T.
Chainwire   v Brintons
Cl'bury Mort.   v Vine
Droitwich   v Highley
S'bridge Soc   v K'minster V.

Saturday July 14th 1.30pm
Badsey   v Droitwich
Brintons   v Highley
K'minster V.   v Chainwire
K'ton on T.   v Cl'bury Mort.
Vine   v S'bridge Soc

Saturday July 21st 1.30pm
Badsey   v Chainwire
Brintons   v Droitwich
K'ton on T.   v K'minster V.
S'bridge Soc   v Cl'bury Mort.
Vine   v Highley

Saturday July 28th 1.30pm
Brintons   v Badsey
Cl'bury Mort.   v Droitwich
Highley   v K'minster V.
S'bridge Soc   v Chainwire
Vine   v K'ton on T.

Saturday August 4th 1.30pm
Chainwire   v K'ton on T.
Highley   v Cl'bury Mort.
K'minster V.   v Brintons
S'bridge Soc   v Droitwich
Vine   v Badsey

Saturday August 11th 1.30pm
Chainwire   v Droitwich
Cl'bury Mort.   v Badsey
Highley   v K'ton on T.

S'bridge Soc   v Brintons
Vine   v K'minster V.

Saturday August 18th 1.00pm
Brintons   v Cl'bury Mort.
Droitwich   v K'ton on T.
K'minster V.   v Badsey
S'bridge Soc   v Highley
Vine   v Chainwire

Saturday August 25th 1.00pm
Badsey   v S'bridge Soc
Chainwire   v Highley
K'minster V.   v Cl'bury Mort.
K'ton on T.   v Brintons
Vine   v Droitwich

Saturday Sept 1st 1.00pm
Badsey   v K'minster V.
Chainwire   v Vine
Cl'bury Mort.   v Brintons
Highley   v S'bridge Soc
K'ton on T.   v Droitwich

DIVISION SIX

Saturday May 5th 1.30pm
Bewdley   v Colwall
Stone   v Netherton
S'bridge Soc   v Hewell
The Lenches   v Hallow
W. Malvern   v Old Hill

Saturday May 12th 1.30pm
Hallow   v W. Malvern
Hewell   v Colwall
Netherton   v Bewdley
Old Hill   v The Lenches
S'bridge Soc   v Stone

Saturday May 19th 1.30pm
Bewdley   v Hewell
Colwall   v Hallow
S'bridge Soc   v Old Hill
The Lenches   v Netherton
W. Malvern   v Stone

Saturday May 26th 1.30pm
Colwall   v W. Malvern
Hallow   v Bewdley
Hewell   v The Lenches
Netherton   v S'bridge Soc
Old Hill   v Stone

Saturday June 2nd 1.30pm
Bewdley   v Old Hill
Colwall   v Netherton
Hallow   v Hewell
S'bridge Soc   v W. Malvern
The Lenches   v Stone

Saturday June 9th 1.30pm
Hewell   v W. Malvern
Netherton   v Hallow
Old Hill   v Colwall
Stone   v Bewdley
S'bridge Soc   v The Lenches

Saturday June 16th 1.30pm
Bewdley   v S'bridge Soc
Colwall   v Stone
Hallow   v Old Hill
Hewell   v Netherton
W. Malvern   v The Lenches

Saturday June 23rd 1.30pm
Netherton   v W. Malvern
Old Hill   v Hewell
Stone   v Hallow
S'bridge Soc   v Colwall
The Lenches   v Bewdley

Saturday June 30th 1.30pm
Bewdley   v W. Malvern
Colwall   v The Lenches
Hallow   v S'bridge Soc
Hewell   v Stone
Old Hill   v Netherton

Saturday July 7th 1.30pm
Colwall   v Bewdley
Hallow   v The Lenches
Hewell   v S'bridge Soc
Netherton   v Stone
Old Hill   v W. Malvern

Saturday July 14th 1.30pm
Bewdley   v Hallow
Stone   v Old Hill
S'bridge Soc   v Netherton
The Lenches   v Hewell
W. Malvern   v Colwall

Saturday July 21st 1.30pm
Bewdley   v Stone
Colwall   v Old Hill
Hallow   v Netherton
The Lenches   v S'bridge Soc
W. Malvern   v Hewell

Saturday July 28th 1.30pm
Hallow   v Colwall
Hewell   v Bewdley
Netherton   v The Lenches
Old Hill   v S'bridge Soc
Stone   v W. Malvern

Saturday August 4th 1.30pm
Hewell   v Hallow
Netherton   v Colwall
Old Hill   v Bewdley

The Worcestershire County League

Stone   v The Lenches
W. Malvern   v S'bridge Soc

Saturday August 11th 1.30pm
Bewdley   v Netherton
Colwall   v Hewell
Stone   v S'bridge Soc
The Lenches   v Old Hill
W. Malvern   v Hallow

Saturday August 18th 1.00pm
Bewdley   v The Lenches
Colwall   v S'bridge Soc
Hallow   v Stone
Hewell   v Old Hill
W. Malvern   v Netherton

Saturday August 25th 1.00pm
Netherton   v Hewell
Old Hill   v Hallow
Stone   v Colwall
S'bridge Soc   v Bewdley
The Lenches   v W. Malvern

Saturday Sept 1st 1.00pm
Netherton   v Old Hill
Stone   v Hewell
S'bridge Soc   v Hallow
The Lenches   v Colwall
W. Malvern   v Bewdley

DIVISION SEVEN

Saturday 19th May 1.30pm
Astwood B'k   v Worcester
Chadd. Cor.   v Ombersley
Coombs Wd   v Enville
Pershore   v Harborne

Saturday 26th May 1.30pm
Chadd. Cor.   v Astwood B'k
Enville   v Harborne
Ombersley   v Pershore
Worcester   v Coombs Wd

Saturday 2nd June 1.30pm
Chadd. Cor.   v Worcester
Coombs Wd   v Harborne
Ombersley   v Astwood B'k
Pershore   v Enville

Saturday 9th June 1.30pm
Chadd. Cor.   v Enville
Harborne   v Astwood B'k
Ombersley   v Coombs Wd
Worcester   v Pershore

Saturday 16th June 1.30pm
Astwood B'k   v Harborne
Coombs Wd   v Ombersley
Pershore   v Worcester
Enville   v Chadd. Cor.

Saturday 23rd June 1.30pm
Enville   v Coombs Wd
Harborne   v Pershore
Ombersley   v Chadd. Cor.
Worcester   v Astwood B'k

Saturday 30th June 1.30pm
Astwood B'k   v Pershore
Chadd. Cor.   v Coombs Wd
Ombersley   v Enville
Worcester   v Harborne

Saturday 7th July 1.30pm
Astwood B'k   v Enville
Harborne   v Chadd. Cor.
Ombersley   v Worcester
Pershore   v Coombs Wd

Saturday 14th July 1.30pm
Coombs Wd   v Chadd. Cor.
Enville   v Ombersley
Harborne   v Worcester
Pershore   v Astwood B'k

Saturday 21st July 1.30pm
Chadd. Cor.   v Pershore
Coombs Wd   v Astwood B'k
Harborne   v Ombersley
Worcester   v Enville

Saturday 28th July 1.30pm
Astwood B'k   v Coombs Wd
Enville   v Worcester
Ombersley   v Harborne
Pershore   v Chadd. Cor.

Saturday 4th August 1.30pm
Astwood B'k   v Ombersley
Enville   v Pershore
Harborne   v Coombs Wd
Worcester   v Chadd. Cor.

Saturday 11th August 1.30pm
Astwood B'k   v Chadd. Cor.
Coombs Wd   v Worcester
Harborne   v Enville
Pershore   v Ombersley

Saturday 18th August 1.00pm
Chadd. Cor.   v Harborne
Coombs Wd   v Pershore
Enville   v Astwood B'k
Worcester   v Ombersley

DIVISION EIGHT

Saturday 19th May 1.30pm
Alvechurch   v Avoncroft
Amblecote   v Malvern
Worcs Noms   v Astwood B'k

Saturday 26th May 1.30pm
Avoncroft   v Amblecote
Malvern   v Astwood B'k
Worcs Noms   v Alvechurch

Saturday 2nd June 1.30pm
Alvechurch   v Avoncroft
Amblecote   v Malvern
Astwood B'k   v Worcs Noms

Saturday 9th June 1.30pm
Amblecote   v Avoncroft
Malvern   v Astwood B'k
Worcs Noms   v Alvechurch

Saturday 16th June 1.30pm
Astwood B'k   v Alvechurch
Avoncroft   v Malvern
Worcs Noms   v Amblecote

Saturday 23rd June 1.30pm
Alvechurch   v Astwood B'k
Malvern   v Avoncroft
Worcs Noms   v Amblecote

Saturday 30th June 1.30pm
Alvechurch   v Worcs Noms
Amblecote   v Avoncroft
Astwood B'k   v Malvern

Saturday 7th July 1.30pm
Amblecote   v Alvechurch
Avoncroft   v Astwood B'k
Malvern   v Worcs Noms

Saturday 14th July 1.30pm
Astwood B'k   v Amblecote
Malvern   v Alvechurch
Worcs Noms   v Avoncroft

Saturday 21st July 1.30pm
Amblecote   v Alvechurch
Avoncroft   v Astwood B'k
Malvern   v Worcs Noms

Saturday 28th July 1.30pm
Alvechurch   v Amblecote
Astwood B'k   v Avoncroft
Worcs Noms   v Malvern

Saturday 4th August 1.30pm
Avoncroft   v Alvechurch
Malvern   v Amblecote
Worcs Noms   v Astwood B'k

Saturday 11th August 1.30pm
Alvechurch   v Malvern
Astwood B'k   v Amblecote
Avoncroft   v Worcs Noms

Saturday 18th August 1.00pm
Alvechurch   v Malvern
Amblecote   vAstwood B'k
Avoncroft   v Worcs Noms

Saturday 25th August 1.00pm
Amblecote   v Worcs Noms
Astwood B'k   v Alvechurch
Malvern   v Avoncroft

When Cookley went to Lord's

by Richard Matthews

IN AUGUST, 1977 Cookley became the first team from Worcestershire to win the National Village Knock-Out Competition, beating Lindal Moor from Cumbria at Lord's by 28 runs. It was the crowning glory for a team that throughout the early 70s had been virtually unbeatable.

The villagers had won the Kidderminster League for a record fifth consecutive time, the league's Charity Cup for the fourth year in a row and the Edwin Read Cup for the second consecutive year, as well as notching up many other memorable achievements and milestones on the way.

Who would have thought on Sunday, May 1st, 1977, when Cookley played their first match of the Haig Whisky-sponsored competition, that nine matches and almost four months later skipper Mick Hopkins would be holding the Haig Village Cricket Trophy aloft at the home of cricket before two or three thousand fanatical supporters.

It all seemed so far away as Cookley, taking part in the competition for only the second time, easily disposed of Ashton-under-Hill by 127 runs in the first round, just as they had done in the previous year. But this time things were different. While the previous year Cookley were thrashed by Kington in the second round, on this occasion they cruised through to the third round with a 126-run win over Eckington.

A comfortable eight-wicket win over near neighbours Stone saw Cookley through to what looked a tough encounter on the picturesque Avoncroft ground in the fourth round. But it was the rain that won the day here putting an end to the proceedings after Cookley had rattled up what looked like a winning 168-8.

The teams met again the following week and the Cookley score of 173 again looked unbeatable. And it was, with Avoncroft being dismissed for 101 and losing by 72 runs. Cookley's heroes here were not for the first (or last) time Mick Hopkins with 63, Ray Poole (55) and Dave Nicholls with 5-18.

Onto the group final on June 26th with Cookley bidding for revenge against their conquerors of the previous season, Kington Town, but having the home advantage on this occasion. With Kington cruising along at 107-2 things looked bleak for Cookley, but suddenly the visitors collapsed and with paceman Ivan Perks ripping the heart out of the batting with 5-25, Kington were all out for 122. Cookley's 123-6 looked worse than it really was for for they had been almost home with only three wickets down. Once again Mick Hopkins was top scorer with 42.

So Cookley had seemingly achieved all they had set out for. Winners of the final of the Hereford, Worcester and East Wales group and feeling on top of the world. The champagne (and the Haig) flowed but the question was, could they go any further in the competition ?

Only 32 clubs were now left but when Cookley saw who they were playing there seemed little likelihood of them going any further. They faced a trip to Stinchcombe, the winners of the Gloucestershire group and a team that many argued should never have been allowed in the competition. Their all-star line-up of ex-professionals and top flight club players seemed to be hardly a village team.

But what a match it turned out to be. Cookley excelled with a total of 172, with skipper Hopkins getting 47 and burly John Such an invaluable 44, but Stinchcombe looked to be well on the way to victory with their score on 156-6 with three overs remaining of their allotted 40 overs. When Hopkins tossed the ball to David Nicholls to bowl the last over they wanted only three runs to win with four wickets still remaining. Incredibly, David bowled a wicket maiden and Cookley had won amidst almost unbearable tension by two runs.

Three matches from Lord's and round seven brought a trip to Miskin Manor near Cardiff. This time Cookley notched up a much easier victory than anyone had anticipated. The two Micks - Hopkins and Pitt - put on 114 for the first wicket and the match was all over bar the shouting. They went on to a total of 205 (Hopkins 89, Pitt 50,) and Miskin were tumbled out for 148, leaving Cookley winners by 57 runs. Ivan Perks was the best bowler with 4-35.

Into the quarter-final and a home match against the holders and three times champions Troon from Cornwall. The end of the road for

Cookley? Before a crowd of 3,000 the Cookley score of 146, boosted by a fine 44 from John Such, did not look nearly enough. But once again drama struck and with one over of the match remaining Troon needed five to win with the last pair at the wicket. Two runs off the first ball and then the last man caught and bowled by Ivan Perks off the fourth. Cookley had done it again. Another two-run win and now Lord's was beckoning.

Their visitors in the semi-final? Langleybury from Hertfordshire. Although rain forced the match to be put back a week, things looked fine when the match eventually did get under way. But not for long. Cookley were 39-4, the overs were ticking by and it looked like the bubble had at last burst. But Langleybury had reckoned without that man Mick Hopkins. After opening the innings he eventually got to grips with the attack and his 77 plus 29 from Doug Crannage helped Cookley to a score of 194-6 in 40 overs.

Langleybury's total of 137 all out does not reflect the drama of the situation for at one stage, amidst heavy clouds and slight rain, the match looked like being abandoned, which meant Cookley would have lost on the 15-over rule.

Luckily the weather held and Cookley were winners by 57 runs. Mick Hopkins was named man of the match, but what was more important the club had reached their goal and the ambition of any team. They had got to Lord's.

Bank Holiday Monday, August 29th and all roads for Cookley's supporters - including the villagers' now famous Carribean section - led to Lords. The fact that Cookley knew little about their opponents, Lindal Moor from near Barrow-in-Furness, didn't seem to matter.

The players and supporters were rewarded with a clear, blue sky and blazing sun and, of course, that historic Cookley win.

But when run machine Hopkins went cheaply for 12 and Cookley were 31-2 after 12 overs the omens were not good. Sensible batting by John Such and Ray Poole improved the situation and it was left to Such, with a fine 42, helped by Doug Crannage's 19, including the only six of the game, to shoulder the main responsibility of getting the score up to a respectable level.

When he went with the score at 107-5, the tailenders were left to inch the score up to 138 off the 40 overs.

The total never looked anywhere near enough but the Cumbrians had reckoned without the resolve of the Cookley side, who were soon to make early inroads into the Lindal Moor batting line up.

Doug Crannage made the early breakthrough, sending back opener Will Knight with just six runs on the board, and wickets fell steadily before a swooping catch in the gully by Dave Nicholls off Crannage sent back skipper Eric Gardiner to make the score 39-5.

At 69-7 it looked all over, but the tail wagged and Lindal Moor eventually reached 110 - 28 runs short of the Cookley score, Crannage and veteran Reg Brittain finishing with three wickets apiece.

The details:

Cookley: 138 all out (John Such 42);
Lindal Moor: 110 all out (Reg Brittain 3-6, Doug Crannage 3-20).
Cookley won by 28 runs.

The figures were unimportant. Cookley had won the Haig Village Cricket Championship, a dream had come true and the village had never seen anything like it when the team returned home with the trophy the next day

Staffordshire Club Cricket Championship

League Officials

PRESIDENT
Tom Waterhouse (H) 01384 252771

CHAIRMAN
John Priest (H) 01902 336089 email:- ajohn@jpriest.fsworld.co.uk

VICE CHAIRMAN
Bill Tranter (H) 01902 342297

SECRETARY and RESULTS SECRETARY
Mark Reynolds (H) 01902 783941 (M) 07761 361445
Results 01902 822162 email:- godders23@hotmail.com

TREASURER
Chris Rudge (H) 01902 334965 (B) 01902 331117

FIXTURE SECRETARY
Fred Davis (H) 01902 752760

WELFARE OFFICER
Ray Bickley (H) 01902 788991

UMPIRES PANEL SECRETARY
Fred Barrett 01902 398441

Onwards and upwards for Old Wulfs Tettenhall

OLD WULFRUNIANS Tettenhall continued their forward march in the West Midlands Premier League set up by easily winning the Divsion 1 championship in 2006. Their final total of 369 points was 32 more than their nearest rivals, Penkridge, and a massive 119 points in front of fourth placed Aldridge.

The club was formed by the amalgamation of Old Wufrunians CC and Tettenhall Village CC in 2004. The merged club won promotion to the top division in its first season and followed this with the runners up spot to Wombourne in Divison 1 in 2005. There's no doubt that the resources of the two clubs, which includes two grounds, have enabled it to move quickly and should stand them in good stead for their future in the Birmingham League.

Although the original concept of the league was created in 1974 with a single fixture format, the league was truly formed in 1975. Between 1975 and 1983 there was considerable movement of teams both in and out of the league. However, there remained a strong twelve team organisation with second teams until the complete reorganisation of the league in 1992.

Of the original eight founder members, Brewood, Cannock, Fordhouses, Milford Hall, Rugeley, Stafford, Wightwick & Finchfield and Wombourne, only Stafford had departed at this time. Subsequently, Market Drayton, Cannock & Rugeley, Penn and Himley joined. The latter three clubs were to dominate the league during the 80s and early 90s.

The league went through active progression from 1983; 3rd XI fixtures were introduced that year and Knock-Out competitions commenced in 1986.

The most successful clubs have been Fordhouses, who won eight league championships until they were promoted to the Premier League

Staffordshire Club Championship

in 1999, and Penn, who won eight league cups in 10 years until they also departed to premier league cricket in 1999.

Although some modifications have been necessary with the growth of the league following its expansion in 1992, the rules have generally remained fairly constant. The expansion involved incorporating both the Star League and the Wolverhampton Works League, effectively increasing the 12-club, 24-team, 2-division set up to a 90-team, 8-division organisation. Today there are 38 clubs, 88 teams and 8 divisions.

Notable changes have included the introduction of neutral umpires, professional/overseas players, some amendments to overs and bonus points, duty of care and stricter disciplinary codes as the competition becomes more apparent allied to relegation and promotion issues. Unlike many leagues we have not applied fielding restrictions.

Prior to the link as the Staffordshire feeder to the Birmingham and District Premier League in 1999 the league had a superb period of success at representation level, winning the Midland Club Cricket Conference inter league cup in 1993, 1997 and 1999.

Since 1999 Fordhouses, Penn, Penkridge, Himley, Wednesbury, Wheaton Aston and Beacon have been promoted to the Premier League. Added to that Cannock went to the Premier League via the Midland Clubs Championship. Notably, Cannock have already won the Premier Division and Himley in three successive seasons of promotion became runners up in the Premier Division and won the League Challenge Cup.

The league has, over its 28-year history, been stable in it's organisation and administration by ensuring change takes place for the correct reasons and to keep pace with the overall changing philosophy around it.

Many excellent players have graced league grounds including International, First Class, Minor Counties and Youth representatives. The league is pro-active in cricket development, coaching and assisting clubs to 'raise their standards'.

The challenge now is to continue with the excellent progress that has given many of our clubs the opportunity to operate at a higher level and subsequently denuded the league of its strength. We will continue to strive to raise the standards of our member clubs which significantly includes teams from all of our promoted premier league clubs plus Wolverhampton, Smethwick and Cannock.

Sadly the league has been unable to attract a sponsor while lesser leagues have managed to do so, but careful financial management has ensured no diminution in organisational standards.

2006 League Tables

DIVISION 1

	P	W	L	WD	LD	D	T	Ab	Pts
Old Wulfs Tettenhall	22	14	2	2	1			3	369
Penkridge	22	12		4	2	1		3	337
Aldridge	21	9	3	4	2			3	250
Wednesbury	22	7	3	4	4			4	223
Milford Hall	22	6	4	5	3			4	222
Lichfield	22	5	9	4	2			2	199
Highcroft & Gt Barr	21	6	7	1	2			5	168
Whittington*	22	5	11	2				4	167
Cannock & Rugeley	22	4	7	0	5	1		5	142
Brewood +	22	4	10	2	2			4	140
Swindon	22	3	12	1	5			1	131
Coseley	22	3	10	1	2			6	111

* Deducted 3 Points for Slow Over Rate
+ Deducted 2 Points for Slow Over Rate

DIVISION 2

	P	W	L	WD	LD	D	T	Ab	Pts
Hammerwich	22	16	1	3				2	376
Bloxwich	22	14	2	3	1			2	351
W'wick & Finchfield	22	9	4	2	2			5	256
Church Eaton	22	9	8	1				2	213
Springvale	22	8	7	2	2			3	212
Rushall	22	7	9	1	3			2	200
Rugeley	22	8	8		3			3	197
Blakenall	22	5	7	3	1			5	195
Armitage	22	8	10		1			3	189
W'hampton Danes	22	5	12	3	1			1	159
Codsall	22	4	13		1			4	125
Willenhall	22	3	15	1	1			2	106

Staffordshire Club Championship

DIVISION 3

	P	W	L	WD	LD	D	T	Ab	Pts
Himley	22	14	2	3				3	357
Penn	22	12	1	5	2			2	335
Quinton	22	10	6	1	1			4	268
Wombourne	22	9	8	1	1			3	230
Swindon	22	9	5	1	2			5	221
Aldridge	22	9	7	1	1			4	220
Penkridge	22	7	10	1	2		1	1	216
Wednesbury	22	8	7		1			6	202
H'croft & Great Barr	22	6	12	2				2	172
Bloxwich	22	5	10	1	3			3	147
Cannock & Rugeley	21	5	11		3		1	1	132
Fordhouses	21	1	15	2	1			2	73

DIVISION 1a

	P	W	L	WD	LD	D	T	Ab	Pts
Milford Hall	22	11	2	4	3			2	303
Old Wulfs Tettenhall	22	9	1	3	3			6	259
Aldridge	22	9	3	2	4		1	3	258
Penkridge	22	5	5	7	3			2	224
Wednesbury	22	7	6	1	4			4	208
Brewood	22	5	6	5	3		1	2	208
Lichfield	22	6	5	5	1			5	205
Swindon	22	6	8	5				3	203
Hammerwich	22	6	9	2	4			1	199
T'hall Coll Wergs	22	5	9	1	2			5	165
Cannock & Rugeley	22	3	6	2	7			4	147
Coseley	22	1	12	1	5			3	75

DIVISION 2A

	P	W	L	WD	LD	D	T	Ab	Pts
Bloxwich	21	11	3	2	1		1	3	307
H'croft & Gt Barr	22	9	2	6	1			4	286
Rugeley	22	8	6	1	4	1		2	219
Penn	22	5	6	5	1		1	4	201
Whittington	22	6	9	2	3		1	1	197
Beacon	22	5	9	3	1	1	1	2	190
Milford Hall	21	6	8	2	3			2	187
W'wick & Finchfield	21	6	5	3	3			4	185
Springvale	22	6	8	2	2			4	178
Old Wulfs Tettenhall	21	5	5	2	3			6	168
Blakenall	22	6	7		3			6	164
W'hampton Courts	22	4	10	1	3			4	141

DIVISION 3a

	P	W	L	WD	LD	D	T	Ab	Pts
Church Eaton	22	14	3	3	2				370
Codsall	22	14	1	4	2			1	341
Rushall	22	14	4	1				3	337
Armitage	21	11	4	3	1			2	298
Himley	22	11	5	2	2			2	280
Wednesbury	22	7	10		1			4	178
Aldridge	22	7	10		3			2	167
Bloxwich	22	6	12		2			2	157
Penkridge	22	3	9	6	3			1	155
H'croft & Great Barr	22	4	11	2	2			3	151
Wombourne	22	4	13					5	118
Fordhouses	21	2	15		3			1	70

DIVISION 4 - PLATE - GROUP

	P	W	L	WD	LD	D	T	Ab	Pts
Beacon	5	4						1	94
Brewood	5	3	1	1					81
Old Wulfs Tettenhall	5	3		1				1	75
Penn	5	2	3						55
Himley	5	1	4						30
Coseley	5		5						1

DIVISION 4 - PLATE - GROUP 2

	P	W	L	WD	LD	D	T	Ab	Pts
Rugeley	5	4						1	91
Hammerwich	5	3	1					1	74
Cannock	5	2	2		1				53
Smethwick	5	1	1	1				2	41
Aston Unity	5	1	2					2	31
Willenhall	5		5						3

Plate Final held 9th September 2006 - Winners Rugeley CC, Runners-Up Beacon CC

2007 Member clubs

Aldridge
The Stick and Wicket Club
The Green, Off High St
WS9 8NH

Armitage
Westfields Road
Armitage WS15 4AH

Aston Unity
Coppice Lane, Bassett's Pole,
Sutton Coldfield B78 2BS

Beacon
Finchfield Hockey Club,
Trysull Road, Wombourne
WV5 8DQ

Blakenall
Broad Way, High Heath,
Pelsall, Walsall, WS4 1BW

Bloxwich
Stafford Road
Bloxwich, WS3 3NJ

Brewood
Deansfield, Four Ashes Rd
Brewood

Cannock
The Morris Ground,
Church Lane, Hatherton,
Cannock WS11 1RR

Cannock And Rugeley
Rawnsley, Cannock

Church Eaton
Glebelands Sports Assoc
Church Eaton, Staffs

Codsall
Codsall Village Hall,
Wolverhampton Road,
Codsall, WV8 1PW

Coseley
Church Road, Coseley WV14

Essington and Great Wryley
Ground TBC

Fordhouses
Wobaston Road, Pendeford,
Wolverhampton WV9 9EW

Hammerwich
Burntwood Rd
Hammerwich

Highcroft and Great Barr Unity
Highcroft Sports and Social
Club, Slade Rd
Stockland Green, Erdington

Himley
Stourbridge Road (A449),
Himley DY3 3PH

Lichfield
Collins Hill, Eastern Avenue,
Lichfield, WS13 7SG

Milford Hall
Main Road
Milford, ST17 0UW

Old Wulfs Tettenhall
253a Castlecroft Road,
Wolverhampton WV3 8NA

Penkridge
Cannock Road,
Pillaton, Penkridge

Penn
Mount Road, Penn,
Wolverhampton WV4 5RU
Tel: 01902 331546

Quinton

Rugeley
Chaseley Road, Rugeley

Rushall
Carter Park, Pelsall Lane
Rushall

Smethwick
Broomfield, The Uplands,
Smethwick B67 6BJ

Springvale
Millfield Rd
Bilston
WV14 0QS

Swindon
Hinksford Lane
Swindon
Wall Heath
DY3 4NU

Wednesbury
Wood Green Road
Wednesbury

Whittington
Bit End Field,
Fisherwick Road
Whittington WS14

Willenhall
Wingfoot Park,
Stafford Road, Wolverhampton,
WV10 6DH

Wightwick And Finchfield
Castlecroft,
Wolverhampton

Wombourne
Church Road, Wombourne,
Wolverhampton WV5 9EZ

Wolverhampton
Danescourt Road, Tettenhall,
Wolverhampton

2007 Fixtures

DIVISION 1

21-Apr - 1:30 PM
Aldridge	vWednesbury
Beacon	vMilford Hall
Brewood	vPenkridge
Cannock & R	vBloxwich
Hammerwich	vLichfield
H'ft & GtBU	vWhittington

28-Apr - 1:30 PM
Bloxwich	vBeacon
Lichfield	vBrewood
Milford Hall	vH'ft & GtBU
Penkridge	vAldridge
Wednesbury	vCannock & R
Whittington	vHammerwich

05-May - 1:30 PM
Brewood	vBloxwich
Cannock & R	vLichfield
H'ft & GtBU	vBeacon
Milford Hall	vAldridge
Penkridge	vWhittington
Wednesbury	vHammerwich

12-May - 1:30 PM
Aldridge	vBrewood
Beacon	vCannock & R
Hammerwich	vBloxwich
H'ft & GtBU	vWednesbury
Lichfield	vPenkridge
Whittington	vMilford Hall

19-May - 1:30 PM
Beacon	vBrewood
Bloxwich	vAldridge
Hammerwich	vH'ft & GtBU
Milford Hall	vLichfield
Penkridge	vCannock & R
Wednesbury	vWhittington

26-May - 1:30 PM
Bloxwich	vH'ft & GtBU
Brewood	vWednesbury
Cannock & R	vMilford Hall
Lichfield	vAldridge
Penkridge	vHammerwich
Whittington	vBeacon

02-Jun - 1:30 PM
Aldridge	vHammerwich
Beacon	vPenkridge
H'ft & GtBU	vCannock & R
Lichfield	vWednesbury
Milford Hall	vBrewood
Whittington	vBloxwich

09-Jun - 1:30 PM
Aldridge	vBeacon
Cannock & R	vWhittington
Hammerwich	vBrewood
H'ft & GtBU	vLichfield
Milford Hall	vPenkridge
Wednesbury	vBloxwich

16-Jun - 1:30 PM
Beacon	vLichfield
Bloxwich	vMilford Hall
Brewood	vH'ft & GtBU
Cannock & R	vHammerwich
Penkridge	vWednesbury
Whittington	vAldridge

23-Jun - 1:30 PM
Aldridge	vCannock & R
Beacon	vWednesbury
Brewood	vWhittington
H'ft & GtBU	vPenkridge
Lichfield	vBloxwich
Milford Hall	vHammerwich

30-Jun - 1:30 PM
Aldridge	vH'ft & GtBU
Cannock & R	vBrewood
Hammerwich	vBeacon
Penkridge	vBloxwich
Wednesbury	vMilford Hall
Whittington	vLichfield

07-Jul - 1:30 PM
Bloxwich	vCannock & R
Lichfield	vHammerwich
Milford Hall	vBeacon
Penkridge	vBrewood
Wednesbury	vAldridge
Whittington	vH'ft & GtBU

14-Jul - 1:30 PM
Aldridge	vPenkridge
Beacon	vBloxwich
Brewood	vLichfield
Cannock & R	vWednesbury
Hammerwich	vWhittington
H'ft & GtBU	vMilford Hall

21-Jul - 1:30 PM
Aldridge	vMilford Hall
Beacon	vH'ft & GtBU
Bloxwich	vBrewood
Hammerwich	vWednesbury
Lichfield	vCannock & R
Whittington	vPenkridge

28-Jul - 1:30 PM
Bloxwich	vHammerwich
Brewood	vAldridge
Cannock & R	vBeacon
Milford Hall	vWhittington

Penkridge · vLichfield
Wednesbury · vH'ft & GtBU

04-Aug - 1:30 PM
Aldridge	vBloxwich
Brewood	vBeacon
Cannock & R	vPenkridge
H'ft & GtBU	vHammerwich
Lichfield	vMilford Hall
Whittington	vWednesbury

11-Aug - 1:30 PM
Aldridge	vLichfield
Beacon	vWhittington
Hammerwich	vPenkridge
H'ft & GtBU	vBloxwich
Milford Hall	vCannock & R
Wednesbury	vBrewood

18-Aug - 1:00 PM
Bloxwich	vWhittington
Brewood	vMilford Hall
Cannock & R	vH'ft & GtBU
Hammerwich	vAldridge
Penkridge	vBeacon
Wednesbury	vLichfield

25-Aug - 1:00 PM
Beacon	vAldridge
Bloxwich	vWednesbury
Brewood	vHammerwich
Lichfield	vH'ft & GtBU
Penkridge	vMilford Hall
Whittington	vCannock & R

01-Sep - 12:30 PM
Aldridge	vWhittington
Hammerwich	vCannock & R
H'ft & GtBU	vBrewood
Milford Hall	vBloxwich
Lichfield	vBeacon
Wednesbury	vPenkridge

08-Sep - 12:30 PM
Bloxwich	vLichfield
Cannock & R	vAldridge
Hammerwich	vMilford Hall
Penkridge	vH'ft & GtBU
Wednesbury	vBeacon
Whittington	vBrewood

15-Sep - 12:30 PM
Beacon	vHammerwich
Bloxwich	vPenkridge
Brewood	vCannock & R
H'ft & GtBU	vAldridge
Lichfield	vWhittington
Milford Hall	vWednesbury

Staffordshire Club Championship

DIVISION 2

21-Apr - 1:30 PM
Armitage   vWillenhall
Church Eaton vWalsll YPF
Coseley   vW'ton Danes
Rugeley   vSpringvale
Rushall   vW'wick & F.
Swindon   vCodsall

28-Apr - 1:30 PM
Codsall   vChurch Eaton
Springvale   vRushall
Walsll YPF   vCoseley
W'wick & F.   vArmitage
Willenhall   vSwindon
W'ton Danes   vRugeley

05-May - 1:30 PM
Coseley   vChurch Eaton
Rushall   vCodsall
Swindon   vSpringvale
Walsll YPF   vArmitage
W'wick & F.   vW'ton Danes
Willenhall   vRugeley

12-May - 1:30 PM
Armitage   vRushall
Church Eaton vSwindon
Coseley   vWillenhall
Rugeley   vCodsall
Springvale   vW'wick & F.
W'ton Danes   vWalsll YPF

19-May - 1:30 PM
Church Eaton vRushall
Codsall   vArmitage
Rugeley   vCoseley
Walsll YPF   vSpringvale
W'wick & F.   vSwindon
Willenhall   vW'ton Danes

26-May - 1:30 PM
Codsall   vCoseley
Rushall   vWillenhall
Springvale   vArmitage
Swindon   vWalsll YPF
W'wick & F.   vRugeley
W'ton Danes   vChurch Eaton

02-Jun - 1:30 PM
Armitage   vRugeley
Church Eaton vW'wick & F.
Coseley   vSwindon
Springvale   vWillenhall
Walsll YPF   vRushall
W'ton Danes   vCodsall

09-Jun - 1:30 PM
Armitage   vChurch Eaton
Coseley   vSpringvale
Rugeley   vRushall
Swindon   vW'ton Danes
Walsll YPF   vW'wick & F.
Willenhall   vCodsall

16-Jun - 1:30 PM
Church Eaton vSpringvale
Codsall   vWalsll YPF
Rushall   vCoseley
Swindon   vRugeley
W'wick & F.   vWillenhall
W'ton Danes   vArmitage

23-Jun - 1:30 PM
Armitage   vSwindon
Church Eaton vWillenhall
Coseley   vW'wick & F.
Rushall   vW'ton Danes
Springvale   vCodsall
Walsll YPF   vRugeley

30-Jun - 1:30 PM
Armitage   vCoseley
Rugeley   vChurch Eaton
Swindon   vRushall
W'wick & F.   vCodsall
Willenhall   vWalsll YPF
W'ton Danes   vSpringvale

07-Jul - 1:30 PM
Codsall   vSwindon
Springvale   vRugeley
Walsll YPF   vChurch Eaton
W'wick & F.   vRushall
Willenhall   vArmitage
W'ton Danes   vCoseley

14-Jul - 1:30 PM
Armitage   vW'wick & F.
Church Eaton vCodsall
Coseley   vWalsll YPF
Rugeley   vW'ton Danes
Rushall   vSpringvale
Swindon   vWillenhall

21-Jul - 1:30 PM
Armitage   vWalsll YPF
Church Eaton vCoseley
Codsall   vRushall
Rugeley   vWillenhall
Springvale   vSwindon
W'ton Danes   vW'wick & F.

28-Jul - 1:30 PM
Codsall   vRugeley
Rushall   vArmitage
Swindon   vChurch Eaton

Walsll YPF   vW'ton Danes
W'wick & F.   vSpringvale
Willenhall   vCoseley

04-Aug - 1:30 PM
Armitage   vCodsall
Coseley   vRugeley
Rushall   vChurch Eaton
Springvale   vWalsll YPF
Swindon   vW'wick & F.
W'ton Danes   vWillenhall

11-Aug - 1:30 PM
Armitage   vSpringvale
Church Eaton vW'ton Danes
Coseley   vCodsall
Rugeley   vW'wick & F.
Walsll YPF   vSwindon
Willenhall   vRushall

18-Aug - 1:00 PM
Codsall   vW'ton Danes
Rugeley   vArmitage
Rushall   vWalsll YPF
Swindon   vCoseley
W'wick & F.   vChurch Eaton
Willenhall   vSpringvale

25-Aug - 1:00 PM
Church Eaton vArmitage
Codsall   vWillenhall
Rushall   vRugeley
Springvale   vCoseley
W'wick & F.   vWalsll YPF
W'ton Danes   vSwindon

01-Sep - 12:30 PM
Armitage   vW'ton Danes
Coseley   vRushall
Rugeley   vSwindon
Springvale   vChurch Eaton
Walsll YPF   vCodsall
Willenhall   vW'wick & F.

08-Sep - 12:30 PM
Codsall   vSpringvale
Rugeley   vWalsll YPF
Swindon   vArmitage
W'wick & F.   vCoseley
Willenhall   vChurch Eaton
W'ton Danes   vRushall

15-Sep - 12:30 PM
Church Eaton vRugeley
Codsall   vW'wick & F.
Coseley   vArmitage
Rushall   vSwindon
Springvale   vW'ton Danes
Walsll YPF   vWillenhall

DIVISION 3

21-Apr - 1:30 PM
Aldridge   vSwindon
Cannock & R   v Penn
Ess. & GtWy   vWednesbury
H'ft & GtBU   vBloxwich
Himley   vPenkridge
Quinton   vWombourne

28-Apr - 1:30 PM
Bloxwich   vAldridge
Penkridge   vEss. & GtWy
Penn   vH'ft & GtBU
Swindon   vQuinton
Wednesbury   vCannock & R
Wombourne   vHimley

05-May - 1:30 PM
Ess. & GtWy   vBloxwich
H'ft & GtBU   vPenkridge
Penn   vHimley
Quinton   vAldridge
Swindon   vCannock & R
Wednesbury   vWombourne

12-May - 1:30 PM
Aldridge   vH'ft & GtBU
Cannock & R   vEss. & GtWy
Himley   vBloxwich
Penkridge   vWednesbury
Quinton   v Penn
Wombourne   vSwindon

19-May - 1:30 PM
Aldridge   vEss. & GtWy
Bloxwich   vCannock & R
Himley   vQuinton
Penn   vWombourne
Swindon   vPenkridge
Wednesbury   vH'ft & GtBU

26-May - 1:30 PM
Bloxwich   vQuinton
Ess. & GtWy   v Penn
H'ft & GtBU   vSwindon
Penkridge   vCannock & R
Wednesbury   vHimley
Wombourne   vAldridge

02-Jun - 1:30 PM
Aldridge   vWednesbury
Cannock & R   vHimley
Penkridge   v Penn
Quinton   vH'ft & GtBU
Swindon   vEss. & GtWy
Wombourne   vBloxwich

09-Jun - 1:30 PM
Cannock & R   vAldridge
H'ft & GtBU   vWombourne
Himley   vEss. & GtWy
Penn   vBloxwich
Quinton   vPenkridge
Swindon   vWednesbury

16-Jun - 1:30 PM
Aldridge   vPenkridge
Bloxwich   vSwindon
Ess. & GtWy   vQuinton
H'ft & GtBU   vHimley
Wednesbury   v Penn
Wombourne   vCannock & R

23-Jun - 1:30 PM
Aldridge   v Penn
Cannock & R   vH'ft & GtBU
Ess. & GtWy   vWombourne
Penkridge   vBloxwich
Quinton   vWednesbury
Swindon   vHimley

30-Jun - 1:30 PM
Cannock & R   vQuinton
H'ft & GtBU   vEss. & GtWy
Himley   vAldridge
Penn   vSwindon
Wednesbury   vBloxwich
Wombourne   vPenkridge

07-Jul - 1:30 PM
Bloxwich   vH'ft & GtBU
Penkridge   vHimley
Penn   vCannock & R
Swindon   vAldridge
Wednesbury   vEss. & GtWy
Wombourne   vQuinton

14-Jul - 1:30 PM
Aldridge   vBloxwich
Cannock & R   vWednesbury
Ess. & GtWy   vPenkridge
H'ft & GtBU   v Penn
Himley   vWombourne
Quinton   vSwindon

21-Jul - 1:30 PM
Aldridge   vQuinton
Bloxwich   vEss. & GtWy
Cannock & R   vSwindon
Himley   v Penn
Penkridge   vH'ft & GtBU
Wombourne   vWednesbury

28-Jul - 1:30 PM
Bloxwich   vHimley
Ess. & GtWy   vCannock & R
H'ft & GtBU   vAldridge

Penn   vQuinton
Penn   vQuinton
Swindon   vWombourne
Wednesbury   vPenkridge

04-Aug - 1:30 PM
Cannock & R   vBloxwich
Ess. & GtWy   vAldridge
H'ft & GtBU   vWednesbury
Penkridge   vSwindon
Quinton   vHimley
Wombourne   v Penn

11-Aug - 1:30 PM
Aldridge   vWombourne
Cannock & R   vPenkridge
Himley   vWednesbury
Penn   vEss. & GtWy
Quinton   vBloxwich
Swindon   vH'ft & GtBU

18-Aug - 1:00 PM
Bloxwich   vWombourne
Ess. & GtWy   vSwindon
H'ft & GtBU   vQuinton
Himley   vCannock & R
Penn   vPenkridge
Wednesbury   vAldridge

25-Aug - 1:00 PM
Aldridge   vCannock & R
Bloxwich   v Penn
Ess. & GtWy   vHimley
Penkridge   vQuinton
Wednesbury   vSwindon
Wombourne   vH'ft & GtBU

08-Sep - 12:30 PM
Bloxwich   vPenkridge
H'ft & GtBU   vCannock & R
Himley   vSwindon
Penn   vAldridge
Wednesbury   vQuinton
Wombourne   vEss. & GtWy

01-Sep - 12:30 PM
Cannock & R   vWombourne
Himley   vH'ft & GtBU
Penkridge   vAldridge
Penn   vWednesbury
Quinton   vEss. & GtWy
Swindon   vBloxwich

15-Sep - 12:30 PM
Aldridge   vHimley
Bloxwich   vWednesbury
Ess. & GtWy   vH'ft & GtBU
Penkridge   vWombourne
Quinton   vCannock & R
Swindon   v Penn

Staffordshire Club Championship

DIVISION 1A

21-Apr - 1:30 PM
Bloxwich	vSwindon
Lichfield	vHammerwich
Milford Hall	vBeacon
Penkridge	vBrewood
Tett Coll Ws	vH'ft & GtBU
Wednesbury	vAldridge

28-Apr - 1:30 PM
Aldridge	vPenkridge
Beacon	vBloxwich
Brewood	vLichfield
Hammerwich	vTett Coll Ws
H'ft & GtBU	vMilford Hall
Swindon	vWednesbury

05-May - 1:30 PM
Aldridge	vMilford Hall
Beacon	vH'ft & GtBU
Bloxwich	vBrewood
Hammerwich	vWednesbury
Lichfield	vSwindon
Tett Coll Ws	vPenkridge

12-May - 1:30 PM
Bloxwich	vHammerwich
Brewood	vAldridge
Milford Hall	vTett Coll Ws
Penkridge	vLichfield
Swindon	vBeacon
Wednesbury	vH'ft & GtBU

19-May - 1:30 PM
Aldridge	vBloxwich
Brewood	vBeacon
H'ft & GtBU	vHammerwich
Lichfield	vMilford Hall
Swindon	vPenkridge
Tett Coll Ws	vWednesbury

26-May - 1:30 PM
Aldridge	vLichfield
Beacon	vTett Coll Ws
Hammerwich	vPenkridge
H'ft & GtBU	vBloxwich
Milford Hall	vSwindon
Wednesbury	vBrewood

02-Jun - 1:30 PM
Bloxwich	vTett Coll Ws
Brewood	vMilford Hall
Hammerwich	vAldridge
Penkridge	vBeacon
Swindon	vH'ft & GtBU
Wednesbury	vLichfield

09-Jun - 1:30 PM
Beacon	vAldridge
Bloxwich	vWednesbury
Brewood	vHammerwich
Lichfield	vH'ft & GtBU
Penkridge	vMilford Hall
Tett Coll Ws	vSwindon

16-Jun - 1:30 PM
Aldridge	vTett Coll Ws
Hammerwich	vSwindon
H'ft & GtBU	vBrewood
Milford Hall	vBloxwich
Lichfield	vBeacon
Wednesbury	vPenkridge

23-Jun - 1:30 PM
Bloxwich	vLichfield
Hammerwich	vMilford Hall
Penkridge	vH'ft & GtBU
Swindon	vAldridge
Tett Coll Ws	vBrewood
Wednesbury	vBeacon

30-Jun - 1:30 PM
Beacon	vHammerwich
Bloxwich	vPenkridge
Brewood	vSwindon
H'ft & GtBU	vAldridge
Lichfield	vTett Coll Ws
Milford Hall	vWednesbury

07-Jul - 1:30 PM
Aldridge	vWednesbury
Beacon	vMilford Hall
Brewood	vPenkridge
Hammerwich	vLichfield
H'ft & GtBU	vTett Coll Ws
Swindon	vBloxwich

14-Jul - 1:30 PM
Bloxwich	vBeacon
Lichfield	vBrewood
Milford Hall	vH'ft & GtBU
Penkridge	vAldridge
Tett Coll Ws	vHammerwich
Wednesbury	vSwindon

21-Jul - 1:30 PM
Brewood	vBloxwich
H'ft & GtBU	vBeacon
Milford Hall	vAldridge
Penkridge	vTett Coll Ws
Swindon	vLichfield
Wednesbury	vHammerwich

28-Jul - 1:30 PM
Aldridge	vBrewood
Beacon	vSwindon
Hammerwich	vBloxwich
H'ft & GtBU	vWednesbury
Lichfield	vPenkridge
Tett Coll Ws	vMilford Hall

04-Aug - 1:30 PM
Beacon	vBrewood
Bloxwich	vAldridge
Hammerwich	vH'ft & GtBU
Milford Hall	vLichfield
Penkridge	vSwindon
Wednesbury	vTett Coll Ws

11-Aug - 1:30 PM
Bloxwich	vH'ft & GtBU
Brewood	vWednesbury
Lichfield	vAldridge
Penkridge	vHammerwich
Swindon	vMilford Hall
Tett Coll Ws	vBeacon

18-Aug - 1:00 PM
Aldridge	vHammerwich
Beacon	vPenkridge
H'ft & GtBU	vSwindon
Lichfield	vWednesbury
Milford Hall	vBrewood
Tett Coll Ws	vBloxwich

25-Aug - 1:00 PM
Aldridge	vBeacon
Hammerwich	vBrewood
H'ft & GtBU	vLichfield
Milford Hall	vPenkridge
Swindon	vTett Coll Ws
Wednesbury	vBloxwich

01-Sep - 12:30 PM
Beacon	vLichfield
Bloxwich	vMilford Hall
Brewood	vH'ft & GtBU
Penkridge	vWednesbury
Swindon	vHammerwich
Tett Coll Ws	vAldridge

08-Sep - 12:30 PM
Aldridge	vSwindon
Beacon	vWednesbury
Brewood	vTett Coll Ws
H'ft & GtBU	vPenkridge
Lichfield	vBloxwich
Milford Hall	vHammerwich

15-Sep - 12:30 PM
Aldridge	vH'ft & GtBU
Hammerwich	vBeacon
Penkridge	vBloxwich
Swindon	vBrewood
Tett Coll Ws	vLichfield
Wednesbury	vMilford Hall

DIVISION 2A

21-Apr - 1:30 PM
Codsall	vCannock & R
Old W Tett.	vChurch Eaton
Penn	vBeacon
Springvale	vRugeley
Whittington	vCoseley
W'wick & F.	vMilford Hall

28-Apr - 1:30 PM
Beacon	vW'wick & F.
Cannock & R	vPenn
Church Eaton	vCodsall
Coseley	vOld W Tett.
Milford Hall	vSpringvale
Rugeley	vWhittington

05-May - 1:30 PM
Beacon	vOld W Tett.
Church Eaton	vCoseley
Codsall	vMilford Hall
Rugeley	vPenn
Springvale	vCannock & R
Whittington	vW'wick & F.

12-May - 1:30 PM
Cannock & R	vChurch Eaton
Codsall	vRugeley
Milford Hall	vBeacon
Old W Tett.	vWhittington
Penn	vCoseley
W'wick & F.	vSpringvale

19-May - 1:30 PM
Beacon	vCodsall
Cannock & R	vW'wick & F.
Coseley	vRugeley
Milford Hall	vChurch Eaton
Springvale	vOld W Tett.
Whittington	vPenn

26-May - 1:30 PM
Beacon	vSpringvale
Church Eaton	vWhittington
Coseley	vCodsall
Old W Tett.	vCannock & R
Penn	vMilford Hall
Rugeley	vW'wick & F.

02-Jun - 1:30 PM
Cannock & R	vCoseley
Codsall	vWhittington
Milford Hall	vOld W Tett.
Penn	vSpringvale
Rugeley	vBeacon
W'wick & F.	vChurch Eaton

09-Jun - 1:30 PM
Church Eaton	vBeacon
Codsall	vPenn
Milford Hall	vRugeley
Springvale	vCoseley
Whittington	vCannock & R
W'wick & F.	vOld W Tett.

16-Jun - 1:30 PM
Beacon	vWhittington
Coseley	vMilford Hall
Old W Tett.	vCodsall
Penn	vW'wick & F.
Rugeley	vCannock & R
Springvale	vChurch Eaton

23-Jun - 1:30 PM
Cannock & R	vBeacon
Codsall	vSpringvale
Penn	vChurch Eaton
Rugeley	vOld W Tett.
Whittington	vMilford Hall
W'wick & F.	vCoseley

30-Jun - 1:30 PM
Church Eaton	vRugeley
Codsall	vW'wick & F.
Coseley	vBeacon
Milford Hall	vCannock & R
Old W Tett.	vPenn
Springvale	vWhittington

07-Jul - 1:30 PM
Beacon	vPenn
Cannock & R	vCodsall
Church Eaton	vOld W Tett.
Coseley	vWhittington
Milford Hall	vW'wick & F.
Rugeley	vSpringvale

14-Jul - 1:30 PM
Codsall	vChurch Eaton
Old W Tett.	vCoseley
Penn	vCannock & R
Springvale	vMilford Hall
Whittington	vRugeley
W'wick & F.	vBeacon

21-Jul - 1:30 PM
Cannock & R	vSpringvale
Coseley	vChurch Eaton
Milford Hall	vCodsall
Old W Tett.	vBeacon
Penn	vRugeley
W'wick & F.	vWhittington

28-Jul - 1:30 PM
Beacon	vMilford Hall
Church Eaton	vCannock & R
Coseley	vPenn

04-Aug - 1:30 PM
Rugeley	vCodsall
Springvale	vW'wick & F.
Whittington	vOld W Tett.

04-Aug - 1:30 PM
Church Eaton	vMilford Hall
Codsall	vBeacon
Old W Tett.	vSpringvale
Penn	vWhittington
Rugeley	vCoseley
W'wick & F.	vCannock & R

11-Aug - 1:30 PM
Cannock & R	vOld W Tett.
Codsall	vCoseley
Milford Hall	vPenn
Springvale	vBeacon
Whittington	vChurch Eaton
W'wick & F.	vRugeley

18-Aug - 1:00 PM
Beacon	vRugeley
Church Eaton	vW'wick & F.
Coseley	vCannock & R
Old W Tett.	vMilford Hall
Springvale	vPenn
Whittington	vCodsall

25-Aug - 1:00 PM
Beacon	vChurch Eaton
Cannock & R	vWhittington
Coseley	vSpringvale
Old W Tett.	vW'wick & F.
Penn	vCodsall
Rugeley	vMilford Hall

01-Sep - 12:30 PM
Cannock & R	vRugeley
Church Eaton	vSpringvale
Codsall	vOld W Tett.
Milford Hall	vCoseley
Whittington	vBeacon
W'wick & F.	vPenn

08-Sep - 12:30 PM
Beacon	vCannock & R
Church Eaton	vPenn
Coseley	vW'wick & F.
Milford Hall	vWhittington
Old W Tett.	vRugeley
Springvale	vCodsall

15-Sep - 12:30 PM
Beacon	vCoseley
Cannock & R	vMilford Hall
Penn	vOld W Tett.
Rugeley	vChurch Eaton
Whittington	vSpringvale
W'wick & F.	vCodsall

Staffordshire Club Championship

DIVISION 3A

21-Apr - 1:30 PM
Bloxwich   vH'ft & GtBU
Fordhouses   vArmitage
Penkridge   vHimley
Walsall YPF   vAldridge
Wednesbury   vRushall
W'ton Courts   vBlakenall

28-Apr - 1:30 PM
Aldridge   vBloxwich
Armitage   vWednesbury
Blakenall   vWalsall YPF
H'ft & GtBU   vFordhouses
Himley   vW'ton Courts
Rushall   vPenkridge

05-May - 1:30 PM
Aldridge   vBlakenall
Armitage   vWalsall YPF
Bloxwich   vRushall
Himley   vFordhouses
Penkridge   vH'ft & GtBU
W'ton Courts   vWednesbury

12-May - 1:30 PM
Bloxwich   vHimley
Fordhouses   vBlakenall
H'ft & GtBU   vAldridge
Rushall   vArmitage
Walsall YPF   vW'ton Courts
Wednesbury   vPenkridge

19-May - 1:30 PM
Armitage   vBloxwich
Blakenall   vHimley
H'ft & GtBU   vWednesbury
Penkridge   vWalsall YPF
Rushall   vAldridge
W'ton Courts   vFordhouses

26-May - 1:30 PM
Aldridge   vW'ton Courts
Armitage   vPenkridge
Blakenall   vBloxwich
Fordhouses   vRushall
Himley   vWednesbury
Walsall YPF   vH'ft & GtBU

02-Jun - 1:30 PM
Bloxwich   vW'ton Courts
Fordhouses   vPenkridge
H'ft & GtBU   vBlakenall
Himley   vArmitage
Rushall   vWalsall YPF
Wednesbury   vAldridge

09-Jun - 1:30 PM
Aldridge   vArmitage
Bloxwich   vFordhouses
Penkridge   vBlakenall
Rushall   vHimley
Wednesbury   vWalsall YPF
W'ton Courts   vH'ft & GtBU

16-Jun - 1:30 PM
Armitage   vW'ton Courts
Blakenall   vRushall
Fordhouses   vWednesbury
Himley   vH'ft & GtBU
Penkridge   vAldridge
Walsall YPF   vBloxwich

23-Jun - 1:30 PM
Bloxwich   vPenkridge
Fordhouses   vAldridge
H'ft & GtBU   vArmitage
Himley   vWalsall YPF
Wednesbury   vBlakenall
W'ton Courts   vRushall

30-Jun - 1:30 PM
Aldridge   vHimley
Blakenall   vArmitage
Bloxwich   vWednesbury
Penkridge   vW'ton Courts
Rushall   vH'ft & GtBU
Walsall YPF   vFordhouses

07-Jul - 1:30 PM
Aldridge   vWalsall YPF
Armitage   vFordhouses
Blakenall   vW'ton Courts
H'ft & GtBU   vBloxwich
Himley   vPenkridge
Rushall   vWednesbury

14-Jul - 1:30 PM
Bloxwich   vAldridge
Fordhouses   vH'ft & GtBU
Penkridge   vRushall
Walsall YPF   vBlakenall
Wednesbury   vArmitage
W'ton Courts   vHimley

21-Jul - 1:30 PM
Blakenall   vAldridge
Fordhouses   vHimley
H'ft & GtBU   vPenkridge
Rushall   vBloxwich
Walsall YPF   vArmitage
Wednesbury   vW'ton Courts

28-Jul - 1:30 PM
Aldridge   vH'ft & GtBU
Armitage   vRushall
Blakenall   vFordhouses

Himley   vBloxwich
Penkridge   vWednesbury
W'ton Courts   vWalsall YPF

04-Aug - 1:30 PM
Aldridge   vRushall
Bloxwich   vArmitage
Fordhouses   vW'ton Courts
Himley   vBlakenall
Walsall YPF   vPenkridge
Wednesbury   vH'ft & GtBU

11-Aug - 1:30 PM
Bloxwich   vBlakenall
H'ft & GtBU   vWalsall YPF
Penkridge   vArmitage
Rushall   vFordhouses
Wednesbury   vHimley
W'ton Courts   vAldridge

18-Aug - 1:00 PM
Aldridge   vWednesbury
Armitage   vHimley
Blakenall   vH'ft & GtBU
Penkridge   vFordhouses
Walsall YPF   vRushall
W'ton Courts   vBloxwich

25-Aug - 1:00 PM
Armitage   vAldridge
Blakenall   vPenkridge
Fordhouses   vBloxwich
H'ft & GtBU   vW'ton Courts
Himley   vRushall
Walsall YPF   vWednesbury

01-Sep - 12:30 PM
Aldridge   vPenkridge
Bloxwich   vWalsall YPF
H'ft & GtBU   vHimley
Rushall   vBlakenall
Wednesbury   vFordhouses
W'ton Courts   vArmitage

08-Sep - 12:30 PM
Aldridge   vFordhouses
Armitage   vH'ft & GtBU
Blakenall   vWednesbury
Penkridge   vBloxwich
Rushall   vW'ton Courts
Walsall YPF   vHimley

15-Sep - 12:30 PM
Armitage   vBlakenall
Fordhouses   vWalsall YPF
H'ft & GtBU   vRushall
Himley   vAldridge
Wednesbury   vBloxwich
W'ton Courts   vPenkridge

DIVISION 4

19-May - 1:30 PM
Hammerwich vSmethwick
Old W Tett.   vWillenhall
Penn   vBrewood
Wombourne   vCannock

26-May - 1:30 PM
Brewood   vHammerwich
Cannock   vPenn
Smethwick   vOld W Tett.
Willenhall   vWombourne

02-Jun - 1:30 PM
Brewood   vCannock
Old W Tett.   vPenn
Smethwick   vWombourne
Willenhall   vHammerwich

09-Jun - 1:30 PM
Cannock   vOld W Tett.
Hammerwich vWombourne
Penn   vWillenhall
Smethwick   vBrewood

16-Jun - 1:30 PM
Brewood   vWillenhall
Cannock   vSmethwick
Hammerwich vPenn
Wombourne   vOld W Tett.

23-Jun - 1:30 PM
Old W Tett.   vHammerwich
Penn   vSmethwick
Willenhall   vCannock
Wombourne   vBrewood

30-Jun - 1:30 PM
Brewood   vOld W Tett.
Hammerwich vCannock
Penn   vWombourne
Smethwick   vWillenhall

07-Jul - 1:30 PM
Brewood   vPenn
Cannock   vWombourne
Old W Tett.   vWillenhall
Smethwick   vHammerwich

14-Jul - 1:30 PM
Hammerwich vBrewood
Penn   vCannock
Smethwick   vOld W Tett.
Wombourne   vWillenhall

21-Jul - 1:30 PM
Cannock   vBrewood
Hammerwich vWillenhall
Penn   vOld W Tett.
Smethwick   vWombourne

28-Jul - 1:30 PM
Brewood   vSmethwick
Old W Tett.   vCannock
Penn   vWillenhall
Wombourne   vHammerwich

04-Aug - 1:30 PM
Old W Tett.   vWombourne
Penn   vHammerwich
Smethwick   vCannock
Willenhall   vBrewood

11-Aug - 1:30 PM
Brewood   vWombourne
Cannock   vWillenhall
Hammerwich vOld W Tett.
Smethwick   vPenn

18-Aug - 1:00 PM
Brewood   vOld W Tett.
Cannock   vHammerwich
Smethwick   vWillenhall
Wombourne   vPenn

DIVISION 5

19-May - 1:30 PM
Coseley   vAston Unity
Rugeley   vBeacon
Springvale   vHimley
W'wick & F.   vFordhouses

26-May - 1:30 PM
Aston Unity   vSpringvale
Coseley   vFordhouses
Himley   vBeacon
Rugeley   vW'wick & F.

02-Jun - 1:30 PM
Coseley   vHimley
Rugeley   vAston Unity
Springvale   vFordhouses
W'wick & F.   vBeacon

09-Jun - 1:30 PM
Aston Unity   vW'wick & F.
Beacon   vSpringvale
Coseley   vRugeley
Himley   vFordhouses

16-Jun - 1:30 PM
Aston Unity   vFordhouses
Coseley   vBeacon
Rugeley   vHimley
Springvale   vW'wick & F.

23-Jun - 1:30 PM
Aston Unity   vHimley
Beacon   vFordhouses
Springvale   vRugeley
W'wick & F.   vCoseley

30-Jun - 1:30 PM
Beacon   vAston Unity
Fordhouses   vRugeley
Springvale   vCoseley
W'wick & F.   vHimley

07-Jul - 1:30 PM
Aston Unity   vCoseley
Fordhouses   vW'wick & F.
Himley   vSpringvale
Rugeley   vBeacon

14-Jul - 1:30 PM
Beacon   vHimley
Coseley   vFordhouses
Springvale   vAston Unity
W'wick & F.   vRugeley

21-Jul - 1:30 PM
Aston Unity   vRugeley
Beacon   vW'wick & F.
Coseley   vHimley
Springvale   vFordhouses

28-Jul - 1:30 PM
Fordhouses   vHimley
Rugeley   vCoseley
Springvale   vBeacon
W'wick & F.   vAston Unity

04-Aug - 1:30 PM
Aston Unity   vFordhouses
Beacon   vCoseley
Himley   vRugeley
W'wick & F.   vSpringvale

11-Aug - 1:30 PM
Coseley   vW'wick & F.
Fordhouses   vBeacon
Himley   vAston Unity
Rugeley   vSpringvale

18-Aug - 1:00 PM
Aston Unity   vBeacon
Coseley   vSpringvale
Himley   vW'wick & F.
Rugeley   vFordhouses

When Wednesbury hosted the World

by Chris Williams

IT'S HARD TO believe that 25 years ago Wednesbury Cricket Club hosted a number of matches in the ICC qualifying competition for the Cricket World Cup. On the 16th June 1982, Bermuda took on Malaysia and on 13th June 1986 Bangladesh took on Kenya. It is interesting to note that out of the four international teams that played at Wednesbury, Bangladesh is now a Test playing nation and Kenya and Bermuda will be playing in the World Cup in 2007 to be played in the West Indies.

I can remember that preparation for the first Bermuda v Malaysia match started well before the event and a wicket was chosen right in the centre of the square for the match. It must have been an excellent wicket as Bermuda smashed a massive 348-9 in 60 overs. This was probably a

At the toss for Bermuda v Malaysia

Len Middleton, Chairman of Wednesbury Sports Union outside the pavillion on the day. Note the flags of the two countries flying in the background.

record for the ground at the time and the highlight of the innings was an opening stand of 211 between Gladstone Brown (100) and Winston Reid (128).

Interestingly, there was no ball stop fencing at the ground at the time and I am sure that plenty of balls must have been hit into the neighbours' gardens. I can't remember any complaints at the time so perhaps our neighbours were a little more tolerant in those days. Zainon Mat (3-54) was the most successful of the Malaysia bowlers in his 12 over stint.

I suppose in those days 348 was a massive total to chase, and so it proved for Malaysia as they were bowled out for just 64 in reply. P.Banzeri (34) was the only Malaysian batsman to reach double figures and Elvin James took 5 wickets for just 2 runs in 7 overs to decimate the Malaysian innings. By the look of his bowling figures, Elvin was probably a little bit too quick for the Malaysian middle order! My only other memory of the match is one of the spectators sitting on the roof of the club next to the scoreboard and getting extremely drunk and waving a national flag around. I think it was one of the Malaysian supporters - perhaps it was their version of the barmy army. All clubs were given a stock of ties to sell to commemorate the world cup and I have still got mine and wear it on occasions for work.

Staffordshire Club Championship

The 1986 game was a low-scoring affair between Bangladesh and Kenya on what was a typical slow and low Wednesbury wicket. Bangladesh batted first and struggled to 143 all out in 54.4 overs. Minhajul Abadin (50) top scored with a gritty half-century and went on to play 27 one day internationals for his Country. Kenya finished just 10 runs short of the target as they were bowled out for 134 in 59 overs. Hitesh Mehta (32) and Edward Odumbe (27) top scored and the wickets were shared around the Bangladesh bowling attack.

The 1986 World Cup was also notable as Wednesbury took on Hong Kong in one of the warm up matches and won, probably the only success against an international team in the history of the club.

Stone clinch title

by Allan Smith

LONG TIME LEADERS Stone deservedly clinched the **North Staffs and South Cheshire Cricket League** premiership title having won 12 of their 22 matches to finish the season with a commanding 59 point lead over second placed Knypersley. Ten of their 12 successes were achieved batting second.

Led by Chris Banks, Stone also added the Staffordshire Cup and the Twenty/20 Trophy to their list of honours for the season. Their spin trio of professional Mo Hussain, Steve Dawson and talented teenager Russ Ballard played a key role in their success. Mo Hussain, as ever, contributed well with the bat and received good support from Shaun Jenkinson, Brian Sims and Phil Cheadle, who all topped the 500 run mark.

Knypersley took advantage of a final day eighth win of the season to jump up into second place. Professional Qaiser Abbas topped the 1000 run mark with Jonathon Cumberbatch the leading amateur batsman. Rob James managed to remain relatively injury free to claim 40 wickets whilst Neil Dutton went past the 500 mark in league wickets for the club. The club also lifted the Sentinel Talbot Cup to complete a fine season.

Three times champions Longton suffered there worst season for many years and only managed to pull clear of the bottom two spots in the closing stages. Runs weren't a particular problem with professional Sridharan Sriram topping 1000 and Peter Wilshaw and Mike Longmore both scoring heavily. The loss of departing professional Alfonso Thomas's wickets, coupled with the non appearance through injury of Dave Edwards, found their bowling resources stretched to the limit.

Checkley slip back into Division One after a seven year run in the top division. Goolam Bodi scored heavily for them with strong support from

"

Mo Hussain of Stone, whose bowling and batting helped Stone to the league title and Staffordshire Cup double.

Nick Hunt but, like a number of clubs, the lack of wicket taking was key to their demise.

It was a similar story for Little Stoke where Richard Harvey, in his first season as a professional topped the 1000 run mark, with Phil Walklate not far short of four figures. Despite Nick Bratt's efforts they were ineffective with the ball and they managed just one win all season and return to Division One after gaining promotion in 2002.

In Division 1, after finishing in third place in 2005, Wood Lane made no mistake this time around clinching their place in the premiership by

Sentinel Talbot Cup winners and Premier Division runners up, Knypersley.

finishing champions with a massive 98 point lead at the top of the table. Captain Jamie Jervis led from the front with the bat as he and Matt Hagan topped the 500 run tally. Gagandeep Singh was the destroyer with the ball, his 84 league wickets including all ten in the match against Stafford.

Hem Heath were indebted to a last day win over nearest rivals Leycett to snatch the second promotion spot. Aakash Chopra was another professional to go past the 1000 mark whilst left arm spinner Gareth Morris produced the goods with the ball following his switch from Longton to help the Double HH side to take their place with the big boys for the first time.

Leycett's early season problems without a professional probably cost them dear in the end as they paid for a poor run in and ended one place outside the promotion spots. Sumit Panda made his mark for the club whilst 16 year old Dan Redfern demonstrated his outstanding batting ability to hit 1000 runs in a season which saw him make a first team appearance for Derbyshire.

Norton slip into Division Two after a traumatic pre season which stretched their resources to the limit. The experienced Tony Dutton contributed usefully to their efforts as did Mark Graham and Greg Willott but to no avail.

Betley made it two successive relegations as their off the field tribulations, which saw their side decimated, found them facing an uphill struggle they were unable to overcome despite the gallant efforts of Adrian Butler.

It was a happy return for Bignall End and Caverswall, who clinched the promotion places from the newly formed Division Two. With all four leagues having come together under the North Staffs & South Cheshire League these two former members of the NSSCCL will be delighted to be back in the top two divisions.

After suffering relegation last year, as the third club to go down to help with the reorganisation, Bignall End have wasted no time in bouncing back up again led by the all round efforts of Tahir Mughal. Their 12 wins enabled Simon Howle's side lift the championship by 30 points.

Caverswall also bounce back at the first time of asking, but only by the narrowest of margins. After finishing level on points with Silverdale they clinched second place by virtue of having recorded one more victory than their rivals. Despite the loss of professional Abdul Rehman, replacement Arsalan Mir stepped into fill the gap handsomely, with the bat in particular. Richie Jervis was to the forefront with the ball for Danny Edge's side.

Blythe fielded no less than three different professionals during the season but still face life in Division Three after recording just three wins in a disappointing season. Hanford also picked up just three wins as they join Blythe in Division Three next year despite the battling efforts of Roger Davies.

After one season in the bottom division, Oakamoor are back up into Division Two after clinching the Division Three title by 18 points. All rounder Shadab Jakati was instrumental in ensuring John Wood's team bounced back at the first attempt. Eccleshall clinched the second promotion place with Mohit Goel once more playing a leading role for Carl Beasley's side to ensure their step up.

2006 League Tables

PREMIER DIVISION A

	P	wbf	wbs	lbf	lbs	d	a	BaP	BoP	Pen	Pts
Stone	22	2	10	3	0	5	2	36	24	0	310
Knypersley	22	4	4	4	2	5	3	43	29	1	251
Porthill Park	22	4	3	4	1	8	2	59	30	0	249
Audley	22	4	4	6	0	5	3	36	31	6	241
Leek	22	2	6	2	0	9	3	42	24	0	236
Barlaston	22	4	1	3	2	10	2	58	46	0	224
Moddershall	22	3	2	2	5	8	2	60	50	1	224
Burslem	22	0	7	5	3	4	3	47	28	0	215
Meir Heath	22	3	3	4	5	5	2	38	40	1	212
Longton	22	0	4	4	1	12	1	68	42	0	190
Checkley	22	1	2	2	5	9	3	53	49	1	166
Little Stoke	22	1	0	7	4	8	2	79	56	2	158

DIVISION 1 A

	P	wbf	wbs	lbf	lbs	d	a	BaP	BoP	Pen	Pts
Wood Lane	22	9	4	3	1	4	1	32	30	3	364
Hem Heath	22	1	9	0	4	4	4	27	34	0	266
Leycett	22	3	6	3	4	3	3	38	27	0	260
Cheadle	22	2	6	2	3	6	3	41	37	0	248
Crewe	22	3	5	2	4	6	2	40	32	5	242
Stafford	22	4	3	6	3	5	1	47	37	2	242
Kidsgrove	22	5	2	3	3	5	4	44	36	4	241
Elworth	22	3	4	5	3	5	2	44	38	1	236
Rode Park & Lawton	22	4	1	5	3	7	2	67	48	2	233
Sandyford	22	4	1	7	1	7	2	52	48	0	220
Norton, Staffs	22	2	3	4	5	7	1	56	43	0	209
Betley	22	0	2	6	6	7	1	53	54	0	147

DIVISION 2 A

	P	wbf	lbs	wbs	lbf	d	a	t	BaP	BoP	Pen	Pts
Bignall End	22	10	2	2	3	3	2	0	33	22	2	343
Caverswall	22	2	1	10	2	6	1	0	35	29	1	313
Silverdale	22	7	2	4	3	2	3	1	31	23	1	313
Oulton	22	6	3	3	2	6	2	0	45	37	5	287
Ashcombe Park	22	4	2	5	2	7	2	0	49	31	7	273
Whitmore	22	3	4	6	1	6	2	0	39	35	1	268
Haslington	22	3	2	3	6	5	3	0	47	36	2	216
Newcastle and H'hill	22	1	5	5	5	4	2	0	46	48	3	216
Weston	22	4	3	0	8	6	1	0	60	48	0	208
J G Meakin	22	1	5	4	3	6	3	0	58	40	1	202
Blythe	22	1	6	2	6	4	2	1	58	48	2	174
Hanford	22	0	7	3	6	3	3	0	68	35	3	160

DIVISION 3 A

	P	wbf	lbs	wbs	lbf	d	a	t	BaP	BoP	Pen	Pts
Oakamoor	20	5	3	5	2	4	1	0	29	30	0	284
Eccleshall	20	3	3	6	0	5	2	1	41	35	0	276
Endon	20	6	1	3	2	5	3	0	36	27	3	270
Woore	20	2	3	6	3	5	1	0	37	37	0	244
Bagnall	20	4	1	3	4	5	3	0	44	28	1	231
Stanfields	20	3	2	3	0	10	2	0	51	37	0	223
Norton-in-Hales	20	2	2	3	5	6	2	0	58	36	0	204
Wedgwood	20	0	2	3	3	9	2	1	51	48	0	164
Buxton	20	1	2	3	5	6	3	0	40	37	1	161
Swynnerton Park	20	1	4	1	9	4	1	0	61	47	0	153
Fenton	20	0	4	1	4	9	2	0	70	57	0	147

PREMIER DIVISION B

	P	wbf	wbs	lbf	lbs	d	a	BaP	BoP	Pen	Pts
Leek	22	4	10	2	2	2	2	26	16	0	342
Stone	22	2	9	4	1	4	2	39	27	0	296
Porthill Park	22	3	7	3	2	3	4	34	26	0	275
Moddershall	22	1	7	3	0	8	3	46	36	3	244
Knypersley	22	2	5	4	2	6	3	48	39	1	236
Barlaston	22	3	1	5	1	9	3	67	50	0	212
Checkley	22	3	2	10	1	4	2	62	28	1	204
Little Stoke	22	2	4	3	1	7	5	47	28	2	203
Audley	22	2	2	2	3	9	4	57	44	0	191
Burslem	22	1	3	3	3	8	4	47	44	1	175
Longton	22	0	2	6	4	6	4	40	42	0	122
Meir Heath	22	1	0	7	4	6	4	52	31	0	108

DIVISION 1 B

	P	wbf	wbs	lbf	lbs	d	a	BaP	BoP	Pen	Pts
Elworth	22	7	6	3	2	3	1	28	25	0	348
Rode Park & Lawton	22	6	7	1	3	3	2	26	24	0	340
Hem Heath	22	5	3	5	2	4	3	47	37	0	269
Leycett	22	5	4	1	3	4	5	31	27	0	263
Wood Lane	22	5	4	5	0	3	5	25	21	0	251
Cheadle	22	4	4	2	7	1	4	34	31	0	245
Stafford	22	4	3	3	1	8	3	40	32	1	231
Norton	22	5	2	3	5	3	4	39	37	25	216
Kidsgrove	21	2	5	5	3	3	3	29	34	2	211
Sandyford	22	3	2	4	8	3	2	40	41	1	195
Crewe	22	3	2	6	5	2	4	36	31	0	182
Betley	21	0	0	4	10	3	4	55	54	0	109

DIVISION 2 B

	P	wbf	wbs	lbf	lbs	d	a	BaP	BoP	Pen	Pts
Ashcombe Park	22	4	0	9	2	5	2	28	24	1	331
Oulton	22	3	1	7	2	6	3	37	31	1	282
Caverswall	22	7	2	1	4	6	2	43	37	0	275
Silverdale	22	6	2	3	2	5	4	36	26	0	272
J G Meakin	22	1	3	9	2	4	3	35	28	0	268
Newcastle and H'hill	22	2	3	5	2	6	4	56	37	0	243
Weston	22	2	4	6	5	2	3	42	29	0	241
Haslington	22	3	4	3	3	5	4	44	34	0	213
Whitmore	22	3	1	3	6	6	3	42	35	2	210
Blythe	22	1	2	2	9	5	3	50	33	0	148
Bignall End	22	1	5	1	7	5	3	49	40	1	133
Hanford	22	0	6	1	6	5	4	51	39	0	110

DIVISION 3 B

	P	wbf	wbs	lbf	lbs	d	a	BaP	BoP	Pen	Pts
Woore	20	5	3	5	0	5	2	30	27	0	282
Bagnall	20	6	3	3	1	3	4	20	32	0	262
Fenton	20	4	2	4	3	5	2	36	33	0	249
Wedgwood	20	4	3	4	2	3	4	32	27	1	238
Buxton	20	4	1	4	4	3	4	26	22	0	228
Norton-in-Hales	20	3	5	2	5	3	2	38	41	0	194
Swynnerton Park	20	2	3	3	4	7	1	38	38	1	185
Eccleshall	20	1	2	5	6	4	2	30	26	0	181
Endon	20	1	4	4	4	4	3	32	38	1	174
Oakamoor	20	0	2	4	7	3	4	44	31	0	155
Stanfields	20	1	3	4	6	4	2	30	19	0	154

Fenton face stiff challenge in Staffs Cup

FORTY-FIVE CLUBS have entered the Staffordshire Cup competition for the coming season. The first round on Sunday April 22nd will consist of 13 matches with 19 clubs receiving byes into the second round.

Fenton, who finished bottom of Championship Division 3 face the daunting task of entertaining Premiership champions and cup holders Stone at their Wheildon Road ground. Amongst the pick of the other first round ties there is an all North Staffs & South Cheshire League Premier Division clash between Leek and Audley whilst Barlaston travel to play Old Hill from the Birmingham League. Last year's runners-up Longton have home advantage over Stafford with Porthill Park entertaining Swynnerton Park from Division 3. Little Stoke and Checkley, who were both relegated from the Premier Division last season, are both drawn away in the opening round to Cheadle and Hanford respectively.

The full first round draw is:
Old Hill v Barlaston
Himley v Bronze
Leek v Audley
Oulton v Fordhouses
Cheadle v Little Stoke
Longton v Stafford
Leycett v Aldridge
Porthill Park v Swynnerton Park
Fenton v Stone
Penkridge v Kidsgrove
Cannock v Walsall
Smethwick v Cannock & Rugeley
Hanford v Checkley

Byes: Bagnall, Bignall End, Burslem, Creda Stanfields, Hem Heath, Knypersley, Lichfield, Meakins, Meir Heath, Moddershall, Newcastle &

Hartshill, Old Wulfs Tettenhall, Penn, Silverdale, West Bromwich Dartmouth, Whitmore, Wolverhampton, Wombourne, Wood Lane.

The draw for the second round to be played on Sunday May 6th is:

Silverdale v Longton or Stafford
West Bromwich Dartmouth v Old Hill or Barlaston
Himley or Bronze v Hem Heath
Wolverhampton v Meakins
Fenton or Stone v Wood Lane
Cannock or Walsall v Moddershall
Creda Stanfields v Bignall End
Whitmore v Burslem
Leycett or Aldridge v Knypersley
Cheadle or Little Stoke v Hanford v Checkley
Penkridge or Kidsgrove v Wombourne
Porthill Park or Swynnerton Park v Leek or Audley
Oulton or Fordhouses v Meir Heath
Old Wulfs Tettenhall v Newcastle & Hartshill
Penn v Smethwick or Cannock & Rugeley
Lichfield v Bagnall

The third round is scheduled to be played on Sunday June 10th.

The Cotswold Hills Cricket League

League Officials

CHAIRMAN
Ron Douglas
The Laurels, Pathlow, Stratford-upon-Avon, Warwickshire, CV37 0ES
Tel: (H) 01789 269233 (M) 07729 220415
Email: chairman@cotswold-hills-league.org

SECRETARY
Brian Parsons
2 Ash Close, Hatton Station, Warwick, CV35 7BL
Tel: (H) 01926 842878 (W) 0121 359 7777 (M) 07714 521415
Email: secretary@cotswold-hills-league.org

TREASURER
John Mould
3 Masters Close, Evesham, Worcestershire, WR11 6EL
Tel: (H) 01386 443352 (M) 07761 117503
Email: treasurer@cotswold-hills-league.org

FIXTURE SECRETARY
Ron Challinor
Sunbridge, The Stables, Moreton Paddox
Moreton Morrell, Warwickshire, CV35 9BU
Tel: (H) 01926 650110 (M) 07831 315889
Email: fixtures@cotswold-hills-league.org

WEBSITE ADDRESS: www.cotswold-hills-league.org

Bretforton make it two titles in a row

BRETFORTON followed their Cotswold Hills League First Division Championship of 2005 with the Premier Division title in 2006 by the astonishing margin of 50 points. Defending champions Exhall & Wixford finished as runners-up, continuing their consistent performance in the league in recent years.

Winchcombe, who were promoted in 2005 with Bretforton, did not manage anywhere near the same level of success and return to the First Division accompanied by Broadway, who had narrowly avoided that fate the previous season and who won just one game in 2006.

Wellesbourne are promoted as champions of the First Division and are joined in the top flight by Alcester & Ragley, who recovered well after relegation in 2005. Twyning appear to be in freefall and are relegated for the second consecutive season along with Claverdon after just a single season in the First Division.

Kineton had the distinction of collecting more points than any other club in all the seven divisions and being the only team to go through the season unbeaten, winning all 14 of their games that were not abandoned to the weather in the Second Division. Elmley Castle are promoted with them, but a lack of players at this club led to the withdrawal of their 2nd XI from the Sixth Division. It was decided that the fairest way to treat all of the Elmley Castle 2nd XI matches was to declare them all null and void and to award no points to any side as a result.

Woodbourne, Fladbury and Blockley won the Third, Fourth and Fifth Divisions respectively, whilst Alvechurch's 3rd XI triumphed in the bottom division.

2006 League Tables

PREMIER DIVISION

	P	W	L	T	A	BaP	BoP	Ded	Pts
Bretforton	18	13	1	0	4	75	79	0	304
Exhall & Wixford	18	10	4	0	4	74	60	0	254
Stratford Bards	18	8	5	0	5	65	58	0	228
Overbury	18	8	6	0	4	56	54	0	210
Moreton-in-Marsh	18	7	7	0	4	63	56	0	209
Earlswood	18	7	5	0	6	58	45	0	203
Shipston-on-Stour	18	7	7	0	4	49	50	0	189
Tanworth-in-Arden	18	5	9	0	4	49	51	0	170
Winchcombe	18	3	10	0	5	44	41	0	140
Broadway	18	1	15	0	2	40	34	0	94

FIRST DIVISION

	P	W	L	T	A	BaP	BoP	Ded	Pts
Wellesbourne	18	11	2	1	4	69	70	0	274
Alcester & Ragley	18	10	3	1	4	76	62	0	263
Ashton-under-Hill	18	11	2	0	5	71	45	0	251
Catherine-de-Barnes	18	9	3	1	5	63	48	0	231
Norton Lindsey	18	7	7	1	3	66	51	0	207
Bidford-on-Avon	18	7	8	0	3	60	51	0	196
Henley-in-Arden	18	6	7	0	5	56	50	0	191
Ebrington	18	3	10	0	5	50	32	0	137
Claverdon	18	1	12	0	5	58	33	0	126
Twyning	18	1	12	0	5	38	28	40	61

SECOND DIVISION

	P	W	L	T	A	BaP	BoP	Ded	Pts
Kineton	18	14	0	0	4	78	72	0	310
Elmley Castle	18	9	5	0	4	69	56	0	235
Warwick CC Staff	18	10	5	0	3	52	60	0	227
Chipping Campden	18	8	7	0	3	59	53	0	207
Leamington III	18	7	7	0	4	49	54	0	193
Rowington	18	6	9	0	3	58	52	0	185
Stratford-upon-Avon III	18	5	10	0	3	59	52	0	176
Long Itchington	18	6	9	0	3	52	48	0	175
Overbury II	18	5	10	0	3	52	51	0	168
Exhall & Wixford II	18	3	1	0	4	40	45	0	135

THIRD DIVISION

	P	W	L	T	A	BaP	BoP	Ded	Pts
Woodbourne	18	12	2	0	4	72	69	5	276
Shipston-on-Stour II	18	10	4	0	4	75	62	0	257
Temple Grafton	18	10	4	0	4	69	64	0	253
Stanway	18	10	4	0	4	59	61	0	240
Wellesbourne II	18	7	7	0	4	57	56	0	203
Norton Lindsey II	18	6	8	0	4	56	54	0	190
Great Alne	18	6	8	0	4	57	49	0	186
FISSC	18	3	10	0	5	38	48	0	141
Bearley Bears	18	4	10	0	4	44	40	20	124
Earlswood II	18	1	12	0	5	26	33	5	89

FOURTH DIVISION

	P	W	L	T	A	BaP	BoP	Ded	Pts
Fladbury	18	12	2	0	4	71	58	0	269
Ashorne	18	10	4	0	4	53	75	0	248
Moreton-in-Marsh II	18	8	5	0	5	53	62	0	220
Alcester & Ragley II	18	7	6	0	5	57	57	0	209
Kenilworth Wardens III	18	7	6	0	5	59	49	0	203
Winchcombe II	18	7	4	0	7	49	40	5	189
Harvington	18	6	6	0	6	48	47	0	185
Twyning II	18	5	7	0	6	29	37	20	126
Rowington II	18	1	12	0	5	26	31	0	92
Hockley Heath	18	2	13	0	3	36	35	45	61

FIFTH DIVISION

	P	W	L	T	A	BaP	BoP	Ded	Pts
Blockley	18	13	1	0	4	73	65	5	283
Cookhill	18	11	2	0	5	65	63	10	253
Tanworth-in-Arden II	18	10	5	0	3	64	64	0	243
Dorridge	18	7	6	0	5	55	50	0	200
Henley-in-Arden II	18	6	7	0	5	52	35	0	172
Ashton-under-Hill II	18	4	10	0	4	58	44	0	162
Bidford-on-Avon II	18	4	8	0	6	47	35	0	152
Stratford Bards II	18	5	8	0	5	49	36	20	140
Mickleton	18	2	10	0	6	44	32	5	121
Eckington	18	4	9	0	5	35	37	30	107

SIXTH DIVISION

	P	W	L	T	A	BaP	BoP	Ded	Pts
Alvechurch III	16	12	1	0	3	55	78	10	258
Bretforton II	16	11	1	0	4	58	59	0	247
Catherine-de-Barnes II	16	7	5	0	4	52	47	0	189
Welford-on-Avon	16	7	4	0	5	44	46	5	180
Kineton II	16	7	5	0	4	43	45	0	178
Claverdon II	16	6	6	0	4	55	28	0	163
Exhall& Wixford III	16	0	9	0	7	17	37	0	89
Kenilworth Wardens IV	16	1	12	0	3	31	38	20	74
Broadway II	16	2	10	0	4	32	29	35	66
Elmley Castle II	0	0	0	0	0	0	0	0	0

How's That Uncle Jack? A celebration of 100 years of cricket in Ashton-under-Hill

by David Hudson-Wood

ASHTON-UNDER-HILL Cricket Club in Worcestershire reaches its century this year…and the players and supporters have certainly got plenty to celebrate.

Located in the shadow of Bredon Hill in the Vale of Evesham, Ashton's ground is one of the most picturesque in the area.

This year Ashton will put out three junior teams for the first time at under-12, under-14 and under-16 level as well as two men's teams in the Cotswold Hills League.

A group of players have put together a 64-page centenary book full of articles about the club, its history and its characters. In addition, a whole host of special matches and events have been organised to mark the centenary, including an all-day match against a Ray Julian Invitation XI, consisting of former Test and County players, on Sunday July 15th, at 11am.

But things were not always so rosy for Ashton Cricket Club. It actually had a stormy first year after the president Frank Collins fell out with a player, Arthur Thomson, after Mr Thomson's cattle broke through a fence into Mr Collins' mowing grass. Mr Thomson was barred from playing for 'disorderly conduct on the field', which nobody could explain, and he left to set up another club in the village, Ashton-under-Hill United Cricket Club. The two clubs joined together in 1910 and thankfully things have been much more friendly since then.

After the First World War, the captain, Mr C Nicklin, put an advert in the Evesham Journal: "Wanted - a blacksmith, preferably one who can play cricket" and Archie Butler arrived from the Forest of Dean. A mighty hitter of the ball, he made history when he hit a six over the scoring hut and it ended up in Gloucester 20 miles away. The ball had landed in an open railway truck as a goods train passed through the station and was found when the train stopped at Gloucester!

After the end of the Second World War, the club restarted on a new ground at the village playing fields and the among the many new players was a teenage Neville Bell, perhaps Ashton's finest ever bowler, who regularly took over 100 wickets in a season and once took all 10 wickets in a local derby match against Beckford.

Mr Bell has many fond memories of those post-war days. One player he has particular memories of was the club's captain, Col Tommy Robertson, who used to take the whole team to away matches in the back of his Army vehicle. He also believes Col Robertson to have been Ashton's finest ever batsman.

"He would get to 50 and he would just leave the field to give somebody else a chance," recalls Mr Bell. "We played Dumbleton once and we threatened him that if he did it that day we wouldn't play the next week. He made a century. He was class."

Up until the 1950s matches were only played on Saturdays and Mr Bell recalls there being "absolute uproar in the village" when the club announced that it wanted to start playing cricket on Sundays and a special meeting was called in the village hall to discuss the matter.

"Everybody from the village came. Everybody from the chapel turned out against it and everybody from the pub turned out in favour. It was eventually agreed to play on a Sunday but we had to stop by 6pm. As soon as the church bells started we had to stop."

Ashton cricket team pictured in 1923 outside the the new pavilion donated by Sir James Curtis.
Back row left to right: Syd Rowland, Chas Stephens, Billy Clements. Middle row: Mr Johnson, Fred Tandy, Frank Barnes, Frank Johnson, Fred Griffin, Albert Driver, George Garland, Ewart Morrison, Hugh Clements, Chas Taylor. Front row: Fred Kempton, Chas Nicklin, J C Nicklin, Sir James Curtis, Noel Rogers, Harry Stratford.

Other Ashton stalwarts to have written articles in the book include Dave Wilson, who has been associated with the club for nearly 50 years; Robbie Hawker, who has played for Ashton since 1963 and is the all-time leading wicket taker with over 1,300 victims; and wicket-keeper batsman Richard Keen, who played for Ashton for 24 years and is the club's second highest run scorer.

And then there is the legendary all-rounder Les Haines, who has just about hung up his boots having played for Ashton since 1962 and is the club's all-time leading batsman with 12,861 runs and second highest wicket-taker with 970 scalps.

Les was in his 44th year playing for Ashton when he scored his one and only century for the club, hitting 127 not out against Overbury in 2004 at the ripe old age of 62.

All the book's statistics have been compiled by Ashton player Alistair Keen, who over the past few years has spent countless hours trawling through old scorebooks and back copies of the Evesham Journal at the town library.

As well as the normal club records section, the book includes a list of more quirky statistics and Alistair himself appears in this section, due to the fact that when he took 8 wickets for 18 runs against Stanton in 1996 he took two wickets in two balls four times. Has any bowler in any cricket match ever been on a hat-trick four times in the same innings?

Ashton's 1st XI in 2006 which made it to the national final of the Sportswise 20-20s competition.
Back row left to right: Cyril Banks (scorer), David Turner, Graeme Wicks, Mahesh Patel, Jason Haines, Darren Haines.
Front row: Ryan Brignull, Richard Wood, Luke Shepherd, Karl Shepherd (captain), Chandu Patel, William Archer, Paresh Patel.

Worcestershire batsman Daryl Mitchell, who began his cricketing career at local rivals Bretforton, has also contributed an article for the book. He has fond memories of scoring a century at Ashton one Saturday afternoon and then hitting two further centuries in two matches the next day. Not a bad weekend's work!

Reports of memorable matches are also featured in the book, including the day in 1995 when Worcestershire and England paceman Neal Radford brought a strong county team to play a benefit game at Ashton with his team including five Test players.

Record-breaking matches featured include the day Ashton scored 367-3 against Woodmancote, a club record, with opening batsman Steve Hardy hitting 201 not out, also a club record.

There are also articles about junior cricket and about the many brothers and fathers and sons who have played for Ashton over the years.

On the lighter side, there is a selection of the best quotes by Ashton players. A major contributor to this section is Matthew Cope, who during his playing days often had his teammates in hysterics with his turn of phrase.

Matthew grew up living next door to Ashton's long-standing umpire Jack Grove and he always referred to him as "Uncle Jack". When bowling one afternoon Matthew hit the batsman's pads and turned round and shouted: "How's that, Uncle Jack?"

Another time, when playing against Fladbury, Matthew had taken five wickets and his elder brother Sam had taken three catches to help Ashton to victory. Coming off the field to applause, Matthew turned to the Fladbury players and said: "I bet you wish you had a Cope playing on your team."

Ashton's centenary book is available for £5 from its editor David Hudson-Wood on (01386) 881839.

2007 Member clubs

ALCESTER & RAGLEY

in the grounds of Ragley Park
Alcester
Tel: 07780 658480

ALVECHURCH & HOPWOOD

Lea End Lane
Hopwood B48 7AS
Tel: 0121 447 8138

ASHORNE & MORETON MORRELL

c/o 6 Wellesbourne Farm
Wellesbourne
Warwickshire CV35 9SL

ASHTON-UNDER-HILL

The Playing Field, Elmley Road
Ashton-under-Hill

BEARLEY BEARS

Mill Field, Snitterfield Road
Bearley, Nr Stratford-upon-Avon CV37 0SE
Tel: 01789 731318

BIDFORD-ON-AVON

The Big Meadow
Honeybourne Road
Bidford-on-Avon

BLOCKLEY

Sparmoor, Station Road
Blockley
Nr. Moreton-in-Marsh

BRETFORTON

Station Road
Bretforton, Worcestershire
Tel: 01386 833410

BROADWAY

Snowshill Road
Broadway

CATHERINE DE BARNES

Rear of Boat Inn
Hampton Lane
Catherine de Barnes, Solihull
Tel: 0121 706 6531

CHIPPING CAMPDEN

Station Road
Chipping Campden
Tel: 01386 841834

CLAVERDON

Recreation Ground
Langley Road, Claverdon

COOKHILL

Neville Arms, The Ridgeway
New End, Redditch

DORRIDGE

c/o Hockley Heath CC
Grove Lane, Lapworth
Solihull B94 6AR

EARLSWOOD

Watery Lane, Cheswick Green
Solihull, B94 6EE

EBRINGTON

Manor Ground, Campden Road
Ebrington, Gloucestershire
GL55 6NF

ECKINGTON

The Recreation Centre
Pershore Road, Eckington
WR10 3AP
Tel: 01386 750746

ELMLEY CASTLE

The Playing Field
Kersoe Lane, Elmley Castle
Worcestershire
Tel: 01386 710209
(Queen Elizabeth pub)

EXHALL & WIXFORD

Exhall, Alcester
Warwickshire, B49 6EA

F.I.S.S.C.

Knights Lane, Tiddington
Warwickshire, CV37 7BJ
Tel: 01789 202940

FLADBURY

Recreation Ground
Station Road, Fladbury

GREAT ALNE

Henley Road, Great Alne
Alcester, B49 6HX

HARVINGTON

Anchor Lane, Harvington
Evesham, WR11 5DH

HENLEY-IN-ARDEN

Stratford Road
Henley-in-Arden, B95 6AP
Tel: 01564 793403

HOCKLEY HEATH

Grove Lane, Lapworth
Solihull, B94 6AR

KENILWORTH WARDENS

Glasshouse Lane
Kenilworth
Tel: 01926 852476

KINETON

Kineton Sports & Social Club
The Sports Ground
Bridge Street
Little Kineton, CV35 0DP
Tel: 01926 640901

LEAMINGTON

Arlington Avenue
Leamington Spa
Warwickshire, CV32 5VG
Tel: 01926 423854

The Cotswold Hills League

LONG ITCHINGTON
White Hall Farm
Stonebridge Lane
Long Itchington
Warwickshire, CV47 9PT

MICKLETON
Stratford Road
Mickleton

MORETON IN MARSH
Batsford Road
Moreton-in-Marsh,
Gloucestershire

NORTON LINDSEY & WOLVERTON
Wolverton Road
Norton Lindsey

OVERBURY
The Playing Field
Overbury, Tewkesbury
Gloucestershire

ROWINGTON
Rowington Green, Rowington
Nr. Warwick, CV35 7DB

SHIPSTON-ON-STOUR
Shipston-on-Stour Sports Club
London Road, Shipston-on-Stour
Tel: 01608 661139

STANWAY
Stanway, Toddington
Gloucestershire

STRATFORD-UPON-AVON
c/o FISSC Cricket Club
Knights Lane, Tiddington
Warwickshire, CV37 7BJ
Tel: 01789 202940

STRATFORD BARDS
Alscot Park, Preston-on-Stour
Warwickshire, CV37 8NB
Tel: 01789 450969

TANWORTH-IN-ARDEN
Tanworth Lane
Tanworth-in-Arden, Solihull

TEMPLE GRAFTON
in the grounds of
Grafton Court

TWYNING
Puckrup, Twyning
Gloucestershire

WARWICK COUNTY COUNCIL STAFF
Myton Hamlet
Myton Road, Warwick
Tel: 01926 491349

WELFORD-ON-AVON
Synder Meadow, Binton Road
Welford-on-Avon
Warwickshire

WELLESBOURNE
Loxley Close
Wellesbourne
Warwickshire
Tel: 01789 840561

WINCHCOMBE
The Pavilion, Corndean Lane
Winchcombe

WOODBOURNE
The Burrows, Rumbush Lane
Earlswood, Solihull B94 5LW
Tel: 01564 703203

2007 Fixtures

Premier Division

Sat 5th May
Ship-on-St.   v More-in-M.
Strat. Bards   v Exhall & W.
Bretforton   v Earlswood
Alc. & R.   v Overbury
W'bourne   v Tan-in-Ard.

Sat 12th May
Alc. & R.   v Ship-on-St.
Tan-in-Ard.   v Exhall & W.
Overbury   v Strat. Bards
Earlswood   v W'bourne
More-in-M.   v Bretforton

Sat 19th May
Ship-on-St.   v Tan-in-Ard.
Exhall & W.   v Earlswood
Strat. Bards   v Alc. & R.
Bretforton   v Overbury
More-in-M.   v W'bourne

Sat 26th May
Bretforton   v Ship-on-St.
Overbury   v Exhall & W.
W'bourne   v Strat. Bards
Tan-in-Ard.   v Earlswood
More-in-M.   v Alc. & R.

Sat 2nd June
W'bourne   v Ship-on-St.
Exhall & W.   v More-in-M.
Earlswood   v Strat. Bards
Bretforton   v Alc. & R.
Tan-in-Ard.   v Overbury

Sat 9th June
Earlswood   v Ship-on-St.
Alc. & R.   v Exhall & W.
More-in-M.   v Overbury
W'bourne   v Bretforton
Strat. Bards   v Tan-in-Ard.

Sat 16th June
Ship-on-St.   v Exhall & W.
Overbury   v W'bourne
Alc. & R.   v Earlswood
Strat. Bards   v More-in-M.
Bretforton   v Tan-in-Ard.

Sat 23rd June
Ship-on-St.   v Strat. Bards
Exhall & W.   v Bretforton
Earlswood   v Overbury
Alc. & R.   v W'bourne
Tan-in-Ard.   v More-in-M.

Sat 30th June
Overbury   v Ship-on-St.
Exhall & W.   v W'bourne
More-in-M.   v Earlswood
Tan-in-Ard.   v Alc. & R.
Strat. Bards   v Bretforton

Sat 7th July
More-in-M.   v Ship-on-St.
Exhall & W.   v Strat. Bards
Earlswood   v Bretforton
Overbury   v Alc. & R.
Tan-in-Ard.   v W'bourne

Sat 14th July
Ship-on-St.   v Alc. & R.
Exhall & W.   v Tan-in-Ard.
Strat. Bards   v Overbury
W'bourne   v Earlswood
Bretforton   v More-in-M.

Sat 21st July
Tan-in-Ard.   v Ship-on-St.
Earlswood   v Exhall & W.
Alc. & R.   v Strat. Bards
Overbury   v Bretforton
W'bourne   v More-in-M.

Sat 28th July
Ship-on-St.   v Bretforton
Exhall & W.   v Overbury
Strat. Bards   v W'bourne
Earlswood   v Tan-in-Ard.
Alc. & R.   v More-in-M.

Sat 4th August
Ship-on-St.   v W'bourne
More-in-M.   v Exhall & W.
Strat. Bards   v Earlswood
Alc. & R.   v Bretforton
Overbury   v Tan-in-Ard.

Sat 11th August
Ship-on-St.   v Earlswood
Exhall & W.   v Alc. & R.
Overbury   v More-in-M.
Bretforton   v W'bourne
Tan-in-Ard.   v Strat. Bards

Sat 18th August
Exhall & W.   v Ship-on-St.
W'bourne   v Overbury
Earlswood   v Alc. & R.
More-in-M.   v Strat. Bards
Tan-in-Ard.   v Bretforton

Sat 25th August
Strat. Bards   v Ship-on-St.
Bretforton   v Exhall & W.
Overbury   v Earlswood
W'bourne   v Alc. & R.
More-in-M.   v Tan-in-Ard.

Sat 1st September
Ship-on-St.   v Overbury
W'bourne   v Exhall & W.
Earlswood   v More-in-M.
Alc. & R.   v Tan-in-Ard.
Bretforton   v Strat. Bards

First Division

Sat 5th May
W'combe   v Kineton
C-de-Barnes   v Henley-in-A.
Elmley Cas.   v Bidf-on-A.
Ebrington   v Broadway
Ash-u-Hill   v Norton Lin.

Sat 12th May
Broadway   v W'combe
Norton Lin.   v Henley-in-A.
Ebrington   v C-de-Barnes
Bidf-on-A.   v Ash-u-Hill
Kineton   v Elmley Cas.

Sat 19th May
W'combe   v Norton Lin.
Henley-in-A.   v Bidf-on-A.
C-de-Barnes   v Broadway
Elmley Cas.   v Ebrington
Kineton   v Ash-u-Hill

Sat 26th May
Elmley Cas.   v W'combe
Ebrington   v Henley-in-A.
Ash-u-Hill   v C-de-Barnes
Norton Lin.   v Bidf-on-A.
Broadway   v Kineton

Sat 2nd June
W'combe   v Ash-u-Hill
Kineton   v Henley-in-A.
Bidf-on-A.   v C-de-Barnes
Broadway   v Elmley Cas.
Norton Lin.   v Ebrington

Sat 9th June
Bidf-on-A.   v W'combe
Henley-in-A.   v Broadway
Ebrington   v Kineton
Ash-u-Hill   v Elmley Cas.
C-de-Barnes   v Norton Lin.

The Cotswold Hills League

Sat 16th June
Henley-in-A. v W'combe
Ebrington v Ash-u-Hill
Broadway v Bidf-on-A.
C-de-Barnes v Kineton
Elmley Cas. v Norton Lin.

Sat 23rd June
W'combe v C-de-Barnes
Henley-in-A. v Elmley Cas.
Bidf-on-A. v Ebrington
Broadway v Ash-u-Hill
Norton Lin. v Kineton

Sat 30th June
W'combe v Ebrington
Ash-u-Hill v Henley-in-A.
Kineton v Bidf-on-A.
Norton Lin. v Broadway
Elmley Cas. v C-de-Barnes

Sat 7th July
Kineton v W'combe
Henley-in-A. v C-de-Barnes
Bidf-on-A. v Elmley Cas.
Broadway v Ebrington
Norton Lin. v Ash-u-Hill

Sat 14th July
W'combe v Broadway
Henley-in-A. v Norton Lin.
C-de-Barnes v Ebrington
Ash-u-Hill v Bidf-on-A.
Elmley Cas. v Kineton

Sat 21st July
Norton Lin. v W'combe
Bidf-on-A. v Henley-in-A.
Broadway v C-de-Barnes
Ebrington v Elmley Cas.
Ash-u-Hill v Kineton

Sat 28th July
W'combe v Elmley Cas.
Henley-in-A. v Ebrington
C-de-Barnes v Ash-u-Hill
Bidf-on-A. v Norton Lin.
Kineton v Broadway

Sat 4th August
Ash-u-Hill v W'combe
Henley-in-A. v Kineton
C-de-Barnes v Bidf-on-A.
Elmley Cas. v Broadway
Ebrington v Norton Lin.

Sat 11th August
W'combe v Bidf-on-A.
Broadway v Henley-in-A.

Kineton v Ebrington
Elmley Cas. v Ash-u-Hill
Norton Lin. v C-de-Barnes

Sat 18th August
W'combe v Henley-in-A.
Ash-u-Hill v Ebrington
Bidf-on-A. v Broadway
Kineton v C-de-Barnes
Norton Lin. v Elmley Cas.

Sat 25th August
C-de-Barnes v W'combe
Elmley Cas. v Henley-in-A.
Ebrington v Bidf-on-A.
Ash-u-Hill v Broadway
Kineton v Norton Lin.

Sat 1st September
Ebrington v W'combe
Henley-in-A. v Ash-u-Hill
Bidf-on-A. v Kineton
Broadway v Norton Lin.
C-de-Barnes v Elmley Cas.

Second Division

Sat 5th May
Strat-upon-A v Ship-on-St.II
Lea'ton III v WCC Staff
L. Itchington v Chipping C.
Woodbourne v Rowington
Twyning v Claverdon

Sat 12th May
Ship-on-St.II v Woodbourne
WCC Staff v Claverdon
Rowington v Lea'ton III
Chipping C. v Twyning
Strat-upon-A v L. Itchington

Sat 19th May
Claverdon v Ship-on-St.II
Chipping C. v WCC Staff
Lea'ton III v Woodbourne
L. Itchington v Rowington
Strat-upon-A v Twyning

Sat 26th May
Ship-on-St.II v L. Itchington
Rowington v WCC Staff
Twyning v Lea'ton III
Claverdon v Chipping C.
Woodbourne v Strat-upon-A

Sat 2nd June
Ship-on-St.II v Twyning
WCC Staff v Strat-upon-A
Chipping C. v Lea'ton III
Woodbourne v L. Itchington
Claverdon v Rowington

Sat 9th June
Ship-on-St.II v Chipping C.
Woodbourne v WCC Staff
Strat-upon-A v Rowington
Twyning v L. Itchington
Lea'ton III v Claverdon

Sat 16th June
WCC Staff v Ship-on-St.II
Rowington v Twyning
Chipping C. v Woodbourne
Lea'ton III v Strat-upon-A
L. Itchington v Claverdon

Sat 23rd June
Lea'ton III v Ship-on-St.II
WCC Staff v L. Itchington
Chipping C. v Rowington
Woodbourne v Twyning
Claverdon v Strat-upon-A

Sat 30th June
Ship-on-St.II v Rowington
Twyning v WCC Staff
Strat-upon-A v Chipping C.
Claverdon v Woodbourne
L. Itchington v Lea'ton III

Sat 7th July
Ship-on-St.II v Strat-upon-A
WCC Staff v Lea'ton III
Chipping C. v L. Itchington
Rowington v Woodbourne
Claverdon v Twyning

Sat 14th July
Woodbourne v Ship-on-St.II
Claverdon v WCC Staff
Lea'ton III v Rowington
Twyning v Chipping C.
L. Itchington v Strat-upon-A

Sat 21st July
Ship-on-St.II v Claverdon
WCC Staff v Chipping C.
Woodbourne v Lea'ton III
Rowington v L. Itchington
Twyning v Strat-upon-A

Sat 28th July
L. Itchington v Ship-on-St.II
WCC Staff v Rowington
Lea'ton III v Twyning
Chipping C. v Claverdon
Strat-upon-A v Woodbourne

Sat 4th August
Twyning v Ship-on-St.II
Strat-upon-A v WCC Staff

Lea'ton III   v Chipping C.
L. Itchington v Woodbourne
Rowington   v Claverdon

Sat 11th August
Chipping C.   v Ship-on-St.II
WCC Staff   v Woodbourne
Rowington   v Strat-upon-A
L. Itchington v Twyning
Claverdon   v Lea'ton III

Sat 18th August
Ship-on-St.II v WCC Staff
Twyning   v Rowington
Woodbourne   v Chipping C.
Strat-upon-A   v Lea'ton III
Claverdon   v L. Itchington

Sat 25th August
Ship-on-St.II v Lea'ton III
L. Itchington v WCC Staff
Rowington   v Chipping C.
Twyning   v Woodbourne
Strat-upon-A   v Claverdon

Sat 1st September
Rowington   v Ship-on-St.II
WCC Staff   v Twyning
Chipping C.   v Strat-upon-A
Woodbourne   v Claverdon
Lea'ton III   v L. Itchington

Third Division

Sat 5th May
Ashorne   v FISSC
Exh. & W. II   v Great Alne
Fladbury   v Temple G.
Overbury II   v Stanway
Norton L. II   v W'bourne II

Sat 12th May
Stanway   v Ashorne
Exh. & W. II   v Norton L. II
Great Alne   v Overbury II
W'bourne II   v Temple G.
Fladbury   v FISSC

Sat 19th May
Norton L. II   v Ashorne
Temple G.   v Exh. & W. II
Stanway   v Great Alne
Overbury II   v Fladbury
W'bourne II   v FISSC

Sat 26th May
Fladbury   v Ashorne
Exh. & W. II   v Overbury II
Great Alne   v W'bourne II
Temple G.   v Norton L. II
FISSC   v Stanway

Sat 2nd June
Ashorne   v W'bourne II
FISSC   v Exh. & W. II
Temple G.   v Great Alne
Stanway   v Fladbury
Overbury II   v Norton L. II

Sat 9th June
Ashorne   v Temple G.
Exh. & W. II   v Stanway
Overbury II   v FISSC
Fladbury   v W'bourne II
Norton L. II   v Great Alne

Sat 16th June
Exh. & W. II   v Ashorne
W'bourne II   v Overbury II
Stanway   v Temple G.
FISSC   v Great Alne
Norton L. II   v Fladbury

Sat 23rd June
Great Alne   v Ashorne
Fladbury   v Exh. & W. II
Overbury II   v Temple G.
W'bourne II   v Stanway
FISSC   v Norton L. II

Sat 30th June
Ashorne   v Overbury II
W'bourne II   v Exh. & W. II
Temple G.   v FISSC
Stanway   v Norton L. II
Great Alne   v Fladbury

Sat 7th July
FISSC   v Ashorne
Great Alne   v Exh. & W. II
Temple G.   v Fladbury
Stanway   v Overbury II
W'bourne II   v Norton L. II

Sat 14th July
Ashorne   v Stanway
Norton L. II   v Exh. & W. II
Overbury II   v Great Alne
Temple G.   v W'bourne II
FISSC   v Fladbury

Sat 21st July
Ashorne   v Norton L. II
Exh. & W. II   v Temple G.
Great Alne   v Stanway
Fladbury   v Overbury II
FISSC   v W'bourne II

Sat 28th July
Ashorne   v Fladbury
Overbury II   v Exh. & W. II

W'bourne II   v Great Alne
Norton L. II   v Temple G.
Stanway   v FISSC

Sat 4th August
W'bourne II   v Ashorne
Exh. & W. II   v FISSC
Great Alne   v Temple G.
Fladbury   v Stanway
Norton L. II   v Overbury II

Sat 11th August
Temple G.   v Ashorne
Stanway   v Exh. & W. II
FISSC   v Overbury II
W'bourne II   v Fladbury
Great Alne   v Norton L. II

Sat 18th August
Ashorne   v Exh. & W. II
Overbury II   v W'bourne II
Temple G.   v Stanway
Great Alne   v FISSC
Fladbury   v Norton L. II

Sat 25th August
Ashorne   v Great Alne
Exh. & W. II   v Fladbury
Temple G.   v Overbury II
Stanway   v W'bourne II
Norton L. II   v FISSC

Sat 1st September
Overbury II   v Ashorne
Exh. & W. II   v W'bourne II
FISSC   v Temple G.
Norton L. II   v Stanway
Fladbury   v Great Alne

Fourth Division

Sat 5th May
M.-in-M. II   v W'combe II
Cookhill   v Harvington
Earlswood II   v Blockley
Ken. Wds III   v Alc. & R. II
Bearley Bs.   v Twyning II

Sat 12th May
W'combe II   v Alc. & R. II
Harvington   v Bearley Bs.
Ken. Wds III   v Cookhill
Twyning II   v Earlswood II
Blockley   v M.-in-M. II

Sat 19th May
Bearley Bs.   v W'combe II
Earlswood II   v Harvington
Alc. & R. II   v Cookhill
Blockley   v Ken. Wds III
Twyning II   v M.-in-M. II

The Cotswold Hills League

Sat 26th May
W'combe II   v Blockley
Harvington   v Ken. Wds III
Cookhill   v Twyning II
Earlswood II   v Bearley Bs.
Alc. & R. II   v M.-in-M. II

Sat 2nd June
Twyning II   v W'combe II
M.-in-M. II   v Harvington
Cookhill   v Earlswood II
Alc. & R. II   v Blockley
Bearley Bs.   v Ken. Wds III

Sat 9th June
W'combe II   v Earlswood II
Harvington   v Alc. & R. II
Ken. Wds III   v M.-in-M. II
Blockley   v Twyning II
Cookhill   v Bearley Bs.

Sat 16th June
W'combe II   v Harvington
Twyning II   v Ken. Wds III
Earlswood II   v Alc. & R. II
M.-in-M. II   v Cookhill
Bearley Bs.   v Blockley |

Sat 23rd June
Cookhill   v W'combe II
Harvington   v Blockley
Ken. Wds III   v Earlswood II
Twyning II   v Alc. & R. II
M.-in-M. II   v Bearley Bs.

Sat 30th June
Ken. Wds III   v W'combe II
Harvington   v Twyning II
Earlswood II   v M.-in-M. II
Alc. & R. II   v Bearley Bs.
Blockley   v Cookhill

Sat 7th July
W'combe II   v M.-in-M. II
Harvington   v Cookhill
Blockley   v Earlswood II
Alc. & R. II   v Ken. Wds III
Twyning II   v Bearley Bs.

Sat 14th July
Alc. & R. II   v W'combe II
Bearley Bs.   v Harvington
Cookhill   v Ken. Wds III
Earlswood II   v Twyning II
M.-in-M. II   v Blockley

Sat 21st July
W'combe II   v Bearley Bs.
Harvington   v Earlswood II

Cookhill   v Alc. & R. II
Ken. Wds III   v Blockley
M.-in-M. II   v Twyning II

Sat 28th July
Blockley   v W'combe II
Ken. Wds III   v Harvington
Twyning II   v Cookhill
Bearley Bs.   v Earlswood II
M.-in-M. II   v Alc. & R. II

Sat 4th August
W'combe II   v Twyning II
Harvington   v M.-in-M. II
Earlswood II   v Cookhill
Blockley   v Alc. & R. II
Ken. Wds III   v Bearley Bs.

Sat 11th August
Earlswood II   v W'combe II
Alc. & R. II   v Harvington
M.-in-M. II   v Ken. Wds III
Twyning II   v Blockley
Bearley Bs.   v Cookhill

Sat 18th August
Harvington   v W'combe II
Ken. Wds III   v Twyning II
Alc. & R. II   v Earlswood II
Cookhill   v M.-in-M. II
Blockley   v Bearley Bs.

Sat 25th August
W'combe II   v Cookhill
Blockley   v Harvington
Earlswood II   v Ken. Wds III
Alc. & R. II   v Twyning II
Bearley Bs.   v M.-in-M. II

Sat 1st September
W'combe II   v Ken. Wds III
Twyning II   v Harvington
M.-in-M. II   v Earlswood II
Bearley Bs.   v Alc. & R. II
Cookhill   v Blockley

Fifth Division

Sat 5th May
Dorridge   v Alvech. III
Hen-in-A. II   v Strat. Bs II
Bidf-on-A. II   v Bretforton II
Rowington II   v Hockley H.
Tan-in-Ard. II   v Ash-u-Hill II

Sat 12th May
Hockley H.   v Alvech. III
Hen-in-A. II   v T-in-Ard. II
Strat. Bs II   v Rowington II
Ash-u-Hill II   v Bidf-on-A. II
Bretforton II   v Dorridge

Sat 19th May
T-in-Ard. II   v Alvech. III
Bidf-on-A. II   v Hen-in-A. II
Hockley H.   v Strat. Bs II
Rowington II   v Bretforton II
Ash-u-Hill II   v Dorridge

Sat 26th May
Alvech. III   v Bretforton II
Hen-in-A. II   v Rowington II
Strat. Bs II   v Ash-u-Hill II
Bidf-on-A. II   v T-in-Ard. II
Dorridge   v Hockley H.

Sat 2nd June
Ash-u-Hill II   v Alvech. III
Hen-in-A. II   v Dorridge
Strat. Bs II   v Bidf-on-A. II
Hockley H.   v Bretforton II
Rowington II   v T-in-Ard. II

Sat 9th June
Alvech. III   v Bidf-on-A. II
Hockley H.   v Hen-in-A. II
Rowington II   v Dorridge
Bretforton II   v Ash-u-Hill II
T-in-Ard. II   v Strat. Bs II

Sat 16th June
Alvech. III   v Hen-in-A. II
Ash-u-Hill II   v Rowington II
Bidf-on-A. II   v Hockley H.
Dorridge   v Strat. Bs II
T-in-Ard. II   v Bretforton II

Sat 23rd June
Strat. Bs II   v Alvech. III
Bretforton II   v Hen-in-A. II
Rowington II   v Bidf-on-A. II
Ash-u-Hill II   v Hockley H.
Dorridge   v T-in-Ard. II

Sat 30th June
Rowington II   v Alvech. III
Hen-in-A. II   v Ash-u-Hill II
Bidf-on-A. II   v Dorridge
Hockley H.   v T-in-Ard. II
Bretforton II   v Strat. Bs II

Sat 7th July
Alvech. III   v Dorridge
Strat. Bs II   v Hen-in-A. II
Bretforton II   v Bidf-on-A. II
Hockley H.   v Rowington II
Ash-u-Hill II   v T-in-Ard. II

Sat 14th July
Alvech. III   v Hockley H.
T-in-Ard. II   v Hen-in-A. II

Rowington II   v Strat. Bs II
Bidf-on-A. II v Ash-u-Hill II
Dorridge   v Bretforton II

Sat 21st July
Alvech. III   v T-in-Ard. II
Hen-in-A. II   v Bidf-on-A. II
Strat. Bs II v Hockley H.
Bretforton II v Rowington II
Dorridge   v Ash-u-Hill II

Sat 28th July
Bretforton II v Alvech. III
Rowington II   v Hen-in-A. II
Ash-u-Hill II v Strat. Bs II
T-in-Ard. II   v Bidf-on-A. II
Hockley H.   v Dorridge

Sat 4th August
Alvech. III   v Ash-u-Hill II
Dorridge   v Hen-in-A. II
Bidf-on-A. II v Strat. Bs II
Bretforton II v Hockley H.
T-in-Ard. II   v Rowington II

Sat 11th August
Bidf-on-A. II v Alvech. III
Hen-in-A. II   v Hockley H.
Dorridge   v Rowington II
Ash-u-Hill II v Bretforton II
Strat. Bs II v T-in-Ard. II

Sat 18th August
Hen-in-A. II   v Alvech. III
Rowington II   v Ash-u-Hill II
Hockley H.   v Bidf-on-A. II
Strat. Bs II v Dorridge
Bretforton II v T-in-Ard. II

Sat 25th August
Alvech. III   v Strat. Bs II
Hen-in-A. II   v Bretforton II
Bidf-on-A. II v Rowington II
Hockley H.   v Ash-u-Hill II
T-in-Ard. II   v Dorridge

Sat 1st September
Alvech. III   v Rowington II
Ash-u-Hill II v Hen-in-A. II
Dorridge   v Bidf-on-A. II
T-in-Ard. II   v Hockley H.
Strat. Bs II v Bretforton II

Sixth Division

Sat 5th May
Kineton II   v Eckington
Exh. & W. III v C-de-B. II
Mickleton   v L. Itching. II
Broadway II   v Ken. Wds IV
Claverdon II   v Wel-on-Avon

Sat 12th May
Eckington   v Broadway II
Claverdon II   v Exh. & W. III
C-de-B. II   v Ken. Wds IV
Wel-on-Avon   v Mickleton
L. Itching. II v Kineton II

Sat 19th May
Eckington   v Claverdon II
Exh. & W. III v Mickleton
Broadway II   v C-de-B. II
Ken. Wds IV   v L. Itching. II
Wel-on-Avon   v Kineton II

Sat 26th May
L. Itching. II v Eckington
Ken. Wds IV   v Exh. & W. III
C-de-B. II   v Wel-on-Avon
Mickleton   v Claverdon II
Kineton II   v Broadway II

Sat 2nd June
Wel-on-Avon   v Eckington
Exh. & W. III v Kineton II
C-de-B. II   v Mickleton
L. Itching. II v Broadway II
Ken. Wds IV   v Claverdon II

Sat 9th June
Eckington   v Mickleton
Broadway II   v Exh. & W. III
Kineton II   v Ken. Wds IV
L. Itching. II v Wel-on-Avon
Claverdon II   v C-de-B. II

Sat 16th June
Exh. & W. III v Eckington
Ken. Wds IV   v Wel-on-Avon
Mickleton   v Broadway II
Kineton II   v C-de-B. II
Claverdon II   v L. Itching. II

Sat 23rd June
C-de-B. II   v Eckington
L. Itching. II v Exh. & W. III
Mickleton   v Ken. Wds IV
Wel-on-Avon   v Broadway II
Kineton II   v Claverdon II

Sat 30th June
Eckington   v Ken. Wds IV
Wel-on-Avon   v Exh. & W. III
Mickleton   v Kineton II
Broadway II   v Claverdon II
C-de-B. II   v L. Itching. II

Sat 7th July
Eckington   v Kineton II
C-de-B. II   v Exh. & W. III

L. Itching. II v Mickleton
Ken. Wds IV   v Broadway II
Wel-on-Avon   v Claverdon II

Sat 14th July
Broadway II   v Eckington
Exh. & W. III v Claverdon II
Ken. Wds IV   v C-de-B. II
Mickleton   v Wel-on-Avon
Kineton II   v L. Itching. II

Sat 21st July
Claverdon II   v Eckington
Mickleton   v Exh. & W. III
C-de-B. II   v Broadway II
L. Itching. II v Ken. Wds IV
Kineton II   v Wel-on-Avon

Sat 28th July
Eckington   v L. Itching. II
Exh. & W. III v Ken. Wds IV
Wel-on-Avon   v C-de-B. II
Claverdon II   v Mickleton
Broadway II   v Kineton II

Sat 4th August
Eckington   v Wel-on-Avon
Kineton II   v Exh. & W. III
Mickleton   v C-de-B. II
Broadway II   v L. Itching. II
Claverdon II   v Ken. Wds IV

Sat 11th August
Mickleton v Eckington
Exh. & W. III v Broadway II
Ken. Wds IV   v Kineton II
Wel-on-Avon   v L. Itching. II
C-de-B. II   v Claverdon II

Sat 18th August
Eckington   v Exh. & W. III
Wel-on-Avon   v Ken. Wds IV
Broadway II   v Mickleton
C-de-B. II   v Kineton II
L. Itching. II v Claverdon II

Sat 25th August
Eckington   v C-de-B. II
Exh. & W. III v L. Itching. II
Ken. Wds IV   v Mickleton
Broadway II   v Wel-on-Avon
Claverdon II   v Kineton II

Sat 1st September
Ken. Wds IV   v Eckington
Exh. & W. III v Wel-on-Avon
Kineton II   v Mickleton
Claverdon II   v Broadway II
L. Itching. II v C-de-B. II

Warwickshire under Woolmer

BOB WOOLMER DIED in a Jamaican hotel room in March straight after the Pakistan team he coached was beaten and dumped out of the World Cup by Ireland. In the glowing tributes that followed his death, it was obvious that one of his greatest achievements, and one that led to his subsequent career as an international coach, was turning round and under-performing Warwickshire county team who scaled heights in the early and mid 1990s which no other county team has equalled. A key member of that squad was all-rounder Paul Smith, no stranger to conflict with authority and whose career came to an unceremonious end with his ban for drug-taking after the departure of Woolmer.

*In this exclusive extract from Smith's recently published autobiography, **Wasted?**, Smith gives a marvellous insight into the mind and methods of Woolmer, as well as the impact of cricket legends Brian Lara and Alan Donald on the Bears' successes.*

NO-ONE LOVED the sport like Woolly. His mentor during his own playing career had been Sir Colin Cowdrey. Apparently Cowdrey used to tell the young Bob that, in order to progress; we should "make this season's weaknesses next summer's strengths." That's a great way of thinking and one which obviously worked for Bob, who started his career as a number 10 or 11 for Kent and later scored Test centuries batting at three for England.

When Bob became coach at Edgbaston he taught us bowlers how you need to keep your nerve and remember game plans, whilst being flexible enough to adjust to last-second innovations by batsmen. Bowling at danger stages of a game will see ups and downs, but in time the good days far outweighed the bad for us.

What Woolly exposed in us were our personal strengths and weaknesses. Sometimes I think we shocked him with what he might have perceived as a lack of professionalism. During a team meeting at

Headingley, Bob asked each of us how many units of alcohol we drank a week. Our answers surprised him - maybe it was our honesty. Clearly he thought we drank too much. We had always been a social bunch, however, and our fitness helped our recovery time. A friend who spent quite a bit of time with me during my benefit year said he reckoned I had drunk about 120 pints the previous week, certainly in excess of 100. And, he warned me, I was on track to drink more in that current week.

Bob used to say that the breakfast of champions is muesli. I couldn't agree with that. I'd been brought up to believe that competition was the breakfast of champions. Soon afterwards I answered a questionnaire for that year's 'Cricketers Who's Who'. I said I did not believe eating bowls of muesli would make me a better cricketer. It caused much laughter in our changing rooms when it made print. It was partially why I wrote it as things like diet were never far from Bob's thinking. In jest I'd often tell Woolly in front of the changing room that the brain uses more energy when you sleep than in waking hours. It's true.

Bob had arrived at Edgbaston as coach in March 1991. The previous coach, Bob Cottam, and the captain, Andy Lloyd, had clashed publicly over that winter. Cottam felt our skipper wasn't always worthy of selection. The discrepancy led to Warwickshire being minus a coach. Within six weeks the club's chairman, Bob Evans, had also gone. An emergency committee meeting was called when Evans was away in Bournemouth and he was voted out. At one stage he had suggested that all interests be declared by those on the committee; some obviously thought it a barbed request. Shame; I always reckoned he was a fine man with the best interests of the club at heart.

So it was a turbulent atmosphere that greeted Woolly when he walked into Edgbaston three months later. Everyone expected South African Clive Rice to be given the coach's job. Yet Woolly's friendship with Dennis Amiss, forged through their mutual experiences in Kerry Packer's World Series, Test and South African rebel cricket, proved telling.

The thing that immediately stood out with Woolly was the time he would spend trying to get his point across. We would debate anything and everything, talking cricket for hours in an attempt to understand what could turn our fortunes. It was time well spent; the four years he spent with

Verde Sports Cricket Ltd

Putting Cricket First

We offer an extensive range of synthetic turf cricket pitches and surfaces constructed to exacting standards using the finest materials and aggregates available. Our range has been developed from more than 25 years of personal experience, enabling us to advise and match customer requirements, ensuring value for money

Design and Construction of Match and Practice Facilities

Permanent and roll up services for Concrete Indoor and Outdoor Surfaces

Permanent, Mobile and Traditional practice Nets

Maintenance, Guidance and Advice

Replacement, Surfacing and Servicing

Gabbotts Farm Barn, Bury Lane, Withnell, Chorley PR6 8SW
Tel: 01254 831666
Fax: 01254 831066
Web Site: www.verdesports.com
E-mail: cricket@verdesports.com
Nottingham: Peter Dury 0115 846 5732

CRICKET COACHING MATS

AFTER A WINTER of back to back cricket with the Ashes series, the One Day Triangular series followed by the World Cup, interest in the game amongst youngsters is still high. Hopefully thousands of youngsters will be queuing up to join the junior section of your club this season wanting to spend the summer practising some of the cover drives, hits through midwicket or hits out of the ground that they have just seen on TV. To cope with the increased interest at club level, the cricket coaching mat, designed by David Cooper, the cricket coach at a Yorkshire club, could be the answer to recruit and retain youngsters and to produce quality cricketers for your clubs First Teams of the future.

The cricket coaching mat is a brand new piece of equipment designed to give youngsters the time to improve their batting techniques on a perfect surface. It works superbly at club level - keeping all the players engaged, focused and employed in the purpose they're there for - playing cricket, improving and enjoying their cricket. It is a fantastic aid for your club coaches as well as it allows them to spot any problems with a youngster's technique which they then quickly and easily remedy.

Johaan Bustin, a coach in South Africa says, "The 'Cricket Coaching Mat' has assisted me tremendously with my coaching as well as assisting the juniors to develop the proper techniques, i.e. stance, feet movement, ball direction and shot selection"

Simon Lowndes of Denton West CC says: "We used the mats for the first time last night on some new youngsters with quite stunning results, repetition of the shots meant that within 4 or 5 tries the new players were playing shots with the correct technique. Excellent - now for the first XI !!!!!!!!!"

Former Yorkshire and England spinner and the ex Head Coach at Lords, Don Wilson, invites David to run batting workshops at the Ampleforth county cricket festival each summer. He describes the mat as "marvellous and the experience for the youngsters being better than a net practice for improving batting techniques".

Iain Stewart, the Lincolnshire County Cricket Board Community Coach, says: "Some under 11 county players have been put through their paces on the mats and their development has progressed rapidly. It's a very good visual coaching aid that assists experienced and less experienced coaches alike."

CRICKET COACHING MATS

"The best thing we have ever bought for our juniors."
South Shore CC Blackpool and Idle CC Bradford

What the Mat does for you:-

◆ You'll **win** more games

◆ By **coaching** every shot in the book

◆ And see immediate **improvements** in batting ability

◆ And keep everyone **involved**

◆ By playing **games**

◆ And be a more **effective** coach thanks to the accompanying CD Coaching Guide

A 2005 Finalist in the ECB Outstanding Services to Cricket Awards (OSCAS) for "innovative ways of developing the game of cricket"

For more information visit: **www.cricketcoachingmats.com**
or contact David Cooper on 01422 244818   07986 234489
Field Head Ogden Halifax HX2 8XJ d.cooper20@ntlworld.com

DON'T GET CAUGHT WITHOUT ONE

"Marvellous, better then a net practice for coaching batting"
Don Wilson Yorkshire and England and former Head Coach at Lords

Flexible Boundary Marker

The No.1 boundary marker in cricket.

F.B.M is a new product which is:

Approximately **40%** cheaper than rope

Only buy what you need (sold in 25m coils with push on connectors)

White in Colour making it easily visible to players and umpires

For Security Personalize your F.B.M

Contact Details

For more information and price list please contact David Williams on:

Mobile: 07775602766

Email: david_fbm@yahoo.co.uk

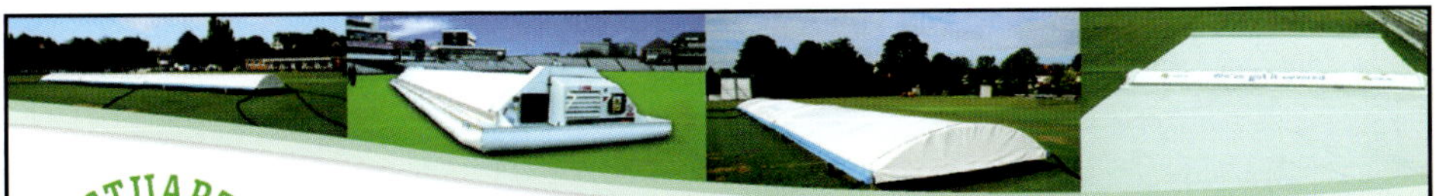

postponed?
Clear standing water fast...

BowDry™

BOW DRY

Bowcom™
game on...
play!

BowDry™ is a revolutionary groundrying
machine, designed specifically to
efficiently and effectively remove
standing water from any surface.

www.bowcom.com   +44 (0)29 2038 8349

The 2007 BOLA Cricket Bowling Machine

→ 12 volt battery or mains operation for use anywhere
→ The very latest speed control technology
→ One mph speed increments for total accuracy
→ 28 ball automatic feeder with remote control & random delivery mode

The Bowling Machine used throughout the West Indies for World Cup 2007

www.bola.co.uk

♣ ClubTurf
ClubTurf Cricket Limited

ClubTurf is the longest-established and market-leading non-turf cricket pitch with around 5,500 installations since 1978

"I am convinced that good non-turf pitches have a vital role to play in the future wellbeing of cricket in this country. This is especially true of cricket in state schools, but good non-turf pitches that produce the changeable playing characteristics of natural turf also have an important place in the public school, university and club scenes."

Derek Underwood
Sales Director

The Nursery Ground at Lord's

When you're choosing an Artificial Pitch or Practice Area for your Club, School or University you'll want to talk to the world-leading experts chosen by the MCC for the Nursery Ground at Lord's and by Cambridge University for Fenner's.

Fenner's Cricket Ground Cambridge University

Visit our web site
www.clubturf.com

Contact us for a brochure or to speak to one of our team

Lea House, 5 Middlewich Road, Sandbach, Cheshire, CW11 1XR
Tel: 01270 753344 | Fax: 01270 753644 | Email: info@clubturf.com

The late Bob Woolmer with Warwickshire's South Africans Shaun Pollock, Brian McMillan and Allan Donald.

us at Edgbaston took the club to a different level. He was superb. A father figure; keen as they come and with a professional approach and attention to detail that was allied to excellent communication skills and a healthy portion of common sense.

Things were now very different. Woolly made a point of encouraging us and generating a positive atmosphere in the dressing room. That really is half the job of a coach. Once the spirit is right, it's also much easier to suggest technical or tactical changes.

One of the first things Woolmer did was insist that a physiotherapist travelled everywhere with the team. In retrospect it seems hard to believe that this wasn't always the case, but before Bob arrived we had been forced to rely on the opponent's physio being honest when treating and advising us. All this whilst he and their team knew the state of play; it led to many occasions when we were told that a bowler would "be better to sit this one out" while an opponent's batsmen made merry. The alterations made by Bob finally made the term "professional cricketer" an appropriate label for Warwickshire cricketers.

He wasn't afraid to be different. He judged Allan Donald's rhythm by listening to the noise the bowler made as he ran up, his feet on the floor and the sound as he passed the umpire. He did this with his back to AD. Over time he fine-tuned Donald's approach to the crease and played a significant part in his development into the world's premier fast bowler. Every delivery AD bowled was like an unwanted alarm call to our opposition. Such was the fear his pace instilled in our opponents that I remember a non-striker coming down the wicket and simply saying to the new, incoming batsman, "We're all doomed."

Bob's attention to detail was fastidious. He embraced new ideas as few men of his age tend to do and was open to any suggestion. He gave us the confidence to try new things and helped us understand what we were doing. The issue of reverse swing was a classic example and, under him, we learnt that chewing Extra Strong Mints helped the ball swing more. We even worked out that the spices in curry lingering in our saliva helped with shining.

Bob also used his experience as a pretty good hockey player. He often talked about batting with hockey techniques, specifically trying to hit the ball when it was directly underneath the eyes, and one day ended up playing a charity game with us just to demonstrate what he was talking about. Trying to make a point in the car on the way to the ground he finally said, "I'll bloody well have to show you what I mean." Besides, his wife and children were in Cape Town at the time and we knew he would be pining for them. The game took place on the Britannic Assurance pitch, just up the road from Edgbaston, and I was at the other end when he came to the crease. I can only say that he really did bat like God that day. I've no doubt that he still had the ability to play professionally at this stage - even though he was in his mid-40s - but his fitness would simply not have allowed it. He smashed it to all parts; it was made more impressive by his repeatedly predicting the outcome of the next delivery he'd face. I'd only seen Lara and Sobers do that. Bob showed that if you worked hard, thought positively and backed yourself, anything was possible.

Bob put the smiles back on faces at Edgbaston, creating an environment where everyone wanted to be involved. The hard work didn't seem that hard. He actually passed on the ability to self-coach if and when things were going against you. He taught us how to asses and correct things within games and taught us about the importance of imagination and affirmation. He was miles ahead of other coaches at that time.

He was always hugely suspicious about what we were up to off the pitch, however. It became an endless source of fun. In Trinidad on his first pre-season tour with us, he announced at 10pm that our accommodation front door key would be left above the entrance door frame at all times. He then moved into the room next to the front door. Eight hours later I returned with a team-mate to find Woolly hadn't kept his promise, he'd retained the key. Our knocking brought a rapidly learning coach to our aid; the excuse that we had gone for a walk to ease our jet-lagged legs didn't totally convince him.

Next year we went to Cape Town. When Bob started worrying that our social life was detracting from our training sessions, he had us relocated to a health spa in the wilderness. Very soon that led to players creeping out in the night and returning to Cape Town.

On one such trip I returned at dawn to find a large, white object crouched down in bushes by the complex entrance. It was Woolmer. He had risen early to catch us as we came in. I crept in around the back and went to bed only to be confronted by an irate coach who asked where I had been and how much sleep I'd had. I denied everything and my tour continued, but what the incident showed was how much he cared. He lived every ball of every game and took great pride in our success.

Bob demanded maximum effort at all times. He gave 100% himself and expected it of all the players. He was forever drumming into us the importance of plenty of sleep and avoiding alcohol, but he knew there had to be times to unwind and have a laugh. I loved working with him. I learned a great deal.

Deep down I'd like to think Bob understood that all players are different. I remember a story I was told by former Australian leg-spinner Kerry O'Keefe. He and team-mate Doug Walters had shared a hotel room during a Test Match in New Zealand. The preparation for their

The bespectacled Paul Smith races off the field after his Man of the Match-winning performance in the 1994 Benson & Hedges Cup Final against local rivals Worcestershire.

performances had been contrasting. O'Keefe had gone to bed early evening, Walters not so. Nearer 6am in fact, when he had collapsed in a heap on top of his room-mate.

Breakfast had been contrasting again, O'Keefe drank orange juice and had cereals; Walters had to be plied with coffee and cigarettes. Walters scored a mammoth 247 without being dismissed. O'Keefe himself was dismissed first ball. Later in the day Walters was a national hero.

****

When the world's premier batsman Brian Lara arrived at Edgbaston in May 1994 we weren't disappointed; time and again he annihilated bowling attacks. Every team would bring on their best bowlers against him, only to be repeatedly smashed to the boundary fences. No one could control Brian on the pitch. He was on a different level. Our season gathered momentum. We were exciting to watch; our crowds grew and our expectations skyrocketed.

It wasn't just Lara, of course. We had the world's premier coach in Woolmer, while Dermot Reeve was streets ahead of other captains. Add to this squad Brian Lara, a hungry one at that, and you had a team worth watching. Every person involved had a passion, a real drive and spirit that eventually took things to unmatched heights.

Warwickshire were only to lose on four occasions over our triumphant summer. Taking into account how many games we played, 43, it's a pretty amazing statistic. We rose 15 places in the table that year - a record - and played a different style to the rest; always aggressive but just as importantly with a sense of humour never far from the surface. Nearly every squad member became a happening cricketer. Everybody had to add urgency to their game just to be considered for selection. It was a breath of fresh air.

Lara scored hundred after hundred. He became the first man to score seven first-class centuries in eight innings and equalled Don Bradman's record of passing 1,000 runs in his seventh innings of the season. In all he scored more than 2,000 at very close to a run a ball. Then we witnessed the genius breaking Hanif Mohammad's world record score of 499 when we played Durham. When the Trinidadian drove a half-volley for four to bring his score to 501 it was a supercharged moment. The hairs stood up on the back of my neck. Bob Woolmer is probably the only person who witnessed both innings. Having been brought up in India, he had been lucky enough to see Hanif's record-breaking innings 36 years earlier.

****

There were times we made fun of Bob. On his first pre-season tour in Trinidad we stopped the team bus at a KFC. Bob, having said he didn't like that sort of food, then took it upon himself to order for the whole team. Or so we thought. Actually, the mountain of dead chicken that he hauled back on to the bus was just for him. Bob liked his food to come by the bucketload. He was a man with a large appetite for life.

Another time he accused me of placing a large traffic cone on top of his brand new car. It wasn't me; it was the team's vice-captain, Tim Munton. In the end I suggested Bob ask to view the hotel's CCTV footage, but he was reluctant as it might just show up the tray of sandwiches he'd had delivered to his room an hour after dinner. Munton eventually owned up and I ordered two breakfasts to be delivered to Woolmer's room in the morning as punishment. I bet he ate them both.

****

Woolly's murder in Jamaica during the World Cup in March 2007 left a scar. Many members of the Warwickshire sides of the mid-90s spoke to each other in the following days; shock was the shared emotion. In amongst that, however, was a sense that we were all incredibly fortunate to have been able to work alongside him and to have seen incredible amounts of success along the way.

I was taking a Prince's Trust session at Edgbaston on the day it was announced that his death was the result of murder. Despite the sense of grief and outrage, his positive influence shone through. I ran the session exactly as I'd seen him run them. The emphasis was on fun, little challenges were set and everyone was involved.

The kids had a great time, but it brought back memories. Fond but painful memories. When I'd been with Bob in Cape Town we would sometimes run sessions together. Other Warwickshire players did the same. We saw how he worked, how he thought and how he communicated. It was a tremendously valuable experience and one I'd damn glad to have had. His methods will live on.

At the time of the murder in the Caribbean I know that Bob was in the process of starting an academy in Cape Town. He won't be around to see it, but I believe everything he planned should still go ahead and his family's announcement of a trust fund to ensure his work endures hopefully will see that happen. He had done so much work in the area - much of it for free - and it would have delighted him to think that future generations of kids could have the chance to play the game that he loved so dearly. I'd go and work in it, if only in his honour. But it will also require funding. A couple of big charity games featuring world stars to raise funds would guarantee its longevity.

WASTED? By Paul Smith (ISBN: 9781905449453) is available from all good bookshops priced at £16.99 or directly from the publishers Know the Score Books - www.knowthescorebooks.com

The East Midlands

DERBYSHIRE

ECB Premier League
Derbyshire County League
Burton & District League
Yorkshire & Derbyshire League

NOTTINGHAMSHIRE

ECB Premier League
South Notts League
Bassetlaw League
Newark Alliance
Mansfield & District Sunday League

LEICESTERSHIRE

ECB Premier League
Leicestershire County League

Ockbrook take nail-biter

by Alan Rowley

THE 2006 SEASON saw club cricket in Derbyshire continue to grow. There is little doubt that the success of the England team in the Ashes series in 2005 led to a much-needed surge in interest and local clubs benefited with increased membership, particularly in the junior sections.

The major league in Derbyshire, the **ECB Derbyshire Premier Cricket League**, went to Ockbrook and Borrowash for the third time in its eight-year history, following wins in the inaugural year, 1999, and 2005. It was a nail-biter of a season, as seems to be the case in the Premier, with Ockbrook battling with old rivals Sandiacre Town for much of the season. Going into the final weekend, Sandiacre held a three-point lead, but a 19-point winning draw for Ockbrook at Spondon, compared to a nine point losing draw for Sandiacre at Quarndon, left Ockbrook seven points clear with one to play.

Sandiacre batted first at home to Ilkeston Rutland and romped home for a 27-pointer. Ockbrook, meanwhile went for safety and batted second against Quarndon, knowing that a 22 point victory would give them the championship. A battling unbeaten 98 from former Derbyshire pro Jonny Owen saw the champions home by four wickets with eight overs to spare.

League newcomers Spondon and Alfreton Town performed with credit in their first seasons at the top flight finishing fourth and fifth respectively. For both clubs this was a major achievement, in particular the young Spondon outfit that had to play all their games away from home as their new ground was deemed to be not ready for the top flight. Their impressive new ground, just down the road from their tiny old ground, will meet the exacting Premier League standards for 2007, and this promising side will be making a bold attempt at the title.

**Johnny Owen in action - his final day undefeated 98
saw Ockbrook to the title.**

Ilkeston Rutland and Marehay were not so lucky. They finished well adrift at the foot of the table and slip down into the County League. They should be leading runners in Division One next season, provided they can hang on to their main players.

Amongst the players, three batsmen passed the 1,000 run mark. Alvaston and Boulton's Anthony Woolley topped the list with 1,066 runs, four runs ahead of Spondon's South African Colin Ingram. Jonny Owen came home in third place with 1,018 runs.

Top wicket taker was Ockbrook's reliable spinner Lian Wharton with 44 wickets, one more than Sandiacre's Naeem Akhtar. Another Ockbrook bowler, Neil Smith, came third with a total of 40 victims.

There was no joy for the Derbyshire clubs in the ECB Cockspur Cup, the national club championship tournament. Previous winners Sandiacre

Town, and Ockbrook and Borrowash, runners-up in 2005, both crashed out at the preliminary round stage.

The Premier Cup final was fought out between the league champions, Ockbrook and Borrowash, and the runners-up, Sandiacre Town. These old rivals played out a tense, hard fought game, with the result in doubt until three overs from the end, and the final rites were not concluded without a little controversy.

Ockbrook posted a total of 190 all out, thanks to 43 from Matt Cassar and 37 from Jonny Owen. When Sandiacre slumped to 17 for 2, the writing looked to be on the wall, but a fighting 36 from Charlie Ault, followed by a rapid 46 from David Jordison, dragged Sandiacre back into the game.

**Matt Cassar, Man of the Match in the
Derbyshire Premier Cup Final.**

With five overs to go Sandiacre had reached 160-7 but they then lost two wickets in two balls and, in the 48th over, with the last pair at the crease Ian Darlington had Irfan Ul Haq leg before with 16 balls left, giving Ockbrook victory by 16 runs. It could have gone either way in the end.

There was a hint of controversy at the very end because Sandiacre felt that the final ball should have been declared no ball, as Ockbrook had not posted four players inside the circle, as required by the rules. However, as we all know, the decision of the umpires is final.

All of Ockbrook's bowlers performed with credit, notably Ian Darlington (3 for 30) and Neil Smith (3 for 46). The Man of the Match award went to Cassar, the Ockbrook captain.

Run machine Bin Nasir slams league record

The Derbyshire County League continued to go from strength to strength. In 2006, the league welcomed Pilsley and Ashover, who transferred over from the largely Nottinghamshire based Bassetlaw League. The Burton and District League continued to decline and seven clubs moved over, Alrewas, Barton-Under-Needwood, Burton, Hilton, Trentside, Walton-on-Trent and Winshill.

Pilsley were highest placed of the newcomers in the northern section, going straight into Division 2 North, mainly on the strength of run scoring machine Saeed Bin Nasir. The free scoring Pakistani hit a league record 1,813 runs from 20 innings, at an average of 120.87. The highlight of this phenomenal performance was a chanceless 196 not out from a 287 total in only 40 overs against luckless Ambergate in June. Bin Nasir's efforts ensured Pilsley a mid-table finish, silencing critics that they were a one-man team destined for relegation.

Of the southern based teams, Barton-Under-Needwood and Alrewas entered the league in Division 2 South. Both teams performed with credit, finishing fourth and fifth respectively. Hilton gained promotion at the first attempt finishing runners-up in Division 3 South to Derby Congregational, only going under by one point. They join their former Burton League rivals in 2 South in 2007.

Saeed Bin Nasir in the sort of explosive action which led to a new league record 1,816 runs for Pilsley in Division 2 North.

Champions of the County League in 2007 were Lullington Park, who cruised home 44 points clear of Elvaston, who in turn were 39 points clear of the third team. These two clubs will be welcomed additions to the Premier League. Lullington have excellent facilites, and although they are situated in remote South Derbyshire, most clubs will be relishing a visit to their attractive ground. Elvaston too have a superb location in the grounds of Elvaston Castle. These former Village Cup champions did well to shake off their 'village' reputation and concentrate on the serious business of league cricket.

In the npower Village Cup, Shipley Hall entered for the first time in many years and reached the semi-finals before crashing out to a rugged Yorkshire outfit from Houghton Main. Despite a brisk unbeaten 61 from Ryan North, and a steady 40 from Simon Walker, Shipley's 189 for 7 from 40 overs never looked like being enough. Richard Jones sealed it for the visitors crashing 57 including 5 sixes and 3 fours. Shipley will be looking to revive their Lord's dream in 2007.

The Premier and County Leagues' Play Cricket website (http://dpcl.play-cricket.com) continues to lead the way. By far the most read league site on the network, the DPCL site is superbly administered by fixture secretary Chris Higginbottom. Chris's dedication ensures that all the results from all 17 divisions are available online by 10:00pm on the day of the game.

2006 Debyshire Premier & County League Tables

KEY:

'p' = Played 'wbf'= Won Batting First (27 points) 'wbs'= Won Batting Second (22 points)
'w11'= Winning draw >75 (11 points) 'w10'= Winning draw 51-75 (10 points)
'w9'= Winning draw 26-50 (9 points) 'w8'= Winning draw 25> (8 points) 't'= Tied (8 points)
'l4'= Losing draw 25> (4 points) 'l3'= Losing draw 26-50 (3 points)
'l2'= Losing draw 51-75 (2 points) 'l1'= Losing draw >75 (1 points)
'can'= Cancelled (5 points) 'ab'= Abandoned (5 points)
'lbs'= Lost Batting Second (0 points) 'lbf'= Lost Batting First (0 points)
'bp' = Bonus Points 'pen' = Penalty Points 'nrr' = Net Run Rate
'pts' = Total Points

ECB Derbyshire Premier Cricket League - Sponsored by : Beechwood SAAB

	P	wbf	wbs	w11	w10	w9	w8	t	l4	l3	l2	l1	can	ab	lbs	lbf	BP	Pen	Pts
Ockbrook & B'sh - 1st XI	22	4	7	3	1	0	1	0	1	0	0	0	0	4	1	0	77	0	414
Sandiacre Town - 1st XI	22	6	6	2	1	1	0	1	0	1	0	0	0	1	0	3	66	5	412
Dunstall - 1st XI	22	3	5	0	1	1	3	1	0	0	1	0	1	3	1	2	78	0	342
Spondon - 1st XI	22	0	10	0	1	0	0	0	0	0	1	0	0	5	1	4	61	5	313
Alfreton - 1st XI	22	3	3	1	1	0	0	0	2	0	1	1	1	3	1	5	79	0	278
Quarndon - 1st XI	22	3	1	0	1	2	0	0	0	1	3	0	1	5	0	5	101	0	271
Clifton Derby - 1st XI	22	0	6	0	0	2	0	0	0	1	0	1	3	3	3	3	70	0	254
Chesterfield - 1st XI	22	1	3	0	1	0	0	0	0	2	1	2	3	4	2	3	86	1	233
Denby - 1st XI	22	1	2	0	2	0	2	0	0	1	0	0	2	4	1	7	90	0	230
A'ton & Boulton - 1st XI	22	1	4	0	0	0	1	0	2	0	0	0	1	3	2	8	76	0	227
Marehay - 1st XI	22	1	1	0	0	1	0	0	1	1	1	2	1	5	5	3	102	0	201
Ilkeston Rutland - 1st XI	22	1	0	0	0	1	0	0	1	1	1	0	3	2	7	5	99	0	169

Derbyshire County Cricket League Division 1 - Sponsored by : Abbey Glass

	P	wbf	wbs	w11	w10	w9	w8	l4	l3	l2	l1	can	ab	lbs	lbf	BP	Pen	Pts
Lullington Park - 1st XI	22	5	5	0	1	5	1	0	1	1	0	0	2	0	1	81	0	404
Elvaston - 1st XI	22	4	7	0	0	1	0	1	1	0	1	0	3	1	3	66	0	360
Sawley & LE Pk - 1st XI	22	1	7	2	0	0	0	0	2	0	1	1	4	0	4	86	0	321
Swarkestone - 1st XI	22	2	4	2	1	1	0	0	0	1	1	1	2	2	5	106	0	307
Ticknall - 1st XI	22	1	5	1	1	1	1	0	0	1	1	1	4	2	3	98	0	301
Rolleston - 1st XI	22	1	6	0	0	1	1	0	4	1	0	1	3	1	3	90	0	300
Aston on Trent - 1st XI	22	2	3	1	2	1	0	1	0	0	0	0	4	2	6	119	3	300

	P	wbf	wbs	w11	w10	w9	w8	l4	l3	l2	l1	can	ab	lbs	lbf	BP	Pen	Pts
Nutbrook - 1st XI	22	0	8	0	0	0	0	0	0	2	0	1	2	5	4	76	0	271
Matlock - 1st XI	22	1	4	0	1	1	1	1	1	0	2	2	2	0	6	93	0	264
Duffield - 1st XI	22	1	4	0	0	2	0	2	2	0	0	1	2	1	7	97	0	259
Tutbury - 1st XI	22	4	1	1	0	0	0	0	1	0	0	2	3	2	8	90	0	259
Staveley Welfare - 1st XI	22	0	2	0	0	1	1	0	2	0	1	2	1	6	6	99	0	182

Division 2 North - Sponsored by : Ow-Zat Cricket Shop

	P	wbf	wbs	w11	w10	w9	w8	l4	l3	l2	l1	can	ab	lbs	lbf	BP	Pen	Pts
Shipley Hall - 1st XI	22	4	8	1	0	3	0	1	0	0	0	1	2	0	2	57	0	398
Denby - 2nd XI	22	3	2	0	4	0	4	1	1	1	1	2	2	0	1	101	0	328
Belper Meadows - 1st XI	22	2	4	1	1	0	2	0	0	2	1	2	2	0	5	91	0	295
South Wingfield - 1st XI	22	1	8	0	0	0	0	1	1	2	0	2	2	4	1	60	0	294
Heanor Town - 1st XI	22	0	7	0	0	1	0	2	3	0	1	0	2	1	5	94	0	285
Pilsley - 1st XI	22	3	1	0	1	2	2	1	0	0	0	3	1	3	5	91	0	262
Wirksworth - 1st XI	22	0	4	1	1	1	1	2	0	0	0	2	3	2	5	102	0	261
Chesterfield - 2nd XI	22	1	3	0	0	1	1	1	2	2	0	3	5	0	3	91	0	255
Riddings - 1st XI	22	1	4	0	1	1	1	0	1	2	0	4	1	2	4	75	0	249
Ambergate - 1st XI	22	0	3	0	2	0	2	3	0	1	0	2	1	2	6	114	2	243
Quarndon - 2nd XI	22	1	2	0	1	1	2	2	1	1	1	1	3	2	4	99	0	239
Clay Cross - 1st XI	22	2	1	1	1	0	0	1	1	1	0	2	4	2	6	84	0	220

Division 2 South - Sponsored by : Burton Glass

	P	wbf	wbs	w11	w10	w9	w8	t	l4	l3	l2	l1	can	ab	lbs	lbf	BP	Pen	Pts
Rolls- Royce - 1st XI	22	3	9	0	4	0	0	0	2	0	1	1	1	1	0	0	64	0	404
Stainsby Hall - 1st XI	22	6	5	1	2	0	1	0	1	0	1	0	1	2	1	1	68	0	400
Ockbrook & B'sh - 2nd XI	22	3	5	2	2	0	1	1	0	0	1	0	3	1	1	2	73	0	344
Barton U. N'wood - 1st XI	22	4	4	0	2	1	0	0	1	1	0	0	1	1	2	5	79	0	321
Alrewas - Sat 1st XI	22	4	1	2	2	0	2	0	1	0	0	0	2	3	2	3	91	0	308
Sandiacre Town - 2nd XI	22	0	6	0	0	1	3	0	0	0	1	0	1	5	0	5	92	0	289
B'ford & Ednaston - 1st XI	22	3	5	0	0	0	0	1	1	1	1	1	2	2	1	4	59	0	288
Spondon - 2nd XI	22	2	6	0	0	1	0	0	0	0	2	1	2	1	2	5	66	3	278
Allestree - 1st XI	22	3	1	0	2	1	0	0	0	1	1	1	2	1	3	6	87	0	240
West Hallam WR - 1st XI	22	2	1	0	0	0	2	0	0	2	2	1	2	1	5	4	96	0	214
Burton, Staffs - 1st XI	22	1	2	0	0	1	0	0	1	0	1	0	2	2	7	5	87	0	193
Sawley & LE Pk - 2nd XI	22	0	1	0	0	0	0	0	2	0	3	0	1	2	7	6	111	0	162

Division 3 North - Sponsored by : Viceroy Restaurant

	P	wbf	wbs	w11	w10	w9	w8	l4	l3	l2	l1	can	ab	lbs	lbf	BP	Pen	Pts
Darley Dale - 1st XI	22	9	3	0	3	1	0	0	0	0	0	2	2	1	1	41	0	409
Belper Amateurs - 1st XI	22	4	7	1	1	1	0	0	0	1	1	1	1	2	2	59	0	364
Langley Mill Utd - 1st XI	22	3	1	3	4	3	2	0	1	0	0	1	1	2	1	122	0	354
Ashover - 1st XI	22	4	5	0	2	0	0	0	1	1	0	2	3	1	3	66	0	334
Darley Abbey - 1st XI	22	0	6	1	0	0	1	2	2	0	0	1	2	3	4	90	0	270
Ilkeston Rutland - 2nd XI	22	3	4	0	0	0	0	1	1	1	0	1	2	3	6	71	0	264
Little Eaton - 1st XI	22	2	4	0	0	0	1	0	2	3	0	1	2	2	5	87	0	264
Shipley Hall - 2nd XI	22	1	5	0	0	0	0	1	1	2	0	2	3	1	6	81	0	254
Marehay - 2nd XI	22	0	4	1	1	2	1	1	1	0	2	2	1	3	3	95	0	254
Swanwick Hall - 1st XI	22	2	4	0	0	2	0	0	0	1	2	2	2	3	4	64	0	248
Morton Colliery - 1st XI	22	2	4	0	0	1	0	0	0	2	1	3	2	4	3	59	0	240
Staveley Welfare - 2nd XI	22	1	0	0	0	0	0	0	1	0	0	4	1	6	9	44	0	99

Derbyshire

Division 3 South - Sponsored by : Engments

Team	P	wbf	wbs	w11	w10	w9	w8	l4	l3	l2	l1	can	ab	lbs	lbf	BP	Pen	Pts
Derby Cong. - 1st XI	22	3	5	0	1	3	1	0	0	0	0	1	2	1	5	89	0	340
Hilton, Derbys - 1st XI	22	2	2	2	4	3	2	0	0	1	0	2	2	1	1	114	0	339
A'ton & Boulton - 2nd XI	22	3	7	1	0	0	0	0	0	1	0	2	5	2	1	51	0	334
Elvaston - 2nd XI	22	3	6	1	1	0	2	0	0	0	1	0	3	3	2	68	3	331
D'cott & Hanbury - 1st XI	22	2	6	1	2	0	0	1	1	0	1	3	3	1	1	67	0	322
Walton-on-Trent - 1st XI	22	2	3	0	0	1	0	1	3	1	1	3	3	2	2	90	-10	275
Trentside - 1st XI	22	0	6	2	0	0	0	1	1	2	0	3	1	0	6	74	0	259
Rolleston - 2nd XI	22	1	5	1	0	1	0	1	1	0	1	2	2	2	5	72	0	257
Lullington Park - 2nd XI	22	1	3	1	0	1	2	2	1	0	2	2	2	2	3	93	22	233
Ticknall - 2nd XI	22	2	1	0	0	0	1	1	2	3	2	2	2	2	4	91	0	213
Old Derbeians - 1st XI	22	0	2	1	0	1	1	2	0	1	2	0	3	3	6	119	5	213
Dunstall - 2nd XI	22	1	1	0	2	0	0	0	1	1	0	0	4	1	11	106	6	194

Division 4 North - Sponsored by : Field Sports

Team	P	wbf	wbs	wcn	w11	w10	w9	w8	l4	l3	l2	l1	can	ab	lbs	lbf	lcn	BP	Pen	Pts
Breadsall - 1st XI	22	3	9	1	2	2	0	0	1	1	0	0	1	2	0	0	0	56	0	426
Clowne Town - 1st XI	22	3	6	0	0	4	1	0	0	0	0	1	2	2	1	2	0	69	0	352
Riddings - 2nd XI	22	4	6	0	0	0	0	1	0	1	2	0	3	1	0	4	0	53	0	328
Cromford M'dws - 1st XI	22	2	8	0	0	0	0	1	0	0	1	0	2	1	3	4	0	60	0	315
Alfreton - 2nd XI	22	4	2	0	0	2	1	1	0	0	2	0	2	3	1	3	1	71	0	289
Ashbourne - 1st XI	22	4	2	0	0	0	0	2	0	1	0	0	4	4	2	3	0	64	0	275
Whitmoor RC - 1st XI	22	1	6	1	0	0	0	0	2	0	0	1	3	2	4	2	0	44	0	264
Belper Meadows - 2nd XI	22	1	5	0	0	1	1	0	1	1	0	0	3	1	0	8	0	72	0	255
South Wingfield - 2nd XI	22	2	2	0	0	1	1	0	0	1	2	0	3	2	1	7	0	93	0	242
Tibshelf - 1st XI	22	2	1	1	0	0	0	0	0	0	0	0	6	2	3	7	0	60	0	203
Wirksworth - 2nd XI	22	2	3	0	0	0	1	0	0	1	1	0	2	1	5	5	1	59	27	181
Selston Town - 1st XI	22	0	0	0	0	0	1	0	1	0	2	0	3	1	8	5	1	79	0	116

Division 4 South - Sponsored by : MG Financial Services

Team	P	wbf	wbs	w11	w10	w9	w8	t	l4	l3	l2	l1	can	ab	lbs	lbf	BP	Pen	Pts
Littleover Cents. - 1st XI	22	6	6	3	0	0	1	1	0	0	0	0	2	1	1	1	55	0	413
Etwall - 1st XI	22	5	7	1	0	0	0	0	3	1	0	0	3	1	1	0	46	0	381
Clifton, Derby - 2nd XI	22	2	6	0	1	2	1	0	1	0	0	1	3	2	0	3	69	0	321
Melbourne Town - 1st XI	22	2	6	0	0	1	0	1	0	1	0	1	2	2	3	3	63	0	290
Lullington Park - 3rd XI	22	2	3	1	1	0	2	0	1	0	1	0	1	3	1	6	96	0	279
Winshill - 1st XI	22	1	6	0	1	0	1	0	1	0	1	0	3	2	1	5	59	0	267
Rosehill Meths - 1st XI	22	1	5	0	1	0	0	0	2	1	2	1	2	3	2	2	77	0	265
Ockbrook & B'sh - 3rd XI	22	4	2	0	0	0	1	0	0	1	0	0	3	3	2	6	70	0	263
Aston on Trent - 2nd XI	22	2	2	1	2	1	0	0	0	0	1	0	2	1	5	5	101	0	256
Swarkestone - 2nd XI	22	2	4	0	1	0	1	0	0	0	1	0	2	2	2	7	70	0	252
Sawley & LE Pk - 3rd XI	22	2	1	0	0	0	1	0	1	0	1	1	1	2	4	8	89	0	195
Tutbury - 2nd XI	22	0	2	0	1	0	1	0	0	0	1	2	2	2	7	4	83	0	169

Division 5 North - Sponsored by : Geoff Cox Cars

Team	P	wbf	wbs	w11	w10	w9	w8	l4	l3	l2	l1	can	ab	lbs	lbf	BP	Pen	Pts
Heanor Town - 2nd XI	22	1	9	0	2	0	3	0	0	1	0	1	1	2	2	77	0	358
Darley Abbey - 2nd XI	22	3	8	0	1	0	1	0	0	2	0	2	1	0	4	48	0	342
Butterley United - 1st XI	22	2	4	3	2	3	0	1	0	0	0	3	1	2	1	91	0	337
W'worth S - 1st XI	22	3	4	0	1	1	0	0	1	1	0	3	2	1	5	76	0	294
Denby - 3rd XI	22	2	4	1	3	0	0	0	0	1	0	3	2	0	6	74	0	284
Belper Amateurs - 2nd XI	22	1	7	0	1	0	0	1	2	0	1	2	1	0	6	63	0	280
Codnor - 1st XI	22	1	4	1	1	1	0	0	1	4	0	3	1	0	5	69	0	245
Clay Cross - 2nd XI	22	1	4	0	0	2	0	1	2	1	2	1	2	1	5	83	0	245

	P	wbf	wbs	w11	w10	w9	w8	l4	l3	l2	l1	can	ab	lbs	lbf	BP	Pen	Pts
Ambergate - 2nd XI	22	0	5	0	2	1	0	0	1	2	1	2	1	3	4	80	0	242
Ashover - 2nd XI	22	0	6	0	1	0	0	0	2	0	0	2	2	3	6	64	0	232
Matlock - 2nd XI	22	2	1	0	1	2	0	2	1	2	1	0	2	1	7	85	0	215
West Hallam WR - 2nd XI	22	1	3	0	0	0	1	0	0	1	0	2	2	4	8	78	0	201

Division 5 South - Sponsored by : Savages

	P	wbf	wbs	w11	w10	w9	w8	l4	l3	l2	l1	can	ab	lbs	lbf	BP	Pen	Pts
B'ford & Ednaston - 2nd XI	22	4	11	0	1	0	1	0	2	1	0	0	1	0	1	41	0	422
Nutbrook - 2nd XI	22	3	11	0	1	1	0	0	0	0	0	2	2	1	1	29	0	391
Duffield - 2nd XI	22	3	7	0	2	3	0	0	0	0	1	0	3	0	3	71	0	369
Rolls- Royce - 2nd XI	22	3	3	1	5	1	0	0	0	0	0	1	0	3	5	106	0	328
Littleover Cents. - 2nd XI	22	6	2	0	2	1	0	0	0	1	0	1	0	5	4	85	0	327
Barton U. N'wood - 2nd XI	22	3	5	0	0	0	1	0	0	1	0	2	1	4	5	68	0	284
Rolleston - 3rd XI	22	1	6	0	1	0	0	1	2	2	0	2	1	1	5	69	0	267
Trentside - 2nd XI	22	4	5	0	0	0	0	0	0	0	0	2	3	3	5	49	33	259
Sandiacre Town - 3rd XI	22	3	2	0	0	0	0	1	3	1	0	3	2	2	5	65	0	230
Kirk Langley - 1st XI	22	1	2	0	0	2	0	0	1	4	0	3	1	3	5	88	0	208
Elvaston - 3rd XI	22	2	2	0	0	0	0	0	0	1	0	0	1	7	9	89	0	194
Etwall - 2nd XI	22	2	0	0	0	0	1	1	0	1	0	2	1	6	8	80	0	163

Division 6 North - Sponsored by : People Plus

	P	wbf	wbs	wcn	w11	w10	w9	w8	l4	l3	l2	l1	can	ab	lbs	lbf	lcn	BP	Pen	Pts
Alfreton - 3rd XI	22	1	14	0	0	0	1	0	0	0	1	0	3	1	0	1	0	16	0	382
Clowne Town - 2nd XI	22	4	6	0	1	2	0	0	0	2	0	0	2	2	0	3	0	49	0	346
Stainsby Hall - 2nd XI	22	2	7	0	0	1	1	2	0	0	1	0	1	2	2	3	0	80	0	340
Denby - 4th XI	22	3	6	0	1	1	1	1	0	1	2	0	3	1	1	1	0	56	0	334
Morton Colliery - 2nd XI	22	2	8	0	0	2	0	0	0	0	1	0	1	1	2	5	0	49	0	311
Marehay - 3rd XI	22	2	4	0	1	2	2	0	1	1	0	0	1	1	1	6	0	83	0	291
Swanwick Hall - 2nd XI	22	3	4	0	0	4	1	0	0	0	0	0	2	1	1	6	0	57	0	290
Darley Dale - 2nd XI	22	1	2	2	0	1	0	0	0	2	3	0	3	1	2	5	0	53	0	220
Belper Meadows - 3rd XI	22	3	1	0	0	0	1	0	2	0	3	0	3	1	3	5	0	71	0	217
Langley Mill Utd - 2nd XI	22	2	2	0	0	2	0	0	0	1	2	0	2	1	5	5	0	58	0	198
Cromford M'dws - 2nd XI	22	0	2	1	0	1	0	0	0	0	2	1	2	2	4	7	0	75	0	181
Wirksworth - 3rd XI	22	1	0	0	0	0	0	0	0	0	1	2	1	2	3	9	3	41	0	87

Division 6 Central - Sponsored by : Pope Machinery

	P	wbf	wbs	wcn	w11	w10	w9	w8	l4	l3	l2	l1	can	ab	lbs	lbf	lcn	BP	Pen	Pts
Mickleover - 1st XI	20	4	5	0	4	2	0	1	0	0	0	0	0	1	1	2	0	76	0	371
Breadsall - 2nd XI	20	1	10	1	1	1	0	0	1	0	0	0	0	3	1	1	0	47	0	361
Quarndon - 3rd XI	20	5	2	0	2	2	1	1	2	0	1	0	1	0	1	2	0	80	0	333
Allestree - 2nd XI	20	5	5	0	0	0	0	0	0	0	2	1	2	1	4	0	33	0	295
Mugginton - 1st XI	20	1	10	0	0	0	0	1	0	0	0	1	1	2	2	2	0	38	27	282
Shipley Hall - 3rd XI	20	2	4	0	1	0	0	0	0	1	1	1	0	2	4	4	0	69	0	238
Parwich - 1st XI	20	6	0	0	0	0	0	0	0	0	1	1	2	2	3	5	0	49	0	234
B'ford & Ednaston - 3rd XI	20	3	2	0	0	0	0	0	1	1	1	1	1	1	3	6	0	69	0	214
Ilkeston Rutland - 3rd XI	20	3	2	0	0	0	1	1	0	0	0	0	2	1	5	5	0	55	0	212
West Hallam WR - 3rd XI	20	1	4	0	0	0	0	0	0	0	1	1	2	2	6	3	0	53	0	191
Ashbourne - 2nd XI	20	1	0	0	0	0	0	0	0	0	0	1	2	0	5	10	1	38	0	76

Division 6 South - Sponsored by : Slazenger

	P	wbf	wbs	wcn	w11	w10	w9	w8	l4	l3	l2	l1	can	ab	lbs	lbf	lcn	BP	Pen	Pts
Spondon - 3rd XI	22	3	10	0	1	0	0	0	2	0	0	0	3	2	0	0	1	35	0	380
Alrewas - Sat 2nd XI	22	3	6	1	1	1	1	0	0	0	0	0	2	3	0	4	0	53	0	348
Derby Cong. - 2nd XI	22	2	8	0	0	1	1	0	1	1	1	1	2	1	0	3	0	56	0	330
Castle Don. Town - 1st XI	22	1	4	0	0	5	3	2	0	0	0	0	0	2	0	5	0	101	0	319

Derbyshire

Team	P	wbf	wbs	wcn	w11	w10	w9	w8	l4	l3	l2	l1	can	ab	lbs	lbf	lcn	BP	Pen	Pts
Rosehill Meths - 2nd XI	22	4	3	0	0	2	0	0	1	0	3	0	3	2	1	3	0	60	0	289
A'ton & Boulton - 3rd XI	22	0	6	0	0	1	1	1	0	1	0	0	2	3	1	6	0	77	0	264
Ockbrook & B'sh - 4th XI	22	1	3	1	0	0	1	2	0	1	3	0	1	1	0	8	0	91	0	255
Sawley & LE Pk - 4th XI	22	1	6	0	0	0	0	0	1	2	2	0	3	1	3	3	0	60	0	253
Winshill - 2nd XI	22	2	3	0	0	1	0	0	0	2	2	0	2	2	4	4	0	75	0	235
Burton, Staffs - 2nd XI	22	1	2	0	0	3	1	0	0	0	1	1	1	2	3	7	0	87	0	215
Ticknall - 3rd XI	22	2	2	0	0	1	0	0	0	1	3	0	3	1	3	6	0	69	0	206
St Lukes & St M'ls - 1st XI	22	1	3	0	0	0	1	0	0	1	0	0	2	0	6	7	1	69	0	184

Division 7 North - Sponsored by : Castlemaine XXXX

Team	P	wbf	wbs	wcn	w11	w10	w9	w8	t	l4	l3	l2	l1	can	ab	lbs	lbf	lcn	BP	Pts
Pilsley - 2nd XI	20	5	4	3	0	0	0	0	0	0	0	0	0	3	2	2	1	0	21	350
Butterley United - 2nd XI	20	8	3	1	0	0	0	0	0	0	0	0	0	2	0	2	4	0	27	346
Codnor - 2nd XI	20	2	6	2	0	0	0	1	1	0	2	0	0	2	2	0	2	0	40	322
Calow - 1st XI	20	7	1	0	0	1	0	0	0	0	1	1	0	4	2	1	2	0	35	291
Chesterfield - 3rd XI	20	0	7	0	0	0	0	1	1	0	0	1	0	3	1	3	3	0	48	240
Tibshelf - 2nd XI	20	3	2	0	1	1	1	0	0	0	0	0	0	6	2	2	1	1	37	232
Alfreton - 4th XI	20	2	4	0	0	0	1	0	0	1	0	1	1	3	1	3	3	0	47	225
Middleton, Derbyshire - 1st XI	20	3	0	0	0	3	1	0	0	0	0	0	0	2	3	4	2	2	60	205
Ambergate - 3rd XI	20	2	2	0	0	0	0	0	0	1	0	0	0	2	2	5	3	3	42	164
Riddings - 3rd XI	20	1	1	0	0	1	0	0	0	0	0	0	0	5	1	5	6	0	57	146
Clay Cross - 3rd XI	20	0	0	0	0	0	0	1	0	1	0	3	0	4	2	6	3	0	79	127

Division 7 Central - Sponsored by : Castlemaine XXXX

Team	P	wbf	wbs	wcn	w11	w10	w9	w8	l4	l3	l2	l1	can	ab	lbs	lbf	lcn	BP	Pen	Pts
Marehay - 4th XI	20	3	9	0	1	0	0	1	0	1	0	1	1	0	0	3	0	34	0	341
Nutbrook - 3rd XI	20	5	4	0	0	1	0	0	0	2	0	1	1	3	0	3	0	54	0	314
Spondon - 4th XI	20	4	5	0	2	0	1	0	0	0	0	0	2	1	2	3	0	43	0	307
Duffield - 3rd XI	20	0	7	0	2	1	0	0	1	1	0	0	1	1	4	2	0	70	0	273
A'ton & Boulton - 4th XI	20	4	2	0	0	2	2	0	0	0	1	0	1	1	3	4	0	67	0	269
Sawley & LE Pk - 5th XI	20	1	3	0	0	2	3	2	0	1	1	0	2	2	0	3	0	82	0	263
Kirk Langley - 2nd XI	20	2	4	0	0	0	0	0	1	0	2	1	4	1	1	4	0	42	0	218
Sandiacre Town - 4th XI	20	2	1	0	0	2	1	0	1	1	1	1	1	2	3	3	1	75	0	205
Clifton, Derby - 3rd XI	20	0	4	1	0	0	0	0	0	2	1	2	1	1	2	6	0	59	0	194
Little Eaton - 2nd XI	20	2	2	0	1	0	0	0	0	1	1	0	1	1	6	4	1	70	0	194
Darley Abbey - 3rd XI	20	1	2	1	0	0	2	0	0	0	1	0	1	1	3	8	0	54	0	182

Division 7 South - Sponsored by : Castlemaine XXXX

Team	P	wbf	wbs	wcn	w11	w10	w9	w8	l4	l3	l2	l1	can	ab	lbs	lbf	lcn	BP	Pen	Pts
Hilton, Derbys - 2nd XI	22	5	9	1	0	0	1	1	0	1	0	0	1	1	0	2	0	33	0	423
Swarkestone - 3rd XI	22	3	8	0	1	1	1	0	0	1	0	0	2	2	2	1	0	56	0	366
Walton-on-Trent - 2nd XI	22	1	6	1	2	0	0	0	0	1	0	0	3	1	2	5	0	60	0	291
Lullington Park - 4th XI	22	0	8	1	0	1	1	0	2	0	1	0	3	2	0	3	0	53	22	288
Melbourne Town - 2nd XI	22	1	7	0	0	2	0	0	1	0	0	0	2	2	1	2	4	44	0	269
Tutbury - 3rd XI	22	2	3	2	0	0	0	0	0	1	2	0	3	1	1	5	2	47	0	248
Barton U. N'wood - 3rd XI	22	2	2	0	1	3	0	1	0	0	0	0	2	3	0	8	0	69	0	241
Elvaston - 4th XI	22	1	4	1	0	0	1	1	0	1	1	0	2	2	2	4	2	52	0	236
Ticknall - 4th XI	22	2	2	0	0	1	1	0	1	1	1	3	2	2	1	5	0	85	0	234
Trentside - 3rd XI	22	1	3	0	0	0	1	2	1	1	1	0	2	2	1	6	1	67	0	214
Dunstall - 3rd XI	22	1	2	3	0	0	0	0	0	0	1	0	2	1	5	6	1	39	0	208
Castle Don. Town - 2nd XI	22	0	0	2	0	0	1	0	0	0	1	1	2	3	4	7	1	62	0	153

2006 Debyshire Premier & County League Averages

BATTING: (top 6 - qualification 250 runs)

ECB Premier League

	M	Inns	NO	Runs	HS	Ave
Chris Lewis (Clif)	16	11	4	621	129*	88.71
Bilal Shafayat (Clif)	7	6	3	254	78	84.67
Anthony Woolley (A&B)	21	20	5	1066	139*	71.07
James Adams (Duns)	21	20	8	805	150*	67.08
Colin Ingram (Spon)	20	20	1	1062	155	55.89
Jonny Owen (Ockb)	22	22	3	1018	147	53.58

Division 1

	M	Inns	NO	Runs	HS	Ave
Matthew Cox (Matl)	20	20	3	1360	146	80
Shahid Khan (Ast)	22	20	4	1087	121	67.94
Wayne White (Swark)	12	11	4	383	74*	54.71
Rob Kettlewell (Elv)	21	17	8	462	63	51.33
Ryan Cowley (Tick)	19	16	4	600	93*	50
Ghulam Ali (Tutb)	19	18	2	790	116*	49.38

Division 2 North

	M	Inns	NO	Runs	HS	Ave
Saeed Bin Nasir (Pils)	20	20	5	1813	196*	120.87
Paul Marshall (Hean)	22	19	11	544	80*	68
Zahid Javed (Wirk)	20	18	2	1085	205*	67.81
Stephen Bullock (Den)	6	6	2	254	87*	63.5
A Cowen (BelpM)	20	20	2	989	135*	54.94
James Cokayne (Ship)	17	14	4	549	92*	54.9

Division 2 South

	M	Inns	NO	Runs	HS	Ave
Adrian Marsh (Stai)	19	18	6	1248	169*	104
Muhammad Alvi (RR)	21	21	5	1222	151*	76.38
Tommy Curtis (WHall)	9	9	2	453	111*	64.71
Dave Wood (Ockb)	17	17	3	857	127*	61.21
Muhammad Sultan (RR)	16	16	4	682	143*	56.83
Chris Attwood (Sand)	20	16	5	579	88*	52.64

Division 3 North

	M	Inns	NO	Runs	HS	Ave
Stephen Dymond (BelpA)	19	19	4	1097	154	73.13
Paul Bailey (LMill)	21	21	3	1059	200*	58.83
Tom Wilton (LEat)	21	20	2	712	148*	39.56
Andrew Bailey (LMill)	20	20	1	590	121*	31.05
Stuart Mee (LMill)	15	15	1	582	126	41.57
Jonathan Bradder (Mare)	16	16	3	568	76*	43.69

Clifton skipper Chris Lewis.
The former Notts, Surrey, Leicester and England all-rounder
topped the Premier League batting averages.

Division 3 South

	M	Inns	NO	Runs	HS	Ave
Tom Jones (Trent)	14	13	5	438	96*	54.75
Murray J Hunter (Tick)	7	7	1	318	124	53
Alan Barber (Hilt)	20	19	3	806	126*	50.38
Irfan Janjua (ODerb)	22	20	2	870	148*	48.33
Mark Baines (DCong)	20	15	6	420	85*	46.67
Haq Nawaz (A&B)	19	18	2	705	148	44.06

Division 4 North

	M	Inns	NO	Runs	HS	Ave
Jason Fenn (Ashb)	7	6	2	343	81	85.75
Adrian Hall (Bread)	14	13	3	653	134*	65.3
Shazad Akhtar (Alf)	6	5	1	250	108*	62.5
Rob Swallow (Tibs)	14	14	4	620	155*	62
Adam White (Clow)	20	15	7	452	117*	56.5
Glyn Long (Clow)	18	18	2	847	132	52.94

Division 4 South

	M	Inns	NO	Runs	HS	Ave
Clive Crocker (Ockb)	12	11	3	658	128*	82.25
A Yaqoob (Ast)	10	9	4	299	67*	59.8
Sam Dutton (Clif)	9	8	0	455	151	56.88
Neil Thurlow (Rose)	16	15	2	664	143*	51.08
Mick Meakin (Melb)	17	16	3	651	91*	50.08
Abdul Rehman (Litt)	8	8	1	342	121	48.86

Division 5 North

	M	Inns	NO	Runs	HS	Ave
Lucas Carlisle (Den)	8	8	4	357	88*	89.25
Bjorn Taylor (WingS)	16	16	3	843	122	64.85
Lee Atkin (Den)	8	8	1	439	107	62.71
Andy Matthews (Hean)	21	20	3	900	97	52.94
Dave Longdon (BelpA)	17	17	4	625	111*	48.08
Steve Alcock (DAbb)	20	19	3	734	111*	45.88

Division 5 South

	M	Inns	NO	Runs	HS	Ave
Robin Stevenson (Duff)	21	19	4	827	156*	55.13
Richard Fletcher (KLang)	16	16	6	540	125*	54
Yasir Mahmood (Litt)	8	8	1	370	91	52.86
Ben Goddard (Brai)	12	11	3	417	76*	52.13
Richard Bryan (Roll)	16	16	3	671	146*	51.62
David Hack (Nutb)	15	11	2	448	89	49.78

Division 6 North

	M	Inns	NO	Runs	HS	Ave
Pete Stone (Stai)	10	10	5	461	109	92.2
Michael Glenn (Den)	13	9	5	273	73*	68.25
Martin Quinn (Mort)	10	8	3	332	96	66.4
Richard Wells (Swan)	7	6	1	278	82	55.6
Dave Coxhead (Swan)	17	14	7	299	52*	42.71
John Beard (BelpM)	6	6	0	256	134	42.67

Derbyshire

Division 6 South

	M	Inns	NO	Runs	HS	Ave
John Cooper (Spon)	3	3	2	302	173*	302
Nigel Sulley (Ockb)	2	2	1	258	161*	258
Stephen C Watson (Alrew)	7	7	3	314	117*	78.5
Mushtaq Khan (Rose)	13	11	2	671	138	74.56
Chris Hodgetts (A&B)	13	11	2	630	135	70
Melvyn Ratcliffe (Ockb)	7	6	2	265	85*	66.25

Division 6 Central

	M	Inns	NO	Runs	HS	Ave
Andrew Docherty (Mugg)	10	9	3	517	152	86.17
Richard Eley (All)	8	8	4	286	74*	71.5
Paul Lowe (Qua)	16	16	4	653	117	54.42
Chris Moseley (Bread)	18	16	5	587	101*	53.36
Nick Wilson (All)	11	9	2	345	99	49.29
Sebastian Maudling (Parw)	13	13	2	532	130*	48.36

Division 7 North

	M	Inns	NO	Runs	HS	Ave
Chris Fletcher (Ches)	5	5	3	273	100*	136.5
P Van Rensberg (Tibs)	8	7	3	396	212*	99
Pete Rohun (Tibs)	13	10	3	296	100*	42.29
Ian Lavender (Ridd)	10	10	2	322	72	40.25
David Hopkinson (Midd)	16	15	1	537	91	38.36
Harry Clark-Hallam (Codn)	13	12	3	340	61*	37.78

Division 7 South

	M	Inns	NO	Runs	HS	Ave
Jerry Gregson (Swark)	18	16	9	660	79*	94.29
Paul Slaney (Hilt)	17	13	5	506	97	63.25
Paul Laurie (Melb)	8	7	1	342	87	57
Stephen Berry (Hilt)	14	13	5	444	121*	55.5
Sam van Daesdonk (Bart)	13	12	3	472	110*	52.44
T Hill (Bart)	8	6	0	303	92	50.5

Division 7 Central

	M	Inns	NO	Runs	HS	Ave
Russell Henshaw (Nutb)	3	3	0	250	138	83.33
Chris Woods (Spon)	9	9	2	468	126	66.86
Derren Birch (KLang)	10	9	4	328	108*	65.6
James Riley (Sand)	6	5	1	253	101*	63.25
Terry Tinsley (Mare)	13	13	5	455	107	56.88
Jerry Bygraves (Duff)	6	6	1	279	111*	55.8

BOWLING: (top 6 - qualification 25 wickets)

ECB Premier League

	Ovs	M	Runs	Wkts	BB	Ave
Naeem Akhtar (Sand)	218.1	52	543	43	5/19	12.63
Neil Smith (Ockb)	159.5	23	656	40	6/33	16.4
James Adams (Duns)	165.1	14	575	35	5/14	16.43
Lian Wharton (Ockb)	215.3	43	768	44	6/35	17.45
Ian Parkin (Sand)	162.4	19	590	31	5/21	19.03
James Chapman (Den)	198	52	694	36	6/56	19.28

Division 1

	Ovs	M	Runs	Wkts	BB	Ave
Andrew Goodwin (Lull)	174	20	638	47	5/31	13.57
Shahid Khan (Ast)	268	50	872	61	5/27	14.3
Balraj Johal (Duff)	137.5	15	524	33	5/15	15.88
Brett Crichton (Elv)	168.2	35	580	32	5/59	18.13
Alex Britton (Roll)	185.4	32	697	36	5/42	19.36
Steve Haslam (Matl)	187	32	539	27	4/29	19.96

Division 2 North

	Ovs	M	Runs	Wkts	BB	Ave
Parry Ghadiali (ClayC)	169.2	33	478	30	6/25	15.93
Tim Kirk (Ches)	128.5	16	571	34	7/44	16.79
Liam Chapman (Qua)	182.2	27	552	32	4/38	17.25
Rajesh Ramesh (Amb)	196.4	33	693	40	6/25	17.33
Paul Chapman (Qua)	142.4	18	522	29	4/18	18
John Buckley (Ship)	183	28	654	33	4/27	19.82

Division 2 South

	Ovs	M	Runs	Wkts	BB	Ave
Andrew Barlow (Stai)	166.2	29	572	42	5/23	13.62
Ollie Broadway (Alre)	219.3	38	655	45	5/27	14.56
James Stevenson (Alre)	115	22	457	27	6/62	16.93
Steve Dash (Spon)	172	24	529	30	5/24	17.63
Jeff Wharton (Stai)	246.3	43	971	49	7/49	19.82
Stephen Briggs (Brai)	146.2	26	575	29	4/15	19.83

Division 3 North

	Ovs	M	Runs	Wkts	BB	Ave
Nilantha Cooray (DDale)	203.2	42	528	54	5/5	9.78
Andrew Ball (LMill)	145.2	27	451	38	8/30	11.87
Ben Moulds (Ilk)	175.4	39	543	42	7/25	12.93
Dayle White (Asho)	136.1	15	475	35	6/38	13.57
Rich Leam (Swan)	174.4	41	608	43	8/8	14.14
Scott Sager (BelpA)	266.2	54	834	59	6/30	14.14

Derbyshire

Division 3 South

	Ovs	M	Runs	Wkts	BB	Ave
Rick Crowther (A&B)	150.2	27	434	32	5/16	13.56
Steve Ottewell (A&B)	133.3	24	411	30	5/27	13.7
Steve Baines (DCong)	151	24	439	28	4/17	15.68
Chris Tye (Dray)	220.4	21	805	49	7/21	16.43
Chris Arnold (Hilt)	132.3	21	470	28	5/15	16.79
Edward Chapman (Walt)	224.4	38	790	46	10/55	17.17

Division 4 North

	Ovs	M	Runs	Wkts	BB	Ave
Gary Coxhead (Ridd)	159.3	58	359	37	7/32	9.7
Nieill Cuthbert (Bread)	138.5	23	508	50	7/47	10.16
Henry Guyler (Bread)	176.1	41	504	36	5/14	14
Kevin Barber (Crom)	171	27	567	36	6/21	15.75
Dale Steers (Clow)	178.5	40	545	34	4/36	16.03
Adrian Kershaw (Crom)	121.5	24	411	25	6/57	16.44

Division 4 South

	Ovs	M	Runs	Wkts	BB	Ave
Philip Mead (Etw)	207.3	43	637	65	7/17	9.8
Khuram Butt (Litt)	255.2	59	713	60	6/65	11.88
Chris Lees (Ockb)	129.3	15	497	37	6/26	13.43
Neil Winfield (Wins)	138	18	502	30	5/25	16.73
Mick Meakin (Melb)	131	15	581	33	6/50	17.61
Steve Price (Melb)	174.2	34	574	32	4/25	17.94

Division 5 North

	Ovs	M	Runs	Wkts	BB	Ave
Stuart Bonsall (Butt)	219.3	60	641	49	8/18	13.08
Paul Smith (DAbb)	192.3	34	594	45	6/22	13.2
Maurice Edwards (Hean)	177.3	43	529	39	5/39	13.56
Colin Haw (WingS)	139.5	23	500	35	4/26	14.29
Steve Taylor (WingS)	194	53	531	34	4/42	15.62
Bjorn Taylor (WingS)	184.1	26	730	42	6/46	17.38

Division 5 South

	Ovs	M	Runs	Wkts	BB	Ave
Dave Hughes (Trent)	138.1	26	511	38	6/24	13.45
Julian Humpidge (Bart)	138.5	21	471	35	6/23	13.46
Amir Ali (Litt)	103	17	404	27	6/13	14.96
Richard Fox (Elv)	153.1	23	526	35	5/40	15.03
Gulriaz Hanif (RR)	208.4	56	641	41	5/57	15.63
Adam Brookes (Nutb)	178.2	27	644	40	6/71	16.1

Division 6 North

	Ovs	M	Runs	Wkts	BB	Ave
Paul Linacre (Clow)	107	26	283	30	8/16	9.43
Dave Coxhead (Swan)	138	58	309	29	4/4	10.66
Steven Bennett (Clow)	148.2	36	408	34	5/25	12
Neil Matthews (Mort)	203	59	445	37	4/11	12.03
Daniel Scothern (Stai)	160	38	473	37	4/13	12.78
Ant Parry (Swan)	140.5	44	368	28	8/42	13.14

Division 6 South

	Ovs	M	Runs	Wkts	BB	Ave
David Abell (Alrew)	171.1	49	385	43	6/20	8.95
Michael Cockayne (Sawl)	203.1	49	616	53	6/28	11.62
John Longdon (Spon)	162	54	436	37	6/35	11.78
Martin Richards (Sawl)	82	10	380	32	7/53	11.88
Nick Parkes (StL)	146.3	42	355	27	6/27	13.15
Ben Symcox (CDon)	159.1	40	466	34	6/24	13.71

Division 6 Central

	Ovs	M	Runs	Wkts	BB	Ave
David Hibberd (Qua)	90.3	25	283	29	5/29	9.76
Steven Hogg (Mugg)	86	13	292	25	4/29	11.68
Steven Sargeant (Mugg)	170.3	53	459	39	8/25	11.77
David Hughes (Bread)	171.2	43	462	35	4/8	13.2
Brian Parker (All)	208.2	34	703	53	6/28	13.26
Oliver Dimmick (Mick)	129.1	23	401	29	5/23	13.83

Division 7 North

	Ovs	M	Runs	Wkts	BB	Ave
Kevin Lanyon (Codn)	159.5	42	368	34	4/10	10.82
Gareth Hatton (Pils)	146.3	38	354	32	5/21	11.06
John Johnson (Calow)	150	35	434	37	6/29	11.73
Ashley Hardwick (Butt)	151	34	451	38	8/45	11.87
Andrew Jowett (Codn)	128.4	23	375	31	5/22	12.1
Dave Gretton (Ridd)	137.4	20	519	26	5/60	19.96

Division 7 South

	Ovs	M	Runs	Wkts	BB	Ave
Nick Fryatt (Walt)	142.1	41	331	35	5/43	9.46
Barry Yeomans (Hilt)	181.3	43	487	47	6/12	10.36
Paul Slaney (Hilt)	177.2	47	409	39	7/34	10.49
John Chambers (Walt)	117.3	27	350	30	6/24	11.67
Geoff Leedham (Lull)	204.3	73	433	35	5/11	12.37
James Baker (Elv)	121.2	25	365	28	4/26	13.04

Division 7 Central

	Ovs	M	Runs	Wkts	BB	Ave
Terry Scott (Nutb)	132.3	46	283	28	7/11	10.11
Gordon Toft (Mare)	155.4	37	443	34	6/16	13.03
Robert Gilbert (Nutb)	145	31	531	34	5/27	15.62
Chris Sheldon (Duff)	105	8	463	29	5/30	15.97
Sam Harper (Spon)	120.5	28	416	25	5/46	16.64
Khalil Akbar (LEat)	151.5	29	493	29	4/44	17

Queen's Park then and now.
Above: action from a Derbyshire county game in the 1970s
and, below, the pavilion pictured in 2006.

Derbyshire ECB Premier League Preview of Season 2007

by Gwyn Jones

AT THE END OF last season the Grounds Committee reported that standards at some grounds were slipping below the Grade A+ required in the Premier League. Fortunately the mild Winter has given clubs the opportunity to rectify this and the evidence points to a great deal of activity in improvements at grounds and in facilities. Since Premier clubs have to cater for third and fourth teams in the County League the need for a second ground under their control has become imperative, and there are encouraging signs of real progress in this respect

The relations with the Derbyshire County Cricket Club remain good and the scheme by which a County player is assigned to each Premier club will continue after some slight delay

The League will again be participating in the League Cricket Conference President's Trophy with the opening fixture against neighbours Notts Premier League on 1st July. Roy Fox will be the Manager and Matt Cassar the captain.

Around the Clubs

ALFRETON showed last season that they are a strong club in terms of performance, coming fifth in the in League table with a very young side. They are also looking very strong in their administration, as evidenced by their activities during the Winter. They have reached an agreement with nearby Mortimer Wilson School, which will provide them with good practice facilities and a ground for their third and fourth teams. They are in negotiations with their local Council, Amber Valley, to obtain a long term lease which will give them encouragement to work on further improvements. Their aim is to build a second ground on Alfreton Park. On the field they remain a very young side, captained by Matthew

Lineker, with Jon Aspinall as Vice-Captain.. They are fortunate to have Tanvir Ahmed back as their overseas player. He had a wonderful season with them last time round with bat and ball. There is a real buzz about the place.

For **ALVASTON & BOULTON** 2007 ia a landmark year because they celebrate their 150th anniversary, and to mark this they are producing a commemorative brochure. There will be a cricket week in August with a game against the MCC as the highlight. They could do with a boost in their performances, but they set off without one of their stars because Campbell Ogilvie has transferred to Clifton. Their new captain is Steve Ottewell, who could be said to be approaching the veteran stage, but he has a wealth of experience and he showed last season that he is bowling as well as ever. The club is full of workers and during the interval they have been refurbishing both the showers and the main club room, with the hope of converting the verandah into a conservatory. Much is expected from their young players and they will benefit again from the services of Anthony Woolley, one of the outstanding all-rounders in the League. They have engaged a strong overseas player, Colin Birch, a 24 year old all rounder who plays for Western Province in South Africa. We wish them well in this important year

CHESTERFIELD struggled on the field last season, but there is a lot of experience in the side and they will hope to do better this time. Andy Brown takes over the captaincy from Simon Lacey and theses two former Derbyshire players will provide the backbone of the side. Tom Lungley will be their Derbyshire player - that has already been decided - and they have a new signing, Andrew Gait-Golding, who was previously on Derbyshire's books, having played recently in the London area. Simon King, the wicket-keeper, will be vic-captain. Their ground at Queen's Park is now back on the County circuit and the renovation has been completed with the final third of the square. Their pace attack will benefit from the transfer of Michael Deane from Denby. They will hope that the first class facilities will inspire this experienced side.

CLIFTON have appointed Simon Moore as captain, a post he held before Chris Lewis took over. The position regarding Lewis is not yet clear and if he is not available they have found good cover with the arrival of Campbell Ogilvie from A&B. Ogilvie is a genuine all-rounder, capable of hitting big centuries and with the knack of breaking troublesome partnerships. They have signed an interesting overseas player, Morne van Vuuren, a left arm spinner and right handed batsman who has been playing for Natal Dolphins. They will be disappointed at losing Aqib Afzaal, a young player of genuine promise who has joined the West Indian Cavaliers in Nottingham. There has been much activity carrying out ground improvements pre season

DENBY start the season with two full size grounds on the Copper Yard, which is good for a club with such a large membership. An extension to the Pavilion is in the planning stage in the hope that it will be completed by 2008, and in the meantime the two portacabins have been refurbished. The club will welcome back Stuart Poplar, their former captain, who has been playing for Matlock for two seasons. His experience has been missed and he will be a great help to young captain Ben Perry-Taylor and vice captain Joe Greenhalgh. They have been desperately trying to strengthen the side with the appointment of an overseas player, but sadly they may run out of time. In particular they need to strengthen their seam attack now that Michael Deane has left them. It is a very young side with genuine talent, but is short on experience.

DUNSTALL have signed Jimmy Adams as their overseas player, but they know that he will not be available on a regular basis. He is based in Nottingham and they hope to be able to include him on the odd weekend. However, they have signed Naeem Akhtar, who has had a long spell with Sandiacre, and they will still have a formidable opening attack with Craig Jennings joining Naeem. They have been unfortunate to lose their other paceman, Alan Gough, who has thrown in his lot with Lullington, and to make matters worse Steve Scrimshaw has joined Rolleston. Ex England paceman Devon Malcolm is still with the club but it has been decided to make him captain of the 2nd team where he can use his coaching experience to bring on their promising youngsters. Their highly competent wicket-keeper, Stuart Eustace, will take over the captaincy, and with Jamie and Matthew Benstead in the team they are capable of big totals.

ELVASTON, newly promoted, start the season with a new captain, Lee Archer, their wicket-keeper, with Nick Briars as vice captain. There is little change in the personnel from last season and they are fortunate to have Brett Crichton back from Australia as their overseas player. He had a wonderful season with them last year. They also welcome back to his roots Charlie Ault, who has spent the last two seasons gaining experience of Premier League cricket with Sandiacre. He spent his early years at the club and has matured into a genuine Premier batsman. There are others there, like all-rounder Paul Birch, who are capable of responding to pressure. Their ground in Elvaston Castle is a delight to visit and next season there will be an extra facility which will be welcomed by all visitors, a new car park which has involved cutting down trees in the neighbouring woodland, and has a path leading to the pavilion, all done at the expense of the South Derbyshire Local Authority. So, no more parking on the adjacent road! The entrance will be well signposted.

LULLINGTON PARK, the other promoted team, made a huge impression last season, leading the way as clear favourites to the title in the County League Division 1. They, too, have a delightful ground with excellent facilities. They will be relying mainly on their home grown squad, captained by Jonny Shales. Alan Gough has joined them from neighbours Dunstall to add a bit of zip to their attack and they have obtained an experienced overseas player from New Zealand, Nick Horsley, a batsman who has played regularly for Northern District. It will be interesting to see how they respond to the extra pressure of the Premier League.

OCKBROOK & BORROWASH, the current Champions, will operate with much the same squad as last year. They have lost Tom Lungley but they retain Jake Needham as their official County player. There has been a significant addition to the seam attack with the signing of Oliver Saffell from Ilkeston Rutland. Matt Cassar is their captain and when you look at the tried and tested players available they must be favourites to retain the title, with Jonny Owen, Trevor Smith, Lian Wharton and Dave Hallack with County experience. They have made an interesting overseas signing, Gary Ballance, who played with much success for Spondon last season but was not classed as an overseas player because of his age. Coming from Zimbabwe and now a year older he is a pupil at Harrow Public School and must be classed as overseas. He is a player of immense talent and Ockbrook hope that he will be available during the school holidays. During the Winter members have been busy updating their facilities.

QUARNDON have also been active with a major transformation of their ground. The field next to their main ground has been levelled and seeded and they have been assured of a grant for the square. Work on this should be completed during the Summer and they are hopeful to be playing on it in 18 months time. This year they have a new captain, Robin Williamson, but previous skipper Matt Dowman will still be available. David Adams has left the club but Chris Paget should be available during the vacation from Durham University where he is a student.

SANDIACRE TOWN, last year's runners up, will be aiming for the top spot once again. They have lost two of their main strike bowlers, Naeem Akhtar who has joined Dunstall and Irfan Ul Haq who has not returned. John Jordison is still there and he is one of the most effective strike bowlers in the League. They have also recruited Adam Barton, a seam bowler from the Derbyshire Academy. They had hoped to sign Wayne White and he wanted to join them, but he is now on the Derbyshire staff and the transfer was blocked. Danny Birch, the son of former Notts player John Birch, has also signed for Derbyshire but he may play for Sandiacre

The pavilion at defending champions Ockbrook & Borrowash.

under existing League rules and not be classed as a County player.. Their overseas player is Ryan McFadyean, from South Africa, an opening bowler who played with great success for Spondon a few years ago.

SPONDON will have the luxury of playing all their home fixtures on their delightful new ground now that it has been assessed officially as Grade A+. Last season they came through as a quality side, ending fourth in the League. They are fortunate to welcome back their South African overseas player Colin Ingram, who was a great success with them last year. He plays for Eastern Province in South Africa. Sam Kellogg is the captain and the squad is much the same as last year. They will be expected to do well.

2007 Derbyshire Premier & County League Fixtures

**Premier League and Division 1
start at 1.00pm. All other
divisions start at 1.30pm**

Beechwood SAAB ECB Premier League

Saturday April 28
Alfreton   vDunstall
Chesterfield   vDenby
Elvaston   vAlv & Boulton
Lullington Pk   vClifton
Ock & B'wash   vSandiacre T.
Spondon   vQuarndon

Saturday May 5
Alv & Boulton   vSpondon
Clifton   vElvaston
Denby   vLullington Pk
Dunstall   vChesterfield
Quarndon   vOck & B'wash
Sandiacre T.   vAlfreton

Sunday May 6
Alv & Boulton   vAlfreton
Clifton   vOck & B'wash
Elvaston   vSpondon
Lullington Pk   vDunstall
Quarndon   vChesterfield
Sandiacre T.   vDenby

Saturday May 12
Alfreton   vQuarndon
Chesterfield   vSandiacre T.
Denby   vDunstall
Elvaston   vLullington Pk
Ock & B'wash   vAlv & Boulton
Spondon   vClifton

Saturday May 19
Alfreton   vClifton
Chesterfield   vAlv & Boulton
Denby   vQuarndon
Dunstall   vSandiacre T.
Ock & B'wash   vElvaston
Spondon   vLullington Pk

Saturday May 26
Alv & Boulton   vDenby
Clifton   vChesterfield
Elvaston   vAlfreton
Lullington Pk   vSandiacre T.
Quarndon   vDunstall
Spondon   vOck & B'wash

Saturday June 2
Alfreton   vSpondon
Chesterfield   vElvaston
Denby   vClifton
Dunstall   vAlv & Boulton
Ock & B'wash   vLullington Pk
Sandiacre T.   vQuarndon

Saturday June 9
Alv & Boulton   vSandiacre T.
Clifton   vDunstall
Elvaston   vDenby
Lullington Pk   vQuarndon
Ock & B'wash   vAlfreton
Spondon   vChesterfield

Saturday June 16
Alfreton   vLullington Pk
Chesterfield   vOck & B'wash
Denby   vSpondon
Dunstall   vElvaston
Quarndon   vAlv & Boulton
Sandiacre T.   vClifton

Saturday June 23
Alfreton   vChesterfield
Clifton   vQuarndon
Elvaston   vSandiacre T.
Lullington Pk   vAlv & Boulton
Ock & B'wash   vDenby
Spondon   vDunstall

Saturday June 30
Alv & Boulton   vClifton
Chesterfield   vLullington Pk
Denby   vAlfreton
Dunstall   vOck & B'wash
Quarndon   vElvaston
Sandiacre T.   vSpondon

Saturday July 7
Alv & Boulton   vElvaston
Clifton   vLullington Pk
Denby   vChesterfield
Dunstall   vAlfreton
Quarndon   vSpondon
Sandiacre T.   vOck & B'wash

Saturday July 14
Alfreton   vSandiacre T.
Chesterfield   vDunstall
Elvaston   vClifton
Lullington Pk   vDenby
Ock & B'wash   vQuarndon
Spondon   vAlv & Boulton

Saturday July 21
Alv & Boulton   vOck & B'wash
Clifton   vSpondon
Dunstall   vDenby
Lullington Pk   vElvaston
Quarndon   vAlfreton
Sandiacre T.   vChesterfield

Saturday July 28
Alfreton   vAlv & Boulton
Chesterfield   vQuarndon
Denby   vSandiacre T.

Dunstall   vLullington Pk
Ock & B'wash   vClifton
Spondon   vElvaston

Saturday August 4
Alv & Boulton   vChesterfield
Clifton   vAlfreton
Elvaston   vOck & B'wash
Lullington Pk   vSpondon
Quarndon   vDenby
Sandiacre T.   vDunstall

Saturday August 11
Alfreton   vElvaston
Chesterfield   vClifton
Denby   vAlv & Boulton
Dunstall   vQuarndon
Ock & B'wash   vSpondon
Sandiacre T.   vLullington Pk

Saturday August 18
Alv & Boulton   vDunstall
Clifton   vDenby
Elvaston   vChesterfield
Lullington Pk   vOck & B'wash
Quarndon   vSandiacre T.
Spondon   vAlfreton

Saturday August 25
Alfreton   vOck & B'wash
Chesterfield   vSpondon
Denby   vElvaston
Dunstall   vClifton
Quarndon   vLullington Pk
Sandiacre T.   vAlv & Boulton

Saturday September 1
Alv & Boulton   vQuarndon
Clifton   vSandiacre T.
Elvaston   vDunstall
Lullington Pk   vAlfreton
Ock & B'wash   vChesterfield
Spondon   vDenby

Saturday September 8
Alv & Boulton   vLullington Pk
Chesterfield   vAlfreton
Denby   vOck & B'wash
Dunstall   vSpondon
Quarndon   vClifton
Sandiacre T.   vElvaston

Sunday September 9
Alfreton   vDenby
Clifton   vAlv & Boulton
Elvaston   vQuarndon
Lullington Pk   vChesterfield
Ock & B'wash   vDunstall
Spondon   vSandiacre T.

Abbey Glass Division 1

Saturday April 28
Duffield vIlk'ton R'land
Marehay vAston-on-Tr.
Nutbrook vSwarkestone
Rolleston vS'ley & LE Pk
Rolls Royce vTicknall
Shipley Hall vMatlock

Saturday May 5
Aston-on-Tr. vNutbrook
Ilk'ton R'land vRolleston
Matlock vMarehay
S'ley & LE Pk vShipley Hall
Swarkestone vRolls Royce
Ticknall vDuffield

Saturday May 12
Duffield vSwarkestone
Marehay vShipley Hall
Nutbrook vMatlock
Rolleston vTicknall
Rolls Royce vAston-on-Tr.
S'ley & LE Pk vIlk'ton R'land

Sunday May 13
Aston-on-Tr. vDuffield
Marehay vNutbrook
Matlock vRolls Royce
Shipley Hall vIlk'ton R'land
Swarkestone vRolleston
Ticknall vS'ley & LE Pk

Saturday May 19
Duffield vMatlock
Ilk'ton R'land vTicknall
Nutbrook vShipley Hall
Rolleston vAston-on-Tr.
Rolls Royce vMarehay
S'ley & LE Pk vSwarkestone

Saturday May 26
Aston-on-Tr. vS'ley & LE Pk
Marehay vDuffield
Matlock vRolleston
Nutbrook vRolls Royce
Shipley Hall vTicknall
Swarkestone vIlk'ton R'land

Saturday June 2
Duffield vNutbrook
Ilk'ton R'land vAston-on-Tr.
Rolleston vMarehay
Rolls Royce vShipley Hall
S'ley & LE Pk vMatlock
Ticknall vSwarkestone

Saturday June 9
Aston-on-Tr. vTicknall
Marehay vS'ley & LE Pk
Matlock vIlk'ton R'land
Nutbrook vRolleston
Rolls Royce vDuffield
Shipley Hall vSwarkestone

Saturday June 16
Duffield vShipley Hall
Ilk'ton R'land vMarehay
Rolleston vRolls Royce
S'ley & LE Pk vNutbrook
Swarkestone vAston-on-Tr.
Ticknall vMatlock

Saturday June 23
Duffield vRolleston
Marehay vTicknall
Matlock vSwarkestone
Nutbrook vIlk'ton R'land
Rolls Royce vS'ley & LE Pk
Shipley Hall vAston-on-Tr.

Saturday June 30
Aston-on-Tr. vMatlock
Ilk'ton R'land vRolls Royce
Rolleston vShipley Hall
S'ley & LE Pk vDuffield
Swarkestone vMarehay
Ticknall vNutbrook

Saturday July 7
Aston-on-Tr. vMarehay
Ilk'ton R'land vDuffield
Matlock vShipley Hall
S'ley & LE Pk vRolleston
Swarkestone vNutbrook
Ticknall vRolls Royce

Saturday July 14
Duffield vTicknall
Marehay vMatlock
Nutbrook vAston-on-Tr.
Rolleston vIlk'ton R'land
Rolls Royce vSwarkestone
Shipley Hall vS'ley & LE Pk

Saturday July 21
Aston-on-Tr. vRolls Royce
Ilk'ton R'land vS'ley & LE Pk
Matlock vNutbrook
Shipley Hall vMarehay
Swarkestone vDuffield
Ticknall vRolleston

Saturday July 28
Duffield vAston-on-Tr.
Ilk'ton R'land vShipley Hall
Nutbrook vMarehay
Rolleston vSwarkestone

Rolls Royce vMatlock
S'ley & LE Pk vTicknall

Saturday August 4
Aston-on-Tr. vRolleston
Marehay vRolls Royce
Matlock vDuffield
Shipley Hall vNutbrook
Swarkestone vS'ley & LE Pk
Ticknall vIlk'ton R'land

Saturday August 11
Duffield vMarehay
Ilk'ton R'land vSwarkestone
Rolleston vMatlock
Rolls Royce vNutbrook
S'ley & LE Pk vAston-on-Tr.
Ticknall vShipley Hall

Saturday August 18
Aston-on-Tr. vIlk'ton R'land
Marehay vRolleston
Matlock vS'ley & LE Pk
Nutbrook vDuffield
Shipley Hall vRolls Royce
Swarkestone vTicknall

Saturday August 25
Duffield vRolls Royce
Ilk'ton R'land vMatlock
Rolleston vNutbrook
S'ley & LE Pk vMarehay
Swarkestone vShipley Hall
Ticknall vAston-on-Tr.

Saturday September 1
Aston-on-Tr. vSwarkestone
Marehay vIlk'ton R'land
Matlock vTicknall
Nutbrook vS'ley & LE Pk
Rolls Royce vRolleston
Shipley Hall vDuffield

Saturday September 8
Aston-on-Tr. vShipley Hall
Ilk'ton R'land vNutbrook
Rolleston vDuffield
S'ley & LE Pk vRolls Royce
Swarkestone vMatlock
Ticknall vMarehay

Sunday September 9
Duffield vS'ley & LE Pk
Marehay vSwarkestone
Matlock vAston-on-Tr.
Nutbrook vTicknall
Rolls Royce vIlk'ton R'land
Shipley Hall vRolleston

Ow-Zat Cricket Shop
Division 2N

Saturday April 28
Ambergate   vDarley Dale
Belper Ams.   vPilsley
Denby   vChesterfield
Riddings   vHeanor Town
S. Wingfield   vBelper Mdws
Wirksworth   vStaveley Wel.

Saturday May 5
Belper Mdws   vWirksworth
Chesterfield   vS. Wingfield
Darley Dale   vRiddings
Heanor Town   vDenby
Pilsley   vAmbergate
Staveley Wel.   vBelper Ams.

Saturday May 12
Ambergate   vStaveley Wel.
Belper Ams.   vBelper Mdws
Heanor Town   vDarley Dale
Riddings   vPilsley
S. Wingfield   vDenby
Wirksworth   vChesterfield

Sunday May 13
Belper Mdws   vAmbergate
Chesterfield   vBelper Ams.
Denby   vDarley Dale
Pilsley   vHeanor Town
S. Wingfield   vWirksworth
Staveley Wel.   vRiddings

Saturday May 19
Ambergate   vChesterfield
Belper Ams.   vS. Wingfield
Darley Dale   vPilsley
Heanor Town   vStaveley Wel.
Riddings   vBelper Mdws
Wirksworth   vDenby

Saturday May 26
Belper Mdws   vHeanor Town
Chesterfield   vRiddings
Denby   vPilsley
S. Wingfield   vAmbergate
Staveley Wel.   vDarley Dale
Wirksworth   vBelper Ams.

Saturday June 2
Ambergate   vWirksworth
Belper Ams.   vDenby
Darley Dale   vBelper Mdws
Heanor Town   vChesterfield
Pilsley   vStaveley Wel.
Riddings   vS. Wingfield

Saturday June 9
Belper Ams.   vAmbergate
Belper Mdws   vPilsley
Chesterfield   vDarley Dale
Denby   vStaveley Wel.
S. Wingfield   vHeanor Town
Wirksworth   vRiddings

Saturday June 16
Ambergate   vDenby
Darley Dale   vS. Wingfield
Heanor Town   vWirksworth
Pilsley   vChesterfield
Riddings   vBelper Ams.
Staveley Wel.   vBelper Mdws

Saturday June 23
Ambergate   v Riddings
Belper Ams.   vHeanor Town
Chesterfield   vStaveley Wel.
Denby   vBelper Mdws
S. Wingfield   vPilsley
Wirksworth   vDarley Dale

Saturday June 30
Belper Mdws   vChesterfield
Darley Dale   vBelper Ams.
Heanor Town   vAmbergate
Pilsley   vWirksworth
Riddings   vDenby
Staveley Wel.   vS. Wingfield

Saturday July 7
Belper Mdws   vS. Wingfield
Chesterfield   vDenby
Darley Dale   vAmbergate
Heanor Town   vRiddings
Pilsley   vBelper Ams.
Staveley Wel.   vWirksworth

Saturday July 14
Ambergate   vPilsley
Belper Ams.   vStaveley Wel.
Denby   vHeanor Town
Riddings   vDarley Dale
S. Wingfield   vChesterfield
Wirksworth   vBelper Mdws

Saturday July 21
Belper Mdws   vBelper Ams.
Chesterfield   vWirksworth
Darley Dale   vHeanor Town
Denby   vS. Wingfield
Pilsley   vRiddings
Staveley Wel.   vAmbergate

Saturday July 28
Ambergate   vBelper Mdws
Belper Ams.   vChesterfield
Darley Dale   vDenby

Heanor Town   vPilsley
Riddings   vStaveley Wel.
Wirksworth   vS. Wingfield

Saturday August 4
Belper Mdws   vRiddings
Chesterfield   vAmbergate
Denby   vWirksworth
Pilsley   vDarley Dale
S. Wingfield   vBelper Ams.
Staveley Wel.   vHeanor Town

Saturday August 11
Ambergate   vS. Wingfield
Belper Ams.   vWirksworth
Darley Dale   vStaveley Wel.
Heanor Town   vBelper Mdws
Pilsley   vDenby
Riddings   vChesterfield

Saturday August 18
Belper Mdws   vDarley Dale
Chesterfield   vHeanor Town
Denby   vBelper Ams.
S. Wingfield   vRiddings
Staveley Wel.   vPilsley
Wirksworth   vAmbergate

Saturday August 25
Ambergate   vBelper Ams.
Darley Dale   vChesterfield
Heanor Town   vS. Wingfield
Pilsley   vBelper Mdws
Riddings   vWirksworth
Staveley Wel.   vDenby

Saturday September 1
Belper Ams.   vRiddings
Belper Mdws   vStaveley Wel.
Chesterfield   vPilsley
Denby   vAmbergate
S. Wingfield   vDarley Dale
Wirksworth   vHeanor Town

Saturday September 8
Belper Mdws   vDenby
Darley Dale   vWirksworth
Heanor Town   vBelper Ams.
Pilsley   vS. Wingfield
Riddings   vAmbergate
Staveley Wel.   vChesterfield

Sunday September 9
Ambergate   vHeanor Town
Belper Ams.   vDarley Dale
Chesterfield   vBelper Mdws
Denby   vRiddings
S. Wingfield   vStaveley Wel.
Wirksworth   vPilsley

Burton Glass
Division 2S

Saturday April 28

Allestree	vSpondon
Barton	vW. Hall. WR
Brailsford	vAlrewas
Derby Congs	vHilton
Sandiacre T.	vOck & B'wash
Stainsby Hall	vTutbury

Saturday May 5

Alrewas	vSandiacre T.
Hilton	vStainsby Hall
Ock & B'wash	vAllestree
Spondon	vDerby Congs
Tutbury	vBarton
W. Hall. WR	vBrailsford

Saturday May 12

Allestree	vAlrewas
Brailsford	vBarton
Derby Congs	vOck & B'wash
Sandiacre T.	vW. Hall. WR
Stainsby Hall	vSpondon
Tutbury	vHilton

Sunday May 13

Alrewas	vDerby Congs
Barton	vHilton
Brailsford	vSandiacre T.
Ock & B'wash	vStainsby Hall
Spondon	vTutbury
W. Hall. WR	vAllestree

Saturday May 19

Allestree	vBrailsford
Derby Congs	vW. Hall. WR
Hilton	vSpondon
Sandiacre T.	vBarton
Stainsby Hall	vAlrewas
Tutbury	vOck & B'wash

Saturday May 26

Alrewas	vTutbury
Barton	vSpondon
Brailsford	vDerby Congs
Ock & B'wash	vHilton
Sandiacre T.	vAllestree
W. Hall. WR	vStainsby Hall

Saturday June 2

Allestree	vBarton
Derby Congs	vSandiacre T.
Hilton	vAlrewas
Spondon	vOck & B'wash
Stainsby Hall	vBrailsford
Tutbury	vW. Hall. WR

Saturday June 9

Allestree	vDerby Congs
Alrewas	vSpondon
Barton	vOck & B'wash
Brailsford	vTutbury
Sandiacre T.	vStainsby Hall
W. Hall. WR	vHilton

Saturday June 16

Derby Congs	vBarton
Hilton	vBrailsford
Ock & B'wash	vAlrewas
Spondon	vW. Hall. WR
Stainsby Hall	vAllestree
Tutbury	vSandiacre T.

Saturday June 23

Allestree	vTutbury
Barton	vAlrewas
Brailsford	vSpondon
Derby Congs	vStainsby Hall
Sandiacre T.	vHilton
W. Hall. WR	vOck & B'wash

Saturday June 30

Alrewas	vW. Hall. WR
Hilton	vAllestree
Ock & B'wash	vBrailsford
Spondon	vSandiacre T.
Stainsby Hall	vBarton
Tutbury	vDerby Congs

Saturday July 7

Alrewas	vBrailsford
Hilton	vDerby Congs
Ock & B'wash	vSandiacre T.
Spondon	vAllestree
Tutbury	vStainsby Hall
W. Hall. WR	vBarton

Saturday July 14

Allestree	vOck & B'wash
Barton	vTutbury
Brailsford	vW. Hall. WR
Derby Congs	vSpondon
Sandiacre T.	vAlrewas
Stainsby Hall	vHilton

Saturday July 21

Alrewas	vAllestree
Barton	vBrailsford
Hilton	vTutbury
Ock & B'wash	vDerby Congs
Spondon	vStainsby Hall
W. Hall. WR	vSandiacre T.

Saturday July 28

Allestree	vW. Hall. WR
Derby Congs	vAlrewas
Hilton	vBarton
Sandiacre T.	vBrailsford
Stainsby Hall	vOck & B'wash
Tutbury	vSpondon

Saturday August 4

Alrewas	vStainsby Hall
Barton	vSandiacre T.
Brailsford	vAllestree
Ock & B'wash	vTutbury
Spondon	vHilton
W. Hall. WR	vDerby Congs

Saturday August 11

Allestree	vSandiacre T.
Derby Congs	vBrailsford
Hilton	vOck & B'wash
Spondon	vBarton
Stainsby Hall	vW. Hall. WR
Tutbury	vAlrewas

Saturday August 18

Alrewas	vHilton
Barton	vAllestree
Brailsford	vStainsby Hall
Ock & B'wash	vSpondon
Sandiacre T.	vDerby Congs
W. Hall. WR	vTutbury

Saturday August 25

Derby Congs	vAllestree
Hilton	vW. Hall. WR
Ock & B'wash	vBarton
Spondon	vAlrewas
Stainsby Hall	vSandiacre T.
Tutbury	vBrailsford

Saturday September 1

Allestree	vStainsby Hall
Alrewas	vOck & B'wash
Barton	vDerby Congs
Brailsford	vHilton
Sandiacre T.	vTutbury
W. Hall. WR	vSpondon

Saturday September 8

Alrewas	vBarton
Hilton	vSandiacre T.
Ock & B'wash	vW. Hall. WR
Spondon	vBrailsford
Stainsby Hall	vDerby Congs
Tutbury	vAllestree

Sunday September 9

Allestree	vHilton
Barton	vStainsby Hall
Brailsford	vOck & B'wash
Derby Congs	vTutbury
Sandiacre T.	vSpondon
W. Hall. WR	vAlrewas

Viceroy Restaurant Division 3N

Saturday April 28
Darley Abbey vBreadsall
Ilk'ton R'land vAshover
Lang. M. Utd vMarehay
Little Eaton vShipley Hall
Quarndon vClay Cross
S'wick Hall vClowne Town

Saturday May 5
Ashover vDarley Abbey
Breadsall vQuarndon
Clay Cross vLang. M. Utd
Clowne Town vIlk'ton R'land
Marehay vLittle Eaton
Shipley Hall vS'wick Hall

Saturday May 12
Darley Abbey vClowne Town
Ilk'ton R'land vS'wick Hall
Lang. M. Utd vBreadsall
Little Eaton vClay Cross
Quarndon vAshover
Shipley Hall vMarehay

Sunday May 13
Ashover vLang. M. Utd
Breadsall vLittle Eaton
Clay Cross vShipley Hall
Clowne Town vQuarndon
Ilk'ton R'land vDarley Abbey
S'wick Hall vMarehay

Saturday May 19
Darley Abbey vS'wick Hall
Lang. M. Utd vClowne Town
Little Eaton vAshover
Marehay vClay Cross
Quarndon vIlk'ton R'land
Shipley Hall vBreadsall

Saturday May 26
Ashover vShipley Hall
Breadsall vMarehay
Clowne Town vLittle Eaton
Darley Abbey vQuarndon
Ilk'ton R'land vLang. M. Utd
S'wick Hall vClay Cross

Saturday June 2
Clay Cross vBreadsall
Lang. M. Utd vDarley Abbey
Little Eaton vIlk'ton R'land
Marehay vAshover
Quarndon vS'wick Hall
Shipley Hall vClowne Town

Saturday June 9
Ashover vClay Cross
Clowne Town vMarehay
Darley Abbey vLittle Eaton
Ilk'ton R'land vShipley Hall
Quarndon vLang. M. Utd
S'wick Hall vBreadsall

Saturday June 16
Breadsall vAshover
Clay Cross vClowne Town
Lang. M. Utd vS'wick Hall
Little Eaton vQuarndon
Marehay vIlk'ton R'land
Shipley Hall vDarley Abbey

Saturday June 23
Clowne Town vBreadsall
Darley Abbey vMarehay
Ilk'ton R'land vClay Cross
Lang. M. Utd vLittle Eaton
Quarndon vShipley Hall
S'wick Hall vAshover

Saturday June 30
Ashover vClowne Town
Breadsall vIlk'ton R'land
Clay Cross vDarley Abbey
Little Eaton vS'wick Hall
Marehay vQuarndon
Shipley Hall vLang. M. Utd

Saturday July 7
Ashover vIlk'ton R'land
Breadsall vDarley Abbey
Clay Cross vQuarndon
Clowne Town vS'wick Hall
Marehay vLang. M. Utd
Shipley Hall vLittle Eaton

Saturday July 14
Darley Abbey vAshover
Ilk'ton R'land vClowne Town
Lang. M. Utd vClay Cross
Little Eaton vMarehay
Quarndon vBreadsall
S'wick Hall vShipley Hall

Saturday July 21
Ashover vQuarndon
Breadsall vLang. M. Utd
Clay Cross vLittle Eaton
Clowne Town vDarley Abbey
Marehay vShipley Hall
S'wick Hall vIlk'ton R'land

Saturday July 28
Darley Abbey vIlk'ton R'land
Lang. M. Utd vAshover
Little Eaton vBreadsall

Marehay vS'wick Hall
Quarndon vClowne Town
Shipley Hall vClay Cross

Saturday August 4
Ashover vLittle Eaton
Breadsall vShipley Hall
Clay Cross vMarehay
Clowne Town vLang. M. Utd
Ilk'ton R'land vQuarndon
S'wick Hall vDarley Abbey

Saturday August 11
Clay Cross vS'wick Hall
Lang. M. Utd vIlk'ton R'land
Little Eaton vClowne Town
Marehay vBreadsall
Quarndon vDarley Abbey
Shipley Hall vAshover

Saturday August 18
Ashover vMarehay
Breadsall vClay Cross
Clowne Town vShipley Hall
Darley Abbey vLang. M. Utd
Ilk'ton R'land vLittle Eaton
S'wick Hall vQuarndon

Saturday August 25
Breadsall vS'wick Hall
Clay Cross vAshover
Lang. M. Utd vQuarndon
Little Eaton vDarley Abbey
Marehay vClowne Town
Shipley Hall vIlk'ton R'land

Saturday September 1
Ashover vBreadsall
Clowne Town vClay Cross
Darley Abbey vShipley Hall
Ilk'ton R'land vMarehay
Quarndon vLittle Eaton
S'wick Hall vLang. M. Utd

Saturday September 8
Ashover vS'wick Hall
Breadsall vClowne Town
Clay Cross vIlk'ton R'land
Little Eaton vLang. M. Utd
Marehay vDarley Abbey
Shipley Hall vQuarndon

Sunday September 9
Clowne Town vAshover
Darley Abbey vClay Cross
Ilk'ton R'land vBreadsall
Lang. M. Utd vShipley Hall
Quarndon vMarehay
S'wick Hall vLittle Eaton

Engments
Division 3S

Saturday April 28
Alv & Boulton vElvaston
Burton vWalton-on-T.
Etwall vLullington Pk
L'over Cents vDray. & H'ry
S'ley & LE Pk vRolleston
Ticknall vTrentside

Saturday May 5
Dray. & H'ry vTicknall
Elvaston vEtwall
Lullington Pk vS'ley & LE Pk
Rolleston vL'over Cents
Trentside vBurton
Walton-on-T. vAlv & Boulton

Saturday May 12
Alv & Boulton vTrentside
Burton vDray. & H'ry
Etwall vWalton-on-T.
L'over Cents vS'ley & LE Pk
Lullington Pk vElvaston
Ticknall vRolleston

Sunday May 13
Dray. & H'ry vAlv & Boulton
L'over Cents vTicknall
Rolleston vBurton
S'ley & LE Pk vElvaston
Trentside vEtwall
Walton-on-T. vLullington Pk

Saturday May 19
Alv & Boulton vRolleston
Burton vL'over Cents
Elvaston vWalton-on-T.
Etwall vDray. & H'ry
Lullington Pk vTrentside
Ticknall vS'ley & LE Pk

Saturday May 26
Dray. & H'ry vLullington Pk
L'over Cents vAlv & Boulton
Rolleston vEtwall
S'ley & LE Pk vWalton-on-T.
Ticknall vBurton
Trentside vElvaston

Saturday June 2
Alv & Boulton vTicknall
Burton vS'ley & LE Pk
Elvaston vDray. & H'ry
Etwall vL'over Cents
Lullington Pk vRolleston
Walton-on-T. vTrentside

Saturday June 9
Burton vAlv & Boulton
Dray. & H'ry vWalton-on-T.
L'over Cents vLullington Pk
Rolleston vElvaston
S'ley & LE Pk vTrentside
Ticknall vEtwall

Saturday June 16
Alv & Boulton vS'ley & LE Pk
Elvaston vL'over Cents
Etwall vBurton
Lullington Pk vTicknall
Trentside vDray. & H'ry
Walton-on-T. vRolleston

Saturday June 23
Alv & Boulton vEtwall
Burton vLullington Pk
L'over Cents vWalton-on-T.
Rolleston vTrentside
S'ley & LE Pk vDray. & H'ry
Ticknall vElvaston

Saturday June 30
Dray. & H'ry vRolleston
Elvaston vBurton
Etwall vS'ley & LE Pk
Lullington Pk vAlv & Boulton
Trentside vL'over Cents
Walton-on-T. vTicknall

Saturday July 7
Dray. & H'ry vL'over Cents
Elvaston vAlv & Boulton
Lullington Pk vEtwall
Rolleston vS'ley & LE Pk
Trentside vTicknall
Walton-on-T. vBurton

Saturday July 14
Alv & Boulton vWalton-on-T.
Burton vTrentside
Etwall vElvaston
L'over Cents vRolleston
S'ley & LE Pk vLullington Pk
Ticknall vDray. & H'ry

Saturday July 21
Dray. & H'ry vBurton
Elvaston vLullington Pk
Rolleston vTicknall
S'ley & LE Pk vL'over Cents
Trentside vAlv & Boulton
Walton-on-T. vEtwall

Saturday July 28
Alv & Boulton vDray. & H'ry
Burton vRolleston
Elvaston vS'ley & LE Pk

Etwall vTrentside
Lullington Pk vWalton-on-T.
Ticknall vL'over Cents

Saturday August 4
Dray. & H'ry vEtwall
L'over Cents vBurton
Rolleston vAlv & Boulton
S'ley & LE Pk vTicknall
Trentside vLullington Pk
Walton-on-T. vElvaston

Saturday August 11
Alv & Boulton vL'over Cents
Burton vTicknall
Elvaston vTrentside
Etwall vRolleston
Lullington Pk vDray. & H'ry
Walton-on-T. vS'ley & LE Pk

Saturday August 18
Dray. & H'ry vElvaston
L'over Cents vEtwall
Rolleston vLullington Pk
S'ley & LE Pk vBurton
Ticknall vAlv & Boulton
Trentside vWalton-on-T.

Saturday August 25
Alv & Boulton vBurton
Elvaston vRolleston
Etwall vTicknall
Lullington Pk vL'over Cents
Trentside vS'ley & LE Pk
Walton-on-T. vDray. & H'ry

Saturday September 1
Burton vEtwall
Dray. & H'ry vTrentside
L'over Cents vElvaston
Rolleston vWalton-on-T.
S'ley & LE Pk vAlv & Boulton
Ticknall vLullington Pk

Saturday September 8
Dray. & H'ry vS'ley & LE Pk
Elvaston vTicknall
Etwall vAlv & Boulton
Lullington Pk vBurton
Trentside vRolleston
Walton-on-T. vL'over Cents

Sunday September 9
Alv & Boulton vLullington Pk
Burton vElvaston
L'over Cents vTrentside
Rolleston vDray. & H'ry
S'ley & LE Pk vEtwall
Ticknall vWalton-on-T.

Field Sports Division 4N

Saturday April 28
Ashbourne   vWhitmoor RC
Belper Mdws   vS. Wingfield
Cromf. Mdws vMorton Coll.
Heanor Town vRiddings
Staveley Wel. vDarley Abbey
Tibshelf   vAlfreton

Saturday May 5
Alfreton   vCromf. Mdws
Darley Abbey vBelper Mdws
Morton Coll.   vStaveley Wel.
Riddings   vTibshelf
S. Wingfield   vAshbourne
Whitmoor RC vHeanor Town

Saturday May 12
Ashbourne   vDarley Abbey
Belper Mdws   vMorton Coll.
Cromf. Mdws vRiddings
Staveley Wel. vAlfreton
Tibshelf   vHeanor Town
Whitmoor RC vS. Wingfield

Sunday May 13
Alfreton   vBelper Mdws
Darley Abbey vWhitmoor RC
Heanor Town vS. Wingfield
Morton Coll.   vAshbourne
Riddings   vStaveley Wel.
Tibshelf   vCromf. Mdws

Saturday May 19
Ashbourne   vAlfreton
Belper Mdws   vRiddings
Cromf. Mdws vHeanor Town
S. Wingfield   vDarley Abbey
Staveley Wel. vTibshelf
Whitmoor RC vMorton Coll.

Saturday May 26
Alfreton   vWhitmoor RC
Cromf. Mdws vStaveley Wel.
Heanor Town vDarley Abbey
Morton Coll.   vS. Wingfield
Riddings   vAshbourne
Tibshelf   vBelper Mdws

Saturday June 2
Ashbourne   vTibshelf
Belper Mdws   vCromf. Mdws
Darley Abbey vMorton Coll.
S. Wingfield   vAlfreton
Staveley Wel. vHeanor Town
Whitmoor RC vRiddings

Saturday June 9
Alfreton   vDarley Abbey
Cromf. Mdws vAshbourne
Heanor Town vMorton Coll.
Riddings   vS. Wingfield
Staveley Wel. vBelper Mdws
Tibshelf   vWhitmoor RC

Saturday June 16
Ashbourne   vStaveley Wel.
Belper Mdws   vHeanor Town
Darley Abbey vRiddings
Morton Coll.   vAlfreton
S. Wingfield   vTibshelf
Whitmoor RC vCromf. Mdws

Saturday June 23
Belper Mdws   vAshbourne
Cromf. Mdws vS. Wingfield
Heanor Town vAlfreton
Riddings   vMorton Coll.
Staveley Wel. vWhitmoor RC
Tibshelf   vDarley Abbey

Saturday June 30
Alfreton   vRiddings
Ashbourne   vHeanor Town
Darley Abbey vCromf. Mdws
Morton Coll.   vTibshelf
S. Wingfield   vStaveley Wel.
Whitmoor RC vBelper Mdws

Saturday July 7
Alfreton   vTibshelf
Darley Abbey vStaveley Wel.
Morton Coll.   vCromf. Mdws
Riddings   vHeanor Town
S. Wingfield   vBelper Mdws
Whitmoor RC vAshbourne

Saturday July 14
Ashbourne   vS. Wingfield
Belper Mdws   vDarley Abbey
Cromf. Mdws vAlfreton
Heanor Town vWhitmoor RC
Staveley Wel. vMorton Coll.
Tibshelf   vRiddings

Saturday July 21
Alfreton   vStaveley Wel.
Darley Abbey vAshbourne
Heanor Town vTibshelf
Morton Coll.   vBelper Mdws
Riddings   vCromf. Mdws
S. Wingfield   vWhitmoor RC

Saturday July 28
Ashbourne   vMorton Coll.
Belper Mdws   vAlfreton
Cromf. Mdws vTibshelf

S. Wingfield   vHeanor Town
Staveley Wel. vRiddings
Whitmoor RC vDarley Abbey

Saturday August 4
Alfreton   vAshbourne
Darley Abbey vS. Wingfield
Heanor Town vCromf. Mdws
Morton Coll.   vWhitmoor RC
Riddings   vBelper Mdws
Tibshelf   vStaveley Wel.

Saturday August 11
Ashbourne   vRiddings
Belper Mdws   vTibshelf
Darley Abbey vHeanor Town
S. Wingfield   vMorton Coll.
Staveley Wel. vCromf. Mdws
Whitmoor RC vAlfreton

Saturday August 18
Alfreton   vS. Wingfield
Cromf. Mdws vBelper Mdws
Heanor Town vStaveley Wel.
Morton Coll.   vDarley Abbey
Riddings   vWhitmoor RC
Tibshelf   vAshbourne

Saturday August 25
Ashbourne   vCromf. Mdws
Belper Mdws   vStaveley Wel.
Darley Abbey vAlfreton
Morton Coll.   vHeanor Town
S. Wingfield   vRiddings
Whitmoor RC vTibshelf

Saturday September 1
Alfreton   vMorton Coll.
Cromf. Mdws vWhitmoor RC
Heanor Town vBelper Mdws
Riddings   vDarley Abbey
Staveley Wel. vAshbourne
Tibshelf   vS. Wingfield

Saturday September 8
Alfreton   vHeanor Town
Ashbourne   vBelper Mdws
Darley Abbey vTibshelf
Morton Coll.   vRiddings
S. Wingfield   vCromf. Mdws
Whitmoor RC vStaveley Wel.

Sunday September 9
Belper Mdws   vWhitmoor RC
Cromf. Mdws vDarley Abbey
Heanor Town vAshbourne
Riddings   vAlfreton
Staveley Wel. vS. Wingfield
Tibshelf   vMorton Coll.

MG Financial Services
Division 4S

Saturday April 28
Aston-on-Tr.   vBrailsford
Clifton   vR'hill Meths
Dunstall   vOck & B'wash
Lullington Pk vO. Derbeians
Melbourne T.   vWinshill
Swarkestone   vNutbrook

Saturday May 5
Brailsford   vClifton
Nutbrook   vAston-on-Tr.
Ock & B'wash   vMelbourne T.
O. Derbeians   vDunstall
R'hill Meths   vLullington Pk
Winshill   vSwarkestone

Saturday May 12
Aston-on-Tr.   vWinshill
Clifton   vNutbrook
Dunstall   vLullington Pk
Melbourne T.   vO. Derbeians
R'hill Meths   vBrailsford
Swarkestone   vOck & B'wash

Sunday May 13
Dunstall   vMelbourne T.
Lullington Pk vBrailsford
Nutbrook   vR'hill Meths
Ock & B'wash   vAston-on-Tr.
O. Derbeians   vSwarkestone
Winshill   vClifton

Saturday May 19
Aston-on-Tr.   vO. Derbeians
Brailsford   vNutbrook
Clifton   vOck & B'wash
Melbourne T.   vLullington Pk
R'hill Meths   vWinshill
Swarkestone   vDunstall

Saturday May 26
Dunstall   vAston-on-Tr.
Lullington Pk vNutbrook
Melbourne T.   vSwarkestone
Ock & B'wash   vR'hill Meths
O. Derbeians   vClifton
Winshill   vBrailsford

Saturday June 2
Aston-on-Tr.   vMelbourne T.
Brailsford   vOck & B'wash
Clifton   vDunstall
Nutbrook   vWinshill
R'hill Meths   vO. Derbeians
Swarkestone   vLullington Pk

Saturday June 9
Dunstall   vR'hill Meths
Lullington Pk vWinshill
Melbourne T.   vClifton
Ock & B'wash   vNutbrook
O. Derbeians   vBrailsford
Swarkestone   vAston-on-Tr.

Saturday June 16
Aston-on-Tr.   vLullington Pk
Brailsford   vDunstall
Clifton   vSwarkestone
Nutbrook   vO. Derbeians
R'hill Meths   vMelbourne T.
Winshill   vOck & B'wash

Saturday June 23
Aston-on-Tr.   vClifton
Dunstall   vNutbrook
Lullington Pk vOck & B'wash
Melbourne T.   vBrailsford
O. Derbeians   vWinshill
Swarkestone   vR'hill Meths

Saturday June 30
Brailsford   vSwarkestone
Clifton   vLullington Pk
Nutbrook   vMelbourne T.
Ock & B'wash   vO. Derbeians
R'hill Meths   vAston-on-Tr.
Winshill   vDunstall

Saturday July 7
Brailsford   vAston-on-Tr.
Nutbrook   vSwarkestone
Ock & B'wash   vDunstall
O. Derbeians   vLullington Pk
R'hill Meths   vClifton
Winshill   vMelbourne T.

Saturday July 14
Aston-on-Tr.   vNutbrook
Clifton   vBrailsford
Dunstall   vO. Derbeians
Lullington Pk vR'hill Meths
Melbourne T.   vOck & B'wash
Swarkestone   vWinshill

Saturday July 21
Brailsford   vR'hill Meths
Lullington Pk vDunstall
Nutbrook   vClifton
Ock & B'wash   vSwarkestone
O. Derbeians   vMelbourne T.
Winshill   vAston-on-Tr.

Saturday July 28
Aston-on-Tr.   vOck & B'wash
Brailsford   vLullington Pk
Clifton   vWinshill
Melbourne T.   vDunstall
R'hill Meths   vNutbrook
Swarkestone   vO. Derbeians

Saturday August 4
Dunstall   vSwarkestone
Lullington Pk vMelbourne T.
Nutbrook   vBrailsford
Ock & B'wash   vClifton
O. Derbeians   vAston-on-Tr.
Winshill   vR'hill Meths

Saturday August 11
Aston-on-Tr.   vDunstall
Brailsford   vWinshill
Clifton   vO. Derbeians
Nutbrook   vLullington Pk
R'hill Meths   vOck & B'wash
Swarkestone   vMelbourne T.

Saturday August 18
Dunstall   vClifton
Lullington Pk vSwarkestone
Melbourne T.   vAston-on-Tr.
Ock & B'wash   vBrailsford
O. Derbeians   vR'hill Meths
Winshill   vNutbrook

Saturday August 25
Aston-on-Tr.   vSwarkestone
Brailsford   vO. Derbeians
Clifton   vMelbourne T.
Nutbrook   vOck & B'wash
R'hill Meths   vDunstall
Winshill   vLullington Pk

Saturday September 1
Dunstall   vBrailsford
Lullington Pk vAston-on-Tr.
Melbourne T.   vR'hill Meths
Ock & B'wash   vWinshill
O. Derbeians   vNutbrook
Swarkestone   vClifton

Saturday September 8
Brailsford   vMelbourne T.
Clifton   vAston-on-Tr.
Nutbrook   vDunstall
Ock & B'wash   vLullington Pk
R'hill Meths   vSwarkestone
Winshill   vO. Derbeians

Sunday September 9
Aston-on-Tr.   vR'hill Meths
Dunstall   vWinshill
Lullington Pk vClifton
Melbourne T.   vNutbrook
O. Derbeians   vOck & B'wash
Swarkestone   vBrailsford

Geoff Cox Cars
Division 5N

Saturday April 28
Alfreton	vCodnor
Breadsall	vWirksworth
Butterley Utd	vAmbergate
Clay Cross	vBelper Ams.
Clowne Town	vDenby
Wing'worth S	vSelston Town

Saturday May 5
Ambergate	vClay Cross
Belper Ams.	vBreadsall
Codnor	vClowne Town
Denby	vWing'worth S
Selston Town	vButterley Utd
Wirksworth	vAlfreton

Saturday May 12
Alfreton	vBelper Ams.
Breadsall	vAmbergate
Butterley Utd	vWing'worth S
Clay Cross	vSelston Town
Clowne Town	vWirksworth
Denby	vCodnor

Sunday May 13
Ambergate	vAlfreton
Belper Ams.	vClowne Town
Butterley Utd	vClay Cross
Selston Town	vBreadsall
Wing'worth S	vCodnor
Wirksworth	vDenby

Saturday May 19
Alfreton	vSelston Town
Breadsall	vButterley Utd
Clay Cross	vWing'worth S
Clowne Town	vAmbergate
Codnor	vWirksworth
Denby	vBelper Ams.

Saturday May 26
Ambergate	vDenby
Belper Ams.	vCodnor
Butterley Utd	vAlfreton
Clay Cross	vBreadsall
Selston Town	vClowne Town
Wing'worth S	vWirksworth

Saturday June 2
Alfreton	vClay Cross
Breadsall	vWing'worth S
Clowne Town	vButterley Utd
Codnor	vAmbergate
Denby	vSelston Town
Wirksworth	vBelper Ams.

Saturday June 9
Ambergate	vWirksworth
Breadsall	vAlfreton
Butterley Utd	vDenby
Clay Cross	vClowne Town
Selston Town	vCodnor
Wing'worth S	vBelper Ams.

Saturday June 16
Alfreton	vWing'worth S
Belper Ams.	vAmbergate
Clowne Town	vBreadsall
Codnor	vButterley Utd
Denby	vClay Cross
Wirksworth	vSelston Town

Saturday June 23
Alfreton	vClowne Town
Breadsall	vDenby
Butterley Utd	vWirksworth
Clay Cross	vCodnor
Selston Town	vBelper Ams.
Wing'worth S	vAmbergate

Saturday June 30
Ambergate	vSelston Town
Belper Ams.	vButterley Utd
Clowne Town	vWing'worth S
Codnor	vBreadsall
Denby	vAlfreton
Wirksworth	vClay Cross

Saturday July 7
Ambergate	vButterley Utd
Belper Ams.	vClay Cross
Codnor	vAlfreton
Denby	vClowne Town
Selston Town	vWing'worth S
Wirksworth	vBreadsall

Saturday July 14
Alfreton	vWirksworth
Breadsall	vBelper Ams.
Butterley Utd	vSelston Town
Clay Cross	vAmbergate
Clowne Town	vCodnor
Wing'worth S	vDenby

Saturday July 21
Ambergate	vBreadsall
Belper Ams.	vAlfreton
Codnor	vDenby
Selston Town	vClay Cross
Wing'worth S	vButterley Utd
Wirksworth	vClowne Town

Saturday July 28
Alfreton	vAmbergate
Breadsall	vSelston Town
Clay Cross	vButterley Utd

Clowne Town vBelper Ams.
Codnor	vWing'worth S
Denby	vWirksworth

Saturday August 4
Ambergate	vClowne Town
Belper Ams.	vDenby
Butterley Utd	vBreadsall
Selston Town	vAlfreton
Wing'worth S	vClay Cross
Wirksworth	vCodnor

Saturday August 11
Alfreton	vButterley Utd
Breadsall	vClay Cross
Clowne Town	vSelston Town
Codnor	vBelper Ams.
Denby	vAmbergate
Wirksworth	vWing'worth S

Saturday August 18
Ambergate	vCodnor
Belper Ams.	vWirksworth
Butterley Utd	vClowne Town
Clay Cross	vAlfreton
Selston Town	vDenby
Wing'worth S	vBreadsall

Saturday August 25
Alfreton	vBreadsall
Belper Ams.	vWing'worth S
Clowne Town	vClay Cross
Codnor	vSelston Town
Denby	vButterley Utd
Wirksworth	vAmbergate

Saturday September 1
Ambergate	vBelper Ams.
Breadsall	vClowne Town
Butterley Utd	vCodnor
Clay Cross	vDenby
Selston Town	vWirksworth
Wing'worth S	vAlfreton

Saturday September 8
Ambergate	vWing'worth S
Belper Ams.	vSelston Town
Clowne Town	vAlfreton
Codnor	vClay Cross
Denby	vBreadsall
Wirksworth	vButterley Utd

Sunday September 9
Alfreton	vDenby
Breadsall	vCodnor
Butterley Utd	vBelper Ams.
Clay Cross	vWirksworth
Selston Town	vAmbergate
Wing'worth S	vClowne Town

Savages
Division 5S

Saturday April 28

Alrewas vL'over Cents
Mickleover vBarton
Rolleston vDuffield
Sandiacre T. vRolls Royce
Trentside vSpondon
Tutbury vS'ley & LE Pk

Saturday May 5

Barton vTutbury
Duffield vSandiacre T.
L'over Cents vMickleover
Rolls Royce vTrentside
S'ley & LE Pk vRolleston
Spondon vAlrewas

Saturday May 12

Alrewas vRolls Royce
Barton vL'over Cents
Mickleover vSpondon
Rolleston vTutbury
Sandiacre T. vS'ley & LE Pk
Trentside vDuffield

Sunday May 13

Duffield vAlrewas
Rolleston vSandiacre T.
Rolls Royce vMickleover
S'ley & LE Pk vTrentside
Spondon vBarton
Tutbury vL'over Cents

Saturday May 19

Alrewas vS'ley & LE Pk
Barton vRolls Royce
L'over Cents vSpondon
Mickleover vDuffield
Sandiacre T. vTutbury
Trentside vRolleston

Saturday May 26

Duffield vBarton
Rolleston vAlrewas
Rolls Royce vL'over Cents
Sandiacre T. vTrentside
S'ley & LE Pk vMickleover
Tutbury vSpondon

Saturday June 2

Alrewas vSandiacre T.
Barton vS'ley & LE Pk
L'over Cents vDuffield
Mickleover vRolleston
Spondon vRolls Royce
Trentside vTutbury

Saturday June 9

Duffield vSpondon
Rolleston vBarton
Sandiacre T. vMickleover
S'ley & LE Pk vL'over Cents
Trentside vAlrewas
Tutbury vRolls Royce

Saturday June 16

Alrewas vTutbury
Barton vSandiacre T.
L'over Cents vRolleston
Mickleover vTrentside
Rolls Royce vDuffield
Spondon vS'ley & LE Pk

Saturday June 23

Alrewas vMickleover
Rolleston vSpondon
Sandiacre T. vL'over Cents
S'ley & LE Pk vRolls Royce
Trentside vBarton
Tutbury vDuffield

Saturday June 30

Barton vAlrewas
Duffield vS'ley & LE Pk
L'over Cents vTrentside
Mickleover vTutbury
Rolls Royce vRolleston
Spondon vSandiacre T.

Saturday July 7

Barton vMickleover
Duffield vRolleston
L'over Cents vAlrewas
Rolls Royce vSandiacre T.
S'ley & LE Pk vTutbury
Spondon vTrentside

Saturday July 14

Alrewas vSpondon
Mickleover vL'over Cents
Rolleston vS'ley & LE Pk
Sandiacre T. vDuffield
Trentside vRolls Royce
Tutbury vBarton

Saturday July 21

Duffield vTrentside
L'over Cents vBarton
Rolls Royce vAlrewas
S'ley & LE Pk vSandiacre T.
Spondon vMickleover
Tutbury vRolleston

Saturday July 28

Alrewas vDuffield
Barton vSpondon
L'over Cents vTutbury

Mickleover vRolls Royce
Sandiacre T. vRolleston
Trentside vS'ley & LE Pk

Saturday August 4

Duffield vMickleover
Rolleston vTrentside
Rolls Royce vBarton
S'ley & LE Pk vAlrewas
Spondon vL'over Cents
Tutbury vSandiacre T.

Saturday August 11

Alrewas vRolleston
Barton vDuffield
L'over Cents vRolls Royce
Mickleover vS'ley & LE Pk
Spondon vTutbury
Trentside vSandiacre T.

Saturday August 18

Duffield vL'over Cents
Rolleston vMickleover
Rolls Royce vSpondon
Sandiacre T. vAlrewas
S'ley & LE Pk vBarton
Tutbury vTrentside

Saturday August 25

Alrewas vTrentside
Barton vRolleston
L'over Cents vS'ley & LE Pk
Mickleover vSandiacre T.
Rolls Royce vTutbury
Spondon vDuffield

Saturday September 1

Duffield vRolls Royce
Rolleston vL'over Cents
Sandiacre T. vBarton
S'ley & LE Pk vSpondon
Trentside vMickleover
Tutbury vAlrewas

Saturday September 8

Barton vTrentside
Duffield vTutbury
L'over Cents vSandiacre T.
Mickleover vAlrewas
Rolls Royce vS'ley & LE Pk
Spondon vRolleston

Sunday September 9

Alrewas vBarton
Rolleston vRolls Royce
Sandiacre T. vSpondon
S'ley & LE Pk vDuffield
Trentside vL'over Cents
Tutbury vMickleover

Pope Machinery
Division 6C

Saturday April 28
Ilk'ton R'land vParwich
Mugginton   vKirk Langley
Ock & B'wash vBrailsford
Shipley Hall   vNutbrook
Spondon   vAllestree
W. Hall. WR   vQuarndon

Saturday May 5
Allestree   vShipley Hall
Brailsford   vW. Hall. WR
Kirk Langley   vIlk'ton R'land
Nutbrook   vOck & B'wash
Parwich   vSpondon
Quarndon   vMugginton

Saturday May 12
Ilk'ton R'land vMugginton
Ock & B'wash vAllestree
Quarndon   vBrailsford
Shipley Hall   vParwich
Spondon   vKirk Langley
W. Hall. WR   vNutbrook

Sunday May 13
Allestree   vW. Hall. WR
Ilk'ton R'land vSpondon
Kirk Langley   vShipley Hall
Mugginton   vBrailsford
Nutbrook   vQuarndon
Parwich   vOck & B'wash

Saturday May 19
Brailsford   vNutbrook
Ock & B'wash vKirk Langley
Quarndon   vAllestree
Shipley Hall   vIlk'ton R'land
Spondon   vMugginton
W. Hall. WR   vParwich

Saturday May 26
Allestree   vBrailsford
Ilk'ton R'land vOck & B'wash
Kirk Langley   vW. Hall. WR
Mugginton   vNutbrook
Parwich   vQuarndon
Spondon   vShipley Hall

Saturday June 2
Brailsford   vParwich
Nutbrook   vAllestree
Ock & B'wash vSpondon
Quarndon   vKirk Langley
Shipley Hall   vMugginton
W. Hall. WR   vIlk'ton R'land

Saturday June 9
Ilk'ton R'land vQuarndon
Kirk Langley   vBrailsford
Mugginton   vAllestree
Parwich   vNutbrook
Shipley Hall   vOck & B'wash
Spondon   vW. Hall. WR

Saturday June 16
Allestree   vParwich
Brailsford   vIlk'ton R'land
Nutbrook   vKirk Langley
Ock & B'wash vMugginton
Quarndon   vSpondon
W. Hall. WR   vShipley Hall

Saturday June 23
Ilk'ton R'land vNutbrook
Kirk Langley   vAllestree
Mugginton   vParwich
Ock & B'wash vW. Hall. WR
Shipley Hall   vQuarndon
Spondon   vBrailsford

Saturday June 30
Allestree   vIlk'ton R'land
Brailsford   vShipley Hall
Nutbrook   vSpondon
Parwich   vKirk Langley
Quarndon   vOck & B'wash
W. Hall. WR   vMugginton

Saturday July 7
Allestree   vSpondon
Brailsford   vOck & B'wash
Kirk Langley   vMugginton
Nutbrook   vShipley Hall
Parwich   vIlk'ton R'land
Quarndon   vW. Hall. WR

Saturday July 14
Ilk'ton R'land vKirk Langley
Mugginton   vQuarndon
Ock & B'wash vNutbrook
Shipley Hall   vAllestree
Spondon   vParwich
W. Hall. WR   vBrailsford

Saturday July 21
Allestree   vOck & B'wash
Brailsford   vQuarndon
Kirk Langley   vSpondon
Mugginton   vIlk'ton R'land
Nutbrook   vW. Hall. WR
Parwich   vShipley Hall

Saturday July 28
Brailsford   vMugginton
Ock & B'wash vParwich
Quarndon   vNutbrook

Saturday August 4
Allestree   vQuarndon
Ilk'ton R'land vShipley Hall
Kirk Langley   vOck & B'wash
Mugginton   vSpondon
Nutbrook   vBrailsford
Parwich   vW. Hall. WR

Saturday August 11
Brailsford   vAllestree
Nutbrook   vMugginton
Ock & B'wash vIlk'ton R'land
Quarndon   vParwich
Shipley Hall   vSpondon
W. Hall. WR   vKirk Langley

Saturday August 18
Allestree   vNutbrook
Ilk'ton R'land vW. Hall. WR
Kirk Langley   vQuarndon
Mugginton   vShipley Hall
Parwich   vBrailsford
Spondon   vOck & B'wash

Saturday August 25
Allestree   vMugginton
Brailsford   vKirk Langley
Nutbrook   vParwich
Ock & B'wash vShipley Hall
Quarndon   vIlk'ton R'land
W. Hall. WR   vSpondon

Saturday September 1
Ilk'ton R'land vBrailsford
Kirk Langley   vNutbrook
Mugginton   vOck & B'wash
Parwich   vAllestree
Shipley Hall   vW. Hall. WR
Spondon   vQuarndon

Saturday September 8
Allestree   vKirk Langley
Brailsford   vSpondon
Nutbrook   vIlk'ton R'land
Parwich   vMugginton
Quarndon   vShipley Hall
W. Hall. WR   vOck & B'wash

Sunday September 9
Ilk'ton R'land vAllestree
Kirk Langley   vParwich
Mugginton   vW. Hall. WR
Ock & B'wash vQuarndon
Shipley Hall   vBrailsford
Spondon   vNutbrook

People Plus Division 6N

Saturday April 28
Ashover vButterley Utd
Darley Dale vLang. M. Utd
Denby vStainsby Hall
Matlock vS'wick Hall
Morton Coll. vCromf. Mdws
Pilsley vMarehay

Saturday May 5
Butterley Utd vMatlock
Cromf. Mdws vAshover
Lang. M. Utd vPilsley
Marehay vMorton Coll.
Stainsby Hall vDarley Dale
S'wick Hall vDenby

Saturday May 12
Ashover vMarehay
Darley Dale vDenby
Matlock vCromf. Mdws
Morton Coll. vLang. M. Utd
Pilsley vStainsby Hall
S'wick Hall vButterley Utd

Sunday May 13
Cromf. Mdws vS'wick Hall
Darley Dale vPilsley
Denby vButterley Utd
Lang. M. Utd vAshover
Marehay vMatlock
Stainsby Hall vMorton Coll.

Saturday May 19
Ashover vStainsby Hall
Butterley Utd vCromf. Mdws
Matlock vLang. M. Utd
Morton Coll. vDarley Dale
Pilsley vDenby
S'wick Hall vMarehay

Saturday May 26
Darley Dale vAshover
Denby vCromf. Mdws
Lang. M. Utd vS'wick Hall
Marehay vButterley Utd
Pilsley vMorton Coll.
Stainsby Hall vMatlock

Saturday June 2
Ashover vPilsley
Butterley Utd vLang. M. Utd
Cromf. Mdws vMarehay
Matlock vDarley Dale
Morton Coll. vDenby
S'wick Hall vStainsby Hall

Saturday June 9
Darley Dale vS'wick Hall
Denby vMarehay
Lang. M. Utd vCromf. Mdws
Morton Coll. vAshover
Pilsley vMatlock
Stainsby Hall vButterley Utd

Saturday June 16
Ashover vDenby
Butterley Utd vDarley Dale
Cromf. Mdws vStainsby Hall
Marehay vLang. M. Utd
Matlock vMorton Coll.
S'wick Hall vPilsley

Saturday June 23
Ashover vMatlock
Darley Dale vCromf. Mdws
Denby vLang. M. Utd
Morton Coll. vS'wick Hall
Pilsley vButterley Utd
Stainsby Hall vMarehay

Saturday June 30
Butterley Utd vMorton Coll.
Cromf. Mdws vPilsley
Lang. M. Utd vStainsby Hall
Marehay vDarley Dale
Matlock vDenby
S'wick Hall vAshover

Saturday July 7
Butterley Utd vAshover
Cromf. Mdws vMorton Coll.
Lang. M. Utd vDarley Dale
Marehay vPilsley
Stainsby Hall vDenby
S'wick Hall vMatlock

Saturday July 14
Ashover vCromf. Mdws
Darley Dale vStainsby Hall
Denby vS'wick Hall
Matlock vButterley Utd
Morton Coll. vMarehay
Pilsley vLang. M. Utd

Saturday July 21
Butterley Utd vS'wick Hall
Cromf. Mdws vMatlock
Denby vDarley Dale
Lang. M. Utd vMorton Coll.
Marehay vAshover
Stainsby Hall vPilsley

Saturday July 28
Ashover vLang. M. Utd
Butterley Utd vDenby
Matlock vMarehay

Morton Coll. vStainsby Hall
Pilsley vDarley Dale
S'wick Hall vCromf. Mdws

Saturday August 4
Cromf. Mdws vButterley Utd
Darley Dale vMorton Coll.
Denby vPilsley
Lang. M. Utd vMatlock
Marehay vS'wick Hall
Stainsby Hall vAshover

Saturday August 11
Ashover vDarley Dale
Butterley Utd vMarehay
Cromf. Mdws vDenby
Matlock vStainsby Hall
Morton Coll. vPilsley
S'wick Hall vLang. M. Utd

Saturday August 18
Darley Dale vMatlock
Denby vMorton Coll.
Lang. M. Utd vButterley Utd
Marehay vCromf. Mdws
Pilsley vAshover
Stainsby Hall vS'wick Hall

Saturday August 25
Ashover vMorton Coll.
Butterley Utd vStainsby Hall
Cromf. Mdws vLang. M. Utd
Marehay vDenby
Matlock vPilsley
S'wick Hall vDarley Dale

Saturday September 1
Darley Dale vButterley Utd
Denby vAshover
Lang. M. Utd vMarehay
Morton Coll. vMatlock
Pilsley vS'wick Hall
Stainsby Hall vCromf. Mdws

Saturday September 8
Butterley Utd vPilsley
Cromf. Mdws vDarley Dale
Lang. M. Utd vDenby
Marehay vStainsby Hall
Matlock vAshover
S'wick Hall vMorton Coll.

Sunday September 9
Ashover vS'wick Hall
Darley Dale vMarehay
Denby vMatlock
Morton Coll. vButterley Utd
Pilsley vCromf. Mdws
Stainsby Hall vLang. M. Utd

Slazenger
Division 6S

Saturday April 28
Alv & Boulton vUttoxeter
Elvaston   vBurton
Hilton   vDerby Congs
R'hill Meths   vEtwall
S'ley & LE Pk vCastle Don. T.
Winshill   vSwarkestone

Saturday May 5
Castle Don. T.vR'hill Meths
Derby Congs vElvaston
Etwall   vHilton
Swarkestone vAlv & Boulton
Uttoxeter   vS'ley & LE Pk

Saturday May 12
Alv & Boulton vBurton
Castle Don. T.vUttoxeter
Elvaston   vEtwall
Hilton   vR'hill Meths
S'ley & LE Pk vSwarkestone
Winshill   vDerby Congs

Sunday May 13
Burton   vS'ley & LE Pk
Derby Congs vAlv & Boulton
Etwall   vWinshill
Hilton   vElvaston
R'hill Meths   vUttoxeter
Swarkestone vCastle Don. T.

Saturday May 19
Alv & Boulton vEtwall
Castle Don. T.vBurton
Elvaston   vR'hill Meths
S'ley & LE Pk vDerby Congs
Uttoxeter   vSwarkestone
Winshill   vHilton

Saturday May 26
Burton   vUttoxeter
Derby Congs vCastle Don. T.
Elvaston   vWinshill
Etwall   vS'ley & LE Pk
Hilton   vAlv & Boulton
R'hill Meths   vSwarkestone

Saturday June 2
Alv & Boulton vElvaston
Castle Don. T.vEtwall
S'ley & LE Pk vHilton
Swarkestone vBurton
Uttoxeter   vDerby Congs
Winshill   vR'hill Meths

Saturday June 9
Derby Congs vSwarkestone
Elvaston   vS'ley & LE Pk
Etwall   vUttoxeter
Hilton   vCastle Don. T.
R'hill Meths   vBurton
Winshill   vAlv & Boulton

Saturday June 16
Alv & Boulton vR'hill Meths
Burton   vDerby Congs
Castle Don. T.vElvaston
S'ley & LE Pk vWinshill
Swarkestone vEtwall
Uttoxeter   vHilton

Saturday June 23
Alv & Boulton vS'ley & LE Pk
Elvaston   vUttoxeter
Etwall   vBurton
Hilton   vSwarkestone
R'hill Meths   vDerby Congs
Winshill   vCastle Don. T.

Saturday June 30
Burton   vHilton
Castle Don. T.vAlv & Boulton
Derby Congs vEtwall
S'ley & LE Pk vR'hill Meths
Swarkestone vElvaston
Uttoxeter   vWinshill

Saturday July 7
Burton   vElvaston
Castle Don. T.vS'ley & LE Pk
Derby Congs vHilton
Etwall   vR'hill Meths
Swarkestone vWinshill
Uttoxeter   vAlv & Boulton

Saturday July 14
Alv & Boulton vSwarkestone
Elvaston   vDerby Congs
Hilton   vEtwall
R'hill Meths   vCastle Don. T.
S'ley & LE Pk vUttoxeter
Winshill   vBurton

Saturday July 21
Burton   vAlv & Boulton
Derby Congs vWinshill
Etwall   vElvaston
R'hill Meths   vHilton
Swarkestone vS'ley & LE Pk
Uttoxeter   vCastle Don. T.

Saturday July 28
Alv & Boulton vDerby Congs
Castle Don. T.vSwarkestone
Elvaston   vHilton

Saturday August 4
S'ley & LE Pk vBurton
Uttoxeter   vR'hill Meths
Winshill   vEtwall

Saturday August 4
Burton   vCastle Don. T.
Derby Congs vS'ley & LE Pk
Etwall   vAlv & Boulton
Hilton   vWinshill
R'hill Meths   vElvaston
Swarkestone vUttoxeter

Saturday August 11
Alv & Boulton vHilton
Castle Don. T.vDerby Congs
S'ley & LE Pk vEtwall
Swarkestone vR'hill Meths
Uttoxeter   vBurton
Winshill   vElvaston

Saturday August 18
Burton   vSwarkestone
Derby Congs vUttoxeter
Elvaston   vAlv & Boulton
Etwall   vCastle Don. T.
Hilton   vS'ley & LE Pk
R'hill Meths   vWinshill

Saturday August 25
Alv & Boulton vWinshill
Burton   vR'hill Meths
Castle Don. T.vHilton
S'ley & LE Pk vElvaston
Swarkestone vDerby Congs
Uttoxeter   vEtwall

Saturday September 1
Derby Congs vBurton
Elvaston   vCastle Don. T.
Etwall   vSwarkestone
Hilton   vUttoxeter
R'hill Meths   vAlv & Boulton
Winshill   vS'ley & LE Pk

Saturday September 8
Burton   vEtwall
Castle Don. T.vWinshill
Derby Congs vR'hill Meths
S'ley & LE Pk vAlv & Boulton
Swarkestone vHilton
Uttoxeter   vElvaston

Sunday September 9
Alv & Boulton vCastle Don. T.
Elvaston   vSwarkestone
Etwall   vDerby Congs
Hilton   vBurton
R'hill Meths   vS'ley & LE Pk
Winshill   vUttoxeter

Castlemaine XXXX Division 7E

Saturday April 28
Awsworth vSandiacre T.
Darley Abbey vS'ley & LE Pk
Duffield vMarehay
W. Hall. WR vLittle Eaton

Saturday May 5
Little Eaton vCodnor
Marehay vDarley Abbey
Sandiacre T. vDuffield
S'ley & LE Pk vW. Hall. WR
Stainsby Hall vAwsworth

Saturday May 12
Codnor vW. Hall. WR
Darley Abbey vSandiacre T.
Duffield vStainsby Hall
S'ley & LE Pk vMarehay

Sunday May 13
Little Eaton vAwsworth
Sandiacre T. vS'ley & LE Pk
Stainsby Hall vDarley Abbey
W. Hall. WR vMarehay

Saturday May 19
Awsworth vCodnor
Duffield vLittle Eaton
Marehay vSandiacre T.
S'ley & LE Pk vStainsby Hall

Saturday May 26
Codnor vDuffield
Little Eaton vDarley Abbey
Stainsby Hall vMarehay
W. Hall. WR vSandiacre T.

Saturday June 2
Awsworth vW. Hall. WR
Darley Abbey vCodnor
Sandiacre T. vStainsby Hall
S'ley & LE Pk vLittle Eaton

Saturday June 9
Awsworth vDuffield
Codnor vS'ley & LE Pk
Little Eaton vMarehay
W. Hall. WR vStainsby Hall

Saturday June 16
Darley Abbey vAwsworth
Duffield vW. Hall. WR
Marehay vCodnor
Sandiacre T. vLittle Eaton

Saturday June 23
Awsworth vS'ley & LE Pk
Codnor vSandiacre T.
Duffield vDarley Abbey
Little Eaton vStainsby Hall

Saturday June 30
Darley Abbey vW. Hall. WR
Marehay vAwsworth
S'ley & LE Pk vDuffield
Stainsby Hall vCodnor

Saturday July 7
Little Eaton vW. Hall. WR
Marehay vDuffield
Sandiacre T. vAwsworth
S'ley & LE Pk vDarley Abbey

Saturday July 14
Awsworth vStainsby Hall
Codnor vLittle Eaton
Darley Abbey vMarehay
Duffield vSandiacre T.
W. Hall. WR vS'ley & LE Pk

Saturday July 21
Marehay vS'ley & LE Pk
Sandiacre T. vDarley Abbey
Stainsby Hall vDuffield
W. Hall. WR vCodnor

Saturday July 28
Awsworth vLittle Eaton
Darley Abbey vStainsby Hall
Marehay vW. Hall. WR
S'ley & LE Pk vSandiacre T.

Saturday August 4
Codnor vAwsworth
Little Eaton vDuffield
Sandiacre T. vMarehay
Stainsby Hall vS'ley & LE Pk

Saturday August 11
Darley Abbey vLittle Eaton
Duffield vCodnor
Marehay vStainsby Hall
Sandiacre T. vW. Hall. WR

Saturday August 18
Codnor vDarley Abbey
Little Eaton vS'ley & LE Pk
Stainsby Hall vSandiacre T.
W. Hall. WR vAwsworth

Saturday August 25
Duffield vAwsworth
Marehay vLittle Eaton
S'ley & LE Pk vCodnor
Stainsby Hall vW. Hall. WR

Saturday September 1
Awsworth vDarley Abbey
Codnor vMarehay
Little Eaton vSandiacre T.
W. Hall. WR vDuffield

Saturday September 8
Darley Abbey vDuffield
Sandiacre T. vCodnor
S'ley & LE Pk vAwsworth
Stainsby Hall vLittle Eaton

Sunday September 9
Awsworth vMarehay
Codnor vStainsby Hall
Duffield vS'ley & LE Pk
W. Hall. WR vDarley Abbey

Castlemaine XXXX Division 7N

Saturday April 28
Belper Mdws vClay Cross
Calow vAlfreton
Chesterfield vAmbergate
Middleton vClowne Town
Riddings vWirksworth

Saturday May 5
Alfreton vChesterfield
Ambergate vBelper Mdws
Clowne Town vCalow
Tibshelf vRiddings
Wirksworth vMiddleton

Saturday May 12
Belper Mdws vAlfreton
Calow vMiddleton
Chesterfield vClowne Town
Riddings vClay Cross
Wirksworth vTibshelf

Sunday May 13
Ambergate vRiddings
Calow vChesterfield
Clay Cross vWirksworth
Clowne Town vBelper Mdws
Middleton vTibshelf

Saturday May 19
Belper Mdws vCalow
Chesterfield vMiddleton
Riddings vAlfreton
Tibshelf vClay Cross
Wirksworth vAmbergate

Saturday May 26
Alfreton   vWirksworth
Ambergate   vTibshelf
Chesterfield   vBelper Mdws
Clowne Town   vRiddings
Middleton   vClay Cross

Saturday June 2
Belper Mdws   vMiddleton
Clay Cross   vAmbergate
Riddings   vCalow
Tibshelf   vAlfreton
Wirksworth   vClowne Town

Saturday June 9
Alfreton   vClay Cross
Calow   vWirksworth
Chesterfield   vRiddings
Clowne Town   vTibshelf
Middleton   vAmbergate

Saturday June 16
Ambergate   vAlfreton
Clay Cross   vClowne Town
Riddings   vBelper Mdws
Tibshelf   vCalow
Wirksworth   vChesterfield

Saturday June 23
Belper Mdws   vWirksworth
Calow   vClay Cross
Chesterfield   vTibshelf
Clowne Town   vAmbergate
Middleton   vAlfreton

Saturday June 30
Alfreton   vClowne Town
Ambergate   vCalow
Clay Cross   vChesterfield
Riddings   vMiddleton
Tibshelf   vBelper Mdws

Saturday July 7
Alfreton   vCalow
Ambergate   vChesterfield
Clay Cross   vBelper Mdws
Clowne Town   vMiddleton
Wirksworth   vRiddings

Saturday July 14
Belper Mdws   vAmbergate
Calow   vClowne Town
Chesterfield   vAlfreton
Middleton   vWirksworth
Riddings   vTibshelf

Saturday July 21
Alfreton   vBelper Mdws
Clay Cross   vRiddings
Clowne Town   vChesterfield

Middleton   vCalow
Tibshelf   vWirksworth

Saturday July 28
Belper Mdws   vClowne Town
Chesterfield   vCalow
Riddings   vAmbergate
Tibshelf   vMiddleton
Wirksworth   vClay Cross

Saturday August 4
Alfreton   vRiddings
Ambergate   vWirksworth
Calow   vBelper Mdws
Clay Cross   vTibshelf
Middleton   vChesterfield

Saturday August 11
Belper Mdws   vChesterfield
Clay Cross   vMiddleton
Riddings   vClowne Town
Tibshelf   vAmbergate
Wirksworth   vAlfreton

Saturday August 18
Alfreton   vTibshelf
Ambergate   vClay Cross
Calow   vRiddings
Clowne Town   vWirksworth
Middleton   vBelper Mdws

Saturday August 25
Ambergate   vMiddleton
Clay Cross   vAlfreton
Riddings   vChesterfield
Tibshelf   vClowne Town
Wirksworth   vCalow

Saturday September 1
Alfreton   vAmbergate
Belper Mdws   vRiddings
Calow   vTibshelf
Chesterfield   vWirksworth
Clowne Town   vClay Cross

Saturday September 8
Alfreton   vMiddleton
Ambergate   vClowne Town
Clay Cross   vCalow
Tibshelf   vChesterfield
Wirksworth   vBelper Mdws

Sunday September 9
Belper Mdws   vTibshelf
Calow   vAmbergate
Chesterfield   vClay Cross
Clowne Town   vAlfreton
Middleton   vRiddings

Castlemaine XXXX
Division 7S

Saturday April 28
Castle Don. T. vMickleover
Derby Congs   vAlv & Boulton
Elvaston   vSt Ls & St Ms
Ticknall   vMelbourne T.
Trentside   vLullington Pk

Saturday May 5
Alv & Boulton   vSwarkestone
Lullington Pk   vCastle Don. T.
Melbourne T.   vElvaston
Mickleover   vDerby Congs
St Ls & St Ms   vTrentside

Saturday May 12
Derby Congs   vCastle Don. T.
Lullington Pk   vSt Ls & St Ms
Swarkestone   vMickleover
Ticknall   vAlv & Boulton
Trentside   vMelbourne T.

Sunday May 13
Alv & Boulton   vElvaston
Castle Don. T. vSt Ls & St Ms
Derby Congs   vSwarkestone
Melbourne T.   vLullington Pk
Mickleover   vTicknall

Saturday May 19
Elvaston   vMickleover
St Ls & St Ms   vMelbourne T.
Swarkestone   vCastle Don. T.
Ticknall   vDerby Congs
Trentside   vAlv & Boulton

Saturday May 26
Alv & Boulton   vLullington Pk
Castle Don. T. vMelbourne T.
Derby Congs   vElvaston
Mickleover   vTrentside
Swarkestone   vTicknall

Saturday June 2
Elvaston   vSwarkestone
Lullington Pk   vMickleover
St Ls & St Ms   vAlv & Boulton
Ticknall   vCastle Don. T.
Trentside   vDerby Congs

Saturday June 9
Alv & Boulton   vMelbourne T.
Derby Congs   vLullington Pk
Mickleover   vSt Ls & St Ms
Swarkestone   vTrentside
Ticknall   vElvaston

Derbyshire

Saturday June 16
Elvaston vCastle Don. T.
Lullington Pk vSwarkestone
Melbourne T. vMickleover
St Ls & St Ms vDerby Congs
Trentside vTicknall

Saturday June 23
Castle Don. T.vAlv & Boulton
Derby Congs vMelbourne T.
Elvaston vTrentside
Swarkestone vSt Ls & St Ms
Ticknall vLullington Pk

Saturday June 30
Alv & Boulton vMickleover
Lullington Pk vElvaston
Melbourne T. vSwarkestone
St Ls & St Ms vTicknall
Trentside vCastle Don. T.

Saturday July 7
Alv & Boulton vDerby Congs
Lullington Pk vTrentside
Melbourne T. vTicknall
Mickleover vCastle Don. T.
St Ls & St Ms vElvaston

Saturday July 14
Castle Don. T.vLullington Pk
Derby Congs vMickleover
Elvaston vMelbourne T.
Swarkestone vAlv & Boulton
Trentside vSt Ls & St Ms

Saturday July 21
Alv & Boulton vTicknall
Castle Don. T.vDerby Congs
Melbourne T. vTrentside
Mickleover vSwarkestone
St Ls & St Ms vLullington Pk

Saturday July 28
Elvaston vAlv & Boulton
Lullington Pk vMelbourne T.
St Ls & St Ms vCastle Don. T.
Swarkestone vDerby Congs
Ticknall vMickleover

Saturday August 4
Alv & Boulton vTrentside
Castle Don. T.vSwarkestone
Derby Congs vTicknall
Melbourne T. vSt Ls & St Ms
Mickleover vElvaston

Saturday August 11
Elvaston vDerby Congs
Lullington Pk vAlv & Boulton
Melbourne T. vCastle Don. T.

Ticknall vSwarkestone
Trentside vMickleover

Saturday August 18
Alv & Boulton vSt Ls & St Ms
Castle Don. T.vTicknall
Derby Congs vTrentside
Mickleover vLullington Pk
Swarkestone vElvaston

Saturday August 25
Elvaston vTicknall
Lullington Pk vDerby Congs
Melbourne T. vAlv & Boulton
St Ls & St Ms vMickleover
Trentside vSwarkestone

Saturday September 1
Castle Don. T.vElvaston
Derby Congs vSt Ls & St Ms
Mickleover vMelbourne T.
Swarkestone vLullington Pk
Ticknall vTrentside

Saturday September 8
Alv & Boulton vCastle Don. T.
Lullington Pk vTicknall
Melbourne T. vDerby Congs
St Ls & St Ms vSwarkestone
Trentside vElvaston

Sunday September 9
Castle Don. T.vTrentside
Elvaston vLullington Pk
Mickleover vAlv & Boulton
Swarkestone vMelbourne T.
Ticknall vSt Ls & St Ms

Castlemaine XXXX Division 7W

Saturday April 28
Barton vDunstall
Dray. & H'ry vTutbury
Uttoxeter vClifton
Walton-on-T. vTicknall

Saturday May 5
Ashbourne vUttoxeter
Clifton vWalton-on-T.
Dunstall vDray. & H'ry
Ticknall vBarton
Tutbury vKirk Langley

Saturday May 12
Barton vClifton
Dray. & H'ry vTicknall
Kirk Langley vDunstall
Walton-on-T. vAshbourne

Sunday May 13
Ashbourne vBarton
Clifton vDray. & H'ry
Ticknall vKirk Langley
Uttoxeter vWalton-on-T.

Saturday May 19
Barton vUttoxeter
Dray. & H'ry vAshbourne
Kirk Langley vClifton
Tutbury vDunstall

Saturday May 26
Ashbourne vKirk Langley
Ticknall vTutbury
Uttoxeter vDray. & H'ry
Walton-on-T. vBarton

Saturday June 2
Dray. & H'ry vWalton-on-T.
Dunstall vTicknall
Kirk Langley vUttoxeter
Tutbury vClifton

Saturday June 9
Ashbourne vTutbury
Barton vDray. & H'ry
Clifton vDunstall
Walton-on-T. vKirk Langley

Saturday June 16
Dunstall vAshbourne
Kirk Langley vBarton
Ticknall vClifton
Tutbury vUttoxeter

Saturday June 23
Ashbourne vTicknall
Dray. & H'ry vKirk Langley
Uttoxeter vDunstall
Walton-on-T. vTutbury

Saturday June 30
Clifton vAshbourne
Dunstall vWalton-on-T.
Ticknall vUttoxeter
Tutbury vBarton

Saturday July 7
Clifton vUttoxeter
Dunstall vBarton
Ticknall vWalton-on-T.
Tutbury vDray. & H'ry

Saturday July 14
Barton vTicknall
Dray. & H'ry vDunstall
Kirk Langley vTutbury
Uttoxeter vAshbourne
Walton-on-T. vClifton

Saturday July 21
Ashbourne   vWalton-on-T.
Clifton   vBarton
Dunstall   vKirk Langley
Ticknall   vDray. & H'ry

Saturday July 28
Barton   vAshbourne
Dray. & H'ry vClifton
Kirk Langley vTicknall
Walton-on-T. vUttoxeter

Saturday August 4
Ashbourne   vDray. & H'ry
Clifton   vKirk Langley
Dunstall   vTutbury
Uttoxeter   vBarton

Saturday August 11
Barton   vWalton-on-T.
Dray. & H'ry vUttoxeter
Kirk Langley vAshbourne
Tutbury   vTicknall

Saturday August 18
Clifton   vTutbury
Ticknall   vDunstall
Uttoxeter   vKirk Langley
Walton-on-T. vDray. & H'ry

Saturday August 25
Dray. & H'ry vBarton
Dunstall   vClifton
Kirk Langley vWalton-on-T.
Tutbury   vAshbourne

Saturday September 1
Ashbourne   vDunstall
Barton   vKirk Langley
Clifton   vTicknall
Uttoxeter   vTutbury

Saturday September 8
Dunstall   vUttoxeter
Kirk Langley vDray. & H'ry
Ticknall   vAshbourne
Tutbury   vWalton-on-T.

Sunday September 9
Ashbourne   vClifton
Barton   vTutbury
Uttoxeter   vTicknall
Walton-on-T. vDunstall

The pavilion at Belper Amateurs, which will be the home of Division 2 North cricket in 2007 after their promotion.

2007 Derbyshire Premier & County League Cup Competition draws

Premier Cup and XXXX Trophy games start at 1.30pm, all other Cup games start at 2 pm

Sunday May 20

Castlemaine XXXX Trophy Prelim Round

Ambergate	v	W Hallam WR
Belper Ams	v	Hilton
Derby Congs	v	Darley Dale

Derby Evening Telegraph Bayley Cup Prelim Round

Alfreton	v	Lull'ton Pk 3
Winshill	v	Ashbourne

Sunday June 3

Derbyshire Premier Cup

Group A Round 1

Alfreton	v	Ock & B'wash
Mansfield HM	v	Denby

Group B Round 1

Papp & Linby	v	Alvaston & B
Quarndon	v	Sandiacre T

Group C Round 1

Clifton	v	Dunstall
Kimberley I	v	Lull'ton Pk

Group D Round 1

Caythorpe	v	Elvaston
Chesterfield	v	Spondon

Castlemaine XXXX Trophy 1st Round

Duffield	v	D Congs/ D Dale
Marehay	v	Tutbury
Nutbrook	v	Ambergate/W Hallam

Rolleston	v	Aston-on-T
Shipley Hall	v	Chesterfield
Ticknall	v	Spondon
Belper Ams/Hilton	v	Riddings
Denby	v	Staveley Wel
Heanor Town	v	Belper Mds
S Wingfield	v	Ilkeston Rut
Wirksworth	v	Pilsley
Allestree	v	Rolls Royce
Barton	v	Sawl & LE Pk
Brailsford	v	Matlock
Sandiacre T	v	Swarkestone
Stainsby Hall	v	Ock & B'wash

Derby Evening Telegraph Bayley Cup 1st Round

Breadsall	v	Little Eaton
Clowne Town	v	Marehay
Ilkeston Rut	v	Walton-on-T
Alv & Boulton	v	Rolleston
Burton	v	Darley Abbey
Draycott & Hanbury	v	Little. Cents
Lull'ton Pk 2	v	Elvaston
Saw & LE Pk	v	Swanwick H
Trentside	v	Shipley Hall
Cromford Mds	v	Quarndon
Morton Coll	v	Etwall
Riddings	v	Clay Cross
Staveley Wel	v	Alfreton/ Lullington 3
Melbourne T	v	Ticknall
Old Derbeians	v	Clifton
Winshill/Ashbourne	v	Langley Mi U

Ripley & Heanor News Wright Cup 1st Round

Belper Mds	v	Heanor Town
Darley Abbey	v	Win'worth S
Tibshelf	v	Denby
Whitmoor RC	v	Duffield
Aston-on-T	v	Spondon
Ock & B'wash	v	Sandiacre T
Swarkestone	v	Breadsall
Ambergate	v	Nutbrook
Butterley Utd	v	Trentside
Clay Cross	v	Wirksworth
Codnor	v	Brailsford
Little. Cents	v	Barton
Mickleover	v	S Wingfield

Rolls Royce	v	Alfreton
Saw & LE Pk	v	Belper Ams
Tutbury	v	Rosehill M

James Harwood Cup 1st Round

Brailsford	v	Shipley Hall
Parwich	v	Butterley Utd
W Hallam WR	v	Nutbrook
Denby	v	Stainsby Hall
Langley M U	v	Hilton
Marehay	v	Allestree
Matlock	v	Winshill
Pilsley	v	Castle Don T
Swanwick H	v	Quarndon
Alvaston & B	v	Kirk Langley
Derby Congs	v	Swarkestone
Elvaston	v	Burton
Etwall	v	Morton Coll
Rosehill M	v	Ilkeston R
Uttoxeter	v	Ock & B'wash

Slazenger Harry Lund Cup 1st Round

Duffield	v	Marehay
Stainsby Hall	v	Derby Congs
W Hallam WR	v	Dray & Hanb
Belper Mds	v	Codnor
Lull'ton Pk	v	Riddings
St Ls & St Ms	v	Tibshelf
Barton	v	Swarkestone
Kirk Langley	v	Elvaston
Walton-on-T	v	Mickleover

Sunday June 17

Derbyshire Premier Cup

Group A Round 2

Alfreton	v	Denby
Ock & B'wash	v	Mansfield HM

Group B Round 2

Alvaston & B	v	Quarndon
Sandiacre T	v	Papp & Linby

Group C Round 2

Dunstall	v	Kimberley I
Lull'ton Pk	v	Clifton

Group D Round 2

Elvaston	v	Chesterfield
Spondon	v	Caythorpe

Castlemaine XXXX Trophy 2nd Round

Derby Evening Telegraph Bayley Cup 2nd Round

Ripley & Heanor News Wright Cup 2nd Round

James Harwood Cup 2nd Round

Slazenger Harry Lund Cup 2nd Round

Sunday July 8

Derbyshire Premier Cup

Group A Round 3

Denby	v	Ock & B'wash
Mansfield HM	v	Alfreton

Group B Round 3

Alvaston & B	v	Sandiacre T
Papp & Linby	v	Quarndon

Group C Round 3

Kimberley I	v	Clifton
Lull'ton Pk	v	Dunstall

Group D Round 3

Caythorpe	v	Chesterfield
Elvaston	v	Spondon

Castlemaine XXXX Trophy Quarter-finals

Derby Evening Telegraph Bayley Cup Quarter-finals

Ripley & Heanor News Wright Cup Quarter-finals

James Harwood Cup Quarter-finals

Slazenger Harry Lund Cup Quarter-finals

Sunday July 29

Derbyshire Premier Cup Quarter-finals

Castlemaine XXXX Trophy Semi-finals

Derby Evening Telegraph Bayley Cup Semi-finals

Ripley & Heanor News Wright Cup Semi-finals

James Harwood Cup Semi-finals

Slazenger Harry Lund Cup Semi-finals

Sunday August 12

James Harwood Cup Final

Sunday August 19

Derbyshire Premier Cup Semi-finals

Ripley & Heanor News Wright Cup Final

Sunday August 26

Derby Evening Telegraph Bayley Cup Final

Monday August 27

Castlemaine XXXX Trophy Final

Sunday Sept 2

Slazenger Harry Lund Cup Final

Saturday Sept 15

Derbyshire Premier Cup Final

Burton League suffers decline

by Alan Rowley

THE **BURTON and District Cricket League** continues its decline. With many teams defecting to the County League, the 2006 season saw only three divisions, each consisting of eight teams. Worse is to follow in 2007 when Division 2 will have only seven teams, and division 3 will have only six. Only five years ago, this once proud league had 52 teams competing in five divisions. Sad!

In the Inchcape Kia First Division, eventual champions Medina made a faltering start, in part due to the weather, and it wasn't until the 10th June that they managed to head the table. Once there, however, they dominated, although Uttoxeter stayed in the hunt until a wet Saturday 2nd September left Medina 29 points clear with two games remaining.

Appleby Magna finished strongly to finish level on points with Uttoxeter, some 42 points adrift of the champions. Magna were, however, the only side to inflict a defeat on the Abbot Beyne-based club. Marstons were competitive in fourth, losing fewer games than both Uttoxeter and Magna. The top four were head and shoulders above the rest.

S & A Foods headed the table for a month but tailed off badly to finish a distant fifth, just ahead of Packington, who twice gave the champions a scare. Hartshorne and Abbots Bromley filled the bottom two places but will escape relegation because of the impending departure of both Uttoxeter and Appleby Magna.

Anderson-Dixon & Roe Division Two was competitive from start to finish but on the final weekend Medina 2nds just managed to squeeze a point ahead of Yoxall. In the final matches, a few more runs in Yoxall's favour against Uttoxeter 2nds and another wicket lost by Medina 2nds at home to Tamworth 3rds would have seen the trophy going to a different home.

Uttoxeter 2nds finished a close third and were 'there or thereabouts' for much of the season. Despite a heavy last match defeat, Tamworth 3rds ended the year strongly in fourth - Lichfield 3rds, leaders early on, tailed off to fifth place much like S & A Foods in Division One. Appleby Magna 2nds managed to steer themselves clear of the relegation zone in the final weeks meaning a bottom two of Kings Bromley and Ashby Town. Both clubs suffered bad weather throughout and both got off to a bad start. Neither recovered and Bromley, for obvious reasons, will wish to draw a line under the 2006 season. Two wins in July hinted at a revival for Ashby but these turned out to be their only successes.

The Maidstones Accountants Third Division was dominated by S & A Foods 2nds and Hartshorne 2nds. S & A always seemed in control but Hartshorne pushed them all the way to the final Saturday. Lichfield 4ths began well and were fairly consistent in finishing third. In mid-table Draycott & Hanbury 2nds, Abbots Bromley 2nds and Yoxall 2nds had many ups and downs, as did seventh placed Marstons 2nds whose end of season was marred by a shortage of available players. North Warwickshire 3rds had some good results but they finished some 26 points adrift at the foot of the table.

2006 Burton League Tables

Division 1

	P	w	l	c	a	wcn	lcn	BP	Pen	Pts
Medina	21	15	1	3	1	1	0	55	0	184
Uttoxeter	21	9	7	2	1	2	0	46	0	142
Appleby Magna	21	11	6	3	1	0	0	53	0	142
Marstons	21	11	5	3	2	0	0	41	0	133
S & A Foods	21	7	10	1	3	0	0	31	0	92
Packington	21	6	10	3	0	0	2	38	0	89
Hartshorne	21	4	9	3	5	0	0	20	0	72
Abbots Bromley	21	1	16	2	1	0	1	36	0	52

Division 2

	P	w	l	c	a	wcn	lcn	T	BP	Pen	Pts
Medina 2nd XI	21	12	4	3	2	0	0	0	50	0	149
Yoxall	21	12	6	1	0	0	1	1	43	0	148
Uttoxeter 2nd XI	21	11	4	4	1	0	0	1	42	0	140

Derbyshire

	P	w	l	c	a	wcn	lcn	BP	Pen	Pts
Tamworth 3rd XI	21	9	9	2	1	0	0	0	49	0	121
Lichfield 3rd XI	21	8	9	3	0	0	1	0	42	0	119
Appleby Magna 2nd XI	21	5	12	0	1	0	2	1	25	0	93
Kings Bromley	21	3	7	4	2	2	0	3	24	0	81
Ashby Town 1st XI	21	2	11	3	3	2	0	0	35	0	67

Division 3

	P	w	l	c	a	wcn	lcn	BP	Pen	Pts
S & A Foods 2nd XI	21	13	1	3	2	0	2	53	0	183
Hartshorne 2nd XI	21	12	4	3	1	0	1	52	0	160
Lichfield 4th XI	21	8	6	2	2	1	2	32	0	124
Dray & Hanbury 2nd XI	21	7	8	3	1	1	1	37	0	110
Abbots Bromley 2nd XI	21	4	7	3	2	3	2	30	0	97
Yoxall 2nd XI	21	4	11	1	2	0	3	23	0	96
Marstons 2nd XI	21	5	6	3	1	5	1	25	0	84
N. Warwickshire 3rd XI	21	3	13	2	1	2	0	28	0	58

2006 Burton League Averages

Batting: (top 6 - qualification9 innings, 300 runs)

Division One

	Inns	NO	Runs	HS	Avge
Ansar Majid (Medina)	10	3	465	103*	66.43
Ishtiaq Kazmi (Medina)	11	5	363	118	60.50
Kev Sanders (Marstons)	15	6	527	96*	58.56
Mick Hodgkinson (Uttoxeter)	11	1	553	159*	55.30
Moh'd Waseem (Medina)	15	4	582	146*	52.91
Andy Gagie (Uttoxeter)	13	1	548	89*	45.67

Division Two

	Inns	NO	Runs	HS	Avge
Greg Thompson (Kings Brom)	11	3	415	94*	51.88
John Woolley (Uttoxeter)	14	3	493	108*	44.82
Gareth Lewis (Yoxall)	19	3	699	95	43.69
Ian Bailey (Uttoxeter)	16	2	609	128	43.50
Richard Cust (Lichfield)	14	2	511	114*	42.58
J Smith (Tamworth)	14	2	473	83	39.42

Division Three

	Inns	NO	Runs	HS	Avge
Mark Smith (D & H)	10	5	438	110	87.60
Moh'd Kaleem (S & A Foods)	15	5	615	92	61.50
Alan Markey (Marstons)	9	2	405	77*	57.86
Rob Lewis (Yoxall)	12	2	548	99	54.80
Simon Staley (D & H)	12	1	485	98	44.09
Neil Fairbrother (Hartshorne)	10	3	336	72	48.00

Bowling: (top 6 - qualification 15 wickets)

Division One

	Os	M	Wkts	Runs	BB	Ave
Moh'd Nusrat (Medina)	75.2	26	27	146	5-18	5.41
Mick Hodgkinson (Uttoxeter)	117.3	35	28	253	5-16	9.04
Matt Richardson (App Magna)	150	29	31	408	5-10	13.16
Andy Whittingham (Packington)	125.3	23	33	448	5-18	13.58
Stan Kirkland (App Magna)	133.2	21	34	462	5-37	13.59
Ehsan Ul-Haq (S & A Foods)	116.3	27	26	389	6-37	14.96

Division Two

	Os	M	Wkts	Runs	BB	Ave
Asqhar Ali (Medina)	73.2	8	27	217	7-16	8.03
Kev Moughan (Yoxall)	159.3	26	46	556	6-47	12.09
Simon Archer (Yoxall)	72	7	20	270	5-13	13.50
Ian Bailey (Uttoxeter)	135.4	26	29	400	5-51	13.79
S Norchi (Tamworth)	161.5	35	34	470	5-16	13.82
Steve Cooper (Uttoxeter)	105.5	22	21	316	5-26	15.05

Division Three

	Os	M	Wkts	Runs	BB	Ave
Moh'd Kaleem (S & A Foods)	152	36	37	415	6-21	11.22
Gareth Woolley (Yoxall)	52.4	5	16	205	4-29	12.81
Allen Clark (D & H)	127.1	29	29	376	4-10	12.97
Martin Cooper (Marstons)	59.1	8	16	243	4-5	15.19
Malik Nazir (S & A Foods)	112	16	24	366	5-25	15.25
Moh'd Shakeel (S & A Foods)	134.2	20	30	465	5-16	15.50

2007 Burton League Fixtures

(2:00pm start unless stated otherwise)

Division One

28 April
Hartshorne	v Marstons
Tamworth 3	v Packington
S & A Foods	v Abbots Brom
Yoxall	v Medina

5 May
Abbots Brom	v Medina
Marstons	v Packington
S & A Foods	v Hartshorne
Tamworth 3	v Yoxall

12 May
Hartshorne	v Abbots Brom
Medina	v Tamworth 3
Packington	v S & A Foods
Yoxall	v Marstons

19 May
Abbots Brom	v Yoxall
Marstons	v S & A Foods
Medina	v Packington
Tamworth 3	v Hartshorne

26 May
Hartshorne	v Medina
Marstons	v Abbots Brom
Packington	v Yoxall
S & A Foods	v Tamworth 3

2 June
Abbots Brom	v Packington
Medina	v S & A Foods
Tamworth 3	v Marstons
Yoxall	v Hartshorne

9 June
Packington	v Hartshorne
Marstons	v Medina
S & A Foods	v Yoxall
Tamworth 3	v Abbots Brom

16 June
Hartshorne	v S & A Foods
Medina	v Abbots Brom
Packington	v Marstons
Yoxall	v Tamworth 3

23 June
Abbots Brom	v Hartshorne
Marstons	v Yoxall
S & A Foods	v Packington
Tamworth 3	v Medina

30 June
Abbots Brom	v S & A Foods
Marstons	v Hartshorne
Medina	v Yoxall
Packington	v Tamworth 3

7 July
Hartshorne	v Tamworth 3
Packington	v Medina
S & A Foods	v Marstons
Yoxall	v Abbots Brom

14 July
Abbots Brom	v Marstons
Medina	v Hartshorne
Tamworth 3	v S & A Foods
Yoxall	v Packington

21 July
Hartshorne	v Yoxall
Marstons	v Tamworth 3
Packington	v Abbots Brom
S & A Foods	v Medina

28 July
Abbots Brom	v Tamworth 3
Medina	v Marstons
Hartshorne	v Packington
Yoxall	v S & A Foods

4 Aug
Abbots Brom	v Medina
Marstons	v Packington
S & A Foods	v Hartshorne
Tamworth 3	v Yoxall

11 Aug
Hartshorne	v Abbots Brom
Medina	v Tamworth 3
Packington	v S & A Foods
Yoxall	v Marstons

18 Aug - 1:30pm
Hartshorne	v Marstons
Packington	v Tamworth 3
S & A Foods	v Abbots Brom
Yoxall	v Medina

25 Aug - 1:30pm
Abbots Brom	v Yoxall
Marstons	v S & A Foods
Medina	v Packington
Tamworth 3	v Hartshorne

1 Sept - 1:30pm
Hartshorne	v Medina
Marstons	v Abbots Brom
Packington	v Yoxall
S & A Foods	v Tamworth 3

8 Sept - 1:00pm
Abbots Brom	v Packington
Medina	v S & A Foods
Tamworth 3	v Marstons
Yoxall	v Hartshorne

15 Sept - 1:00pm
Packington	v Hartshorne
Marstons	v Medina
S & A Foods	v Yoxall
Tamworth 3	v Abbots Brom

Division Two

28 April
Abbots B. 2	v Yoxall 2
Kings Brom	v Lichfield 3
Medina 2	v Hartshorne 2

5 May
Lichfield 3	v Ashby Town
Medina 2	v Abbots B. 2
Yoxall 2	v Kings Brom

12 May
Abbots Br 2	v Hartshorne 2
Ashby Town	v Yoxall 2
Kings Brom	v Medina 2

19 May
Hartshorne 2	v Ashby Town
Lichfield 3	v Abbots B. 2
Yoxall 2	v Medina 2

26 May
Kings Brom	v Ashby Town
Medina 2	v Lichfield 3
Yoxall 2	v Hartshorne 2

2 June
Ashby Town	v Abbots Br 2
Hartshorne 2	v Kings Brom
Lichfield 3	v Yoxall 2

9 June
Abbots B. 2	v Kings Brom
Hartshorne 2	v Lichfield 3
Ashby Town	v Medina 2

16 June
Abbots B. 2	v Medina 2
Ashby Town	v Lichfield 3
Kings Brom	v Yoxall 2

23 June
Hartshorne 2 v Abbots Br 2
Medina 2 v Kings Brom
Yoxall 2 v Ashby Town

30 June
Hartshorne 2 v Medina 2
Lichfield 3 v Kings Brom
Yoxall 2 v Abbots B. 2

7 July
Abbots B. 2 v Lichfield 3
Ashby Town v Hartshorne 2
Medina 2 v Yoxall 2

14 July
Ashby Town v Kings Brom
Hartshorne 2 v Yoxall 2
Lichfield 3 v Medina 2

21 July
Abbots Br 2 v Ashby Town
Kings Brom v Hartshorne 2
Yoxall 2 v Lichfield 3

28 July
Ashby Town v Medina 2
Lichfield 3 v Hartshorne 2
Kings Brom v Abbots B. 2

4 Aug
Lichfield 3 v Ashby Town
Medina 2 v Abbots B. 2
Yoxall 2 v Kings Brom

11 Aug
Abbots Br 2 v Hartshorne 2
Ashby Town v Yoxall 2
Kings Brom v Medina 2

18 Aug - 1:30pm
Abbots B. 2 v Yoxall 2
Kings Brom v Lichfield 3
Medina 2 v Hartshorne 2

25 Aug - 1:30pm
Hartshorne 2 v Ashby Town
Lichfield 3 v Abbots B. 2
Yoxall 2 v Medina 2

1 Sept - 1:30pm
Kings Brom v Ashby Town
Medina 2 v Lichfield 3
Yoxall 2 v Hartshorne 2

8 Sept - 1:00pm
Ashby Town v Abbots Br 2
Hartshorne 2 v Kings Brom
Lichfield 3 v Yoxall 2

15 Sept - 1:00pm
Abbots B. 2 v Kings Brom
Hartshorne 2 v Lichfield 3
Medina 2 v Ashby Town

Division Three

28 April
Hilton 3 v Trentside 4
Lichfield 4 v Alrewas Hs.
Marstons 2 v Ashby H 3

5 May
Alrewas Hs. v Hilton 3
Ashby H 3 v Lichfield 4
Trentside 4 v Marstons 2

12 May
Hilton 3 v Ashby H 3
Lichfield 4 v Trentside 4
Marstons 2 v Alrewas Hs.

19 May
Alrewas Hs. v Trentside 4
Hilton 3 v Marstons 2

26 May
Ashby H 3 v Alrewas Hs.
Lichfield 4 v Marstons 2
Trentside 4 v Hilton 3

2 June
Ashby H 3 v Trentside 4
Hilton 3 v Alrewas Hs.

9 June
Alrewas Hs. v Marstons 2
Ashby H 3 v Hilton 3
Trentside 4 v Lichfield 4

16 June
Lichfield 4 v Ashby H 3
Marstons 2 v Trentside 4

23 June
Ashby H 3 v Marstons 2
Hilton 3 v Lichfield 4
Trentside 4 v Alrewas Hs.

30 June
Alrewas Hs. v Lichfield 4
Hilton 3 v Marstons 2

7 July
Lichfield 4 v Hilton 3
Trentside 4 v Ashby H 3

14 July
Alrewas Hs. v Ashby H 3
Marstons 2 v Lichfield 4

21 July
No games

28 July
No games

4 Aug
No games

11 Aug
Hilton 3 v Alrewas Hs.
Lichfield 4 v Ashby H 3
Marstons 2 v Trentside 4

18 Aug - 1:30pm
Trentside 4 v Lichfield 4
Ashby H 3 v Hilton 3
Marstons 2 v Alrewas Hs.

25 Aug - 1:30pm
Alrewas Hs. v Trentside 4
Ashby H 3 v Marstons 2
Hilton 3 v Lichfield 4

1 Sept - 1:30pm
Ashby H 3 v Alrewas Hs.
Lichfield 4 v Marstons 2
Trentside 4 v Hilton 3

8 Sept - 1:00pm
Alrewas Hs. v Lichfield 4
Marstons 2 v Hilton 3

15 Sept - 1:00pm
Trentside 4 v Ashby H 3

Stanton in the Peak romp to title

by Alan Rowley

THE **YORKSHIRE and Derbyshire Cricket League** is a Saturday league established in 1969, with four divisions and 47 teams, spread over Sheffield and North East Derbyshire, from as far north as the town of Stocksbridge to as far south as the village of Stanton in the Peak.

The 2006 season started in rain and ended the same way. A dousing on the final Saturday of the season condemned Sheffield Centralians to Division Two. They had to win at Calver to stay in Division One, but the downpour prevented any play on the final day.

By far and away the team of the season were Stanton In The Peak, who romped to the title by a phenomenal 77 points from Ashford in the Water who were worthy runners-up.

University Staff were Division Two champions and also promoted were Sheffield Collegiate III, easily the best two teams in the Division. Dronfield Woodhouse and Sheffield Centralians II went down.

Division Three champions are Ridgeway with second spot going to Walkley. Both teams should go well in Division Two next term. Sheffield Transport and Stocksbridge II drop to Division Four. Whittington Wanderers II are Division Four champions, with Sheepbridge II joining them in Division Three in 2007 as runners-up.

The cup final at Olive Grove Road saw Calver take on Ashford in the Water On a funereally slow pitch, Works reached a useful 149-8 from their allotted 40 overs (Lee Stewart 49). Calver were in the game until skipper Dougie Howie was run out, then they folded to 79 all out, Lee Stewart spinning out 3-13 to take the Man of the Match award.

2006 Yorkshire & Derbyshire League Tables

Division 1

	P	ow	iw	c	a	t	il	ol	BP	Pen	Pts
Stanton in the Peak	22	12	4	1	2	0	1	2	12	0	416
Sheffield Works Dept	22	6	7	2	1	0	2	4	25	0	339
Hundall	22	9	1	2	1	0	5	4	49	0	318
Parkhead	22	7	3	3	3	0	1	5	32	0	315
De La Salle Sheffield	22	6	4	4	2	0	2	4	21	0	299
Holmesfield	22	8	0	2	1	1	5	5	54	0	293
Ashford in the Water	22	5	4	3	2	1	4	3	33	0	293
Hathersage	22	5	2	4	3	0	2	6	27	0	248
Stocksbridge	22	4	3	2	2	0	4	7	39	0	231
Calver	22	5	1	3	3	0	1	9	22	0	215
Sheffield Centralians	22	1	5	2	2	0	5	7	52	0	209
Millhouses	22	2	0	2	2	0	2	14	59	0	141

Division 2

	P	ow	w	iw	c	a	t	il	l	ol	BP	Pen	Pts
Sheffield University Staff	22	11	1	4	2	2	0	1	0	1	14	0	426
Sheffield Collegiate IV	22	10	1	3	3	2	0	2	0	1	21	0	396
Bakewell	22	9	0	2	3	2	0	1	0	5	26	0	331
Sheepbridge	22	6	0	4	4	1	0	2	0	5	31	0	301
Chesterfield Barbarians	22	6	0	4	3	1	1	0	0	7	16	0	293
Parkhead II	22	7	0	2	2	2	0	2	1	6	31	0	278
Grindleford	22	5	0	4	3	2	0	2	0	6	22	0	267
Sheffield Works Dept II	22	4	0	3	4	1	1	3	0	6	34	0	249
Baslow	22	7	0	0	5	1	0	2	1	6	23	0	246
De La Salle Sheffield II	22	3	0	2	5	1	0	3	0	8	27	0	190
Dronfield Woodhouse	22	1	0	1	3	3	0	9	0	5	35	25	103
Sheffield Centralians II	22	0	0	0	5	2	0	2	0	13	29	76	9

Division 3

	P	ow	iw	c	a	t	il	ol	BP	Pen	Pts
Ridgeway	18	8	3	3	1	0	1	2	17	0	309
Walkley	18	7	2	4	2	1	0	2	8	0	286
Hundall II	18	8	1	3	1	0	2	3	14	0	266
Millhouses II	18	6	1	2	2	0	0	7	35	0	237
Hathersage II	18	4	3	2	3	0	3	3	19	0	219
Whittington Wanderers	18	4	1	4	2	0	3	4	25	0	193
Hallam III	18	3	1	4	1	1	3	5	31	0	181
Sheffield Collegiate V	18	6	0	3	2	0	2	5	32	50	172
Sheffield Transport	18	2	3	3	1	0	0	9	22	0	164
Stocksbridge II	18	0	2	4	1	0	3	8	40	25	95

Derbyshire

Division 4

	P	ow	w	iw	c	a	t	il	l	ol	BP	Pen	Pts
Whittington Wanderers II	16	7	0	3	4	0	0	0	0	2	5	0	272
Sheepbridge II	16	7	1	0	2	1	0	0	0	5	26	0	250
Sheffield Zingari	16	4	0	4	3	2	0	0	0	3	17	0	237
Chesterfield Barbarians II	16	6	0	1	2	1	0	2	0	4	10	0	204
Sheffield Uni Staff II	16	5	0	0	3	2	0	3	0	3	16	0	181
Coal Aston III	16	5	0	0	4	1	0	2	0	4	27	25	167
Baslow II	16	2	0	1	3	1	1	1	0	7	46	0	163
Dronfield Sp. Contact II	16	4	0	0	4	1	0	1	0	6	32	25	147
Stocksbridge III	16	1	0	1	3	1	1	1	1	7	23	0	115

2007 Yorkshire & Derbyshire League Fixtures

Division 1

Sat 28 April
Ashford v Sheff W Dept
Calver v Holmesfield
Parkhead v Hundall
Sheff Col III v De La Salle
Stanton v Hathersage
Stocksbridge v Sheffield US

Sat 5 May
De La Salle v Calver
Hathersage v Parkhead
Holmesfield v Stanton
Hundall v Ashford
Sheffield US v Sheff Col III
Ashford v Stocksbridge

Mon 7 May
Hathersage v Calver
Holmesfield v De La Salle
Hundall v Stanton
(at Carr Lane,
Dronfield Woodhouse CC)
Sheffield US v Ashford
Ashford v Parkhead
Stocksbridge v Sheff Col III

Sat 12 May
Calver v Ashford
De La Salle v Hundall
Holmesfield v Hathersage
Parkhead v Stocksbridge
Sheff Col III v Ashford
Stanton v Sheffield US

Sat 19 May
Ashford v De La Salle
Parkhead v Calver
Sheff Col III v Stanton
Sheffield US v Hathersage
Ashford v Hundall
Stocksbridge v Holmesfield

Sat 26 May
Ashford v Parkhead
Hathersage v Sheff Col III
Holmesfield v Hundall
Sheffield US v Calver
Ashford v De La Salle
Stocksbridge v Stanton

Mon 28 May
Ashford v Stocksbridge
Calver v Hundall
De La Salle v Hathersage
Parkhead v Sheffield US
Sheff Col III v Holmesfield
Stanton v Ashford

Sat 2 June
Ashford v Calver
Parkhead v Stanton
Sheff Col III v Hundall
Sheffield US v Holmesfield
Ashford v Hathersage
Stocksbridge v De La Salle

Sat 9 June
Calver v Stanton
De La Salle v Parkhead
Hathersage v Stocksbridge
Holmesfield v Ashford
Hundall v Sheffield US
Ashford v Sheff Col III

Sat 16 June
Calver v Stocksbridge
De La Salle v Sheffield US
Hathersage v Hundall
Holmesfield v Ashford
Sheff Col III v Parkhead
Stanton v Ashford

Sat 23 June
Ashford v Hathersage
Parkhead v Holmesfield
Sheff Col III v Calver
Sheffield US v Ashford
Stanton v De La Salle
Stocksbridge v Hundall

Sat 30 June
Calver v Parkhead
De La Salle v Ashford
Hathersage v Sheffield US
Holmesfield v Stocksbridge
Hundall v Ashford
Stanton v Sheff Col III

Sat 7 July
Ashford v Holmesfield
Parkhead v De La Salle
Sheff Col III v Ashford
Sheffield US v Hundall
Stanton v Calver
Stocksbridge v Hathersage

Sat 14 July
De La Salle v Sheff Col III
Hathersage v Stanton
Holmesfield v Calver
Hundall v Parkhead
Sheffield US v Stocksbridge
Ashford v Ashford

Sat 21 July
Ashford v Hundall
Calver v De La Salle
Parkhead v Hathersage
Sheff Col III v Sheffield US
Stanton v Holmesfield
Stocksbridge v Ashford

Sat 28 July

Ashford	v	Sheff Col III
Hathersage	v	Holmesfield
Hundall	v	De La Salle
Sheffield US	v	Stanton
Ashford	v	Calver
Stocksbridge	v	Parkhead

Sat 4 Aug

Calver	v	Sheff Col III
De La Salle	v	Stanton
Hathersage	v	Ashford
Holmesfield	v	Parkhead
Hundall	v	Stocksbridge
Ashford	v	Sheffield US

Sat 11 Aug

Ashford	v	Sheffield US
Calver	v	Hathersage
De La Salle	v	Holmesfield
Parkhead	v	Ashford
Sheff Col III	v	Stocksbridge
Stanton	v	Hundall

Sat 18 Aug

Hathersage	v	De La Salle
Holmesfield	v	Sheff Col III
Hundall	v	Calver
Sheffield US	v	Parkhead
Ashford	v	Stanton
Stocksbridge	v	Ashford

Sat 25 Aug

Ashford	v	Stanton
Hundall	v	Hathersage
Parkhead	v	Sheff Col III
Sheffield US	v	De La Salle
Ashford	v	Holmesfield
Stocksbridge	v	Calver

Mon 27 Aug

Calver	v	Sheffield US
De La Salle	v	Ashford
Hundall	v	Holmesfield
Parkhead	v	Ashford
Sheff Col III	v	Hathersage
Stanton	v	Stocksbridge

Sat 1 Sept

Calver	v	Ashford
De La Salle	v	Stocksbridge
Hathersage	v	Ashford
Holmesfield	v	Sheffield US
Hundall	v	Sheff Col III
Stanton	v	Parkhead

Division 2

Sat 28 April

Bakewell	v	Walkley
Baslow	v	Sheepbridge
De La Salle II	v	Ridgeway
Grindleford	v	Chester'd Ba
Sheff. Cents	v	Millhouses
Ashford II	v	Parkhead II

Sat 5 May

Chester'd Ba	v	Sheff. Cents
Millhouses	v	De La Salle II
Parkhead II	v	Grindleford
Ridgeway	v	Baslow
Sheepbridge	v	Bakewell
Walkley	v	Ashford II

Mon 7 May

Chester'd Ba	v	Ashford II
De La Salle II	v	Baslow
Millhouses	v	Grindleford
Parkhead II	v	Bakewell
Ridgeway	v	Sheff. Cents
Walkley	v	Sheepbridge

Sat 12 May

Bakewell	v	Millhouses
Baslow	v	Sheff. Cents
Grindleford	v	De La Salle II
Sheepbridge	v	Chester'd Ba
Ashford II	v	Ridgeway
Walkley	v	Parkhead II

Sat 19 May

Baslow	v	Ashford II
De La Salle II	v	Walkley
Grindleford	v	Bakewell
Millhouses	v	Chester'd Ba
Ridgeway	v	Parkhead II
Sheff. Cents	v	Sheepbridge

Sat 26 May

Chester'd Ba	v	Walkley
De La Salle II	v	Ashford II
Millhouses	v	Sheepbridge
Parkhead II	v	Baslow
Ridgeway	v	Bakewell
Sheff. Cents	v	Grindleford

Mon 28 May

Grindleford	v	Ridgeway
Bakewell	v	Chester'd Ba
Baslow	v	Walkley
Sheepbridge	v	Parkhead II
Sheff. Cents	v	De La Salle II
Ashford II	v	Millhouses

Sat 2 June

Baslow	v	Chester'd Ba
De La Salle II	v	Sheepbridge
Grindleford	v	Ashford II
Millhouses	v	Parkhead II
Ridgeway	v	Walkley
Sheff. Cents	v	Bakewell

Sat 9 June

Bakewell	v	Ashford II
Chester'd Ba	v	Ridgeway
Millhouses	v	Baslow
Parkhead II	v	De La Salle II
Sheepbridge	v	Grindleford
Walkley	v	Sheff. Cents

Sat 16 June

Bakewell	v	De La Salle II
Baslow	v	Grindleford
Parkhead II	v	Chester'd Ba
Sheepbridge	v	Ridgeway
Ashford II	v	Sheff. Cents
Walkley	v	Millhouses

Sat 23 June

Baslow	v	Bakewell
De La Salle II	v	Chester'd Ba
Grindleford	v	Walkley
Ridgeway	v	Millhouses
Sheff. Cents	v	Parkhead II
Ashford II	v	Sheepbridge

Sat 30 June

Bakewell	v	Grindleford
Chester'd Ba	v	Millhouses
Parkhead II	v	Ridgeway
Sheepbridge	v	Sheff. Cents
Ashford II	v	Baslow
Walkley	v	De La Salle II

Sat 7 July

Baslow	v	Millhouses
De La Salle II	v	Parkhead II
Grindleford	v	Sheepbridge
Ridgeway	v	Chester'd Ba
Sheff. Cents	v	Walkley
Ashford II	v	Bakewell

Sat 14 July

Chester'd Ba	v	Grindleford
Millhouses	v	Sheff. Cents
Parkhead II	v	Ashford II
Ridgeway	v	De La Salle II
Sheepbridge	v	Baslow
Walkley	v	Bakewell

Sat 21 July

Bakewell	v	Sheepbridge
Baslow	v	Ridgeway
De La Salle II	v	Millhouses

Derbyshire

Division 3

Grindleford   v   Parkhead II
Sheff. Cents   v   Chester'd Ba
Ashford II   v   Walkley

Sat 28 July
Chester'd Ba   v   Sheepbridge
De La Salle II   v   Grindleford
Millhouses   v   Bakewell
Parkhead II   v   Walkley
Ridgeway   v   Ashford II
Sheff. Cents   v   Baslow

Sat 4 Aug
Bakewell   v   Baslow
Chester'd Ba   v   De La Salle II
Millhouses   v   Ridgeway
Parkhead II   v   Sheff. Cents
Sheepbridge   v   Ashford II
Walkley   v   Grindleford

Sat 11 Aug
Bakewell   v   Parkhead II
Baslow   v   De La Salle II
Grindleford   v   Millhouses
Sheepbridge   v   Walkley
Sheff. Cents   v   Ridgeway
Ashford II   v   Chester'd Ba

Sat 18 Aug
Chester'd Ba   v   Bakewell
De La Salle II   v   Sheff. Cents
Millhouses   v   Ashford II
Parkhead II   v   Sheepbridge
Ridgeway   v   Grindleford
Walkley   v   Baslow

Sat 25 Aug
Chester'd Ba   v   Parkhead II
De La Salle II   v   Bakewell
Grindleford   v   Baslow
Millhouses   v   Walkley
Ridgeway   v   Sheepbridge
Sheff. Cents   v   Ashford II

Mon 27 Aug
Bakewell   v   Ridgeway
Baslow   v   Parkhead II
Grindleford   v   Sheff. Cents
Sheepbridge   v   Millhouses
Ashford II   v   De La Salle II
Walkley   v   Chester'd Ba

Sat 1 Sept
Bakewell   v   Sheff. Cents
Chester'd Ba   v   Baslow
Parkhead II   v   Millhouses
Sheepbridge   v   De La Salle II
Ashford II   v   Grindleford
Walkley   v   Ridgeway

Division 3

Sat 28 April
Hathersage II v Dronfield W
Hundall II v Duck. Lodge
(at Carr Lane, Dronfield W CC)
Millhouses II v Hallam III
Sh'pbridge II v Whitt. Wds II
Sheff Coll V v Sheff Tran
Whitt. Wds v Sheff Cents II

Sat 5 May
Dronfield W v Sheff Coll V
Duck. Lodge v Whitt. Wds
Hallam III v Hathersage II
Sheff Cents II v Millhouses II
Sheff Tran v Sh'pbridge II
Whitt. Wds II v Hundall II

Sat 12 May
Duck. Lodge v Dronfield W
Hathersage II v Sh'pbridge II
Hundall II v Sheff Coll V
(at Carr Lane, Dronfield W CC)
Millhouses II v Whitt. Wds II
Sheff Cents II v Hallam III
Whitt. Wds v Sheff Tran

Sat 19 May
Hathersage II v Whitt. Wds
Hundall II v Millhouses II
(at Carr Lane, Dronfield W CC)

Sh'pbridge II v Sheff Cents II
Sheff Coll V v Duck. Lodge
Sheff Tran v Dronfield W
Whitt. Wds II v Hallam III

Sat 26 May
Dronfield W v Sheff Cents II
Hallam III v Hundall II
Sh'pbridge II v Millhouses II
Sheff Coll V v Hathersage II
Sheff Tran v Duck. Lodge
Whitt. Wds II v Whitt. Wds

Sat 2 June
Hathersage II v Millhouses II
Hundall II v Dronfield W
(at Carr Lane, Dronfield W CC)
Sh'pbridge II v Duck. Lodge
Sheff Coll V v Whitt. Wds
Sheff Tran v Hallam III
Whitt. Wds II v Sheff Cents II

Sat 9 June
Dronfield W v Whitt. Wds II
Duck. Lodge v Hathersage II

Hallam III v Sh'pbridge II
Sheff Cents II v Sheff Coll V
Sheff Tran v Hundall II
Whitt. Wds v Millhouses II

Sat 16 June
Duck. Lodge v Whitt. Wds II
Hallam III v Dronfield W
Hundall II v Hathersage II
(at Carr Lane, Dronfield W CC)
Millhouses II v Sheff Coll V
Sheff Cents II v Sheff Tran
Whitt. Wds v Sh'pbridge II

Sat 23 June
Hallam III v Sheff Coll V
(at Sandygate, Hallam CC)
Hathersage II v Sheff Cents II
Hundall II v Whitt. Wds
(at Carr Lane, Dronfield W CC)
Millhouses II v Duck. Lodge
Sh'pbridge II v Dronfield W
Whitt. Wds II v Sheff Tran

Sat 30 June
Dronfield W v Sheff Tran
Duck. Lodge v Sheff Coll V
Hallam III v Whitt. Wds II
Millhouses II v Hundall II
Sheff Cents II v Sh'pbridge II
Whitt. Wds v Hathersage II

Sat 7 July
Hathersage II v Duck. Lodge
Hundall II v Sheff Tran
Millhouses II v Whitt. Wds
Sh'pbridge II v Hallam III
Sheff Coll V v Sheff Cents II
(at Abbeydale Park,
Sheffield Collegiate CC)
Whitt. Wds II v Dronfield W

Sat 14 July
Dronfield W v Hathersage II
Duck. Lodge v Hundall II
Hallam III v Millhouses II
Sheff Cents II v Whitt. Wds
Sheff Tran v Sheff Coll V
Whitt. Wds II v Sh'pbridge II

Sat 21 July
Hathersage II v Hallam III
Hundall II v Whitt. Wds II
Millhouses II v Sheff Cents II
Sh'pbridge II v Sheff Tran
Sheff Coll V v Dronfield W
Whitt. Wds v Duck. Lodge

Sat 28 July

Dronfield W	v	Duck. Lodge
Hallam III	v	Sheff Cents II
Sh'pbridge II	v	Hathersage II
Sheff Coll V	v	Hundall II
Sheff Tran	v	Whitt. Wds
Whitt. Wds II	v	Millhouses II

Sat 4 Aug

Dronfield W	v	Sh'pbridge II
Duck. Lodge	v	Millhouses II
Sheff Cents II	v	Hathersage II
Sheff Coll V	v	Hallam III
Sheff Tran	v	Whitt. Wds II
Whitt. Wds	v	Hundall II

Sat 11 Aug

Duck. Lodge	v	Sheff Cents II
Hathersage II	v	Sheff Tran
Hundall II	v	Sh'pbridge II
Millhouses II	v	Dronfield W
Sheff Coll V	v	Whitt. Wds II
Whitt. Wds	v	Hallam III

Sat 18 Aug

Dronfield W	v	Whitt. Wds
Hallam III	v	Duck. Lodge
Sh'pbridge II	v	Sheff Coll V
Sheff Cents II	v	Hundall II
Sheff Tran	v	Millhouses II
Whitt. Wds II	v	Hathersage II

Sat 25 Aug

Dronfield W	v	Hallam III
Hathersage II	v	Hundall II
Sh'pbridge II	v	Whitt. Wds
Sheff Coll V	v	Millhouses II
(at Abbeydale Park,		
Sheffield Collegiate CC)		
Sheff Tran	v	Sheff Cents II
Whitt. Wds II	v	Duck. Lodge

SUNDAY 2 SEPTEMBER
SUNDAY CUP FINAL
Venue to be confirmed

Remarkable year for Caythorpe

by Alan Rowley

2006 Nottinghamshire Premier League Table

	P	w	wd	ld	l	c	a	BaP	BoP	Pen	Pts
Caythorpe	22	11	5	1	2	0	3	65	67	0	334
Kimberley Institute	22	11	4	1	5	0	1	70	69	0	319
West Indian Cavaliers	22	5	7	1	5	2	2	64	51	3	268
Notts Unity Casuals	22	5	5	4	3	1	4	54	44	0	246
Wollaton	22	6	2	2	5	2	5	53	50	0	241
Papplewick and Linby	22	6	3	2	5	2	4	50	52	4	240
Clifton Village	22	1	7	5	2	3	4	58	48	0	240
Welbeck Colliery	22	5	3	4	5	1	4	58	51	11	226
Retford Cricket & Sports	22	7	0	6	6	0	3	53	52	0	219
Mansfield Hosiery Mills	22	4	2	4	6	3	3	61	43	0	216
Long Eaton	22	2	2	5	8	2	3	61	39	3	181
Thoresby Colliery	22	0	0	5	11	2	4	50	31	0	127

THE **NOTTINGHAMSHIRE Premier League** took on a whole new look in 2006. West Indian Cavaliers, champions for the previous five years, were never in the running and finished a disappointing third, 66 points behind champions Caythorpe and 51 points behind runners up Kimberley Institute.

For Caythorpe it was a remarkable year. Signs of a good season ahead were evident in the very first game of the season at home to Kimberley. Caythorpe set a very gettable 170 runs to win, but the visitors were never in the hunt, collapsing to 96 all out. Tom Hemmings, son of former Nottinghamshire CCC stalwart Eddie, did most of the damage taking six wickets for 16 runs.

Star player for the champions was former Nottinghamshire all-rounder Jimmy Hindson who finished second in the batting and bowling averages. His 704 runs came at an average of 64, and he also grabbed 44 wickets at an average of 18.16. Top of the averages were

Kimberley Institute's Nottinghamshire all-rounder Samit Patel finished top of the league batting averages with 943 runs from only 13 innings at an average of 104.78

two Kimberley Institute players. The pick of the batsmen was Nottinghamshire all-rounder Samit Patel, who scored 943 runs from only 13 innings at an average of 104.78. Top of the bowling averages was John Shaw, whose 43 wickets came at an average of 18.07. Shaw also figured prominently in the batting averages scoring 844 runs at an average of 44.42.

The 2005 champions of the Bassetlaw League, Thoresby Colliery, and the South Nottinghamshire League, Long Eaton, both failed miserably in the top flight and drop straight back down for the 2007 season. Thoresby were rooted at the foot of the table, 54 points adrift of Lone Eaton, who in turn were 35 points behind Mansfield Hosiery Mills. Replacing the two relegated sides will be South Nottinghamshire champions Gedling Colliery and Bassetlaw champions Killamarsh Juniors.

Former Nottinghamshire all-rounder Jimmy Hindson's runs and wickets did much to steer Caythorpe to the Premier League title.

Of the remaining clubs, Notts Unity Casuals took the fourth spot, just ahead of Wollaton, Papplewick and Linby and Clifton Village. These four were separated by a mere six points. Welbeck Colliery will be disappointed with a bottom half finish, but will be looking forward to moving to their impressive new ground for the 2007 season.

Retford Cricket and Sports and Mansfield Hosiery Mills both had poor seasons, but neither were ever in any danger of dropping out of the top division.

In the ECB Cockspur Cup, Caythorpe were only one game away from Lord's reaching the semi finals before crashing out to eventual winners South Northumberland. Despite restricting the northerners to only 152 runs, Caythorpe finished well adrift being bowled out for 118 in the 40th over.

Phil "Daffy" DeFreitas turned out for Papplewick & Linby in the Nottinghamshire Premier League in 2006 following his retirement after 20 years in first class cricket the previous summer.

2006 Nottinghamshire Premier League Averages

BATTING (qualification 500 runs - 12 innings):

		Inns	NO	HS	Runs	Ave
S Patel	Kimberley I.	13	4	143*	943	104.78
J Hindson	Caythorpe	19	8	105	704	64.00
P Pollard	Clifton Village	16	1	163	931	62.07
I Hopkins	Long Eaton	18	4	97*	769	54.93
C Kumara	Retford	18	4	100	710	50.71
R Nicol	Wollaton	12	1	129	557	50.64
K Glendenning	Wollaton	16	0	166	782	48.88
F Du Plessis	Mansfield HM	17	1	124	769	48.06
R Harris	Clifton Village	17	6	119*	511	46.45
J Shaw	Kimberley I.	21	2	150	844	44.42
D Irvine	Thoresby Coll	20	1	105	809	42.58
B Scothern	Long Eaton	14	1	74	519	39.92
T Khan	Papp & Linby	18	4	85*	555	39.64
S Musgrove	Mansfield HM	18	1	105	651	38.29
P DeFreitas	Papp & Linby	14	0	130	535	38.21
G Welton	Welbeck Coll	16	1	101	570	38.00
D Williamson	WI Cavaliers	19	2	83*	639	37.59
A Thomas	WI Cavaliers	20	2	111	644	35.78
J Mierkalns	Caythorpe	18	0	97	605	33.61
D Millns	Caythorpe	18	2	84	511	31.94

BOWLING (Qualification 40 wickets):

		Ovs	M	Runs	Wkts	BB	Ave
J Shaw	Kimberley I	186.1	23	777	43	5-49	18.07
J Hindson	Caythorpe	247.4	41	799	44	6-40	18.16
P McMahon	Wollaton	206.0	29	790	43	6-92	18.37
U Hassan	Long Eaton	237.4	24	963	40	6-61	24.08

2007 Nottinghamshire Premier League Fixtures

Saturday 21st April
Kimberley v Papplewick
Retford v Manfield HM
Gedling v Killamarsh
Clifton Village v Notts Unity
W.I. Cavaliers v Wollaton
Caythorpe v Welbeck

Saturday 28th April
Welbeck v Retford
Wollaton v Kimberley
Notts Unity v W.I. Cavaliers
Killamarsh v Clifton Village
Mansfield HM v Gedling
Papplewick v Caythorpe

Saturday 5th May
Kimberley v Notts Unity
Retford v Caythorpe
Gedling v Welbeck
Clifton Village v Mansfield HM
W.I. Cavaliers v Killamarsh
Papplewick v Wollaton

Saturday 12th May
Welbeck v Clifton Village
Retford v Gedling
Notts Unity v Papplewick
Killarmarsh v Kimberley
Mansfield HM v W.I. Cavaliers
Caythorpe v Wollaton

Saturday 19th May
Kimberley v Manfield HM
Wollaton v Notts Unity
Gedling v Caythorpe
Clifton Village v Retford
W.I. Cavaliers v Welbeck
Papplewick v Killamarsh

Saturday 26th May
Welbeck v Kimberley
Retford v W.I. Cavaliers
Gedling v Clifton Village
Killamarsh v Wollaton
Manfield HM v Papplewick
Caythorpe v Notts Unity

Monday 28th May
Kimberley v Retford
Wollaton v Manfield HM
Notts Unity v Killamarsh
Clifton Village v Caythorpe
W.I. Cavaliers v Gedling
Papplewick v Welbeck

Saturday 2nd June
Welbeck v Wollaton
Retford v Papplewick
Gedling v Kimberley
Clifton Village v W.I. Cavaliers
Manfield HM v Notts Unity
Caythorpe v Killamarsh

Saturday 9th June
Kimberley v Clifton Village
Wollaton v Retford
Notts Unity v Welbeck
Killamarsh v Manfield HM
W.I. Cavaliers v Caythorpe
Papplewick v Gedling

Saturday 16th June
Welbeck v Killamarsh
Retford v Notts Unity
Gedling v Wollaton
Clifton Village v Papplewick
W.I. Cavaliers v Kimberley
Caythorpe v Manfield HM

Saturday 23rd June
Kimberley v Caythorpe
Wollaton v Clifton Village
Notts Unity v Gedling
Killamarsh v Retford
Manfield HM v Welbeck
Papplewick v W.I. Cavaliers

Saturday 30th June
Papplewick v Kimberley
Manfield HM v Retford
Killamarsh v Gedling
Notts Unity v Clifton Village
Wollaton v W.I. Cavaliers
Welbeck v Caythorpe

Saturday 7th July
Retford v Welbeck
Kimberley v Wollaton
W.I. Cavaliers v Notts Unity
Clifton Village v Killamarsh
Gedling v Mansfield HM
Caythorpe v Papplewick

Saturday 14th July
Notts Unity v Kimberley
Caythorpe v Retford
Welbeck v Gedling
Mansfield HM v Clifton Village
Killamarsh v W.I. Cavaliers
Wollaton v Papplewick

Saturday 21st July
Clifton Village v Welbeck
Gedling v Retford
Papplewick v Notts Unity
Kimberley v Killarmarsh
W.I. Cavaliers v Mansfield HM
Wollaton v Caythorpe

Saturday 28th July
Manfield HM v Kimberley
Notts Unity v Wollaton
Caythorpe v Gedling
Retford v Clifton Village
Welbeck v W.I. Cavaliers
Killamarsh v Papplewick

Saturday 4th August
Kimberley v Welbeck
W.I. Cavaliers v Retford
Clifton Village v Gedling
Wollaton v Killamarsh
Papplewick v Manfield HM
Notts Unity v Caythorpe

Saturday 11th August
Retford v Kimberley
Manfield HM v Wollaton
Killamarsh v Notts Unity
Caythorpe v Clifton Village
Gedling v W.I. Cavaliers
Welbeck v Papplewick

Saturday 18th August
Wollaton v Welbeck
Papplewick v Retford
Kimberley v Gedling
W.I. Cavaliers v Clifton Village
Notts Unity v Manfield HM
Killamarsh v Caythorpe

Saturday 25th August
Clifton Village v Kimberley
Retford v Wollaton
Welbeck v Notts Unity
Manfield HM v Killamarsh
Caythorpe v W.I. Cavaliers
Gedling v Papplewick

Saturday 1st September
Killamarsh v Welbeck
Notts Unity v Retford
Wollaton v Gedling
Papplewick v Clifton Village
Kimberley v W.I. Cavaliers
Manfield HM v Caythorpe

Saturday 8th September
Caythorpe v Kimberley
Clifton Village v Wollaton
Gedling v Notts Unity
Retford v Killamarsh
Welbeck v Manfield HM
W.I. Cavaliers v Papplewick

Gedling Colliery hope to make better fist of Premier return

by Alan Rowley

THE CHAMPIONS of the **South Nottinghamshire Cricket League** for 2006 are Gedling Colliery, who finished a mammoth 68 points in front of second placed Calverton. Gedling won twelve of their 18 games and had the title wrapped up in early August. They will be hoping to make a better show in the Nottinghamshire Premier than they did in 2005 when they finished bottom.

Calverton will be disappointed not to have pushed Gedling harder for the title, but they did improve on their 2005 third placing. They will be amongst the favourites to lift the title in 2007.

Of the rest, Collingham and District were the most disappointing and they suffer the agony of dropping from the Premier to the SNCL division B in successive seasons. The other relegated side was Bottesford who were well adrift at the foot of the table.

Champions of Division B are Southwell who finished 37 points ahead of Newstead Abbey. These two teams will take their place in Division A in 2007. Dropping out of Division B are Clifton Village 2nds and Bramcote.

2006 South Nottinghamshire League Tables

DIVISION A	P	W	W/D	L/D	T	L	N/R	W+T	B+B	Pts	Ave
GEDLING COLLIERY	18	12	1	0	0	3	2	250	19	269	16.81
CALVERTON	18	7	3	0	0	3	5	170	31	201	15.46
PLUMTREE	18	6	1	3	1	3	4	146	43	189	13.50
BALDERTON	18	6	2	2	0	4	4	144	42	186	13.29
RADCLIFFE ON TRENT	18	4	5	1	0	5	3	132	59	191	12.73
ATTENBOROUGH	18	4	3	2	0	5	4	114	53	167	11.93
EASTWOOD TOWN	18	4	2	1	0	7	4	102	53	155	11.07
ELLERSLIE	18	3	2	2	1	6	4	94	56	150	10.71
COLLINGHAM	18	4	0	4	0	6	4	88	54	142	10.14
BOTTESFORD	18	2	0	4	0	10	2	48	69	117	7.31

DIVISION B

	P	W	W/D	L/D	T	L	N/R	W+T	B+B	Pts	Ave
SOUTHWELL	18	10	3	1	1	0	3	242	31	273	18.20
N'STEAD ABBEY & VILLAGE	18	8	2	2	1	3	2	194	42	236	14.75
GEDLING & SHERWOOD	18	6	4	1	0	5	2	162	56	218	13.63
LOUGHBOROUGH CAR	18	8	1	1	0	5	3	172	31	203	13.53
GOTHAM	17	6	2	1	1	5	2	152	36	188	12.53
ROLLS ROYCE LEISURE	17	5	1	1	1	6	3	122	48	170	12.14
KIMBERLEY INST II	18	6	0	4	1	5	2	138	46	184	11.50
WEST BRIDGFORDIANS	18	4	1	1	1	9	2	102	45	147	9.19
CLIFTON VILLAGE II	18	4	2	1	0	10	1	102	51	153	9.00
BRAMCOTE	18	1	1	4	0	10	2	38	55	93	5.81

DIVISION C

	P	W	W/D	L/D	T	L	N/R	W+T	B+B	Pts	Ave
KIRKBY PORTLAND	18	8	1	3	1	0	5	186	32	218	16.77
KEYWORTH	18	10	2	0	1	3	2	230	38	268	16.75
BELVOIR	18	7	2	1	1	3	4	172	39	211	15.07
WEST INDIAN CARIBS	18	7	2	1	0	4	4	162	49	211	14.00
ATTENBOROUGH II	18	7	1	1	0	5	4	152	35	187	13.36
NOTTINGHAM	18	6	1	1	0	5	5	132	25	157	12.08
PLUMTREE II	18	4	2	1	0	7	4	102	52	154	11.00
HUCKNALL	18	3	2	3	1	8	1	96	79	175	10.29
THRUMPTON	18	3	1	2	0	11	1	74	63	137	8.06
NEWARK	18	1	1	2	0	10	4	34	54	88	6.29

DIVISION D

	P	W	T	L	N/R	W+T	B+B	Pts	Ave
HICKLING	18	13	0	3	2	156	98	254	15.88
LONG WHATTON	18	10	1	4	3	126	94	220	14.67
WILSONS	18	11	0	5	2	132	96	228	14.25
RADCLIFFE ON TRENT II	18	9	0	6	3	108	82	190	12.67
THURGARTON	18	8	1	7	2	102	94	196	12.25
OLD PAVIORS	18	6	0	10	2	72	97	169	10.56
LADY BAY BOOTS	18	6	0	8	4	72	70	142	10.14
STANTON-BY-DALE	18	5	0	10	3	60	77	137	9.13
FARNDON	18	5	0	11	2	60	78	138	8.63
LONG EATON II	18	2	0	11	5	24	60	84	6.46

DIVISION E

	P	W	T	L	N/R	W+T	B+B	Pts	Ave
WILLOUGHBY OTW	18	14	0	1	3	168	99	267	17.80
CALVERTON II	18	9	0	6	3	108	98	206	13.73
UNDERWOOD	17	9	0	6	2	108	84	192	12.80
WOLLATON II	17	7	0	7	3	84	81	165	11.79
COLLINGHAM II	17	7	0	7	3	84	80	164	11.71
HUCKNALL II	17	7	0	8	2	84	89	173	11.53
SOUTHWELL II	18	6	0	8	4	72	85	157	11.21
RISLEY	18	6	0	10	2	72	72	144	9.00
STANTON & AWSWORTH ELKS	18	5	0	10	3	60	64	124	8.27
GEDLING COLLIERY II	18	4	0	11	3	48	66	114	7.60

DIVISION F

	P	W	T	L	N/R	W+T	B+B	Pts	Ave
NUTHALL	18	11	0	4	3	132	99	231	15.40
WEST BRIDGFORD LEG	18	10	0	6	2	120	97	217	13.56
NOTTS UNITY CASUALS II	18	8	1	7	2	102	96	198	12.38
ELLERSLIE II	18	8	0	8	2	96	95	191	11.94
WYMESWOLD	18	8	0	8	2	96	91	187	11.69
LADY BAY BOOTS II	18	8	0	7	3	96	75	171	11.40
RAVENSHEAD	18	8	1	6	3	102	59	161	10.73
EASTWOOD TOWN II	18	6	0	8	4	72	69	141	10.07
WHATTON & ASLOCKTON	18	6	0	9	3	72	72	144	9.60
BRAMCOTE II	18	2	0	12	4	24	45	69	4.93

Ravenshead 30pt deduction from 2005

Nottinghamshire

DIVISION G	P	W	T	L	N/R	W+T	B+B	Pts	Ave
CAYTHORPE III	18	13	0	1	4	156	91	247	17.64
BOTTESFORD II	18	10	0	6	2	120	93	213	13.31
TOTON SYCAMORE	18	9	0	6	3	108	81	189	12.60
LOWDHAM	18	8	0	7	3	96	84	180	12.00
BEESTON	18	7	0	8	3	84	80	164	10.93
SNIBSTON GRANGE	18	6	0	7	5	72	70	142	10.92
GOTHAM II	17	7	0	8	2	84	77	161	10.73
EPPERSTONE	18	5	0	9	4	60	70	130	9.29
ROLLS ROYCE LEISURE II	17	3	0	10	4	36	53	89	6.85
GEDLING & SHERWOOD II	18	4	0	10	4	48	43	91	6.50

DIVISION H	P	W	T	L	N/R	W+T	B+B	Pts	Ave
KINOULTON	18	9	0	5	4	108	92	200	14.29
HOVERINGHAM	18	10	0	5	3	120	85	205	13.67
CHILWELL	18	9	0	6	3	108	81	189	12.60
EAST BRIDGFORD	18	9	0	5	4	108	63	171	12.21
KIRKBY PORTLAND II	18	8	0	7	3	96	86	182	12.13
COTGRAVE	18	7	0	9	2	84	107	191	11.94
EAST LEAKE	18	8	0	6	4	96	70	166	11.86
RAINWORTH WELFARE	18	6	0	8	4	72	61	133	9.50
BESTWOOD VILLAGE	18	5	0	9	4	60	59	119	8.50
RUDDINGTON	18	2	0	13	3	24	56	80	5.33

DIVISION J	P	W	T	L	N/R	W+T	B+B	Pts	Ave
LOUGHBOROUGH CAR II	18	12	1	2	3	150	100	250	16.67
OXTON	18	13	0	3	2	156	105	261	16.31
SUTTON BONINGTON	18	9	0	6	3	108	106	214	14.27
GLADSTONE	18	10	0	4	4	120	74	194	13.86
CAUNTON	18	9	0	6	3	108	73	181	12.07
N'STEAD ABBEY & VILLAGE II	18	5	0	9	4	60	67	127	9.07
EDINGLEY	18	4	0	10	4	48	60	108	7.71
STAPLEFORD	18	4	0	10	4	48	57	105	7.50
NOTTINGHAM II	18	4	0	10	4	48	54	102	7.29
THURGARTON II	18	2	1	12	3	30	64	94	6.27

DIVISION K	P	W	T	L	N/R	W+T	B+B	Pts	Ave
CARRINGTON CAVS	18	10	1	2	5	126	81	207	15.92
LAMBLEY	18	8	1	5	4	102	89	191	13.64
ATTENBOROUGH III	18	11	1	4	2	138	76	214	13.38
BINGHAM	18	10	0	6	2	120	87	207	12.94
WEST BRIDGFORDIANS II	18	9	0	7	2	108	93	201	12.56
BELVOIR II	18	9	0	7	2	108	88	196	12.25
RISLEY II	18	7	1	6	4	90	63	153	10.93
LENTON ABBEY	18	6	0	9	3	72	71	143	9.53
NEWARK II	18	2	0	12	4	24	34	58	4.14
STANTON-BY-DALE II	18	0	0	14	4	0	35	35	2.50

DIVISION L	P	W	T	L	N/R	W+T	B+B	Pts	Ave
BASFORD HALL O B	18	12	0	4	2	144	92	236	14.75
BURTON JOYCE	18	11	0	4	3	132	87	219	14.6
FLINTHAM	18	10	0	5	3	120	93	213	14.2
KIMBERLEY INST III	18	9	0	7	2	108	86	194	12.13
STAN. & A'WORTH ELKS II	18	7	0	8	3	84	73	157	10.47
WOODBOROUGH	18	6	0	9	3	72	68	140	9.333
BREASTON	17	6	0	8	3	72	57	129	9.214
NOTTINGHAM VICTORIA	17	5	0	9	3	60	66	126	9

	P	W	T	L	N/R	W+T	B+B	Pts	Ave
THRUMPTON II	17	5	0	10	2	60	50	110	7.333
BELTON	17	4	0	11	2	48	59	107	7.133

DIVISION M

	P	W	T	L	N/R	W+T	B+B	Pts	Ave
UNDERWOOD II	18	10	0	2	6	120	81	201	16.75
CLIFTON VILLAGE III	18	9	0	5	4	108	81	189	13.5
WILLOUGHBY OTW II	18	8	0	6	4	96	84	180	12.86
KEYWORTH II	18	8	0	7	3	96	86	182	12.13
LONG WHATTON II	18	7	0	6	5	84	64	148	11.38
LAMBLEY II	18	7	0	8	3	84	78	162	10.8
OLD PAVIORS II	18	7	0	7	4	84	63	147	10.5
WILSONS II	18	7	0	9	2	84	68	152	9.5
BALDERTON II	18	5	0	10	3	60	63	123	8.2
SHEPSHED TOWN III	18	4	0	12	2	48	77	125	7.813

DIVISION N

	P	W	T	L	N/R	W+T	B+B	Pts	Ave
FARNDON II	16	10	0	2	4	120	73	193	16.08
SNIBSTON GRANGE II	16	9	0	3	4	108	70	178	14.83
CAYTHORPE IV	16	9	0	4	3	108	70	178	13.69
RADCLIFFE ON TRENT III	16	6	0	7	3	72	64	136	10.46
NEWSTEAD ABBEY & VILL III	16	5	0	6	5	60	55	115	10.45
GEDLING COLLIERY III	16	5	0	8	3	60	65	125	9.62
HUCKNALL III	16	4	0	8	4	48	58	106	8.83
PLUMTREE III	16	4	1	9	2	54	66	120	8.57
CHILWELL II	16	2	1	7	6	30	41	71	7.10
STAN. & A'WORTH ELKS III	0	0	0	0	0	0	0	0	0.00

DIVISION P

	P	W	T	L	N/R	W+T	B+B	Pts	Ave
LOWDHAM II	18	12	0	3	3	144	98	242	16.13
COTGRAVE II	18	11	0	4	3	132	83	215	14.33
ELLERSLIE III	18	9	0	5	4	108	77	185	13.21
LONG EATON III	18	8	0	7	3	96	71	167	11.13
RUDDINGTON II	18	7	0	7	4	84	61	145	10.36
TOTON SYCAMORE II	18	6	0	8	4	72	64	136	9.71
WEST BRIDGFORDIANS III	18	6	0	9	3	72	62	134	8.93
WHATTON & ASLOCKTON II	18	7	0	10	1	84	63	147	8.65
POPLARS	18	5	0	10	3	60	55	115	7.67
BEESTON II	18	3	0	11	4	36	46	82	5.86

DIVISION R

	P	W	T	L	N/R	W+T	B+B	Pts	Ave
KIMBERLEY INST IV	13	8	0	2	3	96	62	158	15.8
KIRKBY PORTLAND III	13	7	0	3	3	84	60	144	14.4
BROAD STREET ARROWS	14	8	0	3	3	96	61	157	14.27
SHEPSHED TOWN IV	13	6	0	2	5	72	40	112	14
EAST LEAKE II	14	7	0	5	2	84	58	142	11.83
WEST BRIDGFORD LEG II	14	7	0	7	0	84	60	144	10.29
BELVOIR III	14	3	0	6	5	36	46	82	9.111
THRUMPTON III	12	4	0	4	4	48	21	69	8.625
COLLINGHAM III	14	4	0	7	3	48	46	94	8.545
EDINGLEY II	14	2	0	10	2	24	32	56	4.667
BINGHAM II	13	2	0	9	2	24	24	48	4.364
NOTTINGHAM III	0	0	0	0	0	0	0	0	0
STANTON & A'WORTH ELKS IV	0	0	0	0	0	0	0	0	0

2007 South Nottinghamshire League Fixtures

DIVISION   A

Sat May 5

A'borough	v N'stead A.
Eastw'd T	v Plumtree
Ellerslie	v Long Eaton
Rad. on T	v Balderton
Southwell	v Calverton

Sat May 12

A'borough	v Eastw'd T
Balderton	v Southwell
Long Eaton	v Calverton
N'stead A.	v Ellerslie
Plumtree	v Rad. on T

Sat May 19

Balderton	v Plumtree
Calverton	v N'stead A.
Ellerslie	v Eastw'd T
Rad. on T	v A'borough
Southwell	v Long Eaton

Sat May 26

A'borough	v Balderton
Eastw'd T	v Calverton
Ellerslie	v Rad. on T
N'stead A.	v Long Eaton
Plumtree	v Southwell

Sat June 2

Balderton	v Ellerslie
Calverton	v Rad. on T
Long Eaton	v Eastw'd T
Plumtree	v A'borough
Southwell	v N'stead A.

Sat June 9

Calverton	v Balderton
Eastw'd T	v N'stead A.
Ellerslie	v Plumtree
Rad. on T	v Long Eaton
Southwell	v A'borough

Sat June 16

A'borough	v Ellerslie
Eastw'd T	v Southwell
Long Eaton	v Balderton
N'stead A.	v Rad. on T
Plumtree	v Calverton

Sat June 23

Balderton	v N'stead A.
Calverton	v A'borough
Long Eaton	v Plumtree
Rad. on T	v Eastw'd T
Southwell	v Ellerslie

Sat June 30

A'borough	v Long Eaton
Eastw'd T	v Balderton
Ellerslie	v Calverton
N'stead A.	v Plumtree
Rad. on T	v Southwell

Sat July 7

Balderton	v Rad. on T
Calverton	v Southwell
Long Eaton	v Ellerslie
N'stead A.	v A'borough
Plumtree	v Eastw'd T
	v

Sat July 14

Calverton	v Long Eaton
Eastw'd T	v A'borough
Ellerslie	v N'stead A.
Rad. on T	v Plumtree
Southwell	v Balderton
	v

Sat July 21

A'borough	v Rad. on T
Eastw'd T	v Ellerslie
Long Eaton	v Southwell
N'stead A.	v Calverton
Plumtree	v Balderton

Sat July 28

Balderton	v A'borough
Calverton	v Eastw'd T
Long Eaton	v N'stead A.
Rad. on T	v Ellerslie
Southwell	v Plumtree

Sat Aug 4

A'borough	v Plumtree
Eastw'd T	v Long Eaton
Ellerslie	v Balderton
N'stead A.	v Southwell
Rad. on T	v Calverton

Sat Aug 11

A'borough	v Southwell
Balderton	v Calverton
Long Eaton	v Rad. on T
N'stead A.	v Eastw'd T
Plumtree	v Ellerslie

Sat Aug 18

Balderton	v Long Eaton
Calverton	v Plumtree
Ellerslie	v A'borough
Rad. on T	v N'stead A.
Southwell	v Eastw'd T

Sat Aug 25

A'borough	v Calverton
Eastw'd T	v Rad. on T
Ellerslie	v Southwell
N'stead A.	v Balderton
Plumtree	v Long Eaton

Sat Sept 1

Balderton	v Eastw'd T
Calverton	v Ellerslie
Long Eaton	v A'borough
Plumtree	v N'stead A.
Southwell	v Rad. on T

DIVISION B

Sat April 28

Kimb I. II	v Bottesford

Sat May 5

RR Leisure	v Lough Car
Collingham	v Kirkby P
W Bridgfs	v Keyworth
Ged & Sher	v Gotham

Sat May 12

Kimb I. II	v RR Leisure
Keyworth	v Ged & Sher
Kirkby P	v Gotham
Bottesford	v Collingham
Lough Car	v W Bridgfs

Sat May 19

Keyworth	v Lough Car
Gotham	v Bottesford
Collingham	v RR Leisure
W Bridgfs	v Kimb I. II
Ged & Sher	v Kirkby P

Sat May 26

Kimb I. II	v Keyworth
RR Leisure	v Gotham
Collingham	v W Bridgfs
Bottesford	v Kirkby P
Lough Car	v Ged & Sher

Sat June 2

Keyworth	v Collingham
Gotham	v W Bridgfs
Kirkby P	v RR Leisure
Kimb I. II	v Lough Car
Ged & Sher	v Bottesford

Sat June 9

Gotham	v Keyworth
RR Leisure	v Bottesford
Collingham	v Lough Car

W Bridgfs v Kirkby P
Ged & Sher v Kimb I. II

Sat June 16
Kimb I. II v Collingham
RR Leisure v Ged & Sher
Kirkby P v Keyworth
Bottesford v W Bridgfs
Lough Car v Gotham

Sat June 23
Keyworth v Bottesford
Gotham v Kimb I. II
Kirkby P v Lough Car
W Bridgfs v RR Leisure
Ged & Sher v Collingham

Sat June 30
Kimb I. II v Kirkby P
RR Leisure v Keyworth
Collingham v Gotham
Bottesford v Lough Car
W Bridgfs v Ged & Sher

Sat July 7
Keyworth v W Bridgfs
Gotham v Ged & Sher
Kirkby P v Collingham
Bottesford v Kimb I. II
Lough Car v RR Leisure

Sat July 14
Gotham v Kirkby P
RR Leisure v Kimb I. II
Collingham v Bottesford
W Bridgfs v Lough Car
Ged & Sher v Keyworth

Sat July 21
RR Leisure v Collingham
Kirkby P v Ged & Sher
Bottesford v Gotham
Lough Car v Keyworth

Sat July 28
Keyworth v Kimb I. II
Gotham v RR Leisure
Kirkby P v Bottesford
W Bridgfs v Collingham
Ged & Sher v Lough Car

Sat Aug 4
Lough Car v Kimb I. II
RR Leisure v Kirkby P
Collingham v Keyworth
Bottesford v Ged & Sher
W Bridgfs v Gotham

Sat Aug 11
Kimb I. II v Ged & Sher
Keyworth v Gotham
Kirkby P v W Bridgfs
Bottesford v RR Leisure
Lough Car v Collingham

Sat Aug 18
Keyworth v Kirkby P
Gotham v Lough Car
Collingham v Kimb I. II
W Bridgfs v Bottesford
Ged & Sher v RR Leisure

Sat Aug 25
Kimb I. II v Gotham
RR Leisure v W Bridgfs
Collingham v Ged & Sher
Bottesford v Keyworth
Lough Car v Kirkby P

Sat Sept 1
Keyworth v RR Leisure
Gotham v Collingham
Kirkby P v Kimb I. II
Lough Car v Bottesford
Ged & Sher v W Bridgfs

Sat Sept 8
Kimb I. II v W Bridgfs

DIVISION C

Sat April 28
Clifton V II v A'borough II
Bramcote v WI Caribs
Hucknall v Hickling

Sat May 5
L Whatton v Hucknall
WI Caribs v Belvoir
Hickling v Bramcote
Plumtree II v Nottingham

Sat May 12
L Whatton v WI Caribs
Nottingham v Hickling
Belvoir v A'borough II
Clifton V II v Hucknall
Bramcote v Plumtree II

Sat May 19
Nottingham v Belvoir
A'borough II v Hucknall
Hickling v WI Caribs
Plumtree II v L Whatton

Sat May 26
L Whatton v Nottingham
WI Caribs v A'borough II

Hickling v Plumtree II
Hucknall v Bramcote
Clifton V II v Belvoir

Sat June 2
Nottingham v Clifton V II
A'borough II v Plumtree II
Belvoir v WI Caribs
Bramcote v L Whatton

Sat June 9
A'borough II v Nottingham
WI Caribs v Hucknall
Hickling v Belvoir
Plumtree II v Bramcote
Clifton V II v L Whatton

Sat June 16
L Whatton v Hickling
WI Caribs v Clifton V II
Belvoir v Nottingham
Hucknall v Plumtree II
Bramcote v A'borough II

Sat June 23
Nottingham v Hucknall
A'borough II v L Whatton
Belvoir v Bramcote
Plumtree II v WI Caribs
Clifton V II v Hickling

Sat June 30
L Whatton v Bramcote
WI Caribs v Nottingham
Hickling v A'borough II
Hucknall v Belvoir
Plumtree II v Clifton V II

Sat July 7
Nottingham v Plumtree II
Bramcote v Clifton V II
Belvoir v Hickling
Hucknall v L Whatton

Sat July 14
A'borough II v Bramcote
WI Caribs v L Whatton
Hickling v Hucknall
Plumtree II v Belvoir
Clifton V II v Nottingham

Sat July 21
L Whatton v Plumtree II
WI Caribs v Hickling
Belvoir v Clifton V II
Hucknall v A'borough II
Bramcote v Nottingham

Nottinghamshire

Sat July 28
Nottingham v L Whatton
A'borough II v WI Caribs
Belvoir v Hucknall
Plumtree II v Hickling
Clifton V II v Bramcote

Sat Aug 4
WI Caribs v Bramcote
Hickling v Nottingham
Hucknall v Clifton V II
Plumtree II v A'borough II

Sat Aug 11
L Whatton v Clifton V II
Nottingham v A'borough II
Belvoir v Plumtree II
Hucknall v WI Caribs
Bramcote v Hickling

Sat Aug 18
Nottingham v Bramcote
A'borough II v Belvoir
Hickling v L Whatton
Plumtree II v Hucknall
Clifton V II v WI Caribs

Sat Aug 25
L Whatton v A'borough II
WI Caribs v Plumtree II
Hickling v Clifton V II
Hucknall v Nottingham
Bramcote v Belvoir

Sat Sept 1
Nottingham v WI Caribs
A'borough II v Hickling
Belvoir v L Whatton
Bramcote v Hucknall
Clifton V II v Plumtree II

Sat Sept 8
A'borough II v Clifton V II
L Whatton v Belvoir

DIVISION D

Sat May 5
Calverton II v Stan-by-D
Thrumpton v Rad. on T II
Thurgarton v Old Paviors
Wilsons v Newark
W'by OTW v Lady BB

Sat May 12
Calverton II v Thrumpton
Newark v W'by OTW
Old Paviors v Lady BB
Stan-by-D v Thurgarton
Rad. on T II v Wilsons

Sat May 19
Newark v Rad. on T II
Lady BB v Stan-by-D
Thurgarton v Thrumpton
Wilsons v Calverton II
W'by OTW v Old Paviors

Sat May 26
Calverton II v Newark
Thrumpton v Lady BB
Thurgarton v Wilsons
Stan-by-D v Old Paviors
Rad. on T II v W'by OTW

Sat June 2
Newark v Thurgarton
Lady BB v Wilsons
Old Paviors v Thrumpton
Rad. on T II v Calverton II
W'by OTW v Stan-by-D

Sat June 9
Lady BB v Newark
Thrumpton v Stan-by-D
Thurgarton v Rad. on T II
Wilsons v Old Paviors
W'by OTW v Calverton II

Sat June 16
Calverton II v Thurgarton
Thrumpton v W'by OTW
Old Paviors v Newark
Stan-by-D v Wilsons
Rad. on T II v Lady BB

Sat June 23
Newark v Stan-by-D
Lady BB v Calverton II
Old Paviors v Rad. on T II
Wilsons v Thrumpton
W'by OTW v Thurgarton

Sat June 30
Calverton II v Old Paviors
Thrumpton v Newark
Thurgarton v Lady BB
Stan-by-D v Rad. on T II
Wilsons v W'by OTW

Sat July 7
Newark v Wilsons
Lady BB v W'by OTW
Old Paviors v Thurgarton
Stan-by-D v Calverton II
Rad. on T II v Thrumpton

Sat July 14
Lady BB v Old Paviors
Thrumpton v Calverton II
Thurgarton v Stan-by-D

Wilsons v Rad. on T II
W'by OTW v Newark

Sat July 21
Calverton II v Wilsons
Thrumpton v Thurgarton
Old Paviors v W'by OTW
Stan-by-D v Lady BB
Rad. on T II v Newark

Sat July 28
Newark v Calverton II
Lady BB v Thrumpton
Old Paviors v Stan-by-D
Wilsons v Thurgarton
W'by OTW v Rad. on T II

Sat Aug 4
Calverton II v Rad. on T II
Thrumpton v Old Paviors
Thurgarton v Newark
Stan-by-D v W'by OTW
Wilsons v Lady BB

Sat Aug 11
Calverton II v W'by OTW
Newark v Lady BB
Old Paviors v Wilsons
Stan-by-D v Thrumpton
Rad. on T II v Thurgarton

Sat Aug 18
Newark v Old Paviors
Lady BB v Rad. on T II
Thurgarton v Calverton II
Wilsons v Stan-by-D
W'by OTW v Thrumpton

Sat Aug 25
Calverton II v Lady BB
Thrumpton v Wilsons
Thurgarton v W'by OTW
Stan-by-D v Newark
Rad. on T II v Old Paviors

Sat Sept 1
Newark v Thrumpton
Lady BB v Thurgarton
Old Paviors v Calverton II
Rad. on T II v Stan-by-D
W'by OTW v Wilsons

DIVISION E

Sat May 5
Underwood v Southwell II
Risley v Long Eaton II
Wollaton II v Collingham II
Nuthall v West B Leg
Hucknall II v Farndon

Sat May 12
Underwood v Risley
West B Leg v Hucknall II
Collingham II v Farndon
Southwell II v Long Eaton II
Wollaton II v Nuthall

Sat May 19
West B Leg v Wollaton II
Farndon v Southwell II
Long Eaton II v Risley
Nuthall v Underwood
Hucknall II v Collingham II

Sat May 26
Underwood v Collingham II
Risley v Farndon
Long Eaton II v Nuthall
Southwell II v West B Leg
Wollaton II v Hucknall II

Sat June 2
West B Leg v Long Eaton II
Farndon v Nuthall
Collingham II v Risley
Wollaton II v Underwood
Hucknall II v Southwell II

Sat June 9
Farndon v West B Leg
Risley v Southwell II
Long Eaton II v Wollaton II
Nuthall v Collingham II
Hucknall II v Underwood

Sat June 16
Underwood v Long Eaton II
Risley v Hucknall II
Collingham II v West B Leg
Southwell II v Nuthall
Wollaton II v Farndon

Sat June 23
West B Leg v Southwell II
Farndon v Underwood
Collingham II v Wollaton II
Nuthall v Risley
Hucknall II v Long Eaton II

Sat June 30
Underwood v West B Leg
Risley v Collingham II
Long Eaton II v Farndon
Southwell II v Wollaton II
Nuthall v Hucknall II

Sat July 7
West B Leg v Nuthall
Farndon v Hucknall II
Collingham II v Long Eaton II

Southwell II v Underwood
Wollaton II v Risley

Sat July 14
Farndon v Collingham II
Risley v Underwood
Long Eaton II v Southwell II
Nuthall v Wollaton II
Hucknall II v West B Leg

Sat July 21
Underwood v Nuthall
Collingham II v Hucknall II
Southwell II v Farndon
West B Leg v Risley

Sat July 28
West B Leg v Underwood
Farndon v Risley
Wollaton II v Southwell II
Nuthall v Long Eaton II

Sat Aug 4
Underwood v Wollaton II
Risley v West B Leg
Long Eaton II v Collingham II
Southwell II v Hucknall II
Nuthall v Farndon

Sat Aug 11
Underwood v Hucknall II
West B Leg v Farndon
Collingham II v Nuthall
Southwell II v Risley
Wollaton II v Long Eaton II

Sat Aug 18
West B Leg v Collingham II
Farndon v Wollaton II
Long Eaton II v Underwood
Nuthall v Southwell II
Hucknall II v Risley

Sat Aug 25
Underwood v Farndon
Risley v Nuthall
Long Eaton II v Hucknall II
Southwell II v Collingham II
Wollaton II v West B Leg

Sat Sept 1
Collingham II v Underwood
Farndon v Long Eaton II
Hucknall II v Wollaton II

Sat Sept 8
Collingham II v Southwell II
Hucknall II v Nuthall
Long Eaton II v West B Leg
Risley v Wollaton II

DIVISION F

Sat, April 28
Ged Coll II v Bottesford II

Sat May 5
Notts U Cs II v Eastw'd T II
Ravenshead v Elks
Caythorpe III v Wymeswold
Bottesford II v Ellerslie II

Sat May 12
Ellerslie II v Ravenshead
Eastw'd T II v Bottesford II
Ged Coll II v Notts U Cs II
Elks v Caythorpe III

Sat May 19
Notts U Cs II v Elks
Wymeswold v Ged Coll II
Caythorpe III v Ravenshead
Bottesford II v Eastw'd T II

Sat May 26
Ravenshead v Wymeswold
Caythorpe III v Ged Coll II
Elks v Ellerslie II
Notts U Cs II v Bottesford II

Sat June 2
Eastw'd T II v Ravenshead
Bottesford II v Ged Coll II
Ellerslie II v Caythorpe III
Wymeswold v Notts U Cs II

Sat June 9
Wymeswold v Eastw'd T II
Ravenshead v Notts U Cs II
Caythorpe III v Elks
Ged Coll II v Ellerslie II

Sat June 16
Ravenshead v Bottesford II
Ellerslie II v Eastw'd T II
Elks v Ged Coll II
Notts U Cs II v Wymeswold

Sat June 23
Eastw'd T II v Notts U Cs II
Ellerslie II v Elks
Ged Coll II v Caythorpe III
Bottesford II v Ravenshead

Sat June 30
Caythorpe III v Ellerslie II
Ravenshead v Eastw'd T II
Bottesford II v Wymeswold
Elks v Notts U Cs II

Sat July 7

Eastw'd T II	v Elks
Wymeswold	v Caythorpe III
Ellerslie II	v Ged Coll II
Notts U Cs II	v Ravenshead

Sat July 14

Wymeswold	v Ellerslie II
Caythorpe III	v Notts U Cs II
Ged Coll II	v Eastw'd T II
Bottesford II	v Elks

Sat July 21

Notts U Cs II	v Ged Coll II
Ravenshead	v Caythorpe III
Ellerslie II	v Wymeswold
Elks	v Bottesford II

Sat July 28

Eastw'd T II	v Caythorpe III
Wymeswold	v Elks
Ged Coll II	v Ravenshead
Bottesford II	v Notts U Cs II

Sat Aug 4

Caythorpe III	v Bottesford II
Ravenshead	v Ellerslie II
Elks	v Eastw'd T II
Ged Coll II	v Wymeswold

Sat Aug 11

Eastw'd T II	v Wymeswold
Ellerslie II	v Bottesford II
Elks	v Ravenshead
Notts U Cs II	v Caythorpe III

Sat Aug 18

Eastw'd T II	v Ellerslie II
Wymeswold	v Ravenshead
Ged Coll II	v Elks
Bottesford II	v Caythorpe III

Sat Aug 25

Elks	v Wymeswold
Ravenshead	v Ged Coll II
Caythorpe III	v Eastw'd T II
Notts U Cs II	v Ellerslie II

Sat Sept 1

Eastw'd T II	v Ged Coll II
Wymeswold	v Bottesford II
Ellerslie II	v Notts U Cs II

DIVISION G

Sat May 5

Gotham II	v Snib. Grge
Whatt & Asl	v Lowdham
Hoveringham	v Epperstone
Bramcote II	v Beeston S.
Kinoulton	v Chilwell

Sat May 12

Gotham II	v Whatt & Asl
Beeston S.	v Kinoulton
Epperstone	v Chilwell
Snib. Grge	v Hoveringham
Lowdham	v Bramcote II

Sat May 19

Beeston S.	v Lowdham
Chilwell	v Snib. Grge
Hoveringham	v Whatt & Asl
Bramcote II	v Gotham II
Kinoulton	v Epperstone

Sat May 26

Gotham II	v Beeston S.
Whatt & Asl	v Chilwell
Hoveringham	v Bramcote II
Snib. Grge	v Epperstone
Lowdham	v Kinoulton

Sat June 2

Beeston S.	v Hoveringham
Chilwell	v Bramcote II
Epperstone	v Whatt & Asl
Lowdham	v Gotham II
Kinoulton	v Snib. Grge

Sat June 9

Chilwell	v Beeston S.
Whatt & Asl	v Snib. Grge
Hoveringham	v Lowdham
Bramcote II	v Epperstone
Kinoulton	v Gotham II

Sat June 16

Gotham II	v Hoveringham
Whatt & Asl	v Kinoulton
Epperstone	v Beeston S.
Snib. Grge	v Bramcote II
Lowdham	v Chilwell

Sat June 23

Beeston S.	v Snib. Grge
Chilwell	v Gotham II
Epperstone	v Lowdham
Bramcote II	v Whatt & Asl
Kinoulton	v Hoveringham

Sat June 30

Gotham II	v Epperstone
Whatt & Asl	v Beeston S.
Hoveringham	v Chilwell
Snib. Grge	v Lowdham
Bramcote II	v Kinoulton

Sat July 7

Beeston S.	v Bramcote II
Chilwell	v Kinoulton
Epperstone	v Hoveringham
Snib. Grge	v Gotham II
Lowdham	v Whatt & Asl

Sat July 14

Chilwell	v Epperstone
Hoveringham	v Snib. Grge
Bramcote II	v Lowdham
Kinoulton	v Beeston S.
Whatt & Asl	v Gotham II

Sat July 21

Gotham II	v Bramcote II
Whatt & Asl	v Hoveringham
Snib. Grge	v Chilwell
Lowdham	v Beeston S.
Epperstone	v Kinoulton

Sat July 28

Beeston S.	v Gotham II
Chilwell	v Whatt & Asl
Epperstone	v Snib. Grge
Bramcote II	v Hoveringham
Kinoulton	v Lowdham

Sat Aug 4

Gotham II	v Lowdham
Whatt & Asl	v Epperstone
Hoveringham	v Beeston S.
Snib. Grge	v Kinoulton
Bramcote II	v Chilwell

Sat Aug 11

Gotham II	v Kinoulton
Beeston S.	v Chilwell
Epperstone	v Bramcote II
Snib. Grge	v Whatt & Asl
Lowdham	v Hoveringham

Sat Aug 18

Beeston S.	v Epperstone
Chilwell	v Lowdham
Hoveringham	v Gotham II
Bramcote II	v Snib. Grge
Kinoulton	v Whatt & Asl

Sat Aug 25

Gotham II	vChilwell
Whatt & Asl	v Bramcote II
Hoveringham	v Kinoulton
Snib. Grge	v Beeston S.
Lowdham	v Epperstone

Sat Sept 1

Beeston S.	v Whatt & Asl
Chilwell	v Hoveringham
Epperstone	v Gotham II
Lowdham	v Snib. Grge
Kinoulton	v Bramcote II

Sat Sept 8
Whatt & Asl   v Gotham II
Epperstone   v Kinoulton

DIVISION H

Sat May 5
Cotgrave   v Ged & Sher II
Beeston S. II v East Leake
Kirkby P II   v Oxton
Lough Car II   v RR Leisure II
Elks II   v E Bridgford

Sat May 12
Cotgrave   v Beeston S. II
RR Leisure II v Elks II
Oxton   v E Bridgford
Ged & Sher II v Kirkby P II
East Leake   v Lough Car II

Sat May 19
RR Leisure II v East Leake
E Bridgford   v Ged & Sher II
Kirkby P II   v Beeston S. II
Lough Car II   v Cotgrave
Elks II   v Oxton

Sat May 26
Cotgrave   v RR Leisure II
Beeston S. II v E Bridgford
Kirkby P II   v Lough Car II
Ged & Sher II v Oxton
East Leake   v Elks II

Sat June 2
RR Leisure II v Kirkby P II
Lough Car II   v E Bridgford
Oxton   v Beeston S. II
East Leake   v Cotgrave
Elks II   v Ged & Sher II

Sat June 9
E Bridgford   v RR Leisure II
Beeston S. II v Ged & Sher II
Kirkby P II   v East Leake
Lough Car II   v Oxton
Elks II   v Cotgrave

Sat June 16
Cotgrave   v Kirkby P II
Beeston S. II v Elks II
Oxton   v RR Leisure II
Ged & Sher II v Lough Car II
East Leake   v E Bridgford

Sat June 23
RR Leisure II v Ged & Sher II
E Bridgford   v Cotgrave
Oxton   v East Leake
Lough Car II   v Beeston S. II
Elks II   v Kirkby P II

Sat June 30
Cotgrave   v Oxton
Beeston S. II v RR Leisure II
Kirkby P II   v E Bridgford
Ged & Sher II v East Leake
Lough Car II   v Elks II

Sat July 7
RR Leisure II v Lough Car II
E Bridgford   v Elks II
Oxton   v Kirkby P II
Ged & Sher II v Cotgrave
East Leake   v Beeston S. II

Sat July 14
E Bridgford   v Oxton
Beeston S. II v Cotgrave
Kirkby P II   v Ged & Sher II
Lough Car II   v East Leake
Elks II   v RR Leisure II

Sat July 21
Cotgrave   v Lough Car II
Beeston S. II v Kirkby P II
Oxton   v Elks II
Ged & Sher II v E Bridgford
East Leake   v RR Leisure II

Sat July 28
RR Leisure II v Cotgrave
E Bridgford   v Beeston S. II
Oxton   v Ged & Sher II
Elks II   v East Leake

Sat Aug 4
Cotgrave   v East Leake
Beeston S. II v Oxton
Kirkby P II   v RR Leisure II
Ged & Sher II v Elks II
E Bridgford   v Lough Car II

Sat Aug 11
Cotgrave   v Elks II
RR Leisure II v E Bridgford
Oxton   v Lough Car II
Ged & Sher II v Beeston S. II
East Leake   v Kirkby P II

Sat Aug 18
RR Leisure II v Oxton
E Bridgford   v East Leake
Kirkby P II   v Cotgrave
Lough Car II   v Ged & Sher II
Elks II   v Beeston S. II

Sat Aug 25
Cotgrave   v E Bridgford
Beeston S. II v Lough Car II
Kirkby P II   v Elks II

Ged & Sher II v RR Leisure II
East Leake   v Oxton

Sat Sept 1
RR Leisure II v Beeston S. II
E Bridgford   v Kirkby P II
Oxton   v Cotgrave
East Leake   v Ged & Sher II
Elks II   v Lough Car II

Sat Sept 8
Lough Car II   v Kirkby P II

DIVISION J

Sat May 5
Sutton Bon   v Caunton
Gladstone   v Lambley
Ruddington   v Bestwood V
Stapleford   v Carr. Cavs
N'stead A. II v Edingley

Sat May 12
Caunton   v Gladstone
Carr. Cavs   v N'stead A. II
Bestwood V   v Edingley
Sutton Bon   v Ruddington
Lambley   v Stapleford

Sat May 19
Carr. Cavs   v Lambley
Edingley   v Sutton Bon
Ruddington   v Gladstone
Stapleford   v Caunton
N'stead A. II v Bestwood V

Sat May 26
Caunton   v Carr. Cavs
Gladstone   v Edingley
Ruddington   v Stapleford
Sutton Bon   v Bestwood V
Lambley   v N'stead A. II

Sat June 2
Carr. Cavs   v Ruddington
Edingley   v Stapleford
Bestwood V   v Gladstone
Lambley   v Caunton
N'stead A. II v Sutton Bon

Sat June 9
Edingley   v Carr. Cavs
Gladstone   v Sutton Bon
Ruddington v Lambley
Stapleford v Bestwood V
N'stead A. II v Caunton

Sat June 16
Caunton   v Ruddington
Gladstone   v N'stead A. II

Nottinghamshire

Bestwood V v Carr. Cavs
Sutton Bon v Stapleford
Lambley v Edingley

Sat June 23
Carr. Cavs v Sutton Bon
Edingley v Caunton
Bestwood V v Lambley
Stapleford v Gladstone
N'stead A. II v Ruddington

Sat June 30
Caunton v Bestwood V
Gladstone v Carr. Cavs
Ruddington v Edingley
Sutton Bon v Lambley
Stapleford v N'stead A. II

Sat July 7
Carr. Cavs v Stapleford
Edingley v N'stead A. II
Bestwood V v Ruddington
Caunton v Sutton Bon
Lambley v Gladstone

Sat July 14
Edingley v Bestwood V
Gladstone v Caunton
Ruddington v Sutton Bon
Stapleford v Lambley
N'stead A. II v Carr. Cavs

Sat July 21
Caunton v Stapleford
Gladstone v Ruddington
Bestwood V v N'stead A. II
Sutton Bon v Edingley
Lambley v Carr. Cavs

Sat July 28
Carr. Cavs v Caunton
Edingley v Gladstone
Bestwood V v Sutton Bon
Stapleford v Ruddington
N'stead A. II v Lambley

Sat Aug 4
Caunton v Lambley
Gladstone v Bestwood V
Ruddington v Carr. Cavs
Sutton Bon v N'stead A. II
Stapleford v Edingley

Sat Aug 11
Caunton v N'stead A. II
Carr. Cavs v Edingley
Bestwood V v Stapleford
Sutton Bon v Gladstone
Lambley v Ruddington

Sat Aug 18
Carr. Cavs v Bestwood V
Edingley v Lambley
Ruddington v Caunton
Stapleford v Sutton Bon
N'stead A. II v Gladstone

Sat Aug 25
Caunton v Edingley
Gladstone v Stapleford
Ruddington v N'stead A. II
Sutton Bon v Carr. Cavs
Lambley v Bestwood V

Sat Sept 1
Carr. Cavs v Gladstone
Edingley v Ruddington
Bestwood V v Caunton
Lambley v Sutton Bon
N'stead A. II v Stapleford
at the Abbey Ground

DIVISION K

Sat May 5
Lenton Ab. v Basf H OB
Belvoir II v Burton Joyce
Bingham v Risley II
A'borough III v Thurgarton II

Sat May 12
Risley II v A'borough III
Burton Joyce v Thurgarton II
Basf H OB v Belvoir II
W Bridgfs II v Bingham

Sat May 19
Risley II v W Bridgfs II
Thurgarton II v Basf H OB
Bingham v Lenton Ab.
A'borough III v Burton Joyce

Sat May 26
Lenton Ab. v Risley II
Belvoir II v Bingham
Basf H OB v Burton Joyce
W Bridgfs II v A'borough III

Sat June 2
Risley II v Belvoir II
Thurgarton II v Bingham
W Bridgfs II v Lenton Ab.
A'borough III v Basf H OB

Sat June 9
Thurgarton II v Risley II
Belvoir II v W Bridgfs II
Bingham v Burton Joyce
A'borough III v Lenton Ab.

Sat June 16
Lenton Ab. v Belvoir II
Burton Joyce v Risley II
Basf H OB v Bingham
W Bridgfs II v Thurgarton II

Sat June 23
Risley II v Basf H OB
Thurgarton II v Lenton Ab.
Burton Joyce v W Bridgfs II
A'borough III v Belvoir II

Sat June 30
Lenton Ab. v Burton Joyce
Belvoir II v Thurgarton II
Basf H OB v W Bridgfs II
Bingham v A'borough III

Sat July 7
Risley II v Bingham
Thurgarton II v A'borough III
Burton Joyce v Belvoir II
Basf H OB v Lenton Ab.

Sat July 14
Thurgarton II v Burton Joyce
Belvoir II v Basf H OB
Bingham v W Bridgfs II
A'borough III v Risley II

Sat July 21
Lenton Ab. v Bingham
Burton Joyce v A'borough III
Basf H OB v Thurgarton II
W Bridgfs II v Risley II

Sat July 28
Risley II v Lenton Ab.
Burton Joyce v Basf H OB
Bingham v Belvoir II
A'borough III v W Bridgfs II

Sat Aug 4
Lenton Ab. v W Bridgfs II
Belvoir II v Risley II
Basf H OB v A'borough III
Bingham v Thurgarton II

Sat Aug 11
Lenton Ab. v A'borough III
Risley II v Thurgarton II
Burton Joyce v Bingham
W Bridgfs II v Belvoir II

Sat Aug 18
Risley II v Burton Joyce
Thurgarton II v W Bridgfs II
Belvoir II v Lenton Ab.
Bingham v Basf H OB

Sat Aug 25
Lenton Ab.   v Thurgarton II
Belvoir II   v A'borough III
Basf H OB   v Risley II
W Bridgfs II   v Burton Joyce

Sat Sept 1
Thurgarton II v Belvoir II
Burton Joyce   v Lenton Ab.
W Bridgfs II   v Basf H OB
A'borough III v Bingham

DIVISION L

Sat May 5
Breaston   v W'by OTW II
Newark II   v Kimb I. III
Woodborough v Flintham
Nott. Vic.   v Clifton V III
Stan-by-D II v Underwood II

Sat May 12
Breaston   v Newark II
Clifton V III v Stan-by-D II
Flintham   v Underwood II
W'by OTW II   v Woodborough
Kimb I. III   v Nott. Vic.

Sat May 19
Clifton V III   v Kimb I. III
Underwood II v W'by OTW II
Woodborough v Newark II
Nott. Vic.   v Breaston
Stan-by-D II v Flintham

Sat May 26
Breaston   v Clifton V III
Newark II   v Underwood II
Woodborough v Nott. Vic.
W'by OTW II   v Flintham
Kimb I. III   v Stan-by-D II

Sat June 2
Clifton V III   v Woodborough
Underwood II v Nott. Vic.
Flintham   v Newark II
Kimb I. III   v Breaston
Stan-by-D II v W'by OTW II

Sat June 9
Underwood II v Clifton V III
Newark II   v W'by OTW II
Woodborough v Kimb I. III
Nott. Vic.   v Flintham
Stan-by-D II v Breaston

Sat June 16
Breaston   v Woodborough
Newark II   v Stan-by-D II
Flintham   v Clifton V III

W'by OTW II   v Nott. Vic.
Kimb I. III   v Underwood II

Sat June 23
Clifton V III   v W'by OTW II
Underwood II v Breaston
Flintham   v Kimb I. III
Nott. Vic.   v Newark II
Stan-by-D II v Woodborough

Sat June 30
Breaston   v Flintham
Newark II   v Clifton V III
Woodborough v Underwood II
W'by OTW II   v Kimb I. III
Nott. Vic.   v Stan-by-D II

Sat July 7
Clifton V III   v Nott. Vic.
Underwood II v Stan-by-D II
Flintham   v Woodborough
W'by OTW II   v Breaston
Kimb I. III   v Newark II

Sat July 14
Underwood II v Flintham
Newark II   v Breaston
Woodborough v W'by OTW II
Nott. Vic.   v Kimb I. III
Stan-by-D II v Clifton V III

Sat July 21
Breaston   v Nott. Vic.
Newark II   v Woodborough
Flintham   v Stan-by-D II
W'by OTW II   v Underwood II
Kimb I. III   v Clifton V III

Sat July 28
Clifton V III   v Breaston
Underwood II v Newark II
Flintham   v W'by OTW II
Nott. Vic.   v Woodborough
Stan-by-D II v Kimb I. III

Sat Aug 4
Breaston   v Kimb I. III
Newark II   v Flintham
Woodborough v Clifton V III
W'by OTW II   v Stan-by-D II
Nott. Vic.   v Underwood II

Sat Aug 11
Breaston   v Stan-by-D II
Clifton V III   v Underwood II
Flintham   v Nott. Vic.
W'by OTW II   v Newark II
Kimb I. III   v Woodborough

Sat Aug 18
Clifton V III   v Flintham
Underwood II v Kimb I. III
Woodborough v Breaston
Nott. Vic.   v W'by OTW II
Stan-by-D II v Newark II

Sat Aug 25
Breaston   v Underwood II
Newark II   v Nott. Vic.
Woodborough v Stan-by-D II
W'by OTW II   v Clifton V III
Kimb I. III   v Flintham

Sat Sept 1
Clifton V III   v Newark II
Underwood II v Woodborough
Flintham   v Breaston
Kimb I. III   v W'by OTW II
Stan-by-D II v Nott. Vic.

DIVISION M

Sat April 28
Keyworth II   v Farndon II

Sat May 5
Farndon II   v Belton
Keyworth II   v Wilsons II
Old Paviors II v Caythorpe IV
Lambley II   v Thrumpton II
Snib. Grge II v L Whatton II

Sat May 12
Farndon II   v Keyworth II
Thrumpton II   v Snib. Grge II
Caythorpe IV v L Whatton II
Belton   v Old Paviors II
Wilsons II   v Lambley II

Sat May 19
Thrumpton II   v Wilsons II
L Whatton II   v Belton
Old Paviors II v Keyworth II
Lambley II   v Farndon II
Snib. Grge II v Caythorpe IV

Sat May 26
Farndon II   v Thrumpton II
Keyworth II   v L Whatton II
Old Paviors II v Lambley II
Belton   v Caythorpe IV
Wilsons II   v Snib. Grge II

Sat June 2
Thrumpton II   v Old Paviors II
L Whatton II   v Lambley II
Caythorpe IV v Keyworth II
Wilsons II   v Farndon II
Snib. Grge II v Belton

Nottinghamshire

Sat June 9
L Whatton II v Thrumpton II
Keyworth II v Belton
Old Paviors II v Wilsons II
Lambley II v Caythorpe IV
Snib. Grge II v Farndon II

Sat June 16
Farndon II v Old Paviors II
Keyworth II v Snib. Grge II
Caythorpe IV v Thrumpton II
Belton v Lambley II
Wilsons II v L Whatton II

Sat June 23
Thrumpton II v Belton
L Whatton II v Farndon II
Caythorpe IV v Wilsons II
Lambley II v Keyworth II
Snib. Grge II v Old Paviors II

Sat June 30
Farndon II v Caythorpe IV
Keyworth II v Thrumpton II
Old Paviors II v L Whatton II
Belton v Wilsons II
Lambley II v Snib. Grge II

Sat July 7
Thrumpton II v Lambley II
L Whatton II v Snib. Grge II
Caythorpe IV v Old Paviors II
Belton v Farndon II
Wilsons II v Keyworth II

Sat July 14
L Whatton II v Caythorpe IV
Old Paviors II v Belton
Lambley II v Wilsons II
Snib. Grge II v Thrumpton II

Sat July 21
Farndon II v Lambley II
Keyworth II v Old Paviors II
Caythorpe IV v Snib. Grge II
Belton v L Whatton II
Wilsons II v Thrumpton II

Sat July 28
Thrumpton II v Farndon II
L Whatton II v Keyworth II
Caythorpe IV v Belton
Lambley II v Old Paviors II
Snib. Grge II v Wilsons II

Sat Aug 4
Farndon II v Wilsons II
Keyworth II v Caythorpe IV
Old Paviors II v Thrumpton II

Belton v Snib. Grge II
Lambley II v L Whatton II

Sat Aug 11
Farndon II v Snib. Grge II
Thrumpton II v L Whatton II
Caythorpe IV v Lambley II
Belton v Keyworth II
Wilsons II v Old Paviors II

Sat Aug 18
Thrumpton II v Caythorpe IV
L Whatton II v Wilsons II
Old Paviors II v Farndon II
Lambley II v Belton
Snib. Grge II v Keyworth II

Sat Aug 25
Farndon II v L Whatton II
Keyworth II v Lambley II
Old Paviors II v Snib. Grge II
Belton v Thrumpton II
Wilsons II v Caythorpe IV

Sat Sept 1
Thrumpton II v Keyworth II
L Whatton II v Old Paviors II
Caythorpe IV v Farndon II
Wilsons II v Belton
Snib. Grge II v Lambley II

DIVISION N

Sat May 5
Elks III v Plumtree III
Balderton II v Hucknall III
Ged Coll III v Rad. on T III
Lowdham II v N'stead A. III
Shepsh. T III v Cotgrave II

Sat May 12
Elks III v Balderton II
N'stead A. III v Shepsh. T III
Rad. on T III v Cotgrave II
Plumtree III v Ged Coll III
Hucknall III v Lowdham II

Sat May 19
N'stead A. III v Hucknall III
Cotgrave II v Plumtree III
Ged Coll III v Balderton II
Lowdham II v Elks III
Shepsh. T III v Rad. on T III

Sat May 26
Elks III v N'stead A. III
Balderton II v Cotgrave II
Ged Coll III v Lowdham II
Rad. on T III v Plumtree III
Hucknall III v Shepsh. T III

Sat June 2
N'stead A. III v Ged Coll III
Cotgrave II v Lowdham II
Rad. on T III v Balderton II
Hucknall III v Elks III
Plumtree III v Shepsh. T III

Sat June 9
Cotgrave II v N'stead A. III
Balderton II v Plumtree III
Ged Coll III v Hucknall III
Lowdham II v Rad. on T III
Shepsh. T III v Elks III

Sat June 16
Elks III v Ged Coll III
Balderton II v Shepsh. T III
Rad. on T III v N'stead A. III
Plumtree III v Lowdham II
Hucknall III v Cotgrave II

Sat June 23
N'stead A. III v Plumtree III
Cotgrave II v Elks III
Rad. on T III v Hucknall III
Lowdham II v Balderton II
Shepsh. T III v Ged Coll III

Sat June 30
Elks III v Rad. on T III
Balderton II v N'stead A. III
Ged Coll III v Cotgrave II
Plumtree III v Hucknall III
Lowdham II v Shepsh. T III

Sat July 7
N'stead A. III v Lowdham II
Cotgrave II v Shepsh. T III
Rad. on T III v Ged Coll III
Plumtree III v Elks III
Hucknall III v Balderton II

Sat July 14
Cotgrave II v Rad. on T III
Balderton II v Elks III
Ged Coll III v Plumtree III
Lowdham II v Hucknall III
Shepsh. T III v N'stead A. III

Sat July 21
Elks III v Lowdham II
Balderton II v Ged Coll III
Rad. on T III v Shepsh. T III
Plumtree III v Cotgrave II
Hucknall III v N'stead A. III

Sat July 28
N'stead A. III v Elks III
Cotgrave II v Balderton II

Plumtree III   v Rad. on T III
Lowdham II   v Ged Coll III
Shepsh. T III   v Hucknall III

Sat Aug 4
Elks III   v Hucknall III
Balderton II   v Rad. on T III
Ged Coll III   v N'stead A. III
Shepsh. T III   v Plumtree III
Lowdham II   v Cotgrave II

Sat Aug 11
Elks III   v Shepsh. T III
N'stead A. III   v Cotgrave II
Rad. on T III   v Lowdham II
Plumtree III   v Balderton II
Hucknall III   v Ged Coll III

Sat Aug 18
N'stead A. III   v Rad. on T III
Cotgrave II   v Hucknall III
Ged Coll III   v Elks III
Lowdham II   v Plumtree III
Shepsh. T III   v Balderton II

Sat Aug 25
Elks III   v Cotgrave II
Balderton II   v Lowdham II
Ged Coll III   v Shepsh. T III
Plumtree III   v N'stead A. III
Hucknall III   v Rad. on T III

Sat Sept 1
Cotgrave II   v Ged Coll III
Rad. on T III   v Elks III
Hucknall III v Plumtree III
Shepsh. T III v Lowdham II

Sat Sept 8
N'stead A. III v Balderton II
at the Abbey Ground

DIVISION P

Sat May 5
Chilwell II   v Beeston S III
Kirkby P III   v L. Eaton III
Ellerslie III   v Ruddington II
Kimb I. IV   v Whatt & A II
Broad St As   v W Bridgfs III

Sat May 12
Chilwell II   v Kirkby P III
Whatt & A II   v Broad St As
Ruddington II v W Bridgfs III
Beeston S III v Ellerslie III
L. Eaton III   v Kimb I. IV

Sat May 19
Whatt & A II   v L. Eaton III
W Bridgfs III   v Beeston S III

Ellerslie III   v Kirkby P III
Kimb I. IV   v Chilwell II
Broad St As   v Ruddington II

Sat May 26
Chilwell II   v Whatt & A II
Kirkby P III   v W Bridgfs III
Ellerslie III   v Kimb I. IV
Beeston S III   v Ruddington II
L. Eaton III   v Broad St As

Sat June 2
Whatt & A II   v Ellerslie III
W Bridgfs III   v Kimb I. IV
Ruddington II v Kirkby P III
L. Eaton III   v Chilwell II
Broad St As   v Beeston S III

Sat June 9
W Bridgfs III   v Whatt & A II
Kirkby P III   v Beeston S III
Ellerslie III   v L. Eaton III
Kimb I. IV   v Ruddington II
Broad St As   v Chilwell II

Sat June 16
Chilwell II   v Ellerslie III
Kirkby P III   v Broad St As
Ruddington II v Whatt & A II
Beeston S III   v Kimb I. IV
L. Eaton III   v W Bridgfs III

Sat June 23
Whatt & A II   v Beeston S III
W Bridgfs III   v Chilwell II
Ruddington II v L. Eaton III
Kimb I. IV   v Kirkby P III
Broad St As   v Ellerslie III

Sat June 30
Chilwell II   v Ruddington II
Kirkby P III   v Whatt & A II
Ellerslie III   v W Bridgfs III
Beeston S III   v L. Eaton III
Kimb I. IV   v Broad St As

Sat July 7
Whatt & A II   v Kimb I. IV
W Bridgfs III   v Broad St As
Ruddington II v Ellerslie III
Beeston S III vChilwell II
L. Eaton III   v Kirkby P III

Sat July 14
W Bridgfs III   v Ruddington II
Kirkby P III   v Chilwell II
Ellerslie III   v Beeston S III
Kimb I. IV   v L. Eaton III
Broad St As   v Whatt & A II

Sat July 21
Chilwell II   v Kimb I. IV
Kirkby P III   v Ellerslie III
Ruddington II v Broad St As
Beeston S III   v W Bridgfs III
L. Eaton III   v Whatt & A II

Sat July 28
Whatt & A II   v Chilwell II
W Bridgfs III   v Kirkby P III
Ruddington II v Beeston S III
Kimb I. IV   v Ellerslie III
Broad St As   v L. Eaton III

Sat Aug 4
Chilwell II   v L. Eaton III
Kirkby P III   v Ruddington II
Ellerslie III   v Whatt & A II
Beeston S III   v Broad St As
Kimb I. IV   v W Bridgfs III

Sat Aug 11
Chilwell II   v Broad St As
Whatt & A II   v W Bridgfs III
Ruddington II v Kimb I. IV
Beeston S III   v Kirkby P III
L. Eaton III   v Ellerslie III

Sat Aug 18
Whatt & A II   v Ruddington II
W Bridgfs III   v L. Eaton III
Ellerslie III   v Chilwell II
Kimb I. IV   v Beeston S III
Broad St As   v Kirkby P III

Sat Aug 25
Chilwell II   v W Bridgfs III
Kirkby P III   v Kimb I. IV
Ellerslie III   v Broad St As
Beeston S III   v Whatt & A II
L. Eaton III   v Ruddington II

Sat Sept 1
Whatt & A II   v Kirkby P III
Ruddington II v Chilwell II
L. Eaton III   v Beeston S III
Broad St As   v Kimb I. IV

Sat Sept 8
W Bridgfs III   v Ellerslie III
at Stamford Road

DIVISION R

Sat May 5
Edingley II   v Kinoulton II
Rad. on T IV   v Notts U Cs III
Poplars   v Hov'ham II
East Leake II   v Bingham II
Wym'wold II   v Shepsh. T IV

Nottinghamshire

Wollaton III   v Coll'ham III
West B Leg II   v Thrumpton III
Young Lions   v Belvoir III

Sat May 12
Edingley II   v Notts U Cs III
Coll'ham III   v Thrumpton III
Hov'ham II   v Belvoir III
Kinoulton II   v Poplars
Wollaton III   v East Leake II
Wym'wold II   v West B Leg II
Shepsh. T IV   v Rad. on T IV
Bingham II   v Young Lions

Sat May 19
Coll'ham III   v Bingham II
Belvoir III   v Kinoulton II
Poplars   v Wym'wold II
East Leake II   v Edingley II
Notts U Cs III   v West B Leg II
Young Lions   v Shepsh. T IV
Thrumpton III v Hov'ham II
Rad. on T IV   v Wollaton III

Sat May 26
Edingley II   v Thrumpton III
Notts U Cs III   v Belvoir III
Poplars   v Rad. on T IV
Kinoulton II   v Hov'ham II
Bingham II   v Wollaton III
Wym'wold II   v Young Lions
West B Leg II   v East Leake II
Shepsh. T IV   v Coll'ham III

Sat June 2
Coll'ham III   v Notts U Cs III
Belvoir III   v West B Leg II
Hov'ham II   v Wym'wold II
Bingham II   v Edingley II
Shepsh. T IV   v Poplars
Young Lions   v Rad. on T IV
Wollaton III   v Kinoulton II
Thrumpton III v East Leake II

Sat June 2
Belvoir III   v Coll'ham III
West B Leg II   v Kinoulton II
Poplars   v Edingley II
East Leake II   v Shepsh. T IV
Young Lions   v Hov'ham II
Rad. on T IV   v Bingham II
Notts U Cs III   v Wollaton III
Thrumpton III v Wym'wold II

Sat June 16
Edingley II   v Rad. on T IV
Hov'ham II   v East Leake II
Kinoulton II   v Thrumpton III
Bingham II   v Belvoir III
Wollaton III   v Young Lions

Wym'wold II   v Coll'ham III
Shepsh. T IV   v Notts U Cs III
West B Leg II   v Poplars

Sat June 23
Coll'ham III   v West B Leg II
Belvoir III   v Wollaton III
Hov'ham II   v Shepsh. T IV
East Leake II   v Rad. on T IV
Wym'wold II   v Kinoulton II
Young Lions   v Edingley II
Notts U Cs III   v Poplars
Thrumpton III v Bingham II

Sat June 30
East Leake II   v Notts U Cs III
Edingley II   v Coll'ham III
Kinoulton II   v Bingham II
Poplars   v Young Lions
Wollaton III   v Wym'wold II
Rad. on T IV   v Thrumpton III
Shepsh. T IV   v Belvoir III
West B Leg II   v Hov'ham II

Sat July 7
Coll'ham III   v Poplars
Belvoir III   v Thrumpton III
Hov'ham II   v Edingley II
Kinoulton II   v Rad. on T IV
Bingham II   v West B Leg II
Young Lions   v East Leake II
Notts U Cs III   v Wym'wold II
Shepsh. T IV   v Wollaton III

Sat July 14
Belvoir III   v Edingley II
Notts U Cs III   v Hov'ham II
Poplars   v Bingham II
East Leake II   v Kinoulton II
Rad. on T IV   v Wym'wold II
Thrumpton III v Wollaton III
West B Leg II   v Shepsh. T IV
Young Lions   v Coll'ham III

Sat July 21
Bingham II   v Notts U Cs III
Edingley II   v West B Leg II
Hov'ham II   v Rad. on T IV
Kinoulton II   v Young Lions
Wollaton III   v Poplars
Wym'wold II   v Belvoir III
Coll'ham III   v East Leake II
Shepsh. T IV   v Thrumpton III

Sat July 28
Coll'ham III   v Kinoulton II
Hov'ham II   v Bingham II
East Leake II   v Poplars
Thrumpton III v Young Lions
Rad. on T IV   v Belvoir III
Wollaton III   v Edingley II

Sat Aug 4
Edingley II   v Wollaton III
Notts U Cs III   v Thrumpton III
Poplars   v Belvoir III
Kinoulton II   v Shepsh. T IV
Rad. on T IV   v Coll'ham III
Wym'wold II   v Bingham II
West B Leg II   v Young Lions

Sat Aug 11
Belvoir III   v East Leake II
Bingham II   v Shepsh. T IV
Hov'ham II   v Wollaton III
Young Lions   v Thrumpton III
Wym'wold II   v Edingley II
Kinoulton II   v Notts U Cs III

Sat Aug 18
Coll'ham III   v Hov'ham II
Rad. on T IV   v West B Leg II
East Leake II   v Wym'wold II
Thrumpton III v Poplars

25 August
Edingley II   v Shepsh. T IV

Killamarsh Juniors 1st XI
Champions of the Bassetlaw League

Back Row (left to right): Steve Ludlam, Pramuka Liyanage, Richard Crabtree, David Allen, Parminder Mudhar, Rodney Cook.

Front Row (left to right): Paul Burdett, Sam Malpass, Adrian Rivington, Adam Burgess, John Wooliscroft.

Lyanage and Mudhar bowl Killamarsh to title

KILLAMARSH JUNIORS became champions of the **Bassetlaw League** in 2006. The key match was against rivals Farnsfield on August 12th. Chasing a respectable 231 for 6, Killamarsh passed their target with three wickets standing. Needing just seven points at Kiveton on the final day of the season, they did exactly that to clinch the title by a single point from Cuckney.

For Killamarsh, Adrian Rivington was an inspirational skipper and the batting revolved around Adam Burgess, 19 year old Sam Malpass and Paul Burdett. Overseas player, Pramuka Liyanage from Sri Lanka, had an excellent season with both bat and ball and in many ways set the tone for the season when, on his arrival for the early season fixture with Glapwell, he took 5 for 27 and made an undefeated 41.

Experienced players such as Rodney Cook, David Allen and Richard Crabtree all made their mark. However, the best of the bowling attack was Parminder Mudhar who had an excellent season, taking 43 wickets. The club made it a double with the 2nd XI winning Division 6.

Runners-up Cuckney had a terrific season. They were fancied at the start, which in itself was a minor miracle as three years ago virtually every member of the club left, but with some shrewd signings and an incredibly good youth policy, they have put things together in great style. There can be no doubt that with the set-up they have they will sooner rather than later qualify for the Premier League. They have one of the best pavilions you will find in any league. There is also a maginificent indoor cricket school which also doubles up as a banqueting suite.

Blidworth are relegated just a year after promotion, but the surprise relegation is that of Edwinstowe, who had finished third in 2005. They are replaced in the top division by Ransome & Marles and Bridon.

Ransome & Marles will have to do without their young South African Francois Le Clus, who arrived here as an unknown at the start and through some prodigious displays became a household name before the end of the season. He is joining Mansfield Hosiery Mills in the Premier League. This must represent a severe blow.

Arguably the club of the year was Mansfield & Pleasley. Their 1st XI are always capable of giving anybody a good game and after a late spurt finished a credible fourth in Division 2 and reached the Tomlin Trophy final. Their 2nd XI won Division 7 and their 3rd XI won Division 9 to show the depth the club has, which bodes well for the future.

2006 Bassetlaw League Tables

Division 1

	P	w	wd	wtr	c	ld	l	BaP	BoP	Pen	Pts
Killamarsh 1st XI	22	9	3	3	3	2	2	66	58	0	302
Cuckney 1st XI	22	10	3	3	1	1	4	63	62	0	301
Farnsfield 1st XI	22	5	8	2	4	1	2	56	54	3	285
Cutthorpe 1st XI	22	10	0	2	3	2	5	54	53	0	261
Notts & Arnold Am 1st XI	22	9	1	3	2	1	6	63	42	0	255
Kiveton Park Colliery 1st XI	22	5	3	5	2	3	4	61	49	0	248
Glapwell Colliery 1st XI	22	6	1	3	2	4	6	57	43	0	220
Bolsover 1st XI	22	3	3	4	2	1	9	39	57	0	200
Worksop 1st XI	22	2	5	1	4	3	7	45	42	0	197
Marshalls Sports 1st XI	22	4	2	4	2	2	8	39	45	0	192
Blidworth Coll. Welf. 1st XI	22	4	0	2	2	6	8	42	45	0	171
Edwinstowe 1st XI	22	4	0	2	3	3	10	31	44	0	159

Division 2

	P	w	wd	wtr	c	ld	l	BaP	BoP	Pen	Pts
Ransome & Marles 1st X1	22	10	6	1	4	0	1	0	66	56	0	334
Bridon 1st XI	22	11	4	2	3	0	2	0	66	67	6	333
Eckington 1st XI	22	9	4	2	4	0	0	3	60	60	9	295
Mansfield & Pleasley 1st XI	22	7	3	4	3	0	2	3	57	48	0	265
Whitwell 1st XI	22	9	1	2	3	0	2	5	63	46	0	261
P'wick and Linby 2nd XI	22	7	1	3	2	0	0	9	45	54	0	223
Anston 1st XI	22	5	0	3	5	1	2	6	55	47	0	220
Mans. Hosiery Mills 2nd XI	22	7	0	2	2	1	2	8	52	44	0	214
Everton 1st XI	22	4	1	1	4	0	4	8	49	40	0	185
NWheatley with Leverton 1st XI	22	4	1	3	4	0	2	8	36	40	0	180
Farnsfield 2nd XI	22	2	0	2	3	0	4	11	38	31	0	131
Notts & Arnold Am. 2nd XI	22	1	0	1	5	0	0	15	30	23	0	101

Division 3

	P	w	wd	wtr	c	ld	l	lcn	wcn	BaP	BoP	Pen	Pts
Waleswood Sports 1st XI	22	12	3	1	3	0	2	0	1	59	60	0	329
Caythorpe 2nd XI	22	12	3	1	2	0	4	0	0	67	60	0	319
Welbeck Colliery Academy	22	10	3	1	4	1	3	0	0	54	46	0	282

	P	w	wd	wtr	c	ld	l	BaP	BoP	Pen	Pts
Thoresby Park 1st XI	22	9	0	1	5	1	6	0	0	27	54	0	227
Teversal 1st XI	22	6	1	2	6	3	4	0	0	44	40	0	220
Grassmoor 1st XI	22	7	0	1	6	2	6	0	0	43	37	0	210
WI Cavaliers 2nd XI	22	5	0	2	4	0	10	0	1	53	45	0	206
Holmewood 1st XI	22	5	1	1	5	4	6	0	0	47	42	0	203
Sherwood Colliery 1st XI	22	2	6	1	4	1	8	0	0	46	37	0	199
Harthill 1st XI	22	4	0	1	5	4	8	0	0	45	38	0	175
Clay Cross Works 1st XI	22	5	0	1	5	2	9	0	0	34	39	2	171
Thurcroft Welfare 1st XI	22	1	1	1	5	0	12	2	0	16	33	20	87

Division 4

	P	w	wd	wtr	c	ld	l	BaP	BoP	Pen	Pts
Retford C. & Sports 2nd XI	22	10	3	2	3	0	4	57	62	0	299
Clumber Park 1st XI	22	8	5	2	3	0	4	57	59	0	292
Bridon 2nd XI	22	9	2	1	5	1	4	50	53	0	269
Worksop 2nd XI	22	7	3	2	5	2	3	47	51	0	258
Milton 1st XI	22	9	1	1	5	1	5	43	48	0	247
Clipstone Welfare 1st XI	22	7	0	1	7	2	5	39	47	0	222
Wadworth 1st XI	22	7	1	2	4	1	7	51	49	10	222
Thoresby Colliery 2nd XI	22	6	0	1	4	5	6	43	44	0	199
Woodsetts Comm. 1st XI	22	4	2	2	4	2	8	37	49	0	194
Welbeck Colliery 2nd XI	22	4	1	2	3	3	9	52	40	0	186
Bolsover 2nd XI	22	3	0	2	4	3	10	45	40	2	161
Edwinstowe 2nd XI	22	2	3	2	3	1	11	32	43	0	161

Division 5

	P	w	wd	wtr	c	ld	l	BaP	BoP	Pen	Pts
Lea Park 1st XI	18	7	5	2	1	1	2	58	43	0	255
Wiseton Wiseton Bas'law XI	18	9	1	2	0	2	4	44	53	0	231
Kiveton Pk Colliery 2nd XI	18	7	2	2	3	0	4	40	41	0	215
Cuckney 2nd XI	18	5	3	1	2	2	5	49	46	0	207
Rose Leisure 1st XI	18	6	2	2	1	1	6	49	40	0	201
Eckington Derbys 2nd XI	18	6	0	1	3	2	6	46	45	0	191
Anston 2nd XI	18	5	2	1	3	1	6	34	40	0	180
Blidworth 2nd XI	18	6	0	1	2	4	5	36	40	0	174
Basford Mill 1st XI	18	5	1	2	1	2	7	35	47	0	174
Notts & Arnold Am. 3rd XI	18	1	0	2	2	1	12	17	22	0	77

Division 6

	P	w	wd	wtr	c	ld	l	lcn	wcn	BaP	BoP	Pen	Pts
Killamarsh 2nd XI	18	12	0	2	2	0	2	0	0	46	57	0	271
Whitwell 2nd XI	18	9	2	2	2	1	2	0	0	48	47	0	249
Marshalls Sports 2nd XI	18	8	3	1	3	0	3	0	0	44	50	0	244
Nomads 1st XI	18	5	2	2	2	1	5	0	1	42	42	0	202
Glapwell Colliery 2nd XI	18	5	2	2	3	2	4	0	0	34	43	0	191
Mans. Hosiery Mills 3rd XI	18	6	0	1	2	2	7	0	0	34	45	0	173
Teversal 2nd XI	18	4	1	2	2	3	5	1	0	37	43	10	158
Milton 2nd XI	18	2	2	2	2	2	8	0	0	32	34	0	138
Bilsthorpe 1st XI	18	2	1	1	6	2	6	0	0	13	26	0	119
Grassmoor 2nd XI	18	1	0	1	4	0	12	0	0	14	27	0	83

Division 7

	P	w	wd	wtr	c	ld	l	BaP	BoP	Pen	Pts
Mansfield & Pleasley 2nd XI	18	10	2	1	2	1	2	46	51	0	257
Clumber Park 2nd XI	18	9	2	0	3	1	3	44	53	0	245
NWheatley with Leverton 1st XI	18	5	3	1	4	1	4	44	45	0	211
Ransome & Marles 2nd X1	18	4	2	1	5	3	3	29	39	0	178
Anston 3rd XI	18	5	1	1	5	0	6	35	34	0	175
Weston 1st XI	18	4	2	1	5	2	4	22	37	0	167
Duckmanton Lodge 1st XI	18	4	1	1	4	2	6	29	40	0	161
Oaklands (Retford) 1st XI	18	3	0	1	6	2	6	19	30	0	131
Cutthorpe 2nd XI	18	1	0	1	4	1	11	14	30	0	88

Division 8

	P	w	wd	wtr	c	ld	l	lcn	wcn	BaP	BoP	Pen	Pts
Worksop 3rd XI	18	10	3	1	1	0	2	0	1	52	56	0	282
Todwick 1st XI	18	10	2	1	1	1	3	0	0	49	49	0	252
Everton 2nd XI	18	8	1	2	2	1	3	0	1	40	54	0	238
Misterton 1st XI	18	8	1	2	1	1	5	0	0	42	52	0	220
South Normanton 1st XI	18	4	2	2	3	2	5	0	0	36	38	0	176
Blyth CC, Notts 1st XI	18	4	0	1	1	1	10	0	1	43	53	0	170
P'wick and Linby 3rd XI	18	4	2	1	2	1	7	1	0	38	38	10	154
Manton 1st XI	18	7	0	1	0	1	7	2	0	34	45	20	151
Holmewood 2nd XI	18	4	0	1	3	1	9	0	0	33	40	0	147
Notts & Arnold Am. 4th XI	18	2	0	2	2	2	10	0	0	28	24	0	104

Division 9

	P	w	wd	wtr	c	ld	l	lcn	wcn	BaP	BoP	Pen	Pts
Mansfield & Pleasley 3rd XI	18	10	0	1	3	1	2	0	1	48	52	0	258
Worksop 4th XI	18	10	0	1	2	0	4	0	1	49	56	0	255
Ollerton Colliery 1st XI	18	9	1	1	4	0	3	0	0	38	50	0	236
Woodsetts Comm. 2nd XI	18	7	0	1	4	0	5	0	1	38	42	0	206
Sherwood Colliery 2nd XI	18	8	0	1	2	0	6	0	1	35	45	0	206
Rockware Glass 1st XI	18	7	0	1	2	0	8	0	0	38	49	0	193
Thoresby Park 2nd XI	18	4	0	1	2	0	10	0	1	31	53	0	162
Wadworth 2nd XI	18	7	0	1	1	0	5	4	0	31	36	40	123
Basford Mill 2nd XI	18	4	0	1	2	0	10	1	0	21	42	10	119
Anston 4th XI	18	1	0	1	2	0	14	0	0	13	31	0	74

Division 10

	P	w	wd	wtr	c	ld	l	lcn	wcn	BaP	BoP	Pen	Pts
Clumber Park 3rd XI	18	11	1	1	2	0	3	0	0	49	53	0	262
Milton 3rd XI	18	8	0	1	3	0	5	0	1	37	45	0	214
Mans. Hosiery Mills 4th XI	18	7	2	2	3	0	4	0	0	38	42	0	214
Waleswood Sports 2nd XI	18	8	1	1	3	0	5	0	0	35	45	0	210
Clumber Park 4th XI	18	6	1	1	2	2	6	0	0	41	51	0	196
Farnsfield 3rd XI	18	5	2	0	4	0	7	0	0	30	47	0	181
Harthill 2nd XI	18	6	0	0	4	1	7	0	0	31	39	0	168
Mansfield & Pleasley 4th XI	18	4	1	3	3	0	7	0	0	25	33	0	152
Duckmanton Lodge 2nd XI	18	3	1	1	4	4	5	0	0	22	37	0	143
Edwinstowe 3rd XI	18	5	0	1	3	2	5	2	0	25	33	20	126
Woodsetts Comm. 3rd XI	18	2	0	1	3	0	11	0	1	21	32	0	113

2006 Bassetlaw League Averages

BATTING (Top 6 - qualification 200 runs):

Division 1

		Inns	N.O.	H.S.	Runs	Ave
Rashid Riaz	Farnsfield	10	3	130*	588	84.00
P. Franks	Farnsfield	10	3	121	580	82.86
A. Khan	Bolsover	17	4	134*	949	73.00
I. Flood	Notts & Arn Am.	18	4	123*	1,020	72.86
L. Baldry	Notts & Arn Am.	19	6	126	876	67.38
A. Thompson	Cutthorpe	18	4	127*	914	65.29

Division 2

		Inns	N.O.	H.S.	Runs	Ave
F. Le Clus	Ransome and Ma	17	5	211	1312	109.33
R. Topham	Bridon	10	7	60*	312	104.00
J. Mimms	Everton	18	4	123	1265	90.36
I. Woodall	Mansfield & Pl	16	7	107*	723	80.33
D. Spooner	Bridon	12	3	110	628	69.78
S. Thomas	Papplewick & Linby	12	4	93*	504	63.00

Division 3

		Inns	N.O.	H.S.	Runs	Ave
G. Botha	Teversal	9	3	170*	487	81.17
F. Khan	Waleswood Spts	17	6	88*	768	69.82
D. Hunt	Welbeck Colliery	11	3	113*	403	57.57
C. French	Welbeck Colliery	13	4	108	449	49.89
P. Bartram	Thoresby Park	7	1	112	281	46.83
I. Cowley	Sherwood Colliery	13	2	134	513	46.63

Division 4

		Inns	N.O.	H.S.	Runs	Ave
M. Ryalls	Bolsover	7	2	152	316	63.20
O. Rossington	Milton	14	3	112	602	54.73
G. Bradbury	Welbeck Colliery	7	2	72	255	51.00
P. Millns	Clipstone Welfare	11	1	97	473	47.30
J. Tomlinson	Bridon	6	0	127	255	42.50
M Deaves	Clumber Park	17	2	80	601	40.07

Division 5

		Inns	N.O.	H.S.	Runs	Ave
J. Lyne	Anston	11	4	121	514	73.42
I. Elliott	Lea Park	14	6	80	537	67.12
A. West	Rose Leisure	14	2	143	662	55.17
D. Richardson	Kiveton Park Coll	11	4	69*	383	54.71
L. Bembridge	Lea Park	6	1	130*	225	45.00
J. Bullivant	Kiveton Park Coll	11	2	73	398	44.22

Division 6

		Inns	N.O.	H.S.	Runs	Ave
B. Smyth	Glapwell Colliery	11	5	65	384	64.00
K. Wright	Nomads	15	5	99*	486	48.60
C. Sadler	Whitwell	14	4	94*	485	48.50
R. Ashley	Whitwell	8	2	90	219	36.50
J. Grlffiths	Killamarsh	13	3	43	310	34.44
D. Shore	Teversal	14	2	78	404	33.66

Division 7

		Inns	N.O.	H.S.	Runs	Ave
W. Ellis	N Wheatley with L	5	1	91*	320	80.00
R. Taylor	Clumber Park	8	1	84	289	41.29
D. Phin	N Wheatley with L	12	2	79*	342	34.20
B. Nichol	Clumber Park	8	2	92	205	34.17
M. Gray	Ransome and Ma	11	3	86	268	33.50
M. Gregory	N Wheatley with L	10	0	103	331	33.10

Division 8

		Inns	N.O.	H.S.	Runs	Ave
B. Smith	Worksop	11	5	186*	461	76.83
M. Falconer	Papp & Linby	6	2	127*	265	66.25
J. Hubble	Worksop	9	2	122*	431	61.57
M. Birkin	Papp & Linby	8	1	106	383	54.71
H. Ashton	South Normanton	6	1	95*	262	52.40
R. Pickersgill	Worksop	9	3	59	313	52.17

Division 9

		Inns	N.O.	H.S.	Runs	Ave
J. Antcliffe	Mansfield & Pl	6	2	128*	258	64.50
D. Evans	Mansfield & Pl	8	2	88	282	47.00
R. Beastall	Thoresby Park	9	2	80	302	43.14
A. Bell	Rockware Glass	14	2	167*	506	42.16
J. Redfern	Worksop	14	3	98	442	40.10
S. Powell	Mansfield & Pl	8	1	92*	215	30.71

Division 10

		Inns	N.O.	H.S.	Runs	Ave
J. Evans	Mansfield & Pl	6	3	135*	344	114.67
R. Hampstead	Clumber Park	5	2	101	229	76.33
G. Bramley	Farnsfield	7	0	112	285	40.71
T. Pressley	Clumber Park	11	1	129	401	40.10
I. Rich	Edwinstowe	9	0	94	321	35.66
D. Shepherd	Clumber Park	14	5	70*	303	33.67

BOWLING (Top 6 - qualification 20 wickets):

Division 1

		Ovs	Ms	Runs	Wkts	Ave
N. Kingham	Cutthorpe	71	12	241	21	11.48
T. Ullyott	Cuckney	127.5	27	368	32	11.50
P. Mudhar	Killamarsh	187.1	40	565	43	13.14
I. O'Brien	Glapwell Colliery	226.3	58	615	39	15.77
G. Saxby	Glapwell Colliery	109.4	24	343	21	16.33
S. Chapman	Cutthorpe	144	41	433	26	17.04

Division 2

		Ovs	Ms	Runs	Wkts	Ave
W. Rana	Papp & Linby	77.1	13	251	22	11.40
W. Dye	Eckington	173.3	25	539	41	13.15
I. Woodall	Mansfield & Pl	158.1	25	494	37	13.35
S. Alford	Pappl & Linby	169.3	54	437	31	14.10
L. Dawson	Eckington	140.5	19	506	35	14.46
G. Lambert	Ransome and Ma	182.5	56	529	34	15.55

Division 3

		Ovs	Ms	Runs	Wkts	Ave
F. Khan	Waleswood Spts	101	36	226	24	9.42
P. Hulme	Thoresby Park	158.3	52	343	30	11.43
M. Storer	Thoresby Park	142.1	30	402	33	12.18
A. Siven	Thoresby Park	143	38	372	28	13.29
G. Lomas	Waleswood Spts	135	41	353	24	14.71
R. Scott	Caythorpe	183.4	30	635	43	14.77

Division 4

		Ovs	Ms	Runs	Wkts	Ave
S. Nicholson	Wadworth	118.4	32	379	36	10.53
D. Powell	Wadworth	83.4	20	260	23	11.30
A. Hall	Woodsetts	90.3	13	301	23	13.09
G Beard	Clumber Park	102.3	26	349	26	13.42
A. Barthorpe	Worksop	145	37	522	38	13.70
S. Evans	Thoresby Coll	102.1	21	350	25	14.00

Division 5

		Ovs	Ms	Runs	Wkts	Ave
M. Spivey	Kiveton Pk Coll	76.5	8	247	20	12.35
R. Bostock	Cuckney	89.3	14	312	22	14.18
T. Roberts	Lea Park	90	16	308	20	15.40
M. Spencer	Rose Leisure	92.3	17	309	20	15.45
R. Breedon	Blidworth Welf	133.2	43	326	21	15.52
S. Allcock	Eckington	100.1	17	421	26	16.19

Division 6

		Ovs	Ms	Runs	Wkts	Ave
A. Anglesea	Whitwell	71.4	20	189	22	8.59
D. Shepphard	Mansfield HM	76.5	17	207	21	9.86
A. McCulloch	Killamarsh	75.2	21	199	20	9.95
M. Forrest	Whitwell	107	34	247	23	10.74
J. Ritchie	Glapwell Colliery	82	16	241	22	10.96
A. Gregory	Killamarsh	105.4	20	343	28	12.25

Division 7

		Ovs	Ms	Runs	Wkts	Ave
R. Stallworthy	Clumber Park	80	2	201	23	8.74
D. Cardwell	Weston	77	15	222	25	8.88
P. Burrell	Ransome & Ma	87.3	21	239	25	9.56
M. Ferry	Mansfield & Pl	116.2	29	285	29	9.83
M. Kilday	Mansfield & Pl	164.2	50	351	31	11.32
I. Tingle	Clumber Park	74.2	12	253	22	11.50

Division 8

		Ovs	Ms	Runs	Wkts	Ave
M. Boscolo	Misterton	59	9	167	20	8.35
S. Blagg	Worksop	97.2	34	203	22	9.23
M. Tordoff	Todwick	155	31	385	36	10.69
D. Williams	Manton	109.4	29	287	26	11.04
R. Lee	Manton	113.2	29	331	28	11.82
M. Hewson	Misterton	170.4	34	475	37	12.84

Division 9

		Ovs	Ms	Runs	Wkts	Ave
S. Gill	Ollerton	82.5	24	232	27	8.59
D. Parnham	Ollerton	114	24	323	32	10.09
M. Brown	Ollerton	84.7	18	241	23	10.47
J. Redfern	Worksop	98	21	316	26	12.10
B. Clark	Thoresby Park	126	26	351	26	13.50
C. Lake	Rockware Glass	71	4	323	20	16.15

Division 10

		Ovs	Ms	Runs	Wkts	Ave
D. Chambers	Waleswood Spts	153.2	42	340	39	8.71
J. Salmon	Mansfield HM	92	23	274	19	14.42
P. Jackson	Woodsetts	120.3	33	335	21	15.95

2007 Bassetlaw League Fixtures

Division 1

Sat 21 April

Bolsover	v	Marshalls
Farnsfield	v	Rans & M
Glapwell	v	Cuckney
Kiveton Park	v	Bridon
Notts & AA	v	Thoresby C
Worksop	v	Cutthorpe

Sat 28 April

Bridon	v	Farnsfield
Cuckney	v	Notts & AA
Cutthorpe	v	Bolsover
Rans & M	v	Glapwell
Thoresby C	v	Marshalls
Worksop	v	Kiveton Pk

Sat 5 May

Bolsover	v	Worksop
Farnsfield	v	Cuckney
Glapwell	v	Bridon
Kiveton Pk	v	Thoresby C
Marshalls	v	Cutthorpe
Notts & AA	v	Rans & M

Mon 7 May

Rans & M	v	Marshalls

Sat 12 May

Bridon	v	Bolsover
Cuckney	v	Marshalls
Cutthorpe	v	Farnsfield
Glapwell	v	Notts & AA
Rans & M	v	Kiveton Pk
Thoresby C	v	Worksop

Sat 19 May

Bolsover	v	Rans & M
Cuckney	v	Cutthorpe
Kiveton Pk	v	Glapwell
Marshalls	v	Farnsfield
Thoresby C	v	Bridon
Worksop	v	Notts & AA

Sat 26 May

Cutthorpe	v	Bridon
Farnsfield	v	Kiveton Pk
Marshalls	v	Bolsover
Notts & AA	v	Glapwell
Worksop	v	Cuckney

Mon 28 May

Cutthorpe	v	Worksop
Glapwell	v	Bolsover
Marshalls	v	Thoresby C

Sat 2 June

Bolsover	v	Farnsfield
Bridon	v	Worksop
Cutthorpe	v	Thoresby C
Marshalls	v	Glapwell
Notts & AA	v	Kiveton Pk
Rans & M	v	Cuckney

Sat 9 June

Cuckney	v	Bridon
Farnsfield	v	Notts & AA
Glapwell	v	Rans & M
Marshalls	v	Kiveton Pk
Thoresby C	v	Bolsover

Sat 16 June

Bolsover	v	Cuckney
Bridon	v	Marshalls
Cutthorpe	v	Notts & AA
Glapwell	v	Thoresby C
Kiveton Pk	v	Rans & M
Worksop	v	Farnsfield

Sat 23 June

Cuckney	v	Thoresby C
Cutthorpe	v	Kiveton Pk
Farnsfield	v	Marshalls
Notts & AA	v	Bolsover
Rans & M	v	Bridon
Worksop	v	Glapwell

Sat 30 June

Bridon	v	Cutthorpe
Cuckney	v	Glapwell
Kiveton Pk	v	Marshalls
Notts & AA	v	Worksop
Rans & M	v	Bolsover
Thoresby C	v	Farnsfield

Sat 7 July

Bolsover	v	Cutthorpe
Bridon	v	Thoresby C
Glapwell	v	Farnsfield
Kiveton Pk	v	Cuckney
Marshalls	v	Notts & AA
Worksop	v	Rans & M

Sat 14 July

Farnsfield	v	Bridon
Glapwell	v	Marshalls
Notts & AA	v	Cuckney
Rans & M	v	Cutthorpe
Thoresby C	v	Kiveton Pk
Worksop	v	Bolsover

Sat 21 July

Bolsover	v	Notts & AA
Bridon	v	Rans & M
Cutthorpe	v	Glapwell
Kiveton Pk	v	Farnsfield
Marshalls	v	Worksop
Thoresby C	v	Cuckney

Sat 28 July

Bridon	v	Notts & AA
Cuckney	v	Kiveton Pk
Cutthorpe	v	Marshalls
Farnsfield	v	Bolsover
Glapwell	v	Worksop
Rans & M	v	Thoresby C

Sat 4 Aug

Bolsover	v	Thoresby C
Cutthorpe	v	Cuckney
Kiveton Pk	v	Notts & AA
Rans & M	v	Farnsfield
Worksop	v	Bridon

Sat 11 Aug

Bridon	v	Kiveton Pk
Cuckney	v	Bolsover
Farnsfield	v	Worksop
Marshalls	v	Rans & M
Notts & AA	v	Cutthorpe
Thoresby C	v	Glapwell

Sat 18 Aug

Bridon	v	Glapwell
Farnsfield	v	Cutthorpe
Kiveton Pk	v	Bolsover
Marshalls	v	Cuckney
Rans & M	v	Worksop
Thoresby C	v	Notts & AA

Sat 25 Aug

Bolsover	v	Bridon
Cuckney	v	Farnsfield
Cutthorpe	v	Rans & M
Glapwell	v	Kiveton Pk
Notts & AA	v	Marshalls
Worksop	v	Thoresby C

Mon 27 Aug

Cuckney	v	Rans & M
Farnsfield	v	Glapwell
Kiveton Pk	v	Worksop
Notts & AA	v	Bridon
Thoresby C	v	Cutthorpe

Sat 1 Sept

Bolsover	v	Glapwell
Bridon	v	Cuckney
Farnsfield	v	Thoresby C

Kiveton Pk   v   Cutthorpe
Rans & M   v   Notts & AA
Worksop   v   Marshalls

Sat 8 Sept
Bolsover   v   Kiveton Pk
Cuckney   v   Worksop
Glapwell   v   Cutthorpe
Marshalls   v   Bridon
Notts & AA   v   Farnsfield
Thoresby C   v   Rans & M

Division 2

Sat 21 April
Anston   v   Eckington
Edwinstowe   v   N W'ley w L
Mans & Pl   v   Caythorpe 2
Mansf HM 2   v   Waleswood
Pappl & L 2   v   Blidworth
Whitwell   v   Everton

Sat 28 April
Blidworth   v   Anston
Caythorpe 2   v   Pappl & L 2
Edwinstowe   v   Mans & Pl
Everton   v   Mansf HM 2
N W'ley w L   v   Eckington
Waleswood   v   Whitwell

Sat 5 May
Anston   v   Everton
Caythorpe 2   v   N W'ley w L
Edwinstowe   v   Blidworth
Mans & Pl   v   Waleswood
Mansf HM 2   v   Eckington
Whitwell   v   Pappl & L 2

Sat 12 May
Eckington   v   Edwinstowe
Everton   v   Mans & Pl
N W'ley w L   v   Blidworth
Pappl & L 2   v   Anston
Waleswood   v   Caythorpe 2
Whitwell   v   Mansf HM 2

Sat 19 May
Anston   v   Edwinstowe
Blidworth   v   Eckington
Caythorpe 2   v   Whitwell
Mans & Pl   v   N W'ley w L
Mansf HM 2   v   Everton
Waleswood   v   Pappl & L 2

Sat 26 May
Anston   v   Mans & Pl
Eckington   v   Everton
Edwinstowe   v   Caythorpe 2
N W'ley w L   v   Waleswood
Pappl & L 2   v   Mansf HM 2
Whitwell   v   Blidworth

Mon 28 May
Anston   v   N W'ley w L
Blidworth   v   Mans & Pl
Waleswood   v   Edwinstowe

Sat 2 June
Blidworth   v   Mansf HM 2
Everton   v   Caythorpe 2
Mans & Pl   v   Edwinstowe
N W'ley w L   v   Whitwell
Pappl & L 2   v   Eckington
Waleswood   v   Anston

Sat 9 June
Blidworth   v   Waleswood
Caythorpe 2   v   Anston
Eckington   v   N W'ley w L
Edwinstowe   v   Whitwell
Everton   v   Pappl & L 2
Mansf HM 2   v   Mans & Pl

Sat 16 June
Anston   v   Blidworth
Edwinstowe   v   Everton
Mansf HM 2   v   Caythorpe 2
Pappl & L 2   v   N W'ley w L
Waleswood   v   Eckington
Whitwell   v   Mans & Pl

Sat 23 June
Anston   v   Mansf HM 2
Caythorpe 2   v   Eckington
Everton   v   Blidworth
Mans & Pl   v   Pappl & L 2
N W'ley w L   v   Edwinstowe
Whitwell   v   Waleswood

Sat 30 June
Blidworth   v   Pappl & L 2
Caythorpe 2   v   Mans & Pl
Eckington   v   Whitwell
Edwinstowe   v   Mansf HM 2
Everton   v   Anston
Waleswood   v   N W'ley w L

Sat 7 July
Eckington   v   Mans & Pl
Everton   v   Edwinstowe
Mansf HM 2   v   N W'ley w L
Pappl & L 2   v   Caythorpe 2
Waleswood   v   Blidworth
Whitwell   v   Anston

Sat 14 July
Anston   v   Waleswood
Eckington   v   Blidworth
Mans & Pl   v   Mansf HM 2
N W'ley w L   v   Everton
Pappl & L 2   v   Edwinstowe

Whitwell   v   Caythorpe 2

Sat 21 July
Caythorpe 2   v   Blidworth
Edwinstowe   v   Anston
Everton   v   Eckington
Mansf HM 2   v   Whitwell
N W'ley w L   v   Pappl & L 2
Waleswood   v   Mans & Pl

Sat 28 July
Anston   v   Caythorpe 2
Blidworth   v   N W'ley w L
Eckington   v   Mansf HM 2
Mans & Pl   v   Everton
Pappl & L 2   v   Waleswood
Whitwell   v   Edwinstowe

Sat 4 Aug
Blidworth   v   Edwinstowe
Caythorpe 2   v   Waleswood
Eckington   v   Anston
Everton   v   Whitwell
Mansf HM 2   v   Pappl & L 2
N W'ley w L   v   Mans & Pl

Sat 11 Aug
Edwinstowe   v   Eckington
Mans & Pl   v   Whitwell
N W'ley w L   v   Caythorpe 2
Pappl & L 2   v   Everton
Waleswood   v   Mansf HM 2

Sat 18 Aug
Anston   v   Pappl & L 2
Caythorpe 2   v   Edwinstowe
Everton   v   Waleswood
Mans & Pl   v   Eckington
Mansf HM 2   v   Blidworth
Whitwell   v   N W'ley w L

Sat 25 Aug
Blidworth   v   Everton
Eckington   v   Caythorpe 2
Edwinstowe   v   Waleswood
Mans & Pl   v   Anston
N W'ley w L   v   Mansf HM 2
Pappl & L 2   v   Whitwell

Mon 27 Aug
Blidworth   v   Whitwell
Caythorpe 2   v   Everton
Eckington   v   Pappl & L 2
Mansf HM 2   v   Anston

Sat 1 Sept
Caythorpe 2   v   Mansf HM 2
Edwinstowe   v   Pappl & L 2
Mans & Pl   v   Blidworth
N W'ley w L   v   Anston

Nottinghamshire

Waleswood   v   Everton
Whitwell   v   Eckington

Sat 8 Sept
Anston   v   Whitwell
Blidworth   v   Caythorpe 2
Eckington   v   Waleswood
Everton   v   N W'ley w L
Mansf HM 2   v   Edwinstowe
Pappl & L 2   v   Mans & Pl

Division 3

Sat 21 April
Clumber Pk   v   Grassmoor
Harthill   v   Notts & AA 2
Teversal   v   Retford 2
Thor'by Pk   v   Farnsfield 2
Welbeck C 2   v   Holmewood

Sat 28 April
Farnsfield 2   v   Sher. Coll
Harthill   v   WI Cavs 2
Holmewood   v   Clumber Pk
Notts & AA 2   v   Welbeck C 2
Retford 2   v   Grassmoor
Thor'by Pk   v   Teversal

Sat 5 May
Clumber Pk   v   Harthill
Grassmoor   v   Sher. Coll
Holmewood   v   Farnsfield 2
Thor'by Pk   v   Notts & AA 2
Welbeck C 2   v   Teversal

Mon 7 May
Retford 2   v   Notts & AA 2
WI Cavs 2   v   Teversal

Sat 12 May
Farnsfield 2   v   Welbeck C 2
Grassmoor   v   Teversal
Harthill   v   Retford 2
Notts & AA 2   v   Clumber Pk
Sher. Coll   v   Thor'by Pk
WI Cavs 2   v   Holmewood

Sat 19 May
Clumber Pk   v   Sher. Coll
Farnsfield 2   v   Teversal
Notts & AA 2   v   Harthill
Retford 2   v   Holmewood
Thor'by Pk   v   Grassmoor
Welbeck C 2   v   WI Cavs 2

Sat 26 May
Clumber Pk   v   Welbeck C 2
Grassmoor   v   Farnsfield 2
Harthill   v   Thor'by Pk
Sher. Coll   v   Notts & AA 2
Teversal   v   Holmewood
WI Cavs 2   v   Retford 2

Mon 28 May
Clumber Pk   v   Thor'by Pk
Harthill   v   Farnsfield 2
Holmewood   v   WI Cavs 2
Teversal   v   Sher. Coll
Welbeck C 2   v   Grassmoor

Sat 2 June
Farnsfield 2   v   Thor'by Pk
Holmewood   v   Notts & AA 2
Sher. Coll   v   Retford 2
Teversal   v   Clumber Pk
WI Cavs 2   v   Grassmoor

Sat 9 June
Clumber Pk   v   WI Cavs 2
Grassmoor   v   Holmewood
Notts & AA 2   v   Farnsfield 2
Retford 2   v   Teversal
Sher. Coll   v   Harthill
Welbeck C 2   v   Thor'by Pk

Sat 16 June
Farnsfield 2   v   WI Cavs 2
Harthill   v   Welbeck C 2
Holmewood   v   Teversal
Notts & AA 2   v   Retford 2
Thor'by Pk   v   Clumber Pk

Sat 23 June
Clumber Pk   v   Teversal
Harthill   v   Holmewood
Retford 2   v   Farnsfield 2
Sher. Coll   v   Grassmoor
Welbeck C 2   v   Notts & AA 2
WI Cavs 2   v   Thor'by Pk

Sat 30 June
Farnsfield 2   v   Harthill
Grassmoor   v   Welbeck C 2
Holmewood   v   Thor'by Pk
Retford 2   v   Sher. Coll
Teversal   v   Notts & AA 2
WI Cavs 2   v   Clumber Pk

Sat 7 July
Farnsfield 2   v   Clumber Pk
Holmewood   v   Sher. Coll
Notts & AA 2   v   Grassmoor
Teversal   v   WI Cavs 2
Thor'by Pk   v   Harthill
Welbeck C 2   v   Retford 2

Sat 14 July
Harthill   v   Teversal
Holmewood   v   Grassmoor
Retford 2   v   Clumber Pk
Sher. Coll   v   Farnsfield 2
Thor'by Pk   v   Welbeck C 2
WI Cavs 2   v   Notts & AA 2

Sat 21 July
Farnsfield 2   v   Holmewood
Grassmoor   v   WI Cavs 2
Notts & AA 2   v   Thor'by Pk
Retford 2   v   Harthill
Welbeck C 2   v   Sher. Coll

Sat 28 July
Clumber Pk   v   Holmewood
Harthill   v   Grassmoor
Notts & AA 2   v   Sher. Coll
Teversal   v   Farnsfield 2
Thor'by Pk   v   Retford 2
WI Cavs 2   v   Welbeck C 2

Sat 4 Aug
Farnsfield 2   v   Grassmoor
Notts & AA 2   v   Holmewood
Retford 2   v   WI Cavs 2
Sher. Coll   v   Clumber Pk
Welbeck C 2   v   Harthill

Sat 11 Aug
Clumber Pk   v   Farnsfield 2
Grassmoor   v   Notts & AA 2
Holmewood   v   Retford 2
Teversal   v   Welbeck C 2
Thor'by Pk   v   Sher. Coll
WI Cavs 2   v   Harthill

Sat 18 Aug
Grassmoor   v   Retford 2
Harthill   v   Clumber Pk
Notts & AA 2   v   WI Cavs 2
Sher. Coll   v   Teversal
Thor'by Pk   v   Holmewood
Welbeck C 2   v   Farnsfield 2

Sat 25 Aug
Clumber Pk   v   Notts & AA 2
Farnsfield 2   v   Retford 2
Grassmoor   v   Thor'by Pk
Holmewood   v   Welbeck C 2
Teversal   v   Harthill
WI Cavs 2   v   Sher. Coll

Mon 27 Aug
Grassmoor   v   Clumber Pk
Harthill   v   Sher. Coll
Retford 2   v   Welbeck C 2
Teversal   v   Thor'by Pk

Sat 1 Sept
Grassmoor   v   Harthill
Notts & AA 2   v   Teversal
Retford 2   v   Thor'by Pk
Sher. Coll   v   Holmewood
Welbeck C 2   v   Clumber Pk
WI Cavs 2   v   Farnsfield 2

Sat 8 Sept
Clumber Pk v Retford 2
Farnsfield 2 v Notts & AA 2
Holmewood v Harthill
Sher. Coll v Welbeck C 2
Teversal v Grassmoor
Thor'by Pk v WI Cavs 2

Sat 15 Sept
Sher. Coll v WI Cavs 2

Division 4

Sat 21 April
Bridon 2 v Woodsetts
Lea Park v Worksop 2
Thurcroft v Milton
Wadworth v Clay C Wks
Welbeck C 3 v Clipstone
Wiseton v Thoresby C 2

Sat 28 April
Lea Park v Clipstone
Milton v Woodsetts
Thurcroft v Thoresby C 2
Wadworth v Bridon 2
Welbeck C 3 v Worksop 2
Wiseton v Clay C Wks

Sat 5 May
Bridon 2 v Welbeck C 3
Clay C Wks v Milton
Clipstone v Wiseton
Lea Park v Woodsetts
Thoresby C 2 v Wadworth
Worksop 2 v Thurcroft

Mon 7 May
Thoresby C 2 v Woodsetts
Welbeck C 3 v Wiseton

Sat 12 May
Clay C Wks v Bridon 2
Clipstone v Milton
Thurcroft v Lea Park
Wiseton v Wadworth
Woodsetts v Welbeck C 3
Worksop 2 v Thoresby C 2

Sat 19 May
Bridon 2 v Thoresby C 2
Milton v Worksop 2
Wadworth v Lea Park
Welbeck C 3 v Clay C Wks
Wiseton v Thurcroft
Woodsetts v Clipstone

Sat 26 May
Bridon 2 v Thurcroft

Clay C Wks v Wiseton
Clipstone v Worksop 2
Lea Park v Welbeck C 3
Thoresby C 2 v Milton
Wadworth v Woodsetts

Sat 2 June
Milton v Wiseton
Thoresby C 2 v Clay C Wks
Thurcroft v Clipstone
Welbeck C 3 v Wadworth
Woodsetts v Lea Park
Worksop 2 v Bridon 2

Sat 9 June
Bridon 2 v Lea Park
Milton v Welbeck C 3
Thurcroft v Woodsetts
Wadworth v Thoresby C 2
Wiseton v Clipstone
Worksop 2 v Clay C Wks

Sat 16 June
Clay C Wks v Thurcroft
Clipstone v Bridon 2
Lea Park v Wiseton
Milton v Wadworth
Thoresby C 2 v Welbeck C 3
Woodsetts v Worksop 2

Sat 23 June
Bridon 2 v Clay C Wks
Thoresby C 2 v Lea Park
Thurcroft v Welbeck C 3
Wadworth v Clipstone
Wiseton v Worksop 2
Woodsetts v Milton

Sat 30 June
Clay C Wks v Lea Park
Clipstone v Thoresby C 2
Milton v Bridon 2
Thurcroft v Wiseton
Welbeck C 3 v Woodsetts
Worksop 2 v Wadworth

Sat 7 July
Clipstone v Lea Park
Thoresby C 2 v Bridon 2
Thurcroft v Worksop 2
Wadworth v Welbeck C 3
Wiseton v Milton
Woodsetts v Clay C Wks

Sat 14 July
Bridon 2 v Wiseton
Clay C Wks v Worksop 2
Lea Park v Wadworth
Milton v Clipstone
Welbeck C 3 v Thurcroft
Woodsetts v Thoresby C 2

Sat 21 July
Clay C Wks v Thoresby C 2
Clipstone v Wadworth
Milton v Lea Park
Thurcroft v Bridon 2
Wiseton v Woodsetts
Worksop 2 v Welbeck C 3

Sat 28 July
Clipstone v Clay C Wks
Lea Park v Thurcroft
Thoresby C 2 v Wiseton
Welbeck C 3 v Bridon 2
Woodsetts v Wadworth
Worksop 2 v Milton

Sat 4 Aug
Bridon 2 v Worksop 2
Clipstone v Woodsetts
Milton v Clay C Wks
Thoresby C 2 v Thurcroft
Wadworth v Wiseton
Welbeck C 3 v Lea Park

Sat 11 Aug
Lea Park v Thoresby C 2
Thurcroft v Clay C Wks
Wadworth v Milton
Wiseton v Welbeck C 3
Woodsetts v Bridon 2
Worksop 2 v Clipstone

Sat 18 Aug
Clay C Wks v Woodsetts
Clipstone v Welbeck C 3
Lea Park v Bridon 2
Milton v Thoresby C 2
Wadworth v Thurcroft
Worksop 2 v Wiseton

Sat 25 Aug
Bridon 2 v Wadworth
Clipstone v Thurcroft
Lea Park v Clay C Wks
Thoresby C 2 v Worksop 2
Welbeck C 3 v Milton
Woodsetts v Wiseton

Mon 27 Aug
Bridon 2 v Clipstone
Clay C Wks v Wadworth
Milton v Thurcroft
Worksop 2 v Lea Park

Sat 1 Sept
Clay C Wks v Welbeck C 3
Lea Park v Milton
Thoresby C 2 v Clipstone
Wadworth v Worksop 2

Nottinghamshire

Wiseton   v   Bridon 2
Woodsetts   v   Thurcroft

Sat 8 Sept
Bridon 2   v   Milton
Clay C Wks   v   Clipstone
Thurcroft   v   Wadworth
Welbeck C 3   v   Thoresby C 2
Wiseton   v   Lea Park
Worksop 2   v   Woodsetts

Division 5

Sat 21 April
Basford Mill   v   Edwinstowe 2
Blidworth 2   v   Kiveton Pk 2
Cuckney 2   v   Rose Leisure
Eckington 2   v   Anston 2
Marshalls 2   v   Bolsover 2

Sat 28 April
Anston 2   v   Blidworth 2
Bolsover 2   v   Edwinstowe 2
Eckington 2   v   Cuckney 2
Kiveton Pk 2   v   Rose Leisure
Marshalls 2   v   Killamarsh 2
Whitwell 2   v   Basford Mill

Sat 5 May
Basford Mill   v   Bolsover 2
Blidworth 2   v   Edwinstowe 2
Cuckney 2   v   Anston 2
Eckington 2   v   Marshalls 2
Killamarsh 2   v   Kiveton Pk 2
Rose Leisure   v   Whitwell 2

Mon 7 May
Killamarsh 2   v   Whitwell 2

Sat 12 May
Anston 2   v   Basford Mill
Blidworth 2   v   Killamarsh 2
Bolsover 2   v   Rose Leisure
Edwinstowe 2   v   Eckington 2
Kiveton Pk 2   v   Whitwell 2
Marshalls 2   v   Cuckney 2

Sat 19 May
Basford Mill   v   Marshalls 2
Eckington 2   v   Blidworth 2
Edwinstowe 2   v   Anston 2
Killamarsh 2   v   Cuckney 2
Rose Leisure   v   Kiveton Pk 2
Whitwell 2   v   Bolsover 2

Sat 26 May
Basford Mill   v   Killamarsh 2
Blidworth 2   v   Marshalls 2
Bolsover 2   v   Anston 2
Cuckney 2   v   Whitwell 2

Kiveton Pk 2   v   Eckington 2
Rose Leisure   v   Edwinstowe 2

Mon 28 May
Cuckney 2   v   Basford Mill
Eckington 2   v   Rose Leisure
Edwinstowe 2   v   Kiveton Pk 2
Whitwell 2   v   Blidworth 2

Sat 2 June
Anston 2   v   Cuckney 2
Eckington 2   v   Basford Mill
Edwinstowe 2   v   Bolsover 2
Killamarsh 2   v   Rose Leisure
Kiveton Pk 2   v   Blidworth 2
Whitwell 2   v   Marshalls 2

Sat 9 June
Anston 2   v   Killamarsh 2
Basford Mill   v   Cuckney 2
Bolsover 2   v   Eckington 2
Kiveton Pk 2   v   Marshalls 2
Rose Leisure   v   Blidworth 2
Whitwell 2   v   Edwinstowe 2

Sat 16 June
Basford Mill   v   Whitwell 2
Blidworth 2   v   Anston 2
Cuckney 2   v   Bolsover 2
Eckington 2   v   Kiveton Pk 2
Killamarsh 2   v   Edwinstowe 2
Marshalls 2   v   Rose Leisure

Sat 23 June
Blidworth 2   v   Cuckney 2
Bolsover 2   v   Basford Mill
Eckington 2   v   Killamarsh 2
Edwinstowe 2   v   Rose Leisure
Kiveton Pk 2   v   Anston 2
Marshalls 2   v   Whitwell 2

Sat 30 June
Anston 2   v   Edwinstowe 2
Basford Mill   v   Kiveton Pk 2
Bolsover 2   v   Killamarsh 2
Marshalls 2   v   Blidworth 2
Rose Leisure   v   Cuckney 2
Whitwell 2   v   Eckington 2

Sat 7 July
Anston 2   v   Whitwell 2
Blidworth 2   v   Eckington 2
Cuckney 2   v   Kiveton Pk 2
Edwinstowe 2   v   Marshalls 2
Killamarsh 2   v   Basford Mill
Rose Leisure   v   Bolsover 2

Sat 14 July
Basford Mill   v   Rose Leisure
Bolsover 2   v   Whitwell 2

Cuckney 2   v   Eckington 2
Kiveton Pk 2   v   Killamarsh 2
Marshalls 2   v   Anston 2

Sat 21 July
Anston 2   v   Rose Leisure
Blidworth 2   v   Basford Mill
Cuckney 2   v   Edwinstowe 2
Eckington 2   v   Bolsover 2
Killamarsh 2   v   Marshalls 2
Whitwell 2   v   Kiveton Pk 2

Sat 28 July
Basford Mill   v   Anston 2
Bolsover 2   v   Blidworth 2
Edwinstowe 2   v   Whitwell 2
Kiveton Pk 2   v   Cuckney 2
Marshalls 2   v   Eckington 2
Rose Leisure   v   Killamarsh 2

Sat 4 Aug
Anston 2   v   Eckington 2
Cuckney 2   v   Blidworth 2
Edwinstowe 2   v   Basford Mill
Killamarsh 2   v   Bolsover 2
Marshalls 2   v   Kiveton Pk 2
Whitwell 2   v   Rose Leisure

Sat 11 Aug
Anston 2   v   Marshalls 2
Blidworth 2   v   Rose Leisure
Bolsover 2   v   Cuckney 2
Eckington 2   v   Edwinstowe 2
Kiveton Pk 2   v   Basford Mill
Whitwell 2   v   Killamarsh 2

Sat 18 Aug
Basford Mill   v   Eckington 2
Blidworth 2   v   Whitwell 2
Bolsover 2   v   Kiveton Pk 2
Cuckney 2   v   Marshalls 2
Edwinstowe 2   v   Killamarsh 2
Rose Leisure   v   Anston 2

Sat 25 Aug
Anston 2   v   Bolsover 2
Killamarsh 2   v   Blidworth 2
Kiveton Pk 2   v   Edwinstowe 2
Marshalls 2   v   Basford Mill
Rose Leisure   v   Eckington 2
Whitwell 2   v   Cuckney 2

Mon 27 Aug
Bolsover 2   v   Marshalls 2
Edwinstowe 2   v   Blidworth 2
Killamarsh 2   v   Anston 2
Rose Leisure   v   Basford Mill

Sat 1 Sept
Anston 2   v   Kiveton Pk 2

Blidworth 2	v	Bolsover 2
Cuckney 2	v	Killamarsh 2
Eckington 2	v	Whitwell 2
Marshalls 2	v	Edwinstowe 2

Sat 8 Sept

Basford Mill	v	Blidworth 2
Edwinstowe 2	v	Cuckney 2
Killamarsh 2	v	Eckington 2
Kiveton Pk 2	v	Bolsover 2
Rose Leisure	v	Marshalls 2
Whitwell 2	v	Anston 2

Division 6

Sat 21 April

Anston 3	v	Bilsthorpe
Mansf HM 3	v	Nomads
Milton 2	v	Mans & Pl 2

Sat 28 April

Anston 3	v	Nomads
Clumber Pk 2	v	Milton 2
Glapwell 2	v	Rans & M 2
Grassmoor 2	v	Mansf HM 3
Mans & Pl 2	v	Bilsthorpe
Teversal 2	v	N W'ley w L 2

Sat 5 May

Mansf HM 3	v	Anston 3
Milton 2	v	Bilsthorpe
Nomads	v	Glapwell 2
N W'ley w L 2	v	Grassmoor 2
Rans & M 2	v	Mans & Pl 2
Teversal 2	v	Clumber Pk 2

Mon 7 May

Clumber Pk 2	v	Mansf HM 3
Glapwell 2	v	Teversal 2
Grassmoor 2	v	Anston 3
N W'ley w L 2	v	Rans & M 2

Sat 12 May

Anston 3	v	Rans & M 2
Clumber Pk 2	v	N W'ley w L 2
Mans & Pl 2	v	Nomads
Mansf HM 3	v	Bilsthorpe
Milton 2	v	Glapwell 2
Teversal 2	v	Grassmoor 2

Sat 19 May

Glapwell 2	v	Bilsthorpe
Grassmoor 2	v	Milton 2
Nomads	v	Clumber Pk 2
N W'ley w L 2	v	Mans & Pl 2
Rans & M 2	v	Mansf HM 3
Teversal 2	v	Anston 3

Sat 26 May

Bilsthorpe	v	Teversal 2
Glapwell 2	v	N W'ley w L 2
Mans & Pl 2	v	Clumber Pk 2
Mansf HM 3	v	Grassmoor 2
Milton 2	v	Nomads
Rans & M 2	v	Anston 3

Mon 28 May

Bilsthorpe	v	Nomads
Grassmoor 2	v	Glapwell 2
Milton 2	v	Clumber Pk 2
Rans & M 2	v	Teversal 2

Sat 2 June

Anston 3	v	Milton 2
Bilsthorpe	v	Mansf HM 3
Clumber Pk 2	v	Teversal 2
Glapwell 2	v	Mans & Pl 2
Grassmoor 2	v	Rans & M 2
Nomads	v	N W'ley w L 2

Sat 9 June

Anston 3	v	Grassmoor 2
Bilsthorpe	v	Clumber Pk 2
Mans & Pl 2	v	Milton 2
N W'ley w L 2	v	Mansf HM 3
Rans & M 2	v	Glapwell 2
Teversal 2	v	Nomads

Sat 16 June

Grassmoor 2	v	Nomads
Mans & Pl 2	v	Anston 3
Mansf HM 3	v	Clumber Pk 2
N W'ley w L 2	v	Bilsthorpe
Rans & M 2	v	Milton 2
Teversal 2	v	Glapwell 2

Sat 23 June

Anston 3	v	Mansf HM 3
Glapwell 2	v	Clumber Pk 2
Grassmoor 2	v	Mans & Pl 2
Milton 2	v	N W'ley w L 2
Nomads	v	Rans & M 2
Teversal 2	v	Bilsthorpe

Sat 30 June

Bilsthorpe	v	Grassmoor 2
Clumber Pk 2	v	Nomads
Glapwell 2	v	Milton 2
Mans & Pl 2	v	Rans & M 2
Mansf HM 3	v	Teversal 2
N W'ley w L 2	v	Anston 3

Sat 7 July

Anston 3	v	Glapwell 2
Clumber Pk 2	v	Grassmoor 2
Mans & Pl 2	v	Teversal 2
Milton 2	v	Mansf HM 3
N W'ley w L 2	v	Nomads
Rans & M 2	v	Bilsthorpe

Sat 14 July

Bilsthorpe	v	Glapwell 2
Clumber Pk 2	v	Rans & M 2
Grassmoor 2	v	N W'ley w L 2
Mansf HM 3	v	Mans & Pl 2
Nomads	v	Anston 3
Teversal 2	v	Milton 2

Sat 21 July

Bilsthorpe	v	Milton 2
Glapwell 2	v	Anston 3
Mans & Pl 2	v	Grassmoor 2
Rans & M 2	v	N W'ley w L 2
Teversal 2	v	Mansf HM 3

Sat 28 July

Anston 3	v	Teversal 2
Bilsthorpe	v	Rans & M 2
Grassmoor 2	v	Clumber Pk 2
Mansf HM 3	v	Milton 2
Nomads	v	Mans & Pl 2
N W'ley w L 2	v	Glapwell 2

Sat 4 Aug

Clumber Pk 2	v	Glapwell 2
Grassmoor 2	v	Bilsthorpe
Mans & Pl 2	v	N W'ley w L 2
Mansf HM 3	v	Rans & M 2
Nomads	v	Milton 2

Sat 11 Aug

Anston 3	v	Clumber Pk 2
Bilsthorpe	v	Mans & Pl 2
Glapwell 2	v	Nomads
Mansf HM 3	v	N W'ley w L 2
Milton 2	v	Teversal 2
Rans & M 2	v	Grassmoor 2

Sat 18 Aug

Bilsthorpe	v	Anston 3
Clumber Pk 2	v	Mans & Pl 2
Glapwell 2	v	Grassmoor 2
Nomads	v	Mansf HM 3
N W'ley w L 2	v	Milton 2
Teversal 2	v	Rans & M 2

Sat 25 Aug

Anston 3	v	Mans & Pl 2
Bilsthorpe	v	N W'ley w L 2
Mansf HM 3	v	Glapwell 2
Milton 2	v	Grassmoor 2
Nomads	v	Teversal 2
Rans & M 2	v	Clumber Pk 2

Mon 27 Aug

Clumber Pk 2	v	Anston 3
Mans & Pl 2	v	Mansf HM 3
Nomads	v	Bilsthorpe
N W'ley w L 2	v	Teversal 2

Nottinghamshire

Sat 1 Sept

Anston 3	v	N W'ley w L 2
Clumber Pk 2	v	Bilsthorpe
Glapwell 2	v	Mansf HM 3
Milton 2	v	Rans & M 2
Nomads	v	Grassmoor 2
Teversal 2	v	Mans & Pl 2

Sat 8 Sept

Grassmoor 2	v	Teversal 2
Mans & Pl 2	v	Glapwell 2
Milton 2	v	Anston 3
N W'ley w L 2	v	Clumber Pk 2
Rans & M 2	v	Nomads

Division 7

Sat 21 April

Blyth	v	East Drayton
Everton 2	v	Misterton
Manton	v	Holmewood 2
Todwick	v	S Normanton
Weston	v	Pappl & L 3

Sat 28 April

Blyth	v	Worksop 3
Manton	v	Cutthorpe 2
Todwick	v	Everton 2
Weston	v	Misterton

Sat 5 May

Cutthorpe 2	v	Pappl & L 3
East Drayton	v	Misterton
Everton 2	v	Manton
Todwick	v	Blyth
Weston	v	S Normanton
Worksop 3	v	Holmewood 2

Mon 7 May

Cutthorpe 2	v	Weston
Holmewood 2	v	Misterton
Pappl & L 3	v	East Drayton
Worksop 3	v	S Normanton

Sat 12 May

Blyth	v	Manton
East Drayton	v	Worksop 3
Holmewood 2	v	Weston
Misterton	v	Cutthorpe 2
Pappl & L 3	v	Todwick
S Normanton	v	Everton 2

Sat 19 May

Cutthorpe 2	v	Blyth
Everton 2	v	Weston
Holmewood 2	v	East Drayton
Manton	v	Todwick
Pappl & L 3	v	Worksop 3
S Normanton	v	Misterton

Sat 26 May

East Drayton	v	Pappl & L 3
Everton 2	v	Cutthorpe 2
Holmewood 2	v	S Normanton
Misterton	v	Blyth
Todwick	v	Weston
Worksop 3	v	Manton

Mon 28 May

Everton 2	v	S Normanton
Worksop 3	v	Todwick

Sat 2 June

Manton	v	East Drayton
Misterton	v	Worksop 3
Pappl & L 3	v	Everton 2
S Normanton	v	Blyth
Todwick	v	Holmewood 2
Weston	v	Cutthorpe 2

Sat 9 June

Blyth	v	Pappl & L 3
Cutthorpe 2	v	Misterton
East Drayton	v	Todwick
Holmewood 2	v	Everton 2
Manton	v	S Normanton
Worksop 3	v	Weston

Sat 16 June

East Drayton	v	Holmewood 2
Everton 2	v	Blyth
Misterton	v	Pappl & L 3
S Normanton	v	Worksop 3
Todwick	v	Cutthorpe 2
Weston	v	Manton

Sat 23 June

Holmewood 2	v	Todwick
Manton	v	Everton 2
Misterton	v	Weston
Pappl & L 3	v	Cutthorpe 2
S Normanton	v	East Drayton
Worksop 3	v	Blyth

Sat 30 June

Blyth	v	Holmewood 2
Cutthorpe 2	v	S Normanton
East Drayton	v	Everton 2
Manton	v	Pappl & L 3
Todwick	v	Misterton
Weston	v	Worksop 3

Sat 7 July

Blyth	v	S Normanton
Cutthorpe 2	v	Manton
Misterton	v	East Drayton
Pappl & L 3	v	Holmewood 2
Worksop 3	v	Everton 2

Sat 14 July

Blyth	v	Todwick
East Drayton	v	Weston
Everton 2	v	Pappl & L 3
Misterton	v	Manton
S Normanton	v	Holmewood 2
Worksop 3	v	Cutthorpe 2

Sat 21 July

Blyth	v	Misterton
Holmewood 2	v	Cutthorpe 2
S Normanton	v	Manton
Todwick	v	East Drayton
Weston	v	Everton 2
Worksop 3	v	Pappl & L 3

Sat 28 July

East Drayton	v	Cutthorpe 2
Everton 2	v	Todwick
Manton	v	Worksop 3
Misterton	v	Holmewood 2
Pappl & L 3	v	S Normanton
Weston	v	Blyth

Sat 4 Aug

Blyth	v	Cutthorpe 2
Holmewood 2	v	Pappl & L 3
Misterton	v	Everton 2
S Normanton	v	Weston
Todwick	v	Manton
Worksop 3	v	East Drayton

Sat 11 Aug

Cutthorpe 2	v	Worksop 3
East Drayton	v	Blyth
Everton 2	v	Holmewood 2
Manton	v	Weston
Pappl & L 3	v	Misterton
S Normanton	v	Todwick

Sat 18 Aug

Blyth	v	Weston
Cutthorpe 2	v	Everton 2
East Drayton	v	S Normanton
Holmewood 2	v	Worksop 3
Misterton	v	Todwick
Pappl & L 3	v	Manton

Sat 25 Aug

Everton 2	v	East Drayton
Manton	v	Blyth
S Normanton	v	Cutthorpe 2
Todwick	v	Pappl & L 3
Weston	v	Holmewood 2
Worksop 3	v	Misterton

Mon 27 Aug

Cutthorpe 2	v	East Drayton
Holmewood 2	v	Manton
Pappl & L 3	v	Blyth
Weston	v	Todwick

Sat 1 Sept
Cutthorpe 2 v Todwick
East Drayton v Manton
Everton 2 v Worksop 3
Holmewood 2 v Blyth
Misterton v S Normanton
Pappl & L 3 v Weston

Sat 8 Sept
Blyth v Everton 2
Cutthorpe 2 v Holmewood 2
Manton v Misterton
S Normanton v Pappl & L 3
Todwick v Worksop 3
Weston v East Drayton

Division 8

Sat 21 April
Notts & AA 3 v Welbeck C 4
Ollerton v Basford Mill 2
Rock. Glass v Clumber Pk 3
Worksop 4 v Sher. Coll 2

Sat 28 April
Cutthorpe 3 v Waleswood 2
Edwinstowe 3 v Clumber Pk 4
Farnsfield 3 v Anston 4
Mans & Pl 4 v Milton 3
Mansf HM 4 v Rans & M 3

Sat 5 May
Clumber Pk 3 v Basford Mill 2
Notts & AA 3 v Ollerton
Rock. Glass v Worksop 4
Sher. Coll 2 v Thor'by Pk 2
Wadworth 2 v Mans & Pl 3
Welbeck C 4 v Woodsetts 2

Mon 7 May
Basford Mill 2 v Notts & AA 3
Mans & Pl 3 v Welbeck C 4
Sher. Coll 2 v Clumber Pk 3
Wadworth 2 v Thor'by Pk 2

Sat 12 May
Basford Mill 2 v Woodsetts 2
Ollerton v Rock. Glass
Thor'by Pk 2 v Notts & AA 3
Wadworth 2 v Sher. Coll 2
Welbeck C 4 v Clumber Pk 3
Worksop 4 v Mans & Pl 3

Sat 19 May
Mans & Pl 3 v Basford Mill 2
Notts & AA 3 v Clumber Pk 3
Ollerton v Thor'by Pk 2
Rock. Glass v Wadworth 2
Sher. Coll 2 v Woodsetts 2
Worksop 4 v Welbeck C 4

Sat 26 May
Clumber Pk 3 v Worksop 4
Ollerton v Notts & AA 3
Rock. Glass v Sher. Coll 2
Thor'by Pk 2 v Mans & Pl 3
Welbeck C 4 v Basford Mill 2
Woodsetts 2 v Wadworth 2

Mon 28 May
Clumber Pk 3 v Wadworth 2
Mans & Pl 3 v Notts & AA 3
Sher. Coll 2 v Worksop 4
Woodsetts 2 v Rock. Glass

Sat 2 June
Basford Mill 2 v Clumber Pk 3
Mans & Pl 3 v Ollerton
Thor'by Pk 2 v Sher. Coll 2
Wadworth 2 v Welbeck C 4
Woodsetts 2 v Notts & AA 3
Worksop 4 v Rock. Glass

Sat 9 June
Mans & Pl 3 v Sher. Coll 2
Notts & AA 3 v Worksop 4
Ollerton v Clumber Pk 3
Thor'by Pk 2 v Wadworth 2
Welbeck C 4 v Rock. Glass
Woodsetts 2 v Basford Mill 2

Sat 16 June
Clumber Pk 3 v Thor'by Pk 2
Mans & Pl 3 v Rock. Glass
Sher. Coll 2 v Basford Mill 2
Wadworth 2 v Ollerton
Welbeck C 4 v Notts & AA 3
Worksop 4 v Woodsetts 2

Sat 23 June
Basford Mill 2 v Rock. Glass
Mans & Pl 3 v Clumber Pk 3
Notts & AA 3 v Wadworth 2
Ollerton v Woodsetts 2
Thor'by Pk 2 v Worksop 4
Welbeck C 4 v Sher. Coll 2

Sat 30 June
Rock. Glass v Ollerton
Sher. Coll 2 v Mans & Pl 3
Thor'by Pk 2 v Basford Mill 2
Wadworth 2 v Clumber Pk 3
Woodsetts 2 v Welbeck C 4
Worksop 4 v Notts & AA 3

Sat 7 July
Basford Mill 2 v Mans & Pl 3
Clumber Pk 3 v Woodsetts 2
Ollerton v Worksop 4
Rock. Glass v Notts & AA 3
Sher. Coll 2 v Wadworth 2
Welbeck C 4 v Thor'by Pk 2

Sat 14 July
Clumber Pk 3 v Welbeck C 4
Mans & Pl 3 v Worksop 4
Notts & AA 3 v Sher. Coll 2
Rock. Glass v Thor'by Pk 2
Wadworth 2 v Basford Mill 2
Woodsetts 2 v Ollerton

Sat 21 July
Basford Mill 2 v Ollerton
Sher. Coll 2 v Rock. Glass
Thor'by Pk 2 v Woodsetts 2
Wadworth 2 v Worksop 4
Welbeck C 4 v Mans & Pl 3

Sat 28 July
Clumber Pk 3 v Mans & Pl 3
Notts & AA 3 v Thor'by Pk 2
Rock. Glass v Welbeck C 4
Sher. Coll 2 v Ollerton
Wadworth 2 v Woodsetts 2
Worksop 4 v Basford Mill 2

Sat 4 Aug
Basford Mill 2 v Wadworth 2
Clumber Pk 3 v Sher. Coll 2
Notts & AA 3 v Rock. Glass
Ollerton v Mans & Pl 3
Thor'by Pk 2 v Welbeck C 4
Woodsetts 2 v Worksop 4

Sat 11 Aug
Basford Mill 2 v Thor'by Pk 2
Clumber Pk 3 v Rock. Glass
Mans & Pl 3 v Woodsetts 2
Sher. Coll 2 v Notts & AA 3
Welbeck C 4 v Ollerton
Worksop 4 v Wadworth 2

Sat 18 Aug
Clumber Pk 3 v Notts & AA 3
Mans & Pl 3 v Wadworth 2
Ollerton v Sher. Coll 2
Rock. Glass v Basford Mill 2
Welbeck C 4 v Worksop 4
Woodsetts 2 v Thor'by Pk 2

Sat 25 Aug
Basford Mill 2 v Worksop 4
Clumber Pk 3 v Ollerton
Sher. Coll 2 v Welbeck C 4
Thor'by Pk 2 v Rock. Glass
Wadworth 2 v Notts & AA 3
Woodsetts 2 v Mans & Pl 3

Nottinghamshire

Mon 27 Aug
Thor'by Pk 2 v Ollerton
Woodsetts 2 v Clumber Pk 3

Sat 1 Sept
Basford Mill 2 v Sher. Coll 2
Notts & AA 3 v Mans & Pl 3
Rock. Glass v Woodsetts 2
Thor'by Pk 2 v Clumber Pk 3
Welbeck C 4 v Wadworth 2
Worksop 4 v Ollerton

Sat 8 Sept
Mans & Pl 3 v Thor'by Pk 2
Notts & AA 3 v Basford Mill 2
Ollerton v Welbeck C 4
Wadworth 2 v Rock. Glass
Woodsetts 2 v Sher. Coll 2
Worksop 4 v Clumber Pk 3

Division 9

Sat 21 April
Cutthorpe 3 v Harthill 2
Edwinstowe 3 v Mansf HM 4
Farnsfield 3 v Woodsetts 3
Mans & Pl 4 v Notts & AA 4
Waleswood 2 v Anston 4

Sat 28 April
Basford Mill 2 v Welbeck C 4
Notts & AA 3 v Woodsetts 2
Ollerton v Wadworth 2
Rock. Glass v Mans & Pl 3
Worksop 4 v Thor'by Pk 2

Sat 5 May
Anston 4 v Edwinstowe 3
Clumber Pk 4 v Mansf HM 4
Mans & Pl 4 v Harthill 2
Milton 3 v Cutthorpe 3
Rans & M 3 v Woodsetts 3
Waleswood 2 v Notts & AA 4

Mon 7 May
Anston 4 v Notts & AA 4
Edwinstowe 3 v Cutthorpe 3
Farnsfield 3 v Mans & Pl 4
Harthill 2 v Woodsetts 3
Mansf HM 4 v Waleswood 2
Milton 3 v Rans & M 3

Sat 12 May
Cutthorpe 3 v Anston 4
Edwinstowe 3 v Milton 3
Mans & Pl 4 v Waleswood 2
Notts & AA 4 v Harthill 2
Rans & M 3 v Farnsfield 3
Woodsetts 3 v Clumber Pk 4

Sat 19 May
Anston 4 v Mans & Pl 4
Farnsfield 3 v Clumber Pk 4
Harthill 2 v Rans & M 3
Mansf HM 4 v Notts & AA 4
Milton 3 v Waleswood 2
Woodsetts 3 v Cutthorpe 3

Sat 26 May
Anston 4 v Harthill 2
Clumber Pk 4 v Mans & Pl 4
Cutthorpe 3 v Farnsfield 3
Notts & AA 4 v Woodsetts 3
Rans & M 3 v Mansf HM 4
Waleswood 2 v Edwinstowe 3

Mon 28 May
Anston 4 v Rans & M 3
Clumber Pk 4 v Edwinstowe 3
Farnsfield 3 v Harthill 2
Mans & Pl 4 v Cutthorpe 3
Mansf HM 4 v Woodsetts 3
Notts & AA 4 v Milton 3

Sat 2 June
Clumber Pk 4 v Milton 3
Harthill 2 v Cutthorpe 3
Mansf HM 4 v Farnsfield 3
Notts & AA 4 v Anston 4
Rans & M 3 v Edwinstowe 3
Woodsetts 3 v Mans & Pl 4

Sat 9 June
Edwinstowe 3 v Woodsetts 3
Harthill 2 v Notts & AA 4
Mans & Pl 4 v Rans & M 3
Mansf HM 4 v Clumber Pk 4
Milton 3 v Anston 4
Waleswood 2 v Cutthorpe 3

Sat 16 June
Anston 4 v Woodsetts 3
Cutthorpe 3 v Clumber Pk 4
Edwinstowe 3 v Harthill 2
Milton 3 v Farnsfield 3
Notts & AA 4 v Mans & Pl 4
Rans & M 3 v Waleswood 2

Sat 23 June
Clumber Pk 4 v Notts & AA 4
Farnsfield 3 v Edwinstowe 3
Mansf HM 4 v Anston 4
Rans & M 3 v Cutthorpe 3
Waleswood 2 v Mans & Pl 4
Woodsetts 3 v Milton 3

Sat 30 June
Anston 4 v Waleswood 2
Farnsfield 3 v Cutthorpe 3
Harthill 2 v Mansf HM 4

Mans & Pl 4 v Clumber Pk 4
Milton 3 v Edwinstowe 3
Notts & AA 4 v Rans & M 3

Sat 7 July
Edwinstowe 3 v Anston 4
Harthill 2 v Mans & Pl 4
Milton 3 v Mansf HM 4
Notts & AA 4 v Waleswood 2
Rans & M 3 v Clumber Pk 4
Woodsetts 3 v Farnsfield 3

Sat 14 July
Anston 4 v Farnsfield 3
Clumber Pk 4 v Woodsetts 3
Cutthorpe 3 v Edwinstowe 3
Mans & Pl 4 v Mansf HM 4
Milton 3 v Notts & AA 4
Waleswood 2 v Harthill 2

Sat 21 July
Anston 4 v Milton 3
Cutthorpe 3 v Mans & Pl 4
Mansf HM 4 v Edwinstowe 3
Notts & AA 4 v Farnsfield 3
Rans & M 3 v Harthill 2
Woodsetts 3 v Waleswood 2

Sat 28 July
Cutthorpe 3 v Rans & M 3
Farnsfield 3 v Mansf HM 4
Mans & Pl 4 v Anston 4
Milton 3 v Harthill 2
Waleswood 2 v Clumber Pk 4
Woodsetts 3 v Notts & AA 4

Sat 4 Aug
Anston 4 v Cutthorpe 3
Clumber Pk 4 v Farnsfield 3
Harthill 2 v Edwinstowe 3
Milton 3 v Mans & Pl 4
Waleswood 2 v Mansf HM 4
Woodsetts 3 v Rans & M 3

Sat 11 Aug
Clumber Pk 4 v Waleswood 2
Harthill 2 v Farnsfield 3
Mans & Pl 4 v Edwinstowe 3
Notts & AA 4 v Cutthorpe 3
Rans & M 3 v Anston 4
Woodsetts 3 v Mansf HM 4

Sat 18 Aug
Cutthorpe 3 v Woodsetts 3
Edwinstowe 3 v Waleswood 2
Farnsfield 3 v Milton 3
Mansf HM 4 v Harthill 2
Notts & AA 4 v Clumber Pk 4
Rans & M 3 v Mans & Pl 4

Sat 25 Aug
Clumber Pk 4 v Rans & M 3
Cutthorpe 3   v Milton 3
Harthill 2   v Anston 4
Notts & AA 4 v Mansf HM 4
Waleswood 2 v Farnsfield 3
Woodsetts 3   v Edwinstowe 3

Mon 27 Aug
Clumber Pk 4 v Harthill 2
Cutthorpe 3   v Mansf HM 4
Edwinstowe 3 v Farnsfield 3
Mans & Pl 4   v Woodsetts 3
Rans & M 3   v Notts & AA 4
Waleswood 2 v Milton 3

Sat 1 Sept
Clumber Pk 4 v Cutthorpe 3
Edwinstowe 3 v Rans & M 3
Farnsfield 3   v Notts & AA 4
Harthill 2   v Waleswood 2
Mansf HM 4   v Milton 3
Woodsetts 3   v Anston 4

Sat 8 Sept
Anston 4   v Clumber Pk 4
Edwinstowe 3 v Notts & AA 4
Farnsfield 3   v Rans & M 3
Harthill 2   v Milton 3
Mansf HM 4   v Mans & Pl 4
Waleswood 2 v Woodsetts 3

Sat 15 Sept
Milton 3   v Clumber Pk 4

2006 Newark Alliance League Tables

Division One

	P	W	L	T	NR	Pts
PCCC	18	11	3	0	4	52
Balderton	18	11	4	0	3	50
Calverton	18	10	4	0	4	48
Madni	18	8	6	0	4	40
Bracebridge Heath	18	8	7	0	3	38
Radcliffe-on-Trent	18	7	6	0	5	38
#Sleaford	18	6	8	0	4	31
Papplewick & Linby ?	18	6	9	0	3	28
##Collingham	18	4	11	0	3	20
#Southwell	18	1	14	0	3	9

Result sheet not received. -1 point deducted
? Fixture not fulfilled -2 points deducted

Division Two

	P	W	L	T	NR	Pts
Retford	18	11	2	0	5	54
#Gedling Colliery	18	10	5	0	3	45
##Kimberley	18	9	5	0	4	42
Ellerslie	18	8	6	0	4	40
##Attenborough ?	18	10	6	0	2	40
#Bottesford ?	18	7	8	0	3	31
Lenton	18	5	8	0	5	30
Boston	18	4	9	0	5	26
Caythorpe Lincs	18	4	11	0	3	22
##Notts & Arnold ??	18	3	11	0	4	14

Result sheet not received. -1 point deducted
? Fixture not fulfilled -2 points deducted

Division Three

	P	W	L	T	NR	Pts
#Caythorpe Notts	18	13	1	0	4	59
Thoresby Colliery ?	18	11	4	0	3	48
#Long Eaton	18	9	6	0	3	41
Radcliffe-on-Trent	18	7	6	1	4	39
East Drayton	18	7	7	1	3	37
Oxton	18	7	7	0	4	36
Fiskerton	18	6	9	0	3	30
Gotham ?	18	6	10	0	2	26
Clifton Village ?	18	5	10	0	3	24
Farndon ???	18	2	13	0	3	8

Result sheet not received. -1 point deducted
? Fixture not fulfilled -2 points deducted

Division Four

	P	W	L	T	NR	Pts
Larwood & Voce Mgs	16	12	3	0	1	50
Plumtree	16	10	3	0	3	46
#Gedling & S'wood ?	16	10	3	0	3	43
Thurgarton	16	8	5	0	3	38
#Newark	16	6	8	0	2	27
#Ransome & Marles	16	5	7	0	4	27
Nuthall	16	4	11	0	1	18
Welby	16	3	10	0	3	18
#Claypole	16	3	11	0	2	15

Result sheet not received. -1 point deducted
? Fixture not fulfilled -2 points deducted

Division Five

	P	W	L	T	NR	Pts
#Sherwood Casuals	18	10	3	0	5	49
PCCC ?	18	10	5	0	3	44
#Rolls Royce ?	18	10	5	0	3	43
#Clumber Park	18	8	6	0	4	39
Lambley	18	7	6	1	4	39
Gedling Colliery	18	6	9	1	2	31
Balderton	18	5	8	0	5	30
Ropsley ?	18	5	9	0	4	26
#Clifton Village ??	18	6	9	0	3	25
##Notts & Arnold	18	4	11	0	3	20

Result sheet not received. -1 point deducted
? Fixture not fulfilled -2 points deducted

Division Six

	P	W	L	T	NR	Pts
East Bridgford	16	11	2	0	3	50
#Wollaton	16	10	2	0	4	47
#Pakistan KCC	16	8	4	0	4	39
Beeston	16	7	6	0	3	34
Bingham	16	6	7	0	3	30
#Southwell ?	16	7	8	0	1	27
Ransome & Marles ?	16	4	8	0	4	22
Fiskerton	16	2	11	0	3	14
###Collingham ?	16	2	9	0	5	13

Result sheet not received. -1 point deducted
? Fixture not fulfilled -2 points deducted

Clubs and county benefit from top players' participation

by Ken Widdows

THE EVERARDS Leicestershire League is to continue with a scheme which they believe is unique in league cricket up and down the country. For the first time last season, they linked up with Leicestershire County Cricket Club, who allowed senior professionals to play at the grass roots. Players were allocated to clubs and when Leicestershire had no game, or players were returning from injury, or were dropped for lack of form, they turned out on a Saturday in the Everards League.

Club captain Jeremy Snape was allocated to Langtons, Darren Maddy and Marc Rosenberg to Leicester Banks, Asif Habib to Illston Abey, World Cup wicket-keeper Paul Nixon to Barrow Town, Stuart Broad, an England paceman of the future, to Loughborugh Town and all-rounder James Allenby to Leicester Ivanhoe.

The idea was to give the weaker clubs a chance of having an even playing field - and it worked exceptionally well. Maddy, who has now signed for Warwickshire, and Rosenberg both scored tons for Leicester Banks, Allenby was a big hit at Leicester Ivanhoe with bat and ball, and Paul Harrison became a big favourite at Stoughton & Thurnby.

League adminstrator Alan Lucas said: "We felt it was a big success and we are to continue doing it again this season. The only difference this season is that where clubs are allocated two players, they are only allowed to play one in any game. The scheme was to bolster the weaker teams and we feel it worked."

The players, too, enjoyed playing club cricket again. Allenby, for instance, said he loved playing for Ivanhoe and for Maddy it was a return to Leicester Banks, his former club before becoming a professional with

Leicestershire. It led to the most competitive Premier Division for many years, but it still didn't prevent Kibworth and Loughborough Town taking the top two places yet again.

Kibworth took the title for the fifth time in nine years, beating off the challenge of 2005 champs Loughborough, who won it three times in those nine years. The only team to break that stranglehold were Leicester Ivanhoe in 1999. But it wasn't a runaway win by any means.

Market Harborough, led by ex-Leicestershire all-rounder Laurie Potter, led the table early on. Loughborough then took over and Kibwoerth dropped to sixth at one stage. But they had a tremendous run-in, winning seven games in succession to pip Loughborough by seven points, with Harborough third 20 points adrift.

It proved to be a magnificent season for Kibworth, the Cockspur National KO winners in 2004, all round. Not only did they win the Premier Division title but their second team ran away with the second division title to become the only club in the history of the league to have teams in the top two tiers next season. The third team also won promotion from division nine of the Northamptonshire County League and the first team added the icing on the cake by winning the inaguaral Leicestershire 20s trophy.

It was fitting that Kibworth took the honours on their new ground, which is situated next to their old one which is earmarked for housing. The new ground, however, boasts a giant pavilion which would be the envy of most clubs in the country and has two playing areas, one for the first team and another for juniors.

Skipper Mike Sutliff said: "The club has spent the last 10 years really anxious to move forward. This year we have had our first season at the new ground and the club has always looked to have a strong junior section. Now we have an outstanding crop of youngsters, five or six under 17 who have played in the first team. With the succcess we have had, it has been a fantastic season."

The Leicestershire 20s competition also proved to be a big success. Based on the national Twenty20 competition, the Premier Division was split into four groups of three teams with the winners going forward to the semi-finals and finals day. Kibworth came out on top, beating

Hinckley Town in the final, but everyone agreed that the concept was good, although in its first season, it was a bit hit and miss with the clubs having to organise their fixtures, fitting them in whenever they could.

Stoughton & Thurnby had the best idea, organising their three games on one Sunday, making it a family day out for the whole village, with a barbecue, bouncy castle and, of course, a bar! Skipper Jim Ardley said: "Takings were very good and we had hundreds of people turn up for the day. We'll definitely do it again this season." It is be hoped it will be better organisded by the league this season because the players enjoyed it, it made the clubs money over the bar and it drew in more spectators.

While the Leicestershire 20s was based on fun, the Premier Division title race was anything but, not surprising with the amount of talent within its ranks. There are many ex-pros sprinkled through the league, although most clubs are now looking to give youngsters the chance of playing at a higher level. Kibworth, for instance, did not rely solely on their experienced players. They played five teenagers at various stages of the season, as did Loughborough, and their top two placings suggests the crop of youngsters coming through in Leicestershire augurs well for the future. In all, there are seven divisions of the Everards League, boasting 84 teams.

Kibworth's Nick Ferraby won the batting averages with 683 runs at 68.3, followed by Leicester Banks' Andy Jackman with 255 at 51.00 and Habib of Illston Abey with 501 at 50.1. Potter won the bowling averages with 41 wickets at 11.41, followeed by 16-year-old left-arm seamer Colin Griggs of Kibworth with 28 wickets at 12.42 and Paul Fisher of Loughborough with 21 wickets at 15.14.

There are two other leagues in the county, the **Leicestershire League** and the **Leicestershire Senior League**, and while not up to the standard of the Everards League, boast some talented cricketers. The Leicestershire League was won by Maher Stars, with Highfield Rangers in second place, 15 points behind. The Senior League was won by Birstall Village.

2006 Everards Leicestershire League Tables

PREMIER DIVISION

	P	W	D	L	A	PTS
KIBWORTH	22	12	5	3	2	375
LOUGHBOROUGH TOWN	22	14	2	5	1	368
ILSTON ABEY	22	12	4	3	3	355
MARKET HARBOROUGH	22	12	3	4	3	355
LEICESTER IVANHOE	22	8	3	8	3	314
LEICESTER BANKS	22	7	5	8	2	289
HINCKLEY TOWN	22	6	5	9	2	259
LUTTERWORTH	22	6	4	10	2	258
SYSTON TOWN	22	5	7	9	1	253
STOUGHTON & THURNBY	22	5	5	10	2	235
BARROW	22	4	9	9	0	186
LANGTONS	22	3	2	16	1	177

DIVISION 1

	P	W	D	L	A	PTS
SILEBY TOWN	22	12	5	5	0	361
ASHBY HASTINGS	22	11	4	6	1	353
BARWELL	22	9	6	5	2	316
EARL SHILTON	22	9	7	3	3	303
COUNTESTHORPE	22	6	7	8	1	300
KEGWORTH TOWN	22	9	3	9	1	297
BITTESWELL	22	7	5	7	3	271
BROOMLEYS	22	6	5	10	1	271
IBSTOCK TOWN	22	5	6	10	1	263
RATBY TOWN	22	8	2	10	2	251
BILLESDON	22	5	4	11	2	243
NEWTOWN LINFORD	22	6	4	9	3	238

Leicestershire

DIVISION 2

	P	W	D	L	A	PTS
KIBWORTH 2	22	11	7	2	2	348
QUORN	22	9	7	5	1	322
NARBORO' & L'THORPE	22	8	10	3	1	317
SHEPSHED MESSENGERS	22	7	9	4	2	313
GRACEDIEU PARK	22	7	7	7	1	297
LEICESTER IVANHOE 2	22	5	9	6	2	277
SHEPSHED TOWN	22	6	7	8	1	275
L'BORO COB	22	4	10	8	0	255
EGERTON PARK	22	6	7	7	2	245
L'BRO TOWN 2	22	4	11	6	1	233
MARKET HARBOROUGH 2	22	5	6	8	3	230
BARDON HILL	22	2	8	10	2	181

DIVISION 3

	P	W	D	L	A	PTS
THORPE ARNOLD	22	10	7	2	3	367
CROPSTON	22	10	7	3	2	357
DUNTON BASSETT	22	8	6	4	4	303
IBSTOCK 2	22	7	9	4	2	283
L'BRO GREENFIELDS	22	8	5	7	2	282
COSBY	22	5	7	7	3	264
KIRBY MUXLOE	22	6	7	6	3	261
ROTHLEY PARK	22	7	6	7	2	255
ELECTRICITY SPORTS	22	7	3	9	3	245
SYSTON TOWN 2	22	6	5	8	3	242
MARKET BOSWORTH	22	4	5	11	2	229
MELTON MOWBRAY	22	3	3	13	3	180

DIVISION 4

	P	W	D	L	A	PTS
HINCKLEY AMATEUR	22	10	9	1	2	347
LUTTERWORTH 2	22	9	8	2	3	335
MOUNTSORREL CASTLE	22	9	7	5	1	318
S'TON & THURNBY 2	22	10	4	6	2	314
COUNTESTHORPE 2	22	6	9	5	2	297
BARKBY UNITED	22	5	9	6	2	296
L'BORO' OUTWOODS	22	8	5	8	1	282
LEICESTER BANKS 2	22	3	10	6	3	252
ENDERBY	22	4	8	8	2	242
BARROW 2	22	6	6	9	1	237
ILLSTON ABEY 2	22	5	7	7	3	236
BROOMLEYS 2	22	2	4	14	2	142

DIVISION 5

	P	W	D	L	A	PTS
SILEBY TOWN 2	22	7	13	1	1	379
KEGWORTH TOWN 2	22	11	8	2	1	357
QUORN 2	22	10	10	2	0	354
SHEPSHED TOWN 2	22	8	6	5	3	302
ASHBY HASTINGS 2	22	9	4	6	3	282
LANGTONS 2	22	5	11	4	2	263
CROFT	22	6	7	5	4	259
NARBORO & LTTLETH'PE 2	22	6	6	8	2	245
EARL SHILTON TOWN 2	22	4	5	11	2	234
BARWELL 2	22	5	5	10	2	228
BILLESDON 2	22	2	6	11	3	169
NEWTOWN LINFORD 2	22	1	9	9	3	165

DIVISION 6

	P	W	D	L	A	PTS
THORPE ARNOLD 2	22	11	8	2	1	383
HINCKLEY TOWN 2	22	12	5	2	3	357
L'BRO CARILLON OB 2	22	8	3	7	4	281
BARKBY UNITED 2	22	6	9	5	2	279
COSBY 2	22	5	9	5	3	279
ELECTRICITY SPORTS 2	22	6	5	8	3	264
CROPSTON 2	22	5	3	10	4	247
RATBY TOWN 2	22	5	6	9	2	247
BITTESWELL 2	22	4	10	5	3	246
MARKET BOSWORTH 2	22	8	6	6	2	242
ENDERBY 2	22	4	7	9	2	214
KIRBY MUXLOE 2	22	5	5	11	1	198

DIVISION 7

	P	W	D	L	A	PTS
HINCKLEY AMATEUR 2	22	15	4	3	0	413
EGERTON PARK 2	22	12	5	3	2	375
SHEPSHED M'GERS 2	22	13	3	3	3	363
DUNTON BASSETT 2	22	8	7	4	3	309
MOUNTSORREL CASTLE 2	22	7	3	9	3	253
ROTHLEY PARK 2	22	7	7	7	1	251
BARDON HILL 2	22	7	3	12	0	245
CROFT 2	22	7	4	8	3	233
GRACEDIEU PARK 2	22	5	6	9	2	229
L'BRO GREENFIELDS 2	22	5	2	12	3	208
MELTON MOWBRAY 2	22	4	5	12	1	186
LOUGH. OUTWOODS 2	22	4	5	12	1	171

2006 Everards Leicestershire League Averages

BATTING (Qualification 10 inns, 200 runs):

Premier Division

		Inns	N.O.	Runs	Ave
N. Ferraby	Kibworth	14	4	683	68.30
A. Jackman	Leicester Banks	10	5	255	51.00
A. Habib	Ilston Abbey	16	6	501	50.10
B. Jonas	St'ton & Thurnby	14	2	538	44.83
M. Craven	Hinckley Town	20	1	840	44.21
S. Perera	Ilston Abbey	15	3	502	41.83

Division 1

		Inns	N.O.	Runs	Ave
T. Higgins	Earl Shilton Town	18	2	947	59.18
D. Bulpitt	Newtown Linford	10	1	526	58.44
R. Moorhouse	Kegworth Town	21	6	864	57.60
D. Miller	Bitteswell	18	3	797	53.13

Division 2

		Inns	N.O.	Runs	Ave
N. Shafiq	Gracedieu Park	11	2	484	53.77
S. Bailey	Loughborough COB	19	2	856	50.35
M. Buck	Gracedieu Park	19	1	890	49.44
B. Robertson	Egerton Park	19	4	731	48.73

Division 3

		Inns	N.O.	Runs	Ave
P. Stockdale	Lough. Greenfield	20	5	892	59.46
M. Pickering	Dunton Bassett	16	3	722	55.53
P. Humphries	Thorpe Arnold	14	1	712	54.76
C. Pole	Cropston	16	5	556	50.54
K. Geary	Cropston	14	3	556	50.54

Division 4

		Inns	N.O.	Runs	Ave
T. Watts	Barrow Town 2	15	6	513	57.00
H. Horsley	Hinckley Ams	20	6	673	48.07
M. Ray	Hinckley Ams	15	1	648	46.28
R. Marshall	Enderby	13	2	504	45.81

Division 5

		Inns	N.O.	Runs	Ave
C. Grimes	Croft	10	5	612	122.40
M. Cobley	Earl Shilton T 2	17	4	875	67.30
J. Willett	Sileby Town 2	15	4	731	66.45
G. Blades	Quorn 2	17	4	827	63.61

Division 6

		Inns	N.O.	Runs	Ave
S. Ward	Cropston 2	10	5	431	86.20
G. Fox	Bitteswell 2	16	6	637	70.77
D. Wilson	Hinckley Town 2	13	2	594	54.00
J. Vann	Enderby 2	19	5	681	48.64

Division 7

		Inns	N.O.	Runs	Ave
G. Tyler	Egerton Park 2	13	6	797	113.85
M. Geary	Gracedieu Park 2	11	1	521	52.10
P. Oliver	Shepshed Mess 2	14	2	613	51.08
W. Spencer	Hinckley Ams 2	21	9	563	46.91

BOWLING (Qualification 20 wickets):

Premier Division

		Ovs	Runs	Wkts	Ave
L. Potter	Market Harb.	183.5	468	41	11.41
C. Griggs	Kibworth	105	348	28	12.42
P. Fisher	Loughborough T	120.1	318	21	15.14
M. Gidley	Loughborough T	85.2	313	20	15.65
S. Renshaw	Kibworth	166	594	35	16.97
I. Fraser	Syston Town	102	387	22	17.59

Division 1

		Ovs	Runs	Wkts	Ave
M. Ryan	Ashby Hastings	283.3	890	73	12.19
M. Wade	Kegworth Town	132	329	22	14.95
L. Copson	Ratby Town	226.5	731	42	17.40
M. Ellis	Sileby Town	139.2	598	34	17.58

Division 2

		Ovs	Runs	Wkts	Ave
R. Cross	Shepshed Town	120	394	30	13.13
D. Broughton	Kibworth 2	159.3	447	31	14.41
S. Bird	L'borough COB	122	508	30	16.93
M. Parnham	Egerton Park	184.4	759	42	18.07

Division 3

		Ovs	Runs	Wkts	Ave
B. Aspell	Rothley Park	63.4	228	20	11.40
A. Benyon	Syston Town 2	150	502	40	12.55
C. Pole	Cropston	189	705	45	15.66
D. Perry	Elec. Sports	136.2	451	27	16.70

Leicestershire

Division 4

		Ovs	Runs	Wkts	Ave
M. Snow	Hinckley Ams	63.5	232	20	11.60
M. Baxter	Lutterworth 2	78	253	20	12.65
D. Baxter	Lutterworth 2	77.2	345	22	15.68
A. Harrison	Hinckley Ams	220.4	867	54	16.05

Division 5

		Ovs	Runs	Wkts	Ave
L. Wilson	Langtons 2	135	519	36	14.41
R. Hands	Sileby Town 2	221.2	703	45	15.62
J. Martin	Quorn 2	277.2	1045	66	15.83
G. Isaac	Kegworth T 2	208.4	762	48	15.87

Division 6

		Ovs	Runs	Wkts	Ave
G. Bateman	Bitteswell 2	171.3	541	35	15.45
D. Clarke	Cosby 2	220.2	669	34	19.67
B. Long	Bitteswello 2	199	742	37	20.05
H. Desai	Hinckley T 2	227.4	838	40	20.95

Division 7

		Ovs	Runs	Wkts	Ave
L. Rastall	Hinckley Ams 2	95	262	25	10.48
M. Butcher	Dunton Bass. 2	139.2	382	35	10.91
G. Bennett	Shep. Mess. 2	127.1	466	35	13.31
J. Cook	Shep. Mess. 2	202.3	798	53	15.05

2007 Everards Leicestershire League Fixtures

Premier Division

Sat 28 April
Leic. Ivan.   vHinckley Town
Ashby Hast.   vKibworth
Lough. Town   vLutterworth
Sileby Town   vIllston Abey
S'ton & ThurnvLeic. Banks
Market Harb. vSyston Town

Sat 5 May
Hinckley TownvAshby Hast.
Syston Town   vLeic. Ivan.
Kibworth   vLough. Town
Lutterworth   vSileby Town
Illston Abey   vS'ton & Thurn
Leic. Banks   vMarket Harb.

Sat 12 May
Lough. Town   vHinckley Town
Ashby Hast.   vLeic. Ivan.
Sileby Town   vKibworth
S'ton & ThurnvLutterworth
Market Harb. vIllston Abey
Leic. Banks   vSyston Town

Sat 19 May
Hinckley TownvSileby Town
Leic. Ivan.   vLough. Town
Syston Town   vAshby Hast.
Kibworth   vS'ton & Thurn
Lutterworth   vMarket Harb.
Illston Abey   vLeic. Banks

Sat 26 May
S'ton & ThurnvHinckley Town
Sileby Town   vLeic. Ivan.
Lough. Town   vAshby Hast.
Market Harb. vKibworth
Leic. Banks   vLutterworth
Illston Abey   vSyston Town

Sat 2 June
Hinckley TownvMarket Harb.
Leic. Ivan.   vS'ton & Thurn
Ashby Hast.   vSileby Town
Syston Town   vLough. Town
Kibworth   vLeic. Banks
Lutterworth   vIllston Abey

Sat 9 June
Leic. Banks   vHinckley Town
Market Harb. vLeic. Ivan.
S'ton & ThurnvAshby Hast.
Sileby Town   vLough. Town
Illston Abey   vKibworth
Lutterworth   vSyston Town

Sat 16 June
Hinckley TownvIllston Abey
Leic. Ivan.   vLeic. Banks
Ashby Hast.   vMarket Harb.
Lough. Town   vS'ton & Thurn
Syston Town   vSileby Town
Kibworth   vLutterworth

Sat 23 June
Lutterworth   vHinckley Town
Illston Abey   vLeic. Ivan.
Leic. Banks   vAshby Hast.
Market Harb. vLough. Town
S'ton & ThurnvSileby Town
Kibworth   vSyston Town

Sun 24 June
Hinckley TownvKibworth
Leic. Ivan.   vLutterworth
Ashby Hast.   vIllston Abey
Lough. Town   vLeic. Banks
Sileby Town   vMarket Harb.
Syston Town   vS'ton & Thurn

Sat 30 June
Syston Town   vHinckley Town
Kibworth   vLeic. Ivan.
Lutterworth   vAshby Hast.
Illston Abey   vLough. Town
Leic. Banks   vSileby Town
Market Harb. vS'ton & Thurn

Sat 7 July
Hinckley TownvLeic. Ivan.
Kibworth   vAshby Hast.
Lutterworth   vLough. Town
Illston Abey   vSileby Town
Leic. Banks   vS'ton & Thurn
Syston Town   vMarket Harb.

Sat 14 July
Ashby Hast.   vHinckley Town
Leic. Ivan.   vSyston Town
Lough. Town   vKibworth
Sileby Town   vLutterworth
S'ton & ThurnvIllston Abey
Market Harb. vLeic. Banks

Sat 21 July
Hinckley TownvLough. Town
Leic. Ivan.   vAshby Hast.
Kibworth   vSileby Town
Lutterworth   vS'ton & Thurn
Illston Abey   vMarket Harb.
Syston Town   vLeic. Banks

Sat 28 July
Sileby Town   vHinckley Town
Lough. Town   vLeic. Ivan.
Ashby Hast.   vSyston Town
S'ton & ThurnvKibworth
Market Harb. vLutterworth
Leic. Banks   vIllston Abey

Sat 4 Aug
Hinckley TownvS'ton & Thurn
Leic. Ivan.   vSileby Town
Ashby Hast.   vLough. Town
Kibworth   vMarket Harb.
Lutterworth   vLeic. Banks
Syston Town   vIllston Abey

Sat 11 Aug
Market Harb. vHinckley Town
S'ton & ThurnvLeic. Ivan.
Sileby Town   vAshby Hast.
Lough. Town   vSyston Town
Leic. Banks   vKibworth
Illston Abey   vLutterworth

Sat 18 Aug
Hinckley TownvLeic. Banks
Leic. Ivan.   vMarket Harb.
Ashby Hast.   vS'ton & Thurn
Lough. Town   vSileby Town
Kibworth   vIllston Abey
Syston Town   vLutterworth

Sat 25 Aug
Illston Abey   vHinckley Town
Leic. Banks   vLeic. Ivan.
Market Harb. vAshby Hast.
S'ton & ThurnvLough. Town
Sileby Town   vSyston Town
Lutterworth   vKibworth

Sat 1 Sept
Hinckley TownvLutterworth
Leic. Ivan.   vIllston Abey
Ashby Hast.   vLeic. Banks
Lough. Town   vMarket Harb.
Sileby Town   vS'ton & Thurn
Syston Town   vKibworth

Sat 8 Sept
Kibworth   v Hinckley Town
Lutterworth   vLeic. Ivan.
Illston Abey   vAshby Hast.
Leic. Banks   vLough. Town
Market Harb. vSileby Town
S'ton & ThurnvSyston Town

Leicestershire

Sat 15 Sept
Hinckley TownvSyston Town
Leic. Ivan.   vKibworth
Ashby Hast.   vLutterworth
Lough. Town   vIllston Abey
Sileby Town   vLeic. Banks
S'ton & ThurnvMarket Harb.

Division One

Sat 28 April
Earl Shilton T vIbstock Town
Coun'thorpe   vKegworth T.
Quorn   vLangtons
Kibworth II   vBarrow Town
Ratby Town   vBarwell
Broomleys   vBitteswell

Sat 5 May
Ibstock Town vCoun'thorpe
Bitteswell   vEarl Shilton T.
Kegworth T.   vQuorn
Langtons   vKibworth II
Barrow Town   vRatby Town
Barwell   vBroomleys

Sat 12 May
Quorn   vIbstock Town
Coun'thorpe   vEarl Shilton T.
Kibworth II   vKegworth T.
Ratby Town   vLangtons
Broomleys   vBarrow Town
Barwell   vBitteswell

Sat 19 May
Ibstock Town vKibworth II
Earl Shilton T.vQuorn
Bitteswell   vCoun'thorpe
Kegworth T.   vRatby Town
Langtons   vBroomleys
Barrow Town   vBarwell

Sat 26 May
Ratby Town   vIbstock Town
Kibworth II   vEarl Shilton T.
Quorn   vCoun'thorpe
Broomleys   vKegworth T.
Barwell   vLangtons
Barrow Town   vBitteswell

Sat 2 June
Ibstock Town vBroomleys
Earl Shilton T.vRatby Town
Coun'thorpe   vKibworth II
Bitteswell   vQuorn
Kegworth T.   vBarwell
Langtons   vBarrow Town

Sat 9 June
Barwell   vIbstock Town
Broomleys   vEarl Shilton T.

Ratby Town   vCoun'thorpe
Kibworth II   vQuorn
Barrow Town   vKegworth T.
Langtons   vBitteswell

Sat 16 June
Ibstock Town vBarrow Town
Earl Shilton T.vBarwell
Coun'thorpe   vBroomleys
Quorn   vRatby Town
Bitteswell   vKibworth II
Kegworth T.   vLangtons

Sat 23 June
Langtons   vIbstock Town
Barrow Town   vEarl Shilton T.
Barwell   vCoun'thorpe
Broomleys   vQuorn
Ratby Town   vKibworth II
Kegworth T.   vBitteswell

Sun 24 June
Ibstock Town vKegworth T.
Earl Shilton T.vLangtons
Coun'thorpe   vBarrow Town
Quorn   vBarwell
Kibworth II   vBroomleys
Bitteswell   vRatby Town

Sat 30 June
Bitteswell   vIbstock Town
Kegworth T.   vEarl Shilton T.
Langtons   vCoun'thorpe
Barrow Town   vQuorn
Barwell   vKibworth II
Broomleys   vRatby Town

Sat 7 July
Ibstock Town vEarl Shilton T
Kegworth T.   vCoun'thorpe
Langtons   vQuorn
Barrow Town   vKibworth II
Barwell   vRatby Town
Bitteswell   vBroomleys

Sat 14 July
Coun'thorpe   vIbstock Town
Earl Shilton T.vBitteswell
Quorn   vKegworth T.
Kibworth II   vLangtons
Ratby Town   vBarrow Town
Broomleys   vBarwell

Sat 21 July
Ibstock Town vQuorn
Earl Shilton T.vCoun'thorpe
Kegworth T.   vKibworth II
Langtons   vRatby Town
Barrow Town   vBroomleys
Bitteswell   vBarwell

Sat 28 July
Kibworth II   vIbstock Town
Quorn   vEarl Shilton T.
Coun'thorpe   vBitteswell
Ratby Town   vKegworth T.
Broomleys   vLangtons
Barwell   vBarrow Town

Sat 4 Aug   v
Ibstock Town vRatby Town
Earl Shilton T.vKibworth II
Coun'thorpe   vQuorn
Kegworth T.   vBroomleys
Langtons   vBarwell
Bitteswell   vBarrow Town

Sat 11 Aug
Broomleys   vIbstock Town
Ratby Town   vEarl Shilton T.
Kibworth II   vCoun'thorpe
Quorn   vBitteswell
Barwell   vKegworth T.
Barrow Town vLangtons

Sat 18 Aug
Ibstock Town vBarwell
Earl Shilton T.vBroomleys
Coun'thorpe   vRatby Town
Quorn   vKibworth II
Kegworth T.   vBarrow Town
Bitteswell   vLangtons

Sat 25 Aug
Barrow Town vIbstock Town
Barwell   vEarl Shilton T.
Broomleys   vCoun'thorpe
Ratby Town   vQuorn
Kibworth II   vBitteswell
Langtons   vKegworth T.

Sat 1 Sept
Ibstock Town vLangtons
Earl Shilton T.vBarrow Town
Coun'thorpe   vBarwell
Quorn   vBroomleys
Kibworth II   vRatby Town
Bitteswell   vKegworth T.

Sat 8 Sept
Kegworth T.   vIbstock Town
Langtons   vEarl Shilton T.
Barrow Town vCoun'thorpe
Barwell   vQuorn
Broomleys   vKibworth II
Ratby Town   vBitteswell

Sat 15 Sept
Ibstock Town vBitteswell
Earl Shilton T.vKegworth T.

Coun'thorpe   vLangtons
Quorn   vBarrow Town
Kibworth II   vBarwell
Ratby Town   vBroomleys

Division Two

Sat 28 April
Billesdon   vNewtown Lin
Cropston   vNarb. & Little.
Shepshed M.   vLough. T. II
Egerton Park vLough. COB
Shepshed T.   vLeic. Ivan. II
Gracedieu Pk.vThorpe Arnold

Sat 5 May
Newtown Lin vCropston
Thorpe ArnoldvBillesdon
Narb. & Little.vShepshed M.
Lough. T. II vEgerton Park
Lough. COB   vShepshed T.
Leic. Ivan. II vGracedieu Pk.

Sat 12 May
Shepshed M. vNewtown Lin
Cropston   vBillesdon
Egerton Park vNarb. & Little.
Shepshed T.   vLough. T. II
Gracedieu Pk.vLough. COB
Leic. Ivan. II vThorpe Arnold

Sat 19 May
Newtown Lin vEgerton Park
Billesdon   vShepshed M.
Thorpe ArnoldvCropston
Narb. & Little.vShepshed T.
Lough. T. II vGracedieu Pk.
Lough. COB   vLeic. Ivan. II

Sat 26 May
Shepshed T. vNewtown Lin
Egerton Park vBillesdon
Shepshed M. vCropston
Gracedieu Pk.vNarb. & Little.
Leic. Ivan. II vLough. T. II
Lough. COB   vThorpe Arnold

Sat 2 June
Newtown Lin vGracedieu Pk.
Billesdon   vShepshed T.
Cropston   vEgerton Park
Thorpe ArnoldvShepshed M.
Narb. & Little.vLeic. Ivan. II
Lough. T. II vLough. COB

Sat 9 June
Leic. Ivan. II vNewtown Lin
Gracedieu Pk.vBillesdon
Shepshed T.   vCropston
Egerton Park vShepshed M.

Lough. COB   vNarb. & Little.
Lough. T. II vThorpe Arnold

Sat 16 June
Newtown Lin vLough. COB
Billesdon   vLeic. Ivan. II
Cropston   vGracedieu Pk.
Shepshed M. vShepshed T.
Thorpe ArnoldvEgerton Park
Narb. & Little.vLough. T. II

Sat 23 June
Lough. T. II vNewtown Lin
Lough. COB   vBillesdon
Leic. Ivan. II vCropston
Gracedieu Pk.vShepshed M.
Shepshed T.   vEgerton Park
Narb. & Little.vThorpe Arnold

Sun 24 June
Newtown Lin vNarb. & Little.
Billesdon   vLough. T. II
Cropston   vLough. COB
Shepshed M. vLeic. Ivan. II
Egerton Park vGracedieu Pk.
Thorpe ArnoldvShepshed T.

Sat 30 June
Thorpe ArnoldvNewtown Lin
Narb. & Little.vBillesdon
Lough. T. II vCropston
Lough. COB   vShepshed M.
Leic. Ivan. II vEgerton Park
Gracedieu Pk.vShepshed T.

Sat 7 July
Newtown Lin vBillesdon
Narb. & Little.vCropston
Lough. T. II vShepshed M.
Lough. COB   vEgerton Park
Leic. Ivan. II vShepshed T.
Thorpe ArnoldvGracedieu Pk.

Sat 14 July
Cropston   vNewtown Lin
Billesdon   vThorpe Arnold
Shepshed M. vNarb. & Little.
Egerton Park vLough. T. II
Shepshed T.   vLough. COB
Gracedieu Pk.vLeic. Ivan. II

Sat 21 July
Newtown Lin vShepshed M.
Billesdon   vCropston
Narb. & Little.vEgerton Park
Lough. T. II vShepshed T.
Lough. COB   vGracedieu Pk.
Thorpe ArnoldvLeic. Ivan. II

Sat 28 July
Egerton Park vNewtown Lin
Shepshed M. vBillesdon
Cropston   vThorpe Arnold
Shepshed T.   vNarb. & Little.
Gracedieu Pk.vLough. T. II
Leic. Ivan. II vLough. COB

Sat 4 Aug   Sat 26 May
Newtown Lin vShepshed T.
Billesdon   vEgerton Park
Cropston   vShepshed M.
Narb. & Little.vGracedieu Pk.
Lough. T. II vLeic. Ivan. II
Thorpe ArnoldvLough. COB

Sat 11 Aug
Gracedieu Pk.vNewtown Lin
Shepshed T.   vBillesdon
Egerton Park vCropston
Shepshed M. vThorpe Arnold
Leic. Ivan. II vNarb. & Little.
Lough. COB   vLough. T. II

Sat 18 Aug
Newtown Lin vLeic. Ivan. II
Billesdon   vGracedieu Pk.
Cropston   vShepshed T.
Shepshed M. vEgerton Park
Narb. & Little.vLough. COB
Thorpe ArnoldvLough. T. II

Sat 25 Aug
Lough. COB   vNewtown Lin
Leic. Ivan. II vBillesdon
Gracedieu Pk.vCropston
Shepshed T.   vShepshed M.
Egerton Park vThorpe Arnold
Lough. T. II vNarb. & Little.

Sat 1 Sept
Newtown Lin vLough. T. II
Billesdon   vLough. COB
Cropston   vLeic. Ivan. II
Shepshed M. vGracedieu Pk.
Egerton Park vShepshed T.
Thorpe ArnoldvNarb. & Little.

Sat 8 Sept
Narb. & Little.vNewtown Lin
Lough. T. II vBillesdon
Lough. COB   vCropston
Leic. Ivan. II vShepshed M.
Gracedieu Pk.vEgerton Park
Shepshed T.   vThorpe Arnold

Sat 15 Sept
Newtown Lin vThorpe Arnold
Billesdon   vNarb. & Little.
Cropston   vLough. T. II

Shepshed M. vLough. COB
Egerton Park vLeic. Ivan. II
Shepshed T. vGracedieu Pk.

Division Three

Sat 28 April
Kirby Muxloe v Market H. II
Rothley Park v Hinckley Amat.
Lutterworth II v Elec. Sports
Bardon Hill   v Dunton Bass.
Syston T. II   v Cosby
Ibstock T. II   v Lough. Green.

Sat 28 April
Kirby Muxloe vMarket H. II
Rothley Park vHinckley Ams
Lutterworth IIvElec. Sports
Bardon Hill   vDunton Bass.
Syston T. II   vCosby
Ibstock T. II vLough. Green.

Sat 5 May
Market H. II vRothley Park
Lough. Green.vKirby Muxloe
Hinckley Ams vLutterworth II
Elec. Sports vBardon Hill
Dunton Bass. vSyston T. II
Cosby   vIbstock T. II

Sat 12 May
Lutterworth IIvMarket H. II
Rothley Park vKirby Muxloe
Bardon Hill   vHinckley Ams
Syston T. II   vElec. Sports
Ibstock T. II vDunton Bass.
Cosby   vLough. Green.

Sat 19 May
Market H. II vBardon Hill
Kirby Muxloe vLutterworth II
Lough. Green.vRothley Park
Hinckley Ams vSyston T. II
Elec. Sports vIbstock T. II
Dunton Bass. vCosby

Sat 26 May
Syston T. II   vMarket H. II
Bardon Hill   vKirby Muxloe
Lutterworth IIvRothley Park
Ibstock T. II vHinckley Ams
Cosby   vElec. Sports
Dunton Bass. vLough. Green.

Sat 2 June
Market H. II vIbstock T. II
Kirby Muxloe vSyston T. II
Rothley Park vBardon Hill
Lough. Green.vLutterworth II

Hinckley Ams vCosby
Elec. Sports vDunton Bass.

Sat 9 June
Cosby   vMarket H. II
Ibstock T. II vKirby Muxloe
Syston T. II   vRothley Park
Bardon Hill   vLutterworth II
Dunton Bass. vHinckley Ams
Elec. Sports vLough. Green.

Sat 16 June
Market H. II vDunton Bass.
Kirby Muxloe vCosby
Rothley Park vIbstock T. II
Lutterworth IIvSyston T. II
Lough. Green.vBardon Hill
Hinckley Ams vElec. Sports

Sat 23 June
Elec. Sports vMarket H. II
Dunton Bass. vKirby Muxloe
Cosby   vRothley Park
Ibstock T. II vLutterworth II
Syston T. II   vBardon Hill
Hinckley Ams vLough. Green.

Sun 24 June
Market H. II vHinckley Ams
Kirby Muxloe vElec. Sports
Rothley Park vDunton Bass.
Lutterworth IIvCosby
Bardon Hill   vIbstock T. II
Lough. Green.vSyston T. II

Sat 30 June
Lough. Green.vMarket H. II
Hinckley Ams vKirby Muxloe
Elec. Sports vRothley Park
Dunton Bass. vLutterworth II
Cosby   vBardon Hill
Ibstock T. II vSyston T. II

Sat 7 July
Market H. II vKirby Muxloe
Hinckley Ams vRothley Park
Elec. Sports vLutterworth II
Dunton Bass. vBardon Hill
Cosby   vSyston T. II
Lough. Green.vIbstock T. II

Sat 14 July
Rothley Park vMarket H. II
Kirby Muxloe vLough. Green.
Lutterworth IIvHinckley Ams
Bardon Hill   vElec. Sports
Syston T. II   vDunton Bass.
Ibstock T. II vCosby

Sat 21 July
Market H. II vLutterworth II
Kirby Muxloe vRothley Park
Hinckley Ams vBardon Hill
Elec. Sports vSyston T. II
Dunton Bass. vIbstock T. II
Lough. Green.vCosby

Sat 28 July
Bardon Hill   vMarket H. II
Lutterworth IIvKirby Muxloe
Rothley Park vLough. Green.
Syston T. II   vHinckley Ams
Ibstock T. II vElec. Sports
Cosby   vDunton Bass.

Sat 4 Aug
Market H. II vSyston T. II
Kirby Muxloe vBardon Hill
Rothley Park vLutterworth II
Hinckley Ams vIbstock T. II
Elec. Sports vCosby
Lough. Green.vDunton Bass.

Sat 11 Aug
Ibstock T. II vMarket H. II
Syston T. II   vKirby Muxloe
Bardon Hill   vRothley Park
Lutterworth IIvLough. Green.
Cosby   vHinckley Ams
Dunton Bass. vElec. Sports

Sat 18 Aug
Market H. II vCosby
Kirby Muxloe vIbstock T. II
Rothley Park vSyston T. II
Lutterworth IIvBardon Hill
Hinckley Ams vDunton Bass.
Lough. Green.vElec. Sports

Sat 25 Aug
Dunton Bass. vMarket H. II
Cosby   vKirby Muxloe
Ibstock T. II vRothley Park
Syston T. II   vLutterworth II
Bardon Hill   vLough. Green.
Elec. Sports vHinckley Ams

Sat 1 Sept
Market H. II vElec. Sports
Kirby Muxloe vDunton Bass.
Rothley Park vCosby
Lutterworth IIvIbstock T. II
Bardon Hill   vSyston T. II
Lough. Green.vHinckley Ams

Sat 8 Sept
Hinckley Ams vMarket H. II
Elec. Sports vKirby Muxloe
Dunton Bass. vRothley Park

Cosby   vLutterworth II
Ibstock T. II vBardon Hill
Syston T. II   vLough. Green.

Sat 15 Sept
Market H. II vLough. Green.
Kirby Muxloe vHinckley Ams
Rothley Park vElec. Sports
Lutterworth IIvDunton Bass.
Bardon Hill   vCosby
Syston T. II   vIbstock T. II

The Leicestershire Senior League Final Tables 2006

V-SPORTS PREMIER DIVISION

	P	W	D	L	NR	Pts
Birstall Village	18	11	4	3	0	324
Leicester Caribbeans	18	7	4	4	3	259
Newbold Verdon	18	7	3	5	3	259
Woodhouse Eaves	18	7	2	7	2	254
Leicester Ivanhoe	18	5	5	7	1	215
Huncote	18	5	2	8	3	213
Hathern Old	18	6	0	9	3	210
Wigston Town	18	4	5	6	4	206
Sharnford	18	5	2	7	4	199
Hinckley	18	7	2	8	1	183

FIRST DIVISION

	P	W	D	L	NR	Pts
Twycross	18	11	1	2	4	324
Bharat Sports	18	9	3	3	3	288
Westonians	18	8	2	6	2	277
Burton on the Wolds	18	5	6	2	5	211
Stoke Golding	18	4	4	7	3	201
Walton le Wolds	18	5	2	7	4	197
Broughton Astley	18	4	3	8	3	195
Leicester Caribbeans 2nd	18	4	5	3	6	185
Birstall Village 2nd	18	4	1	10	3	162
Leicester Taverners	18	2	3	8	5	148

SECOND DIVISION

	P	W	D	L	NR	Pts
Anstey & Glenfield	18	10	2	4	2	305
Whetstone	18	8	3	5	2	278
Great Glen	18	7	2	5	4	250
Burbage	18	6	3	6	3	241
Thornton St. Peters	18	6	5	4	3	239
Huncote 2nd	18	6	3	7	2	227
Newbold Verdon 2nd	18	7	2	6	3	226
Westonians 2nd	18	4	6	7	1	191
Braunstone Cricketers	18	3	5	9	1	177
Sapcote	18	3	3	7	5	148

THIRD DIVISION

	P	W	D	L	NR	Pts
Bharat Sports 2nd	18	8	5	3	2	285
Wigston Town 2nd	18	6	4	3	5	259
Leicester Ivanhoe 2nd	18	7	4	4	3	253
Woodhouse Eaves 2nd	18	7	1	6	4	238
Sharnford 2nd	18	8	5	2	3	229
Great Glen 2nd	18	4	3	6	5	189
Twycross 2nd	18	4	4	9	1	187
Stoke Golding 2nd	18	5	2	7	4	184
Anstey & Glenfield 2nd	18	2	5	7	4	175
Leicester Taverners 2nd	18	4	1	8	5	172

FOURTH DIVISION

	P	W	D	L	NR	Pts
Broughton Astley 2nd	18	10	2	3	3	300
Walton le Wolds 2nd	18	9	4	4	1	294
Burton on the Wolds 2nd	18	8	4	3	3	273
Whetstone 2nd	17	7	3	5	2	242
Hathern Old 2nd	18	6	4	5	3	241
Hinckley 2nd	18	7	2	6	3	237
Burbage 2nd	17	6	4	4	3	209
Sapcote 2nd	18	5	2	10	1	170
Braunstone Cricketers 2nd	18	3	2	9	4	148
Thornton St. Peters 2nd	18	1	3	13	1	59

PREMIER DIVISION

2007 Leicestershire Senior League Fixtures

April 28th

Birstall V.	vTwycross
Leic. Caribs	vSharnford
Leic. Ivan.	vHuncote
Newbold V	vWood. Eaves
Westonians	vBharat Sp.
Wigston T.	vHathern Old

May 5th

Bharat Sp.	vLeic. Caribs
Hathern Old	vLeic. Ivan.
Huncote	vNewbold V
Sharnford	vWigston T.
Twycross	vWestonians
Wood. Eaves	vBirstall V.

May 12th

Birstall V.	vHuncote
Leic. Ivan.	vSharnford
Newbold V	vHathern Old
Twycross	vWood. Eaves
Westonians	vLeic. Caribs
Wigston T.	vBharat Sp.

May 19th

Bharat Sp.	vLeic. Ivan.
Hathern Old	vBirstall V.
Huncote	vTwycross
Leic. Caribs	vWigston T.
Sharnford	vNewbold V
Wood. Eaves	vWestonians

May 26th

Birstall V.	vSharnford
Leic. Ivan.	vLeic. Caribs
Newbold V	vBharat Sp.
Twycross	vHathern Old
Westonians	vWigston T.
Wood. Eaves	vHuncote

June 2nd

Bharat Sp.	vBirstall V.
Hathern Old	vWood. Eaves
Huncote	vWestonians
Leic. Caribs	vNewbold V
Sharnford	vTwycross
Wigston T.	vLeic. Ivan.

June 9th

Birstall V.	vLeic. Caribs
Huncote	vHathern Old
Newbold V	vWigston T.
Twycross	vBharat Sp.
Westonians	vLeic. Ivan.
Wood. Eaves	vSharnford

June 16th

Bharat Sp.	vWood. Eaves
Hathern Old	vWestonians
Leic. Caribs	vTwycross
Leic. Ivan.	vNewbold V
Sharnford	vHuncote
Wigston T.	vBirstall V.

June 17th (Sunday)

Birstall V.	vWestonians
Hathern Old	vLeic. Caribs
Huncote	vWigston T.
Sharnford	vBharat Sp.
Twycross	vNewbold V
Wood. Eaves	vLeic. Ivan.

June 23rd

Birstall V.	vLeic. Ivan.
Hathern Old	vSharnford
Huncote	vBharat Sp.
Twycross	vWigston T.
Westonians	vNewbold V
Wood. Eaves	vLeic. Caribs

June 30th

Bharat Sp.	vHathern Old
Leic. Caribs	vHuncote
Leic. Ivan.	vTwycross
Newbold V	vBirstall V.
Sharnford	vWestonians
Wigston T.	vWood. Eaves

July7th

Birstall V.	vWood. Eaves
Leic. Caribs	vBharat Sp.
Leic. Ivan.	vHathern Old
Newbold V	vHuncote
Westonians	vTwycross
Wigston T.	vSharnford

July14th

Bharat Sp.	vWigston T.
Hathern Old	vNewbold V
Huncote	vBirstall V.
Leic. Caribs	vWestonians
Sharnford	vLeic. Ivan.
Wood. Eaves	vTwycross

July 21st

Birstall V.	vHathern Old
Leic. Ivan.	vBharat Sp.
Newbold V	vSharnford
Twycross	vHuncote
Westonians	vWood. Eaves
Wigston T.	vLeic. Caribs

July 28th

Bharat Sp.	vNewbold V
Hathern Old	vTwycross
Huncote	vWood. Eaves
Leic. Caribs	vLeic. Ivan.
Sharnford	vBirstall V.
Wigston T.	vWestonians

Aug 4th

Birstall V.	vBharat Sp.
Leic. Ivan.	vWigston T.
Newbold V	vLeic. Caribs
Twycross	vSharnford
Westonians	vHuncote
Wood. Eaves	vHathern Old

Aug 11th

Bharat Sp.	vTwycross
Hathern Old	vHuncote
Leic. Caribs	vBirstall V.
Leic. Ivan.	vWestonians
Sharnford	vWood. Eaves
Wigston T.	vNewbold V

Aug 12th (Sunday)

Bharat Sp.	vWestonians
Hathern Old	vWigston T.
Huncote	vLeic. Ivan.
Sharnford	vLeic. Caribs
Twycross	vBirstall V.
Wood. Eaves	vNewbold V

Aug 18th

Birstall V.	vWigston T.
Huncote	vSharnford
Newbold V	vLeic. Ivan.
Twycross	vLeic. Caribs
Westonians	vHathern Old
Wood. Eaves	vBharat Sp.

Aug 25th

Bharat Sp.	vHuncote
Leic. Caribs	vWood. Eaves
Leic. Ivan.	vBirstall V.
Newbold V	vWestonians
Sharnford	vHathern Old
Wigston T.	vTwycross

Sept 1st

Birstall V.	vNewbold V
Hathern Old	vBharat Sp.
Huncote	vLeic. Caribs
Twycross	vLeic. Ivan.
Westonians	vSharnford
Wood. Eaves	vWigston T.

Sept 8th
Bharat Sp.   vSharnford
Leic. Caribs   vHathern Old
Leic. Ivan.   vWood. Eaves
Newbold V   vTwycross
Westonians   vBirstall V.
Wigston T.   vHuncote

DIVISION 1

April 28th
B. on the W.   vLeic. Caribs II
Great Glen   vBirstall V. II
Leic. Tavs   vHinckley
L. Patidar   vBroughton A.
Stoke Gold.   vWhetstone
Walton le W.   vAnstey & G.

May 5th
Anstey & G.   vL. Patidar
Birstall V. II vLeic. Tavs
Broughton A.   vStoke Gold.
Hinckley   vWalton le W.
Leic. Caribs IIvGreat Glen
Whetstone   vB. on the W.

May 12th
B. on the W.   vBroughton A.
Great Glen   vLeic. Tavs
Leic. Caribs IIvWhetstone
L. Patidar   vHinckley
Stoke Gold.   vAnstey & G.
Walton le W.   vBirstall V. II

May 19th
Anstey & G.   vB. on the W.
Birstall V. II vL. Patidar
Broughton A.   vLeic. Caribs II
Hinckley   vStoke Gold.
Leic. Tavs   vWalton le W.
Whetstone   vGreat Glen

May 26th
B. on the W.   vHinckley
Great Glen   vWalton le W.
Leic. Caribs IIvAnstey & G.
L. Patidar   vLeic. Tavs
Stoke Gold.   vBirstall V. II
Whetstone   vBroughton A.

June 2nd
Anstey & G.   vWhetstone
Birstall V. II vB. on the W.
Broughton A.   vGreat Glen
Hinckley   vLeic. Caribs II
Leic. Tavs   vStoke Gold.
Walton le W.   vL. Patidar

June 9th
Broughton A.   vAnstey & G.
B. on the W.   vLeic. Tavs

Great Glen   vL. Patidar
Leic. Caribs IIvBirstall V. II
Stoke Gold.   vWalton le W.
Whetstone   vHinckley

June 16th
Anstey & G.   vGreat Glen
Birstall V. II vWhetstone
Hinckley   vBroughton A.
L. Patidar   vStoke Gold.
Leic. Tavs   vLeic. Caribs II
Walton le W.   vB. on the W.

June 17th (Sunday)
Anstey & G.   vLeic. Tavs
Broughton A.   vWalton le W.
B. on the W.   vGreat Glen
Hinckley   vBirstall V. II
Leic. Caribs IIvStoke Gold.
Whetstone   vL. Patidar

June 23rd
Anstey & G.   vHinckley
Broughton A.   vBirstall V. II
B. on the W.   vL. Patidar
Great Glen   vStoke Gold.
Leic. Caribs IIvWalton le W.
Whetstone   vLeic. Tavs

June 30th
Birstall V. II vAnstey & G.
Hinckley   vGreat Glen
L. Patidar   vLeic. Caribs II
Leic. Tavs   vBroughton A.
Stoke Gold.   vB. on the W.
Walton le W.   vWhetstone

July7th
B. on the W.   vWhetstone
Great Glen   vLeic. Caribs II
Leic. Tavs   vBirstall V. II
L. Patidar   vAnstey & G.
Stoke Gold.   vBroughton A.
Walton le W.   vHinckley

July14th
Anstey & G.   vStoke Gold.
Birstall V. II vWalton le W.
Broughton A.   vB. on the W.
Hinckley   vL. Patidar
Leic. Tavs   vGreat Glen
Whetstone   vLeic. Caribs II

July 21st
B. on the W.   vAnstey & G.
Great Glen   vWhetstone
Leic. Caribs IIvBroughton A.
L. Patidar   vBirstall V. II
Stoke Gold.   vHinckley
Walton le W.   vLeic. Tavs

July 28th
Anstey & G.   vLeic. Caribs II
Birstall V. II vStoke Gold.
Broughton A.   vWhetstone
Hinckley   vB. on the W.
Leic. Tavs   vL. Patidar
Walton le W.   vGreat Glen

Aug 4th
B. on the W.   vBirstall V. II
Great Glen   vBroughton A.
Leic. Caribs IIvHinckley
L. Patidar   vWalton le W.
Stoke Gold.   vLeic. Tavs
Whetstone   vAnstey & G.

Aug 11th
Anstey & G.   vBroughton A.
Birstall V. II vLeic. Caribs II
Hinckley   vWhetstone
Leic. Tavs   vB. on the W.
L. Patidar   vGreat Glen
Walton le W.   vStoke Gold.

Aug 12th (Sunday)
Anstey & G.   vWalton le W.
Birstall V. II vGreat Glen
Broughton A.   vL. Patidar
Hinckley   vLeic. Tavs
Leic. Caribs IIvB. on the W.
Whetstone   vStoke Gold.

Aug 18th
Broughton A.   vHinckley
B. on the W.   vWalton le W.
Great Glen   vAnstey & G.
Leic. Caribs IIvLeic. Tavs
Stoke Gold.   vL. Patidar
Whetstone   vBirstall V. II

Aug 25th
Birstall V. II vBroughton A.
Hinckley   vAnstey & G.
Leic. Tavs   vWhetstone
L. Patidar   vB. on the W.
Stoke Gold.   vGreat Glen
Walton le W.   vLeic. Caribs II

Sept 1st
Anstey & G.   vBirstall V. II
Broughton A.   vLeic. Tavs
B. on the W.   vStoke Gold.
Great Glen   vHinckley
Leic. Caribs IIvL. Patidar
Whetstone   vWalton le W.

Sept 8th
Birstall V. II vHinckley
Great Glen   vB. on the W.

Leic. Tavs   vAnstey & G.
L. Patidar   vWhetstone
Stoke Gold.   vLeic. Caribs II
Walton le W.   vBroughton A.

DIVISION 2

May 5th
Appleby M.   v Bharat Sp. II
Newbold V II v Braunstone C
Thornton StP v Huncote II
Westonians IIv Burbage
Wigston T. II v Sapcote

May 12th
Appleby M.   v Westonians II
Bharat Sp. II v Wigston T. II
Braunstone C v Burbage
Huncote II   v Newbold V II
Sapcote   v Thornton StP

May 19th
Burbage   v Huncote II
Newbold V II v Sapcote
Thornton StP v Bharat Sp. II
Westonians IIv Braunstone C
Wigston T. II v Appleby M.

May 26th
Appleby M.   v Thornton StP
Bharat Sp. II v Newbold V II
Huncote II   v Braunstone C
Sapcote   v Burbage
Wigston T. II v Westonians II

June 2nd
Braunstone C v Sapcote
Burbage   v Bharat Sp. II
Newbold V II v Appleby M.
Thornton StP v Wigston T. II
Westonians IIv Huncote II

June 9th
Appleby M.   v Burbage
Bharat Sp. II v Braunstone C
Sapcote   v Huncote II
Thornton StP v Westonians II
Wigston T. II v Newbold V II

June 16th
Braunstone C v Appleby M.
Burbage   v Wigston T. II
Huncote II   v Bharat Sp. II
Newbold V II v Thornton StP
Westonians IIv Sapcote

June 23rd
Appleby M.   v Huncote II
Bharat Sp. II v Sapcote
Newbold V II v Westonians II
Thornton StP v Burbage
Wigston T. II v Braunstone C

June 30th
Braunstone C v Thornton StP
Burbage   v Newbold V II
Huncote II   v Wigston T. II
Sapcote   v Appleby M.
Westonians IIv Bharat Sp. II

July7th
Bharat Sp. II v Appleby M.
Braunstone C v Newbold V II
Burbage   v Westonians II
Huncote II   v Thornton StP
Sapcote   v Wigston T. II

July14th
Burbage   v Braunstone C
Newbold V II v Huncote II
Thornton StP v Sapcote
Westonians IIv Appleby M.
Wigston T. II v Bharat Sp. II

July 21st
Appleby M.   v Wigston T. II
Bharat Sp. II v Thornton StP
Braunstone C v Westonians II
Huncote II   v Burbage
Sapcote   v Newbold V II

July 28th
Braunstone C v Huncote II
Burbage   v Sapcote
Newbold V II v Bharat Sp. II
Thornton StP v Appleby M.
Westonians IIv Wigston T. II

Aug 4th
Appleby M.   v Newbold V II
Bharat Sp. II v Burbage
Huncote II   v Westonians II
Sapcote   v Braunstone C
Wigston T. II v Thornton StP

Aug 11th
Braunstone C vBharat Sp. II
Burbage   v Appleby M.
Huncote II   v Sapcote
Newbold V II v Wigston T. II
Westonians IIv Thornton StP

Aug 18th
Appleby M.   v Braunstone C
Bharat Sp. II v Huncote II
Sapcote   v Westonians II
Thornton StP v Newbold V II
Wigston T. II v Burbage

Aug 25th
Braunstone C v Wigston T. II
Burbage   v Thornton StP

Huncote II   v Appleby M.
Sapcote   v Bharat Sp. II
Westonians IIv Newbold V II

Sept 1st
Appleby M.   v Sapcote
Bharat Sp. II v Westonians II
Newbold V II v Burbage
Thornton StP v Braunstone C
Wigston T. II v Huncote II

DIVISION 3

May 5th
Great Glen II v Twycross II
Leic. Ivan. II v B'ghton A. II
Leic. Tavs II v Sharnford II
Stoke Gld II v Wd. Eaves II
Walton I-W II v A'tey & G. II

May 12th
A'tey & G. II v Leic. Ivan. II
B'ghton A. II v Stoke Gld II
Leic. Tavs II v Great Glen II
Sharnford II   v Walton I-W II
Wd. Eaves II v Twycross II

May 19th
Great Glen II v Wd. Eaves II
Leic. Ivan. II v Sharnford II
Stoke Gld II v A'tey & G. II
Twycross II   v B'ghton A. II
Walton I-W II v Leic. Tavs II

May 26th
A'tey & G. II v Twycross II
B'ghton A. II v Wd. Eaves II
Leic. Tavs II v Leic. Ivan. II
Sharnford II   v Stoke Gld II
Walton I-W II v Great Glen II

June II
Great Glen II v B'ghton A. II
Leic. Ivan. II v Walton I-W II
Stoke Gld II v Leic. Tavs II
Twycross II   v Sharnford II
Wd. Eaves II v A'tey & G. II

June 9th
A'tey & G. II v B'ghton A. II
Leic. Ivan. II v Great Glen II
Leic. Tavs II v Twycross II
Sharnford II   v Wd. Eaves II
Walton I-W II v Stoke Gld II

June 16th
B'ghton A. II v Sharnford II
Great Glen II v A'tey & G. II
Stoke Gld II v Leic. Ivan. II
Twycross II   v Walton I-W II
Wd. Eaves II v Leic. Tavs II

June 23rd
Leic. Ivan. II v Twycross II
Leic. Tavs II v B'ghton A. II
Sharnford II v A'tey & G. II
Stoke Gld II v Great Glen II
Walton I-W II v Wd. Eaves II

June 30th
A'tey & G. II v Leic. Tavs II
B'ghton A. II v Walton I-W II
Great Glen II v Sharnford II
Twycross II v Stoke Gld II
Wd. Eaves II v Leic. Ivan. II

July7th
A'tey & G. II v Walton I-W II
B'ghton A. II v Leic. Ivan. II
Sharnford II v Leic. Tavs II
Twycross II v Great Glen II
Wd. Eaves II v Stoke Gld II

July14th
Great Glen II v Leic. Tavs II
Leic. Ivan. II v A'tey & G. II
Stoke Gld II v B'ghton A. II
Twycross II v Wd. Eaves II
Walton I-W II v Sharnford II

July 21st
A'tey & G. II v Stoke Gld II
B'ghton A. II v Twycross II
Leic. Tavs II v Walton I-W II
Sharnford II v Leic. Ivan. II
Wd. Eaves II v Great Glen II

July 28th
Great Glen II v Walton I-W II
Leic. Ivan. II v Leic. Tavs II
Stoke Gld II v Sharnford II
Twycross II v A'tey & G. II
Wd. Eaves II v B'ghton A. II

Aug 4th
A'tey & G. II v Wd. Eaves II
B'ghton A. II v Great Glen II
Leic. Tavs II v Stoke Gld II
Sharnford II v Twycross II
Walton I-W II v Leic. Ivan. II

Aug 11th
B'ghton A. II v A'tey & G. II
Great Glen II v Leic. Ivan. II
Stoke Gld II v Walton I-W II
Twycross II v Leic. Tavs II
Wd. Eaves II v Sharnford II

Aug 18th
A'tey & G. II v Great Glen II
Leic. Ivan. II v Stoke Gld II

Leic. Tavs II v Wd. Eaves II
Sharnford II v B'ghton A. II
Walton I-W II v Twycross II

Aug 25th
A'tey & G. II v Sharnford II
B'ghton A. II v Leic. Tavs II
Great Glen II v Stoke Gld II
Twycross II v Leic. Ivan. II
Wd. Eaves II v Walton I-W II

Sept 1st
Leic. Ivan. II v Wd. Eaves II
Leic. Tavs II v A'tey & G. II
Sharnford II v Great Glen II
Stoke Gld II v Twycross II
Walton I-W II v B'ghton A. II

DIVISION 4

May 5th
Br'stone C II v Hathern O II
Burbage II v Hinckley II
B o'the W II v Appleby M. II
L. Patidar II v Th'ton StP II
Sapcote II v Whetstone II

May 12th
Burbage II v B o'the W II
Hathern O II v L. Patidar II
Hinckley II v Br'stone C II
Th'ton StP II v Sapcote II
Whetstone II v Appleby M. II

May 19th
Appleby M. II v Th'ton StP II
Br'stone C II v Burbage II
B o'the W II v Whetstone II
L. Patidar II v Hinckley II
Sapcote II v Hathern O II

May 26th
Br'stone C II v B o'the W II
Burbage II v L. Patidar II
Hathern O II v Appleby M. II
Hinckley II v Sapcote II
Th'ton StP II v Whetstone II

June 2nd
Appleby M. II v Hinckley II
B o'the W II v Th'ton StP II
L. Patidar II v Br'stone C II
Sapcote II v Burbage II
Whetstone II v Hathern O II

June 9th
Br'stone C II v Sapcote II
Burbage II v Appleby M. II
Hathern O II v Th'ton StP II
Hinckley II v Whetstone II
L. Patidar II v B o'the W II

June 16th
Appleby M. II v Br'stone C II
B o'the W II v Hathern O II
Sapcote II v L. Patidar II
Th'ton StP II v Hinckley II
Whetstone II v Burbage II

June 23rd
Br'stone C II v Whetstone II
Burbage II v Th'ton StP II
Hinckley II v Hathern O II
L. Patidar II v Appleby M. II
Sapcote II v B o'the W II

June 30th
Appleby M. II v Sapcote II
B o'the W II v Hinckley II
Hathern O II v Burbage II
Th'ton StP II v Br'stone C II
Whetstone II v L. Patidar II

July7th
Appleby M. II v B o'the W II
Hathern O II v Br'stone C II
Hinckley II v Burbage II
Th'ton StP II v L. Patidar II
Whetstone II v Sapcote II

July14th
Appleby M. II v Whetstone II
Br'stone C II v Hinckley II
B o'the W II v Burbage II
L. Patidar II v Hathern O II
Sapcote II v Th'ton StP II

July 21st
Burbage II v Br'stone C II
Hathern O II v Sapcote II
Hinckley II v L. Patidar II
Th'ton StP II v Appleby M. II
Whetstone II v B o'the W II

July 28th
Appleby M. II v Hathern O II
B o'the W II v Br'stone C II
L. Patidar II v Burbage II
Sapcote II v Hinckley II
Whetstone II v Th'ton StP II

Aug 4th
Br'stone C II v L. Patidar II
Burbage II v Sapcote II
Hathern O II v Whetstone II
Hinckley II v Appleby M. II
Th'ton StP II v B o'the W II

Aug 11th
Appleby M. II v Burbage II
B o'the W II v L. Patidar II

Sapcote II   v Br'stone C II
Th'ton StP II v Hathern O II
Whetstone II v Hinckley II

Aug 18th
Br'stone C II v Appleby M. II
Burbage II   v Whetstone II
Hathern O II v B o'the W II
Hinckley II   v Th'ton StP II
L. Patidar II v Sapcote II

Aug 25th
Appleby M. II v L. Patidar II
B o'the W II v Sapcote II
Hathern O II v Hinckley II
Th'ton StP II v Burbage II
Whetstone II v Br'stone C II

Sept 1st
Br'stone C II v Th'ton StP II
Burbage II   v Hathern O II
Hinckley II   v B o'the W II
L. Patidar II   v Whetstone II
Sapcote II   v Appleby M. II